WORDS IN ACTION

WORDS IN ACTION

SPEECH ACT THEORY AND
BIBLICAL INTERPRETATION

Toward a Hermeneutic of Self-Involvement

RICHARD S. BRIGGS

T&T CLARK
EDINBURGH & NEW YORK

T&T CLARK LTD

A Continuum imprint

59 George Street
Edinburgh EH2 2LQ
Scotland

www.tandtclark.co.uk

370 Lexington Avenue
New York 10017–6503
USA

www.continuumbooks.com

First published 2001

ISBN: 978-0-5670-8345-6

British Library Cataloguing-in-Publication Data
A catalogue record for this book is available from the British Library

Typeset by Waverley Typesetters, Galashiels
Printed and bound in Great Britain by
The Cromwell Press, Trowbridge, Wiltshire

To Melody

Contents

Part 2: Aspects of Self-Involvement in Interpreting New Testament Speech Acts

Preface

This book began life as a Ph.D. thesis submitted to the University of Nottingham under the title 'Speech Act Theory and Biblical Interpretation: Toward a Hermeneutic of Self-Involvement'. I would like to express my immense gratitude to Professor Anthony Thiselton, who as my supervisor was a source of both guidance and inspiration throughout my research. Its initial direction and subsequent development were indebted to him, and I benefited on innumerable occasions from his wise comment and patient consideration of all angles, likely and unlikely. It was a great pleasure to have the privilege of discussing my work with him.

I am also grateful for the constructive comments and encouragement of Alan Torrance and Craig Bartholomew, my examiners, who made several valuable suggestions for ways in which the present work might be taken forward to explore more explicitly theological dimensions of language. Such considerations are clearly raised in what follows, and equally clearly my brief remarks in the conclusion do not adequately address them, but they do, I hope, indicate ways ahead, ways which I look forward to exploring in due course. Craig Bartholomew also convened a consultation on 'Speech Act Theory and Biblical Interpretation', for the hermeneutics unit of the Bible Society Open Book programme, in Cheltenham on 25–7 May 1998. It was an unexpected privilege to have a room full of people concerning themselves with my research topic, and I would like to record my thanks to him and to all those involved who, quite incidentally to their main objectives, stimulated my thinking in a variety of ways.

My studies would not have been possible without the generous award of three-year grants both from the Whitefield Institute in Oxford and from the University of Nottingham Faculty of Arts, as well as the extraordinary generosity of many friends around the world. Special thanks in particular to Dr David Cook and all at the Whitefield Institute for the invigorating experience of having early drafts of chapters 3 and 6 subjected to friendly critique at their seminar days.

Pathway Christian Fellowship in Nottingham was a home to me and my family for the two and a half years during which this project took shape. Their love, their worship and their community meant everything to us. I cannot imagine having completed this without them.

My wife Melody was a wonderful support throughout, and I dedicate this book to her as one small way of saying thank you. Dedication is a fairly conventional speech act: Melody, it does not tell the half of my gratitude; and yes, perhaps one day it will be that best-selling novel I've promised rather than a hermeneutical treatise which will bear your name. Our children Joshua and Kristin (and now Matthew too) have brightened our days in inimitable ways, even claiming that they too 'want to do a Ph.D.' someday.

Finally I wish to acknowledge the support, encouragement and assistance in many and various ways of: Antony Billington, Robert and Maureen Briggs, Graham and Mary Brown, Karla and Cary Campanella, Chris Carroll, Mark Chan, Carrie and John Downing, Mary Elmer, Paul and Judith Lawlor, Mark Lovatt, Chris McBrien, Katie Machell, Hugh and Barbara Mason, Dave Parris, Jo and Steve Porter, Simon and Miranda Portwood, Margaret Swan, Andres Synofzik, George Verwer, Rachel Weiss, Dave and Pam White, and Vera Zabramski. Thank you one and all; without you, the experience of writing this book would not have been the joy that it was.

Abbreviations

AB	Anchor Bible
ABD	David N. Freedman et al. (eds), *Anchor Bible Dictionary*, New York: Doubleday, 1992
BAGD	W. Bauer, W. F. Arndt, F. W. Gingrich and F. W. Danker, *A Greek–English Lexicon of the New Testament and Other Early Christian Literature*, Chicago and London: University of Chicago Press, ^{2}1979
BibInt	*Biblical Interpretation*
Bib Int Ser	Biblical Interpretation Series
BNTC	Black's New Testament Commentaries
CR:BS	*Currents in Research: Biblical Studies*
CSR	*Christian Scholar's Review*
CTJ	*Calvin Theological Journal*
DBI	R. J. Coggins and J. L. Houlden (eds), *A Dictionary of Biblical Interpretation*, London: SCM Press, 1990
DJG	Joel B. Green, Scot McKnight and I. Howard Marshall (eds), *Dictionary of Jesus and the Gospels*, Leicester and Downers Grove: IVP, 1992
DLNTD	Ralph P. Martin and Peter H. Davids (eds), *Dictionary of the Later New Testament and Its Developments*, Leicester and Downers Grove: IVP, 1997

EJTh	*European Journal of Theology*
ET	English translation
ExpT	*Expository Times*
FNT	*Filologia Neotestamentaria*
FRLANT	Forschungen zur Religion und Literatur des Alten und Neuen Testaments
FS	Festschrift
Gos. Thom.	*Gospel of Thomas*
HBTh	*Horizons in Biblical Theology*
HDTW	J. L. Austin, *How to Do Things with Words*, edited by J. O. Urmson and Marina Sbisa, Oxford: Oxford University Press, ²1975 (1962)
HHS	*History of the Human Sciences*
HSM	Harvard Semitic Monographs
HTR	*Harvard Theological Review*
ICC	International Critical Commentary
IDB	George A. Buttrick et al. (eds), *The Interpreter's Dictionary of the Bible*, Nashville: Abingdon, 1962
Int	*Interpretation*
IVP	Inter-Varsity Press
JAAR	*Journal of the American Academy of Religion*
JBL	*Journal of Biblical Literature*
JETS	*Journal of the Evangelical Theological Society*
JP	*Journal of Philosophy*
JPrag	*Journal of Pragmatics*
JRE	*Journal of Religious Ethics*
JSNT	*Journal for the Study of the New Testament*
JSNTS	*Journal for the Study of the New Testament Supplement Series*
JSOTS	*Journal for the Study of the Old Testament Supplement Series*
JTC	*Journal for Theology and the Church*
JTS	*Journal of Theological Studies*
JTSA	*Journal of Theology for Southern Africa*
LCC	Library of Christian Classics
LT	*Literature & Theology*

Mart. Pol.	*Martyrdom of Polycarp*
MLN	*Modern Language Notes*
MTh	*Modern Theology*
NICNT	New International Commentary on the New Testament
NIDNTT	Colin Brown (ed.), *New International Dictionary of New Testament Theology*, Carlisle: Paternoster, 1975–8
NIGTC	New International Greek Testament Commentary
NIV	New International Version
NLH	*New Literary History*
NLR	*New Left Review*
NovT	*Novum Testamentum*
NovTSup	Supplements to *Novum Testamentum*
NRSV	New Revised Standard Version
NS	New Series
NT	New Testament
NTS	*New Testament Studies*
OT	Old Testament
PhQ	*Philosophical Quarterly*
PRS	*Perspectives in Religious Studies*
RelSRev	*Religious Studies Review*
RelStud	*Religious Studies*
REP	Edward Craig (ed.), *Routledge Encyclopedia of Philosophy*, London and New York: Routledge, 1998
RSR	*Recherches de Science Religieuse*
SBET	*Scottish Bulletin of Evangelical Theology*
SBLDS	SBL Dissertation Series
SBLMS	SBL Monograph Series
SBT	Studies in Biblical Theology
SJT	*Scottish Journal of Theology*
SNTSMS	Society for New Testament Studies Monograph Series
SNTU	*Studien zum Neuen Testament und seiner Umwelt*

SNTW	Studies of the New Testament and Its World
StABH	Studies in American Biblical Hermeneutics
Str-B	H. L. Strack and Paul Billerbeck, *Kommentar zum Neuen Testament aus Talmud und Midrasch,* Munich: C. H. Beck, 1922–61
TDNT	G. Kittel and G. Friedrich (eds), *Theological Dictionary of the New Testament,* ET: Grand Rapids: Eerdmans, 1964–76
TynB	*Tyndale Bulletin*
USQR	*Union Seminary Quarterly Review*
WBC	Word Biblical Commentary
WUNT	Wissenschaftliche Untersuchungen zum Neuen Testament
ZNW	*Zeitschrift für die neutestamentliche Wissenschaft*

INTRODUCTION

1

Speech Act Theory and Biblical Interpretation

§1 Introduction

'Speech act theory' is the name given to a type of inquiry brought into focus by the work of J. L. Austin in his 1955 William James lectures at Harvard, and later published as *How to Do Things with Words*.[1] At heart, speech act theory concerns itself with the performative nature of language: with the topic of how language 'utterances' are operative and have effects whether they occur in face-to-face personal conversation or in any communicative action. Typically, the subject is introduced by way of such examples as the uttering of 'I do' at the appropriate point in a marriage ceremony; the naming of a ship by an appointed celebrity who smashes the champagne bottle against the hull and says, 'I name this ship the Titanic'; or the creation of obligation simply through the uttering of the words 'I'll be there at 10.00 tomorrow morning'. In all these cases, an act is performed by, in and through the use of speech.

Austin did not invent speech act theory but, as the subject currently stands, most of its pre-Austin development is of relatively minor significance.[2] Of considerably greater significance

---

[1] J. L. Austin, *How to Do Things with Words*, edited by J. O. Urmson and Marina Sbisa, Oxford: Oxford University Press, [2]1975 (1962). Details of many of the works mentioned in these introductory paragraphs may be found in later discussions, particularly in chapter 2.

[2] I trace that part of it specifically applicable to Austin's work in chapter 2. Alan White has written that 'since the 1980's there has been a growing awareness of interesting anticipations [of speech-act theory] in the work of philosophers influenced by Brentano or Husserl, such as Anton Marty (1847–1914) and Adolf

is the fact that Austin died before he was able to develop fully
his account of 'performative utterances', with the result that at
the very centre of the topic lies a debate concerning the direction
in which his work should be developed. John Searle provides
the most comprehensive statement of a full theory of speech
acts. Another direction was explored most notably by Paul
Grice, who developed a pragmatic approach focusing on the
notion of 'conversational implicature'. More recent writers offer
a variety of ways forward, ranging from conciliatory approaches
such as that of François Recanati to more partisan contributions
such as the logico-linguistic emphasis of Daniel Vanderveken.
Chapter 2 of this study presents a detailed survey of speech act
theory and develops some particular lines of thought within it
which will prove useful in our inquiry.

Beyond the arena of analytic philosophy of language, speech
act theory has developed even greater diversity. Literary theorists
have appealed to it both as a resource (following Grice) and as a
governing paradigm, albeit without always agreeing on its nature.
The work of Mary Louise Pratt and Richard Ohmann is prominent here, as well as the particular contribution of Shoshana
Felman in looking at Austin's unique stylistic approach.[3] In
chapter 3 I consider these various developments and applications, noting also the remarkable degree of attention afforded
to speech act theory by such prominent writers as Jacques
Derrida and Stanley Fish.

One of Austin's own students, Donald Evans, produced an
early study in applications of the ideas of speech act theory to
biblical language,[4] and more recently there has been a growing
literature involving the use of speech act theory in biblical and
theological studies. In my judgment, however, there remains

Reinach (1883–1917)', 'Speech Acts', in Thomas Mautner (ed.), *A Dictionary of Philosophy*, Oxford: Blackwell, 1996, 403–4, here 404. For a helpful survey with a comprehensive bibliography, see Brigitte Nerlich and David D. Clarke, 'Language, Action and Context: Linguistic Pragmatics in Europe and America (1800–1950)', *JPrag* 22 (1994), 439–63.

[3] Shoshana Felman, *The Literary Speech-Act: Don Juan with J. L. Austin, or Seduction in Two Languages*, Ithaca, NY: Cornell University Press, 1983. Felman is concerned particularly with Austinian style and humour as components of his message. Her work is tangential to my own concerns and will not be explored here.

[4] Donald D. Evans, *The Logic of Self-Involvement: A Philosophical Study of Everyday Language with Special Reference to the Christian Use of Language about God as Creator*, London: SCM Press, 1963.

considerable confusion concerning what may or may not be expected of speech act theory and its insights in the area of biblical and theological studies.

First, appeals to 'Austin's idea of performative language' seem to be made by people with diametrically opposed points to make. Secondly, many biblical interpreters seem to suppose that speech act theory is constituted in its entirety by *How to Do Things with Words*, or at least that nothing is lost by adding to this only some footnoted appeals to the work of John Searle. Thirdly, the concerns of a Searlean type of Austin are sometimes assimilated to the pragmatic stylistics of Paul Grice, all under the rubric of 'speech act criticism'. In the face of such varied appropriations of speech act theory in the biblical field, it seems best to take preliminary issues carefully in order to examine precisely what it is that speech act theory can achieve.

My aim in this introduction is therefore to clarify what should and should not be expected of a study which seeks to relate speech act theory to biblical interpretation, both with reference to the nature of speech act theory itself and with respect to its relationship with biblical hermeneutics. In the subtitle 'Toward a Hermeneutic of Self-Involvement', I indicate my own conviction: that the direction suggested by Donald Evans remains the most fruitful for utilising speech act theory in a hermeneutical role in biblical interpretation. My various accounts of the work done in utilising speech act categories and concerns in biblical studies will demonstrate that this has not been the main area in which attention has been focused. I shall consider the relatively few exceptions to this judgment below, and in chapter 5 I will turn to a detailed examination of Evans's own unjustly neglected work. With the framework thus in place for a 'hermeneutic of self-involvement', the remainder of part 2 of the study will then be given over to an exploration of various topics in New Testament interpretation which may be helpfully illuminated by a speech act approach. I conclude with some suggestions for various hermeneutical implications of this approach.

§2 The Philosophy of Language and Biblical and Theological Hermeneutics

It is not my intention to suggest either that speech act theory offers a comprehensive philosophy of language or that it might

serve as a panacea for all hermeneutical problems in biblical
and theological studies. These two points are related, and in
this section I propose to deal with them briefly.

§2.1 *Speech act theory is not a solution to the hermeneutical problem*

The story of the development of hermeneutics as its own distinctive field of inquiry has often been traced, and need not be
repeated here.[5] Perhaps most suggestively it has been seen as
the path taken by the discipline of philosophy after it reached
the limits of its own former approach with Kant.[6] Without
wishing to engage in a study of it here, I take it that one may talk
of 'the hermeneutical problem' as formulated in the tradition
reaching back to Schleiermacher and developed in the thinking
of Heidegger, Gadamer and Ricoeur.[7] This is the problem of
arriving at understanding (be it of texts, of history, of events, or
of people) in a world in which we always operate as a situated
observer, relative to our own horizons and falling short of a
supposedly objective 'view from nowhere'.[8] Hermeneutics, thus
conceived, has engendered a variety of responses, ranging
from the ardent defence of various forms of pre-hermeneutical
objectivity through to doom-laden predictions of the end of
the epistemological world as we knew it, with the collapse of all
criteria except those of community predilection.

[5] A helpful historically orientated account is that of Jean Grondin, *Introduction to Philosophical Hermeneutics* (trans. Joel Weinsheimer), New Haven and London: Yale University Press, 1994 (1991).

[6] On the 'closing of the philosophical canon' with Kant, see Bruce Kuklick, 'Seven Thinkers and How They Grew: Descartes, Spinoza, Leibniz, Locke, Berkeley, Hume, Kant', in Richard Rorty, J. B. Schneewind and Quentin Skinner (eds), *Philosophy in History: Essays on the Historiography of Philosophy*, Cambridge: Cambridge University Press, 1984, 125–39.

[7] I am aware of course that there is fragmentation within the discipline of hermeneutics, but this need not concern us here. See Edward Tingley, 'Types of Hermeneutics', *Southern Journal of Philosophy* 36 (1998), 587–611, and Nicholas H. Smith, *Strong Hermeneutics: Contingency and Moral Identity*, London and New York: Routledge, 1997, especially 15–34, who characterises various hermeneutical traditions as 'strong', 'weak' and 'deep', partly as a way of evaluating their 'ontological commitment', a term which in hermeneutical as distinct from philosophical inquiry relates to the debate concerning the essential role of hermeneutical tradition in constituting human nature. This sense of 'ontology' thus contrasts primarily with 'contingency'.

[8] To use the memorable phrase of Thomas Nagel, *The View from Nowhere*, New York: Oxford University Press, 1986.

Hermeneutics in itself does not require us to adopt either of these extremes in response. In so far as the self has always been situated, and yet anything has ever been understood, then clearly it has proved possible to find resolution to hermeneutical difficulties. Hermeneutical theorising would then be the task of accounting for how this has happened. In contrast, hermeneutics as a discipline has demonstrated that all knowledge is indeed contextual, and the self always is situated. A fortiori there must then be a way through the issues which, in the phrase of Richard Bernstein, moves 'beyond objectivism and relativism'.[9]

The hermeneutical problem cannot be resolved simply by sharper a priori thinking. In fact, if hermeneutics has taught us anything then it is that one may not say in advance of any interpretive situation which method will be required in order to resolve interpretive difficulties. That is, there is no short cut by which we may eliminate *judgment* from the interpretive process. Gadamer says of judgment that

> it cannot be taught in the abstract but only practised from case to case, and is therefore more an ability like the senses. It is something that cannot be learned, because no demonstration from concepts can guide the application of rules.[10]

It cannot be learned, that is, in advance of the particularities of any given case. However, in the particular case, judgment will always be an act of *self-involvement*.

The concept of self-involvement is a central one to which we shall return many times. It occurs as part of the title of Evans's early work on speech act theory and creation language, but, from Evans onwards, is frequently left ambiguous in an unfortunate manner. To anticipate a major theme of this study, it will prove helpful always to bear in mind that there are degrees of self-involvement, and that we do well to distinguish between cases of strong and significant self-involvement and more general cases where we might wish to say that all language is self-involving. The former is a primary concern of speech act theory. The latter only arises when speech act theory is broadened in an attempt

---

[9] Richard J. Bernstein, *Beyond Objectivism and Relativism: Science, Hermeneutics, and Praxis*, Philadelphia: University of Pennsylvania Press, 1983.

[10] Hans-Georg Gadamer, *Truth and Method*, London: Sheed & Ward, [2]1989 (German original 1960), 31.

to develop it into an entire philosophy of language (on which see the next section).

For example, the paradigm case of strong self-involvement in speech acts is the commitment of the person who says, 'I promise to be there tomorrow.' The promise can only be understood and evaluated in connection with the commitments and intentions of the speaker. Very little can be said about this utterance short of investigating the speaker's degree of self-involvement in it. In contrast, a statement such as 'Karl Barth was born in 1886', while it may be said in a particular situation for any number of relevant reasons, is not intrinsically self-involving as a statement in any interesting manner. It may be evaluated or interpreted satisfactorily regardless of who says it. Of course no statement is entirely acontextual: the point is rather that its context may or may not be a particularly interesting aspect of it.

The notion of self-involvement in reading the biblical text, therefore, is less a matter of logic (*pace* Evans) and more a function of certain hermeneutically interesting situations regarding how particular texts are read by particular readers. It is such particular cases which will be considered in part 2 of this study. In saying this, I am distancing myself from those who have argued that self-involvement is a feature of all reading of all texts, but who have not indicated whether this is to be taken as always equally significant. For example, I have considerable sympathy with Ben Meyer's Lonergan-inspired 'critical realism', which emphasises how one must attain a stance towards the text in order to judge it. He writes that before judging

> one must have grasped the concrete data ... This 'grasp' is the crucial antecedent of judgment ... the act of committing oneself to the proposition ... true judgment is paradoxical in being simultaneously impersonal and personal.[11]

In Meyer's opinion, New Testament scholarship has never been so well served for insight, but all this insight is to no avail without concomitant judgment: 'a tower of insight can also be a house of cards, riven from top to bottom with structural faults – the absence of grounded *judgment*'.[12] However, much as I am in agreement with this, I think it is important to realise that this is

---

[11] Ben F. Meyer, *Reality and Illusion in New Testament Scholarship: A Primer in Critical Realist Hermeneutics*, Collegeville, MN: Michael Glazier, Liturgical Press, 1994, 27.

[12] Meyer, *Reality and Illusion*, 153.

not the sense in which speech act theory proposes to handle the notion of self-involvement. While hermeneutics may indeed require of us a situated judgment in any and every case, it is only in certain types of case (which I have indicated that I will note as 'strongly self-involving') that speech act theory will prove relevant.

A similar point must be made about Paul Ricoeur's use of the categories of speech acts as part of his general interpretation theory. He suggests that the difference between *explanation* (of propositional content) and *understanding* (of illocutionary force) may be thrown into relief by speech act theory to precisely the extent that the 'grammar' of illocutions is encoded, or in-scripturated, in the text.[13] To understand the text is to dwell in the world it opens up; whereas to explain it is to penetrate behind it to points of actual reference. This does not, however, make Ricoeur's hermeneutic *self-involving* in anything like the sense in which that term is significant in speech act theory. It requires only a logic of 'possibility' which involves the self in the particular sense that 'I' am part of the projected, possible world.[14] It seems less than coincidental that the particular biblical genres which capture Ricoeur's imagination are those of wisdom and narrative, where the gentler 'self-involvement' of world-projection is at work, rather than the stronger forms of directive prophecy or teaching, where questions of speaker agency come to the forefront. In so far, then, as Ricoeur raises the hermeneutical problem in terms of speech act theory, it is important to see why it is that speech act theory provides no 'solution' in general terms.

§2.2 *Speech act theory is not a comprehensive philosophy of language*

It is not necessary to demonstrate conclusively that the hermen-eutical problem cannot be resolved by sharper a priori thinking

[13] It would be a further debatable issue as to whether Ricoeur is right here to assimilate the well-known *Erklärung-Verstehen* debate to the distinction between propositional content and illocutionary force. On this topic see Karl-Otto Apel, *Understanding and Explanation: A Transcendental-Pragmatic Perspective*, Cambridge, MA, and London: MIT Press, 1984 (1979).

[14] See especially Paul Ricoeur, *Interpretation Theory: Discourse and the Surplus of Meaning*, Fort Worth: Texas Christian University Press, 1976, 87–8, and, with reference to speech act theory, 14–18.

for the purposes of this study, because I also wish to claim that speech act theory will not in any case serve as a comprehensive philosophy of language. This claim will be made in detail in chapter 2, but can be sketched in outline here.

Austin's original focus was on performative utterances: cases where a deed was done in or by the saying of the words. He went on to demonstrate that certain interesting characteristics of such utterances could be seen at work in all language use: degrees of felicity or infelicity, and the role of extra-linguistic conventions, for example. In his sketch-like writings he proposes ways of seeing these issues which have been taken up and systematised by subsequent philosophers, most notably John Searle. For all the structural clarity and explanatory power of Searle's speech act theory, a case can be made for saying that he has erred in attempting to press it into service as a full-scale philosophy of language. Much recent philosophical work on this topic has concentrated on exploring problems with Searle's approach, and developing his work in one of two ways: either seeking to deepen and extend its formal scope to make good perceived deficiencies (Vanderveken) or rethinking certain of his working hypotheses in order to reduce the theory to a humbler and more flexible level.[15] In chapter 2 I shall argue that this latter path is the correct one.

Without entering into the technicalities of speech act theory at this stage, the point can be made with reference to the work of the later Wittgenstein. By focusing insistently on the way language is actually used rather than imposing theories about how it 'should' be used, Wittgenstein demonstrated that the theoretical conceptualities we develop in discussing the philosophy of language are always relative to the particular goals of our discussion. As a particularly pertinent example, he considered the asymmetry of first-person and third-person usages of certain verbs such as 'to feel pain' or 'to believe falsely'.[16] While it makes perfect sense to say 'John believes falsely that phlogiston explains the concept of heat', it makes no sense to say 'I believe it falsely too' since it is part of the grammar of

[15] In particular is this true of several contributors to Savas L. Tsohatzidis (ed.), *Foundations of Speech Act Theory: Philosophical and Linguistic Perspectives,* London and New York: Routledge, 1994.

[16] Ludwig Wittgenstein, *Philosophical Investigations*, Oxford: Blackwell, [3]1967 (1953), pp. 187–92. References to Wittgenstein's works are usually given by § number. In cases such as this reference to the second part of the *Investigations*, which lacks § numbers, I make it explicit that a page reference is intended.

'believe' that the speaker is *involved* in the ascription of belief to himself when using it as a present-tense first-person verb, but not as a third-person verb. However, Wittgenstein did not go on to claim that this indicated an entire field of philosophical inquiry concerning subject-asymmetry in verb uses. Instead it simply indicates that we must learn to be alert to this kind of possibility. His later philosophical work can be seen as the attempt to clarify what actually occurs in language use (amongst other topics) in the belief that in fact if philosophy were successfully to clear up the confusions surrounding ordinary usage then it would find that it had no subject matter of its own to pursue. Wittgenstein's vision for philosophy was that it would 'leave everything as it is', and consist 'in assembling reminders for a particular purpose', namely, whatever the task was to hand.[17] Philosophical ideas, rather like words themselves, are then best seen as tools to unlock certain problems.

While much of this spirit pervades Austin's written work it is notably absent from the approaches of Searle who, for instance, sees system specifically in places where Wittgenstein saw limitless variety.[18]

The field of philosophy of language continues to encompass detailed arguments about all aspects of speech act theory, and it is not my purpose to adjudicate them all.[19] Those germane to my own study will be considered in chapter 2. To state clearly my own conviction, however, I am sympathetic to certain negative conclusions concerning aspects of speech act theory especially where it has pursued reductive approaches concerned with logical calculus or depth grammar, but I believe that its main insights concerning certain types of strongly self-involving language survive these critiques and remain useful for certain purposes.[20] Primary among these purposes are the

---

[17] Wittgenstein, *Philosophical Investigations*, §§124–8, §599.

[18] See John R. Searle, *Expression and Meaning: Studies in the Theory of Speech Acts*, Cambridge: Cambridge University Press, 1979, 29, rejecting Wittgenstein's idea of 'the limitless uses of language'.

[19] See various articles in Bob Hale and Crispin Wright (eds), *A Companion to the Philosophy of Language* (Blackwell Companions to Philosophy), Oxford: Blackwell, 1997, as well as articles in Tsohatzidis (ed.), *Foundations of Speech Act Theory*.

[20] Primary among such critiques is the analysis of two prominent Wittgenstein commentators: G. P. Baker and P. M. S. Hacker, *Language, Sense and Nonsense: A Critical Investigation into Modern Theories of Language*, Oxford: Blackwell, 1984, with which I find myself in considerable agreement, although note James Bogen, 'An Unfavourable Review of *Language, Sense and Nonsense*', *Inquiry* 28 (1985), 467–82.

clarifying of presuppositions, implications and entailments of performative uses of language especially in cases of strong self-involvement. These purposes are sufficient to make speech act theory a worthwhile tool in the field of biblical and theological inquiry.

One final comment is relevant here, concerning my frequent recourse to Wittgensteinian ways of thinking. Wittgenstein was not a speech act theorist, and it is well known that Austin was frequently unimpressed by him.[21] Some authors have specifically directed a Wittgensteinian critique *against* speech act theory.[22] Nevertheless, in my judgment, this is usually against certain formalisations of the theory rather than its central ideas. Wittgenstein's relationship with subsequent analytic philosophy remains debated, and I am inclined to agree with that stream of thought which sees fruitful if limited points of contact between his work and the more 'continental' tradition of hermeneutics: 'his work . . . provides much-needed arguments against the reductionist conceptions of human beings which the hermeneutic tradition rightly abhors'.[23] With respect to biblical interpretation, as against the philosophy of religion,[24] relatively few writers have explored Wittgensteinian resources, although those that have also indicate the relevant 'continental' sympathies.[25] In short, my appeal to speech act theory is not to a comprehensive philosophy of language but to a hermeneutical resource in the manner of the later Wittgenstein, although it stands or falls on its own independent merits.

---

[21] See further ch. 2, §1.1 below.

[22] See G. C. Kerner, 'A Wittgensteinian Critique of Some Recent Developments in the Theory of Speech Acts', in Rudolf Haller and Wolfgang Grassl (eds), *Language, Logic and Philosophy: Proceedings of the Fourth International Wittgenstein Symposium 28 Aug–2 Sep 1979, Kirchberg am Wechsel, Austria*, Dordrecht: D. Reidel Publishing Company, and Vienna: Hölder-Pichler-Tempsky, 1980, 423–5.

[23] Hans-Johann Glock, *A Wittgenstein Dictionary*, Oxford: Blackwell, 1996, 29. More radical, but with some helpful points, is Henry Staten, *Wittgenstein and Derrida*, Oxford: Blackwell, 1985, especially 64–108.

[24] See the helpful survey of Joseph M. Incandela, 'The Appropriation of Wittgenstein's Work by Philosophers of Religion: Towards a Re-Evaluation and an End', *RelStud* 21 (1985), 457–74.

[25] See in particular Anthony C. Thiselton, *The Two Horizons: New Testament Hermeneutics and Philosophical Description*, Grand Rapids: Eerdmans, and Carlisle: Paternoster Press, 1980, 357–438 and also 33–40; Fergus Kerr, 'Language as Hermeneutic in the Later Wittgenstein', *Tijdschrift voor Filosofie* 27 (1965), 491–520; and more broadly idem, *Theology after Wittgenstein*, London: SPCK, ²1997 (1986).

§2.3 *Speech act theory is not a variety of anti-foundationalism*

Finally, discussions of religious language and theological hermeneutics have been greatly preoccupied over the last twenty years by the question of 'foundationalism' and its variant forms. This topic, fertile in American soil particularly, arises as a result of the disintegration of an alleged Enlightenment consensus about the nature of the given in intellectual inquiry.[26] As that consensus disappears, so scholars of all persuasions find themselves confronted with the issue of how to ground their beliefs, whether in rational absolutes, community traditions, personal preferences, or moral standards.

This issue is perhaps so predominant in both philosophy and theology owing to the particular nature of American thought as a self-created discourse with no continuous tradition that can trace itself back beyond the Revolution. This has led to pragmatism as the American philosophy par excellence, and to a great deal of soul-searching in the wake of the demise of a 'modern' consensus.[27] Nancey Murphy is one representative American thinker who has attempted to map the epistemological possibilities of this demise, and to develop criteria by which post-'modern' schemes (in this Anglo-American sense) may be evaluated.[28] One result of her approach is to classify Austin's speech act theory as postmodern, and as representative of the same kind of anti-foundational drift as George Lindbeck's prominent 'postliberal' proposal for understanding religion and doctrines.[29]

[26] See the survey of John E. Thiel, *Nonfoundationalism* (Guides to Theological Inquiry), Minneapolis: Augsburg–Fortress, 1994.

[27] Positive and negative views respectively of this tradition are offered by Robert S. Corrington, *The Community of Interpreters: On the Hermeneutics of Nature and the Bible in the American Philosophical Tradition* (StABH 3), Macon, GA: Mercer University Press, [2]1995 (1987), and Roger Lundin, 'Reading America', unpublished paper at the Crossing the Boundaries conference, Gloucester, MA, 1998. From the vast literature on this subject, an account which seeks to tie in theological with other issues is Jeffrey Stout, *The Flight from Authority: Religion, Morality and the Quest for Autonomy*, Notre Dame, IN: University of Notre Dame Press, 1981.

[28] Her writings are now collected in Nancey Murphy, *Anglo-American Postmodernity: Philosophical Perspectives on Science, Religion, and Ethics*, Colorado: Westview Press, 1997.

[29] Murphy, *Anglo-American Postmodernity*, 2 (where she makes the link), and 23–5, 131–51 on Austin as 'postmodern'. See also the influential article: Nancey Murphy and James Wm McClendon, Jr, 'Distinguishing Modern and Postmodern Theologies', *MTh* 5 (1989), 191–214.

Lindbeck explicitly seeks a way between cognitive-propositional models of religious language and experiential-expressive models, which he characterises as typically conservative and liberal respectively. The one is bound to a restrictive theory of reference and fact, the other to the reporting of internal religious experience.[30] He appeals to a 'cultural-linguistic' model as an alternative: religious language works in thickly descriptive terms, embodied in continuous traditions which give currency to the language.

It is not my purpose to investigate Lindbeck's influential proposal, except to point out that it gets confused in the literature with certain speech-act approaches to language, apparently because it expresses a very similar dissatisfaction with the traditional options: both views propose that the familiar dichotomy between fact-stating language and the language of experience or 'effect' can be transcended by a third way, a kind of *via media*. But in place of Lindbeck's cultural traditions, speech act theory follows the path of looking at how a speaker invests himself or herself in an utterance in terms of personal backing and stance. Might one say that where Lindbeck posits a third axis as a way of making sense of the other two (propositional content and force), speech act theory contents itself with showing ways in which these first two are integrally linked.

Thus in my view it is a mistake to see speech act theory as a variety of anti-foundationalism, and indeed it is a mistake to suppose that it even addresses this issue in particular. My use of speech act theory to address certain hermeneutical questions presupposes that there is no universal foundation to linguistic practice, but I am unpersuaded that this is a startling thesis worthy of epistemological soul-searching. Nevertheless, if one does wish to defend the view that the loss of a supposed absolute certainty need not entail incoherence in religious claims or religious uses of language, whether or not such a defence is self-consciously 'non-foundational', then speech act theory provides one way of so doing.

For example, in his book *Divine Discourse*, Nicholas Wolterstorff proposes the framework of speech action theory, as he calls it, as

---

[30] George A. Lindbeck, *The Nature of Doctrine: Religion and Theology in a Postliberal Age*, London: SPCK, 1984, 16.

a way of articulating how it can be that God speaks through the biblical text, or more precisely in the biblical text.[31] I would like to propose that we see his argument as a defensive polemic against a certain sort of philosophical argument, namely, that it is incoherent to read the Bible in the belief that God may speak to the reader through that process. I am encouraged to think this way by a comment of McClendon and Smith concerning the so-called 'reformed epistemology' in which Wolterstorff has played such a role: the views of reformed epistemologists 'are designed solely to negate or blunt the attack of foundationalist epistemological theories on religious belief'.[32] For example, Plantinga's response to the charge that the reformed epistemologist might as well believe in the Great Pumpkin as in the Christian God is correct as a way of showing that holding one conviction does not entail holding any and every conviction.[33] However, as McClendon and Smith point out, in a wider pluralist world, this falls far short of demonstrating why a particular belief might or might not be justified. To demonstrate precisely this, and to do so using speech act theory, in fact, is the burden of their book.[34]

My concern here is simply to propose a similar judgment concerning the purpose and achievement of *Divine Discourse*. In bald essence, this book mounts an argument that the locutions of the Bible may serve as the vehicles of divine illocutions, thus securing the literal claim that God speaks, since to speak is to engage in the production of illocutionary acts. This much is a successful argument.[35]

What is considerably less clear in Wolterstorff's account is whether this claim enables us to make substantive progress

[31] Nicholas Wolterstorff, *Divine Discourse: Philosophical Reflections on the Claim That God Speaks,* Cambridge: Cambridge University Press, 1995.

[32] James Wm McClendon Jr and James M. Smith, *Convictions: Defusing Religious Relativism,* Valley Forge, PA: Trinity Press International, 1994, 12; cf. Nicholas Wolterstorff, 'What "Reformed Epistemology" Is Not', *Perspectives* (November 1992), 10–16.

[33] Cf. Alvin Plantinga, 'Reason and Belief in God', in Alvin Plantinga and Nicholas Wolterstorff (eds), *Faith and Rationality: Reason and Religious Belief in God,* Notre Dame: University of Notre Dame Press, 1983, 16–93, especially 74–8.

[34] McClendon and Smith, *Convictions,* 12–13, and throughout. See below.

[35] Wolterstorff, *Divine Discourse,* e.g. 75–94 and, on God speaking, 95–129. The precise nature of an 'illocutionary act' need not concern us in this chapter, but will be examined in chapter 2.

towards elucidating what it is that God says.[36] My own view is that
the general claim of God's speaking is secured at the expense of
opening up a considerable gap between the textual locutions
and the divine illocutions. Wolterstorff's claim is that what it is
for a locution to count as a divine illocution is describable
through a fairly tight set of rules which pose no significant
interpretive problems. This is even more his view concerning
the interpretation of discourse for human discourse. Yet in so
arguing he makes points such as the following:

> Our interest as authorial-discourse interpreters is indeed in what
> the speaker said – not in what he intended to say, but in what he did
> say, if anything. But saying is an intentional action. And more
> importantly, we have to know how he was operating, or trying to
> operate, the system.[37]

This, however, is problematic, for how do we in fact know how
the speaker was trying to operate the system? In his elaboration, Wolterstorff is content with 'in coming to know that, a
crucial role is played by our beliefs as to which plan of action
for saying something he probably implemented'. In summary:
'interpreters cannot operate without beliefs about the dis-
courser'.[38]

The key word here is 'beliefs', and while Wolterstorff is surely
right, what follows from this is simply the observation that the
hermeneutical question (or problem) is recast in speech act
terms, rather than solved by it. Stanley Fish, as we shall see in
chapter 4, might wish to take this word 'beliefs' and argue that
we are back at community-relative conventions, but of course
this is to make only one of the possible judgments open at this
point. In chapter 4 I shall argue that one need not follow Fish to
his end of the spectrum.

The only moral I wish to draw from the discussion at this
point is that speech act theory cannot be marshalled as anti-
foundationalist evidence, since it is not in itself a mechanism
for making judgments but rather it is concerned with clarify-

---

[36] This may account for the cautious response to the book by biblical scholars,
such as I. Howard Marshall, ' "To Find Out What God Is Saying": Reflections on the
Authorizing of Scripture', in Roger Lundin (ed.), *Disciplining Hermeneutics:
Interpretation in Christian Perspective*, Grand Rapids: Eerdmans, and Leicester: Apollos,
1997, 49–55.

[37] Wolterstorff, *Divine Discourse*, 199.

[38] Wolterstorff, *Divine Discourse*, 196.

ing presuppositions, entailments and implications in those judgments.[39]

Conclusions

The conclusions of this section are worth stating briefly, in order that we may keep in view the appropriate goals for our own investigation. Speech act theory provides tools for analysing uses of language, in particular uses which are strongly self-involving. Although it has been used in attempts to provide a comprehensive philosophy of language, and although likewise claims have been made about the self-involving nature of all language, I judge these claims to be either mistaken or else true only in a weak sense. One particular use of speech act theory in theological work is thus both acknowledged and set to one side for the purposes of this study: the view that the coherence of religious language can be defended by removing the supposed sting from the anti-foundationalist charge by appeal to speech act theory.[40] I acknowledge the validity of this as a polemical counter-measure, but note that my own interest lies along a different path.

[39] On the prevalence of hermeneutical foreclosure as a result of pressing questions about the 'anti-foundational' agenda see now Anthony C. Thiselton, 'Communicative Action and Promise in Interdisciplinary, Biblical, and Theological Hermeneutics', in Roger Lundin, Clarence Walhout and Anthony C. Thiselton, *The Promise of Hermeneutics*, Grand Rapids: Eerdmans, and Carlisle: Paternoster Press, 1999, 133–239, especially 209–14.

[40] In the light of this, I make here a brief comment on the work, already mentioned, of McClendon and Smith, *Convictions*. Their account has a formal similarity to mine: their view of how to analyse statements such as 'God led Israel across the Sea of Reeds' is that 'such assertions *happily* occur, *can* happily occur, only in connection with the rich involvement in stance, in commitment, and in appropriate effect . . . that make up the happiness of [such a statement]' (70) and in particular they are keen to focus on the idea that there is 'no nonconvictional road to the truths around which our convictions cluster' (69). Their account, self-consciously 'nonfoundational' (9–10), effectively suggests that beliefs and convictions must be judged as parts of whole traditions, and, in much the spirit of MacIntyre (175–8), that the pressing question for a theologian is how to justify a set of convictions as a viable tradition. In my judgment, this is an excellent account of how self-involving claims work within a framework of what I will later call institutional facts, but it appears to suppose that the same degree of institutionality pervades all convictional utterances. While God-language and faith claims may indeed be helpfully explicated for certain purposes within such a perspective, I would insist, following Searle, that the philosophy of speech acts implies very clearly that brute facts must lie at the bottom of the institutional heirarchy. I take up this discussion in chapter 6 below regarding the 'truth' of confessional statements.

These preliminary points suggest that speech act theory, understood in the terms in which I shall describe it, will not offer any method of by-passing the hermeneutical issues of interpretation, or the need for judgment. As will become clear, I therefore offer it not as a hermeneutical method, but as a tool for investigating certain types of strongly self-involving biblical language.

§3 Exegeting Texts or Reconceiving Exegesis?

One further distinction is worth considering at this point. In the context of biblical interpretation, Martin Buss suggests that we might have two different goals with speech act theory: use it to refine our exegetical procedures or step back and utilise it in the theoretical reconceptualisation of exegesis.[41] In the first of these, we already know what exegesis is, and speech act theory helps us to do it better. In the second, more ambitiously, it changes our view of what is required of us as exegetes. I want to propose that although this distinction sounds clear, it in fact disguises the nature of the difference between the two tasks, which are not as different as they first appear.

In the light of the foregoing discussion, I would propose that in the former case, where we are engaged in the process of exegesis, speech act theory will be of use in understanding texts which concern themselves with the kinds of language uses which are strongly self-involving. More generally, it may clarify the issues in certain texts where a point at issue is the existence or non-existence of, for example, essential preparatory conditions for the performing of felicitous speech acts. This has been done, within and without the world of biblical studies, without any necessary reconceptualisation of the task of exegesis itself.[42]

The latter case sounds more ambitious: speech act theory may enable us to reconceive exegesis itself. This is the programme proposed and attempted by Dietmar Neufeld, in a

---

[41] Martin J. Buss, 'Potential and Actual Interactions between Speech Act Theory and Biblical Studies', in Hugh C. White (ed.), *Speech Act Theory and Biblical Criticism* (= *Semeia* 41), Decatur, GA: Scholars Press, 1988, 125–34, here 125.

[42] Cf. Anthony C. Thiselton, 'The Supposed Power of Words in the Biblical Writings', *JTS* 25 (1974), 283–99; Stanley Fish, 'How to Do Things with Austin and Searle: Speech-Act Theory and Literary Criticism', *MLN* 91 (1976), 983–1025, reprinted in Fish, *Is There a Text in This Class? The Authority of Interpretive Communities*, Cambridge, MA: Harvard University Press, 1980, 197–245.

book on 1 John significantly entitled *Reconceiving Texts as Speech Acts*.[43] However, in a summary of Neufeld's purpose, which directly addresses the distinction we are considering, Duane Watson notes:

> Neufeld argues that the author of 1 John incorporates a number of speech-acts in boasts, denials, and confessions to create a literary world of an apocalyptic kind. This world delimits the boundaries of proper and improper confession and ethical behaviour and the apocalyptic consequences of each, often relying heavily upon antithesis for clarification. When entering this world the readers are encouraged to transform their understanding of God, Jesus, the world, their speech, and their conduct. They are challenged to create a proper confession and ethical behaviour rather than become alienated from God.[44]

In so saying Watson, whose view of speech act theory largely treats it as a variety of rhetorical criticism, appears to be representing Neufeld's achievement as a matter of elucidating the way in which *correct understanding* may lead to a transformed lifestyle. In fact Neufeld goes further and wishes to use speech act theory to point up the ethical backing given to confessions of Christ as fundamentally the embodiment of Christian discipleship in counter-distinction to the inauthentic living (and not just teaching) which is indicated by the 'antichrist' in 1 John.[45] That this is a matter of 'reconceiving texts', as Neufeld's study has it, is because the boasts, denials and confessions he considers are all examples of strongly self-involving language used in a document (be it a letter or church instruction (*paraenesis*)) which is directly communicative, that is, where authorial agency is focused on eliciting a response.

I suggest that it is this feature of 1 John which accounts for the apparent distinction between Neufeld's 'reconceiving' of texts, and what Buss considers as the refining of exegetical procedures which are already in place, where the prime examples, cited earlier, all occur in less directive texts (narrative, literary works generally) where authorial agency works less directly. Thus I propose recasting what seems like a fair suggestion in the

---

[43] Dietmar Neufeld, *Reconceiving Texts as Speech Acts: An Analysis of 1 John* (Bib Int Ser 7), Leiden: E. J. Brill, 1994.

[44] Duane F. Watson, 'Rhetorical Criticism of Hebrews and the Catholic Epistles since 1978', *CR:BS* 5 (1997), 175–207; here 199.

[45] Neufeld's specific proposals are considered more fully in ch. 5, §4.2 below.

following terms: the strongly self-involving language of the biblical text may be manifest in two distinct ways. First, it may occur within some narrative world, for example, in blessings or curses pronounced by characters in the biblical narrative, where the self-involvement is on the part of the characters in that biblical world. Second, it may occur as part of the communication between author and reader, as with a work such as 1 John, where the self-involvement at issue is raised in the discussion which takes place between the author and the real-world reader. This way of putting the matter seems to do better justice to the varieties of self-involvement relevant to this study.

§4 Major Theorists in the Field

I conclude this introduction with a brief review of the relevant work of Anthony Thiselton and Kevin Vanhoozer, the two authors who have most consistently proposed the suitability of speech act theory for the various tasks of biblical interpretation and theological hermeneutics, and whose work therefore stands most obviously in direct relationship to my own proposals.[46]

§4.1 Anthony C. Thiselton

Thiselton's conviction is that 'Speech-act theory has suffered undeserved neglect in biblical interpretation, in systematic theology, and in discussions of "religious language" in textbooks on the philosophy of religion'.[47] In a series of works over the last thirty years he has sought to indicate some of the appropriate resources offered by speech act theory for these various tasks.[48]

---

[46] Other authors will be considered at various points in later chapters.

[47] Anthony C. Thiselton, 'Speech-Act Theory and the Claim That God Speaks: Nicholas Wolterstorff's *Divine Discourse*', *SJT* 50 (1997), 97–110, here 97.

[48] A convenient summary of his overall work is provided by Anthony C. Thiselton, 'Thirty Years of Hermeneutics: Retrospect and Prospects', in Joze Krasovec (ed.), *Interpretation of the Bible*, Ljubljana: Slovenska akademija znanosti in umetnosti, and Sheffield: Sheffield Academic Press, 1998, 1559–74. See also Brian J. Walsh, 'Anthony Thiselton's Contribution to Biblical Hermeneutics', *CSR* 14 (1985), 224–35; C. G. Bartholomew, 'Three Horizons: Hermeneutics from the Other End – an Evaluation of Anthony Thiselton's Hermeneutic Proposals', *EJTh* 5 (1996), 121–35; and Dan R. Stiver, 'The Uneasy Alliance between Evangelicalism and Postmodernism: A Reply to Anthony Thiselton', in David S. Dockery (ed.), *The Challenge of Postmodernism: An Evangelical Engagement*, Wheaton: Bridgepoint, 1995, 239–53.

In a 1970 article on the parables, Thiselton draws on some parallels suggested by Robert Funk between the language-event of continental hermeneutics and the performative-utterance approach of Austin.[49] Austin and Wittgenstein offer more nuanced tools for the task: 'the crux of the matter is that *assertions themselves* may function in various ways and with various effects'.[50] Many of the ideas articulated in this article become part of the framework for Thiselton's later work, receiving clearer articulation in a general fashion in his programmatic 1973 article: 'The Use of Philosophical Categories in New Testament Hermeneutics', which sets out essentially the programme of his later *The Two Horizons*.[51]

A clear example of the exegetical relevance of such an approach is provided by his analysis of 'The Supposed Power of Words in the Biblical Writings' in which he subjects to critique the view that Old Testament curses and blessings operated by virtue of a primitive view of language where the speakers believed (mistakenly) that their words had brute causal power (an image often expounded with reference to analogies drawn from military weaponry).[52] Drawing again on Austin, Thiselton suggests that such performative utterances rely on social institutions which create the conditions for institutional processes such as blessing, and therefore the question of why a blessing was seen as efficacious, or why it could not be withdrawn (as, for example, in the case of Isaac and Jacob in Genesis 27), was a matter of the existence or non-existence of social conventions rather than a magical view of language.[53]

Further studies have worked both in exegetical and in more obviously theological areas. In the case of the latter, Thiselton's work has ranged over the performative nature of liturgy,[54] the inadequately grounded nature of functional hermeneutical

---

[49] Anthony C. Thiselton, 'The Parables as Language-Event: Some Comments on Fuchs's Hermeneutics in the Light of Linguistic Philosophy', *SJT* 23 (1970), 437–68.

[50] Thiselton, 'Parables', 439.

[51] Anthony C. Thiselton, 'The Use of Philosophical Categories in New Testament Hermeneutics', *Churchman* 87 (1973), 87–100.

[52] Thiselton, 'Supposed Power of Words', 283–6.

[53] Thiselton, 'Supposed Power of Words', 293–4.

[54] Thiselton, *Language, Liturgy and Meaning* (Grove Liturgical Study 2), Bramcote: Grove Books, [2]1986 (1975).

approaches such as reader-response theory,[55] the pastoral insights available from speech act theory's linking of effect with presupposed states of affairs,[56] and the suggestion that speech act theory offers a way out of the impasse between conservative and functionalist approaches to biblical authority.[57] This last contribution starts from Tyndale's view of speech acts in the Bible itself,[58] and then draws parallels between hermeneutical debates and debates concerning authority. Thiselton notes the crucial nature of the illocutionary/perlocutionary distinction so central to speech act theory yet which lies beyond the reach of the purely functional approach to the effects of language on readers: 'The authority of the Bible, then, derives from the operative statutory or institutional validity of transforming speech-acts in Scripture', corrigible in the light of what has not yet happened, but inviting us forward as a believing community 'towards those verdicts and corroboration of promises and pledges which will become public and revealed as definitive at the last judgement'.[59] This emphasis, drawn from Pannenberg, also invites a critique of the view that all interpretation is self-interested power play, again drawing on the distinction between illocutionary and perlocutionary force.[60]

More specifically exegetical studies have attempted to bring the insights of speech act theory to bear on particular interpretive issues. In his *New Horizons in Hermeneutics*, Thiselton combines a wide-ranging agenda concerning the various paths of hermeneutics in its post-Gadamer forms with a particular argument that the recognition of words as belonging to different illocutionary categories leads us to see that 'The biblical texts

[55] Thiselton, 'Reader-Response Hermeneutics, Action Models, and the Parables of Jesus', in Roger Lundin, Anthony C. Thiselton and Clarence Walhout, *The Responsibility of Hermeneutics*, Grand Rapids: Eerdmans, and Exeter: Paternoster Press, 1985, 79–113.

[56] Thiselton, 'Address and Understanding: Some Goals and Models of Biblical Interpretation as Principles of Vocational Training', *Anvil* 3 (1986), 101–18, especially 116–18.

[57] Thiselton, 'Authority and Hermeneutics: Some Proposals for a More Creative Agenda', in Philip E. Satterthwaite and David F. Wright (eds), *A Pathway into the Holy Scripture*, Grand Rapids: Eerdmans, 1994, 107–41.

[58] The article is in a book celebrating, *inter alia*, the 500 year anniversary of Tyndale's birth.

[59] Thiselton, 'Authority and Hermeneutics', 137.

[60] Thiselton, 'Authority and Hermeneutics', 137–41; cf. also Part 1 of idem, *Interpreting God and the Postmodern Self: On Meaning, Manipulation and Promise*, Edinburgh: T&T Clark, 1995, 3–43.

abound in examples of occurrences of these verbs in institutional, situational, and inter-personal contexts which render them performative speech-acts'.[61] In particular he applies this framework to E. P. Sanders's claims about the Pauline language of the power of the cross, arguing that Sanders has overreacted against 'atonement' language in favour of 'participatory' language, whereas speech act theory suggests that participatory language necessarily presupposes certain interpersonal states of affairs.[62] Similar concerns are evident in Thiselton's later article about synoptic Christology: 'The Synoptic Gospels make promissory language explicit, leaving the possibility of christological assertion to lie hidden *implicitly* behind the overt speech-acts of Jesus.'[63] He again draws out the significance of the illocutionary/perlocutionary distinction by showing how it is institutional status and not causal force which informs Jesus' words and deeds: 'their respective significance for christology is one of almost complete opposition and contrast',[64] since perlocutionary force relies on self-assertiveness, which would undo the very point of Jesus' sacrificial messiahship; and hence the illocutionary aspect of his Christological claims is required by the nature of his mission. Finally, a 1993 article which restricted its observations more to exegetical clarification focused on the way in which first-person utterances in their self-involving way differ from logico-linguistic reflections on the nature of language, and suggested that this throws light on the liar paradox of Titus 1:12–13.[65] In particular, one should see Titus 1:12–13 not as a historically contingent proposition, but as making a logical point: 'the aim is to demonstrate that, *anchored to an inappropriate behaviour context, first-person* utterances can become *self-defeating*'.[66]

---

[61] Thiselton, *New Horizons in Hermeneutics: The Theory and Practice of Transforming Biblical Reading*, London: HarperCollins, 1992, 298–9.

[62] Thiselton, *New Horizons*, 300–4. In chapter 6 below I will be considering more closely this kind of argument and suggesting possible modifications to it.

[63] Thiselton, 'Christology in Luke, Speech-Act Theory, and the Problem of Dualism in Christology after Kant', in Joel B. Green and Max Turner (eds), *Jesus of Nazareth: Lord and Christ*, Carlisle: Paternoster Press, and Grand Rapids: Eerdmans, 1994, 453–72, here 466.

[64] Thiselton, 'Christology in Luke', 462–3. Quote from 463, originally in italics.

[65] Thiselton, 'The Logical Role of the Liar Paradox in Titus 1:12, 13: A Dissent from the Commentaries in the Light of Philosophical and Logical Analysis', *BibInt* 2 (1994), 207–23.

[66] Thiselton, 'Liar Paradox', 219.

Thiselton's most recent work focuses on the significance of the category of *communicative action* in various biblical and theological pursuits, with speech act theory being one prominent way of articulating this category.[67] This lengthy treatment contains several points of contact with my own work, which will be noted at appropriate points.

In brief, I suggest, first, that one of Thiselton's major interests has been the conceptual clarification of the philosophical issues involved in biblical interpretation.[68] Speech act theory has been a major tool to this end, although not the only one. Secondly, exegetical insight has followed with regard to certain types of texts, and in particular to texts which concern themselves with such speech *acts* as promising, blessing or commanding. Thirdly, and perhaps most significantly, he persistently demonstrates that false dichotomies have bedevilled the hermeneutical models brought to bear on biblical interpretation, and he uses speech act theory to bring together what has been unnecessarily separated. By consistently relating texts to the streams of life which produce them, and insisting on this in the reading process too, he attempts to strike a balance which some hermeneutical approaches fail to achieve. Perhaps the most helpful way of expressing these points is to say that Thiselton uses speech act theory as a powerful *resource* for refining and clarifying the varied tasks of hermeneutics.

§4.2 *Kevin J. Vanhoozer*

Kevin Vanhoozer's continuing interest in speech act theory and its implications has been a persistent feature of his writings from his earliest 1986 article through to his comprehensive 'theology of interpretation', *Is There a Meaning in This Text?*[69] In his earliest work, his concern is with the question: 'how does the diversity of Scripture's literary forms affect the way we take biblical propositions and understand scriptural truth?'[70] He argues that

---

[67] Thiselton, 'Communicative Action', especially 144–50 and 223–39.

[68] See explicitly Thiselton, *Two Horizons*, 3–10.

[69] Kevin J. Vanhoozer, *Is There a Meaning in this Text? The Bible, the Reader, and the Morality of Literary Knowledge*, Grand Rapids: Zondervan, 1998.

[70] Vanhoozer, 'The Semantics of Biblical Literature: Truth and Scripture's Diverse Literary Forms', in D. A. Carson and John D. Woodbridge (eds), *Hermeneutics, Authority and Canon*, Leicester: IVP, 1986, 53–104, here 56.

defenders of conservative views of biblical inspiration, wanting to affirm the truth of the Bible against what they see as liberal and/or Barthian conceptions of 'existential' truth, have been led into spurious claims concerning the role of propositions in the Bible, even to 'the heresy of propositional paraphrase'.[71] Drawing on Mary Louise Pratt and Susan Lanser, Vanhoozer suggests that 'there is a correlation between a text's genre, or literary form, and a text's illocutionary point and force'.[72] As a result, 'the propositional content is intended to function or count *as* something in the communicative act'.[73] I shall be taking up these various emphases in later chapters. In fact, Vanhoozer's article turns aside at this point to explore ways in which his approach rehabilitates the concept of 'infallibility' since he here introduces a presupposed doctrine of inerrancy. It seems fair to conclude that this is a concern drawn from elsewhere rather than from speech act theory.

Vanhoozer has also written of the need for philosophical sensitivity in hermeneutics; of biblical theology as a 'poetics of revelation', based around an understanding of speech acts in their biblical genres, which form the bridge between the canon and the concepts of theology, and of the particular epistemological role of the speech act of testimony in John's Gospel.[74] Many of these concerns are drawn together in his 1994 contribution to the volume mentioned earlier celebrating 500 years since Tyndale's birth.[75] Here he considers the issues surrounding a doctrine of Scripture by noting that speech act theory 'allows us to transcend the debilitating dichotomy

---

[71] Vanhoozer, 'Semantics of Biblical Literature', 56–75; cf. the quoted title on 67.

[72] Vanhoozer, 'Semantics of Biblical Literature', 91. On the work of Pratt and Lanser, see chapter 3 below.

[73] Vanhoozer, 'Semantics of Biblical Literature', 92.

[74] Vanhoozer, 'Christ and Concept: Doing Theology and the "Ministry" of Philosophy', in John D. Woodbridge and Thomas Edward McComiskey (eds), *Doing Theology in Today's World: Essays in Honor of Kenneth S. Kantzer*, Grand Rapids: Zondervan, 1991, 99–145; idem, 'From Canon to Concept: "Same" and "Other" in the Relation between Biblical and Systematic Theology', *SBET* 12 (1994), 96–124, especially 111–12; idem, 'The Hermeneutics of I–Witness Testimony: John 21.20–24 and the "Death" of the "Author"', in A. Graeme Auld (ed.), *Understanding Poets and Prophets: Essays in Honour of George Wishart Anderson* (JSOTS 152), Sheffield: Sheffield Academic Press, 1993, 366–87.

[75] Kevin J. Vanhoozer, 'God's Mighty Speech-Acts: The Doctrine of Scripture Today', in Philip E. Satterthwaite and David F. Wright (eds), *A Pathway into the Holy Scripture*, Grand Rapids: Eerdmans, 1994, 143–81.

between revelation as "God saying" and "God doing"', and, reminiscent of his 1986 article, he urges that instead of a narrow focus on truth-telling, we should see 'Scripture [as] rather composed of divine-human speech-acts which, through what they say, accomplish several authoritative cognitive, spiritual and social functions'.[76] This, and indeed many of his reflections here concerning the functional-propositional divide in views of Scripture, mirror Thiselton's comments in the same volume.

In *Is There a Meaning in This Text?* Vanhoozer offers speech act theory as an approach which focuses our attention on the irreducibly communicative role of texts: 'A text . . . is communicative action fixed by writing.'[77] He provides a comprehensive review of Searle's work and adopts and adapts it to his own ends, to develop a theological understanding of text and to restore to its rightful place the authorial prerogative to determine what a text means, not in locutionary or perlocutionary terms, but in illocutionary terms: 'what the author was doing *in* writing, *in* tending to his words in such and such a fashion'.[78] This argument is mounted against the backdrop of a claim that the postmodern displacement of 'meaning' is a theological phenomenon, where the 'death of God' lies directly behind the 'death of the author'.[79] Powerful and suggestive as his analysis is, it remains largely at this level of theological conceptualisation and does not engage with particular interpretive issues in biblical texts. Not all will be persuaded that 'Speech act theory serves as a handmaiden to a trinitarian theology of communication',[80] and nor is it entirely evident that there need be a clear correlation between the Father and the locution, the Son and the illocution and the Spirit and the perlocution, as is suggested both here and elsewhere.[81]

Vanhoozer's approach most notably differs from Thiselton's in its appeal to speech act theory as an overarching perspective

[76] Vanhoozer, 'God's Mighty Speech Acts', 147, 148.
[77] Vanhoozer, *Is There a Meaning in This Text?*, 229; cf. especially 207–14 and 226–9.
[78] Vanhoozer, *Is There a Meaning in This Text?*, 253.
[79] Vanhoozer, *Is There a Meaning in This Text?*, 30, 198–200, and *passim*. He consciously follows here George Steiner, *Real Presences: Is There Anything in What We Say?*, London: Faber & Faber, 1990. It is perhaps debatable whether Steiner's 'theological' reading of deconstruction is entirely conducive to Vanhoozer's own specifically Trinitarian concerns.
[80] Vanhoozer, *Is There a Meaning in This Text?*, 457.
[81] Vanhoozer, *Is There a Meaning in This Text?*, 455–7; cf. Vanhoozer, 'God's Mighty Speech Acts', 169–80.

within which different genres are at work.[82] As such it is more obviously a doctrinal framework than a hermeneutical one, in contrast to Thiselton's view that even without a vantage point exterior to the hermeneutical debate one may still make good use of speech act theory in cases where it addresses issues appropriate to the texts at hand.[83] My own approach will tend towards this more eclectic view, but this is perhaps more a difference of agendas than of estimation of value. In his repeated calls for philosophical clarity in the work of theological interpretation, Vanhoozer has rightly drawn attention to the various ways in which speech act theory may serve as an important conceptual framework.

Before moving on to the biblical investigations of part 2 of this study, I spend the next three chapters exploring the precise nature of the resources of speech act theory, looking in particular at the various questions which arise concerning criteria. I shall take in turn the issues of criteria for speech acts themselves, for speech acts as they relate to texts, and finally for construal, an issue which is placed on our agenda precisely by considering how to appropriate speech act theory for questions concerning texts.

---

[82] Vanhoozer, 'God's Mighty Speech Acts', 180.
[83] This distinction between the approaches of Vanhoozer and of Thiselton is noted by Bartholomew, 'Three Horizons', 134, n. 55.

PART 1

Speech Acts, Texts and Construal:
The Problem of Criteria

2

Speech Act Theory:
Past Forms and
Present Functions

To understand a text as a communicative action is an appealing move in broad terms. It appears to be both straightforward and a useful corrective to overly dominant models of texts as representational or, to borrow Janet Martin Soskice's term, 'reality-depicting'.[1] The philosophical field of inquiry to develop out of this basic insight is *speech act theory*, and its foundational text is J. L. Austin's engagingly titled *How to Do Things with Words*.[2] However, in moving beyond the simple observation captured in Austin's title, that when we speak we do other things too, one encounters considerable debate concerning the criteria which exist for understanding the different dimensions of speech acts. The further claim that texts may be read as speech acts will occupy us in chapter 3. Before one can examine that claim, speech act theory itself needs to be understood.

In this chapter I shall be examining in particular the concept of the *illocutionary act*, perhaps the major analytical tool of speech act theory, along with its associated concepts such as *brute* and *institutional facts*. I suggest that speech act theory offers some helpful resources for the interpretive task, but that attempts to use these tools are hampered by a lack of clarity concerning

---

[1] Janet Martin Soskice, *Metaphor and Religious Language*, Oxford: Clarendon Press, 1985, 97. For Vincent Brümmer also, speech act theory offers us a way of moving from reality being depicted by language to reality serving as a constituting context for effective speech acts: Vincent Brümmer, *Theology & Philosophical Inquiry: An Introduction*, Philadelphia: Westminster Press, 1982, 9–33, 228–48.

[2] Hereafter abbreviated as *HDTW*.

many of the major theoretical ideas pertinent to speech acts, including indeed the very idea of the illocutionary act itself.

My solution to this lack of clarity is to retrace the development of speech act theory and examine its various ideas in context, in the hope that a coherent set of criteria for speech acts may emerge. Such a proposal involves looking at the different forms of speech act theory developed by Austin, Searle and others; and then also examining the particular functions of speech act theory once it is grasped and, to a certain extent, rearticulated as a current live option, independently of the functions its constituent parts may have had when originally introduced.

§1 Speech Act Theory: Background and Introduction

The period after 1945 was a major creative phase of British philosophy and earned a variety of generic names: 'ordinary language' philosophy, Wittgensteinian philosophy, Oxford philosophy and perhaps most generally 'analytic philosophy'. Despite the loose usage of these terms it is worth noting that none of them are interchangeable: all represent particular emphases.[3] Peter Strawson has suggested 'connective' analysis as the most helpful term to cover the variety of emphases included.[4]

These approaches were characterised by concentration on careful elucidation of concepts, a study of language and its uses, and a general aversion towards theory-building on the grand scale.[5] Austin's work in particular falls into this characterisation, as does that of the later Wittgenstein. Austin himself was neither particularly influenced nor impressed by Wittgenstein, but practised philosophy in a way which was certainly congruent with his main emphases.[6] As David Pears has observed, 'they both thought that there was something wrong with the methods

---

[3] A survey and analysis of them all is the subject of P. M. S. Hacker, *Wittgenstein's Place in Twentieth-Century Analytic Thought*, Oxford: Blackwell, 1996. He notes major variations within the various 'traditions' these labels represent; e.g. 148–61, especially 158–9. Source material from this period is collected in Richard Rorty (ed.), *The Linguistic Turn: Recent Essays in Philosophical Method*, Chicago and London: University of Chicago Press, 1967. Contemporary surveys may be found in John Passmore, *A Hundred Years of Philosophy*, Harmondsworth: Penguin, [2]1966 (1957), 424–65; G. J. Warnock, *English Philosophy since 1900*, London: Oxford University Press, [2]1969 (1958).

[4] P. F. Strawson, *Analysis and Metaphysics: An Introduction to Philosophy*, Oxford: Oxford University Press, 1992, 21.

[5] Hacker, *Wittgenstein's Place*, 159–60.

[6] Hacker, *Wittgenstein's Place*, 172–5.

of earlier philosophers, and they both thought that the right method would involve the study of language'.[7]

Austin and method

Austin did not believe that ordinary language was the sole interesting subject matter of philosophy, and his aversion to theory-building did not mean that he was unwilling to introduce any technical vocabulary when he felt it was necessary, as his terms *illocutionary* and *perlocutionary* amply demonstrate. That such views have been attributed to him is in part due to his overall reluctance to offer any wider thoughts on philosophical matters than his piecemeal papers, of which only seven were published in his lifetime; and the fact that on the one occasion where he obviously did offer such reflections, in the introduction to his 1956 presidential address to the Aristotelian Society ('A Plea for Excuses'), he evidently laid himself open to misinterpretation.[8] He observed that in the study of excuses there was plenty of material available in ordinary language for 'field work', as he called it, which, while not the 'last word' in philosophy, was at least the 'first word'. He also famously suggested that 'our common stock of words embodies all the distinctions men have found worth drawing' in explicit contrast to those words thought up by philosophers in their armchairs.[9]

As Geoffrey Warnock has observed, this was intended as a commendation of his subject of the time (excuses), rather than his method. The method was simply there if one chose to follow it.[10] For better or for worse, Austin described his method as 'linguistic phenomenology', by which he meant the procedure of examining '*what we should say when*, and so why and what we should mean by it'.[11] In his study of this aspect of Austin's work, Joseph DiGiovanna makes the point that the study of language itself is not an example of a field of inquiry in which people

---

[7] David Pears, 'Wittgenstein and Austin', in Bernard Williams and Alan Montefiore (eds), *British Analytical Philosophy*, London: Routledge & Kegan Paul, 1966, 17–39, here 17.

[8] J. L. Austin, 'A Plea for Excuses', in his *Philosophical Papers*, edited by J. O. Urmson and G. J. Warnock, Oxford: Oxford University Press, [3]1979 (1961), 175–204, here 177–86.

[9] Austin, 'Plea for Excuses', 182–5.

[10] G. J. Warnock, *J. L. Austin*, London: Routledge & Kegan Paul, [2]1991 (1989), 5.

[11] Austin, 'Plea for Excuses', 182, 181.

naturally draw up their own terms and discussions, and concludes that Austin's work on speech acts should not be viewed as an example of his linguistic phenomenology.[12] I would rather say that DiGiovanna's helpful observation explains why a linguistic phenomenologist can be at one and the same time so attentive to ordinary language use while also capable of bringing such a weight of technical vocabulary to bear on it. This is an important point and an important distinction, for want of which some influential streams of contemporary philosophy have found it apparently easy to dismiss 'ordinary language philosophy'.[13]

What *was* characteristic of Austin was his belief that ordinary language as it stood was not flawed, and neither did it require the philosopher to abandon it and replace it (or reduce it to) some form of logical calculus. In this, connective analysis represented a reaction against the early twentieth-century work of Russell, Frege and, to some extent, Moore, as well as a considerable redirection of the focus of Wittgenstein's earliest work, the *Tractatus*.[14] As Wittgenstein himself came to express it in his later work: 'Philosophy may in no way interfere with the actual use of language; it can in the end only describe it . . . It leaves everything as it is.'[15]

Although these roots are still visible in speech act theory today, there is also a strong tradition of allying its concerns with a formal logico-syntactic approach. Certainly Chomsky's work on syntactic structures was contemporary with early speech act theory and may have been a contributing factor to this development.[16]

---

[12] Joseph J. DiGiovanna, *Linguistic Phenomenology: Philosophical Method in J. L. Austin* (American University Studies, Series V, Philosophy, vol. 63), New York: Peter Lang, 1989, especially 189–94.

[13] In particular see the discussion of the so-called 'paradox of analysis': if a philosophical analysis catches the meaning of the original 'ordinary' expression then it is pointless; if it does not then it is false. A thorough and penetrating critique of 'ordinary language philosophy' which mentions this point, but which appears to exempt speech act theory from it, is provided by Jonathan Rée, 'English Philosophy in the Fifties', *Radical Philosophy* 65 (1993), 3–21; cf. 17 and n. 139 with 16 and n. 136. For a good example of the view that ordinary language carries no philosophical privilege, see W. V. O. Quine, 'Mr Strawson on Logical Theory', *Mind* 62, 248 (1953), 433–51, reprinted in idem, *The Ways of Paradox*, New York: Random House, 1966, 135–55.

[14] Hacker, *Wittgenstein's Place*, 1–38; Rée, 'English Philosophy'. The *Tractatus Logico-Philosophicus* was Wittgenstein's only published book in his lifetime: London: Routledge & Kegan Paul, 1961, trans. D. F. Pears and B. F. McGuinness (1921).

[15] Wittgenstein, *Philosophical Investigations*, §124.

[16] See, *inter alia*, N. Chomsky, *Syntactic Structures*, The Hague: Mouton, 1957.

Equally John Searle's programmatic recasting of Austin's ideas has lent itself to more formal approaches, as we shall see. Further, as Stanley Fish has pointed out, Austin's own work is possessed of a peculiar double structure whereby proposed terms are adapted out of all recognition, and frequently abandoned. He cites the 'double structure' of Austin's text as being

> responsible for the fact that the book has given rise to two versions of speech-act theory, one committed to reabsorbing illocutionary force into a formal theory of the Chomsky type . . . and the other committed to making illocutionary force a function of pragmatic – that is, unformalizable – circumstances.[17]

He cites Katz on one side and writers like H. P. Grice and Mary Louise Pratt on the other. A third stream is represented by those like Searle who have tried to 'reconcile the formal and the pragmatic', and he observes that for Austin it was never possible to reduce the workings of language to 'the operation of a formal mechanism', making a project like Searle's an uneasy marriage at best.[18] Fish's observation is astute, and will in large part be borne out in what follows.

§1.1 *Wittgenstein, Prichard and Austin's early work*

In the *Philosophical Investigations*, in the context of examining first-person utterances, Wittgenstein considered how we express fear, and began to ask about the different purposes we have in speaking. He pointed out the differences between, for example, using the same words as an expression of mourning or as a description or a prayer.[19] He also considered expressions of the form 'I believe . . . ', observing that 'If there were a verb meaning "to believe falsely", it would not have any significant first person present indicative'.[20] To say 'I believe' highlights the investment made by the speaker in the utterance:

---

[17] Stanley Fish, 'With the Compliments of the Author: Reflections on Austin and Derrida', *Critical Inquiry* 8 (1982), 693–721, reprinted in Fish, *Doing What Comes Naturally: Change, Rhetoric and the Practice of Theory in Literary and Legal Studies*, Oxford: Clarendon Press, 1989, 37–67.

[18] Fish, 'With the Compliments of the Author', 67.

[19] Wittgenstein, *Philosophical Investigations*, especially pp. 187–9ff. See also the 'preliminary sketches' of these ideas in idem, *The Blue and Brown Books*, Oxford: Blackwell, [2]1969 (1958), 143–8.

[20] Wittgenstein, *Philosophical Investigations*, 190.

it is not a depiction of some mental state revealed by the speaker's words.[21]

The particular role of first-person verbs like this would also be a feature considered by Austin. For Wittgenstein, the fact that 'My own relation to my words is wholly different from other people's'[22] was partly what enabled him to get away from the false picture of words operating out of mental states as translations of mental concepts which existed pre-linguistically. To anticipate, the speech act, here, is a personal, self-involving act which must be considered within the 'forms of life' where it takes place. Although many of the key elements of speech act theory are in place here, nevertheless, 'for better or for worse, there is barely a mention of speech-act analysis in the whole of Wittgenstein's *oeuvre*'.[23] Hacker, for his part, notes only some unpublished references to greetings and thankings not being statements; a line of thought mentioned without further elaboration in the *Investigations*, at §489.[24] Perhaps this is less significant than it might appear: in due course I shall be arguing that the kinds of concern most helpfully illuminated by speech act theory are best viewed in what might be termed a 'Wittgensteinian perspective'.[25]

Austin himself was White's Professor of Moral Philosophy at Oxford from 1952, a chair which had been held earlier by H. A Prichard. Prichard's influence on Austin is evident from the latter's first written (although unpublished) paper,[26] and it seems probable that in the background of his work on speech acts is Prichard's article, dating from around 1940, 'The Obligation to Keep a Promise'.[27]

Prichard considers how it is that 'In promising, agreeing, or undertaking to do some action we seem to be creating or

---

[21] As if, perhaps, one would have to listen to oneself speak in order to know what one believed. Cf. Wittgenstein, *Philosophical Investigations*, 191–2.

[22] Wittgenstein, *Philosophical Investigations*, 192.

[23] Hacker, *Wittgenstein's Place*, 245.

[24] Hacker, *Wittgenstein's Place*, 328, n. 33, referring to two different unpublished Wittgenstein manuscripts.

[25] See also §3.4 below where I discuss how Searle relates his own work to that of Wittgenstein.

[26] Now ch. 1 of Austin, *Philosophical Papers*, 1–31.

[27] G. J. Warnock, *English Philosophy*, 12; Hacker, *Wittgenstein's Place* 299, n. 86. The article is reprinted in H. A. Prichard, *Moral Obligation: Essays and Lectures*, Oxford: Clarendon Press, 1949, 169–79. On Prichard, see the brief assessment of Warnock, *English Philosophy*, 9–12.

bringing into existence the obligation to do it, so much so that promising seems just to *be* binding ourselves . . . to do it'.[28] His own article pursues the line of arguing that one makes some kind of general prior promise not to utter certain noises without also intending to be bound by certain obligations, which in turn leads him to something like Searle's later notion of Background, with an appeal to general expectations required by interpersonal behaviour. Although hampered by the lack of any particular conceptual apparatus for expressing his ideas, Prichard's article clearly envisages an inquiry along the lines which Austin would take up. Indeed, the act of promising remains the great archetypal speech act, even if the degree to which 'creating an obligation' is viewed as an intentional act remains debated.[29]

In Austin's work itself, two of the papers collected in his posthumous *Philosophical Papers* broach the topic of speech act theory, while a third, 'Other Minds', far from being about other minds, makes preliminary use of his thoughts on knowing, promising and the 'descriptive fallacy'.[30]

'How to Talk – Some Simple Ways' is his first full discussion of speech acts, although it is extremely unusual in his work by virtue of the fact that it confines itself to an imaginary ideal speech situation S_0, where only sentences of the form 'I is a T' are permissible (in a universe of items and types).[31] Within this framework he develops a fourfold schema of speech acts, to demonstrate that, for instance, we need care in understanding exactly what we mean by 'statement'. (His schema is placing, casting, stating and instancing.) He also introduces the notion of *direction of fit,* which is concerned with the difference between fitting names to items and items to names.[32] He notes that the

---

[28] Prichard, *Moral Obligation*, 169.

[29] A helpful survey is provided by Jan Narveson, 'The Agreement to Keep Our Agreements: Hume, Prichard, and Searle', *Philosophical Papers* 23 (1994), 75–87, with particular reference to John Searle's celebrated 'How to Derive an "Ought" from an "Is"', *Philosophical Review* 73 (1964), 43–58, which he adapts into a more comprehensive speech act perspective in his *Speech Acts* (see below), 175–98.

[30] See 'Other Minds', in Austin, *Philosophical Papers*, 76–116, especially 98–103.

[31] Austin, *Philosophical Papers*, 134–53. Warnock judges it 'very strange' and 'extravagantly artificial', while suggesting that it formed a possible background to Austin's views on truth, where he espoused a correspondence theory, G. J. Warnock, *Austin*, 47.

[32] Austin, *Philosophical Papers*, 143.

difference between speech acts often resides principally in the
difference between envisaged speech situations.[33]

The other relevant paper represents a substantial step forward,
and indeed presents in outline the structure of his later *HDTW*.
'Performative Utterances' was originally a BBC radio talk given
in 1956,[34] and is parallelled in considerable measure by a paper
given in 1958: 'Performative-Constative'.[35] Indeed, where *HDTW*
was difficult to reconstruct from Austin's manuscripts these
articles were used instead. Both papers pursue the same path of
setting up a distinction between statements on the one hand
and performative utterances on the other, and then collapsing
it. They then call for an analysis of explicit performative verbs
and a study of the force with which an utterance is used.

§2 J. L. Austin's *How to Do Things with Words*

This unusual style of essentially proposing a series of distinctions
and then abandoning and/or replacing them by others also
forms the structure of *How to Do Things with Words*. It is this
feature of the work which has made such a variety of interpretations of it possible, and thus requires that one distinguish
carefully between the examples Austin used, the point he was
trying to make, and the basic ideas subsequently taken up by
speech act theorists.

The 'descriptive fallacy', that all statements are attempts to
describe states of affairs and as such are either true or false, is in
Austin's sights from the very beginning. It is clear, he argues,
that a great many statements are trying to do something else
altogether. He categorises sentences into *performatives* or
constatives: statements used to perform certain acts, or to describe
states of affairs, respectively.[36]

No sooner is this distinction made than he sets about
undermining it. At least four different approaches to the
performative–constative distinction ultimately suggest that it
needs reconsidering. First, there is the 'doctrine of the

---

[33] Austin, *Philosophical Papers*, 150–1.

[34] Austin, *Philosophical Papers*, 233–52.

[35] Printed in Charles E. Caton (ed.), *Philosophy and Ordinary Language*, Urbana:
University of Illinois Press, 1963, 22–33, with discussion 33–54. Reprinted, without
the discussion, in John R. Searle (ed.), *The Philosophy of Language*, Oxford: Oxford
University Press, 1971, 13–22.

[36] Austin, *HDTW*, 1–4. Further page references to this book are in the text.

infelicities', or '*the things that can be and go wrong* on the occasion of such utterances' (i.e. performatives) (14). These can be 'misfires', where for instance the act in question is only purported but does not properly occur (e.g. someone who is not entitled to name a ship does so); or they can be 'abuses' where the act *is* achieved but not properly (e.g. an insincere promise). But, significantly, these kinds of failings can also apply to constatives (14–20).

Secondly, with regard to performatives, Austin focuses on the issue of conventions:

> There must exist an accepted conventional procedure having a certain conventional effect, that procedure to include the uttering of certain words by certain persons in certain circumstances, and . . . the particular persons and circumstances in a given case must be appropriate for the invocation of the particular procedure invoked. (14–15; cf. discussion on 26–35)

Thirdly, there are the intentions which go along with the utterance (15; cf. discussion on 39–45). On both of these points Austin's conclusion is that philosophers have erred in saying that a statement can be considered true or false in isolation from the total speech act which is being performed (52). This only adds to the drift of the argument that the distinction between performatives and constatives cannot be sustained in its original, simple form.

His remaining approach to the problem is to look for a better clarification of the performative, by asking whether it has any distinguishing grammatical feature. He concludes that it does not (55–66). At this point, still not quite ready to give up the distinction, he embarks on what is perhaps an unfortunate attempt to argue that although 'utterances *as they stand*' are 'hopeless' in terms of exhibiting grammatically significant signs of their performative status, perhaps it is the case that all performative utterances could be 'reduced' to what he calls *explicit performatives*, involving first person present tense singular indicative active verbs of the form 'I promise . . .' or 'I baptise . . .', etc. (67–8). This discussion involves an attempt to find verbs which are themselves performative verbs, before coming to the conclusion that the project is not feasible.

This occasions his celebrated remark, by now over half way through the book, that 'It is time then to make a fresh start on the problem' (91). More seriously, it seems likely that it is this part of his inquiry, albeit presented originally as a dead end, which has given rise to some of the various 'readings' of his work as offering a rationale for the search for 'logical form' analysis of speech acts, replacing language as it stands with a form of language (a 'reduction', or a 'deep structure') which exhibits certain desired features.

§2.1 Locution, illocution and perlocution

The first step of Austin's fresh start is to discuss briefly some points concerning phonetic, phatic and rhetic acts,[37] but it seems that their sole function in his text is that taken together they comprise what he chooses to dub the *locutionary act* (94). This is the normal sense of 'saying something'. He then introduces the term *illocutionary act*: the 'performance of an act *in* saying something as opposed to performance of an act *of* saying something' (99–100). This, he points out, is not necessarily a clearly defined class of acts, but 'to perform a locutionary act is in general, we may say, also and *eo ipso* to perform an *illocutionary* act' (98); and the way in which the language functions in such a case is a question of its *illocutionary force*.

Force, for Austin here, is to be kept distinguished from meaning, where meaning is equivalent to sense and reference (100). This fits with his notion that the locutionary act contains the rhetic (sense and reference) act, leaving force as the additional factor which defines the illocutionary act as a distinctive (though not separate) act. One upshot of this is that it may be possible to determine entirely the locutionary act on any given occasion, but not thereby understand which illocutionary act has been performed (100–1). The first is, in Austin's terms, a traditional question of meaning; while the second may concern whether an act of informing, or ordering, or warning, etc. took place (109).

The third type of act in Austin's schema at this point is introduced thus: 'Saying something will often, or even normally, produce certain consequential effects upon the feelings,

---

[37] He defines these as follows: a *phonetic* act is the act of uttering certain noises; a *phatic* act is 'the act of uttering certain vocables or words . . . in a certain construction . . . with a certain intonation'; and a *rhetic* act is the act of using the pheme (of the phatic act) with a (more or less) definite sense and reference; Austin, *HDTW*, 95–8.

thoughts, or actions of the audience, or of the speaker, or of other persons', and an act performed in this way (possibly intentionally) is a *perlocutionary act* (101).

The differences between the three forces as Austin envisages them are given by some examples:

He said to me, 'Shoot her!'   – locutionary
He urged me to shoot her.   – illocutionary
He persuaded me to shoot her.   – perlocutionary. (102)

Unfortunately these examples are problematic: 'urging' is a particularly unhelpful example of an illocution since it fails, for example, to be a matter of linguistic convention, and has no 'institutional' component. Urging is probably best seen as a perlocutionary act. Indeed in the ensuing discussion it also becomes apparent that Austin's ideas of the locutionary and illocutionary acts are confused. The remainder of the book is then given to clarifying the notion of illocutionary force in two ways: first, and mainly, by delineating more carefully the ways in which an illocutionary act differs from a locutionary or perlocutionary one (103–47); and secondly by looking at the various types of illocutionary force (148–64).

Three points may be made here. First, Austin is working with approximate, and indeed abstract, classifications. What happens in *HDTW* is that an intuitive understanding of the various types of act under discussion, which he admits are not necessarily clearly defined, is approached from different angles each of which provide useful but not final insights. As a result the categories are working at occasional cross-purposes with earlier or later manifestations of themselves. This is undoubtedly a source of much of the subsequent debate in speech act theory. It also follows that these different types of act, as abstractions, need always to be viewed functionally, that is, with regard to the longer-term role they may play in clarification of some other concept. It is this point which is in view when Austin remarks that 'The total speech-act in the total speech-situation is the *only actual* phenomenon which, in the last resort, we are engaged in elucidating' (148).

Secondly, Austin's classification of different types of illocutionary force is clearly a work in progress, which he did not live long enough to make satisfactory. Despite its appearance as the concluding chapter in the book, it does *not* represent the natural concluding stage of his argument, but is, I suggest, best seen as a separate but related inquiry undertaken for different reasons.[38] Austin's approach is to examine performative verbs which could be made to stand for paradigmatic performative utterances of different sorts. His categorisation of verdictives, exercitives, commissives, behabitives and expositives is self-confessedly vague, far from definitive, and perhaps not even mutually exclusive. We shall take up Searle's development of this area below.

Thirdly, and most significantly, Austin's definitions of locution and illocution do not match up either to the examples he gives or his subsequent discussion. Without a doubt, Searle's work in this area has superseded Austin's exploratory discussion, although certain features of Austin's presentation are worth noting.

He notes three particular contrasts between illocutions and perlocutions: the [successful] performance of an illocutionary act involves the securing of *uptake*; we say that the illocutionary act 'takes effect' rather than produces consequences; and finally illocutions invite by convention a response or sequel (117).[39] Two other influential attempts to capture the distinction are as follows: 'Illocutionary acts are conventional acts: perlocutionary acts are *not* conventional' (121); and secondly an illocutionary act is one performed *in* saying something, as against a perlocutionary act which is done *by* saying something (122–32). Both of these criteria, especially the latter with its reversion to the hunt for hidden logical form in contrast to 'surface' manifestations, turn out to be, unsurprisingly, either inconclusive or equivocal.

§2.2 Summary

Because of the confusing structure of Austin's argument, it is important to summarise the major achievements of *HDTW*. First, and in spite of the disputable nature of the definitions of key terms which he offers, his notion of the *illocutionary act* is

---

[38] Warnock has suggested that Austin desired long-term collaborative and cumulative work in philosophy in order to build more substantial results than it had typically produced. Classification and cataloguing, in this perspective, may thus be seen as an essential first step towards longer-lasting philosophical work. See the interview with Warnock in Ved Mehta, *Fly and the Fly-bottle: Encounters with British Intellectuals*, Harmondsworth: Penguin Books, 1965, 53–60, especially 56–7.

[39] Austin's omission of 'successful' here seems to falsify the distinction he actually makes in this very paragraph.

enormously fruitful for analysing the functioning of utterances in social contexts. We take up the disputes below.

Secondly, the idea that utterances are primarily concerned to state facts is challenged. *HDTW* does *not* propose a performative–constative distinction so much as show that fact-stating utterances are but one type of performative. Austin allows that certain types of simple 'archetype' sentences ('"The cat is on the mat", said for no conceivable reason', for example (146)) approximate to either the performative or constative case, but contends that in actual language use we rarely if ever encounter such abstractions. Rather: 'Once we realize that what we have to study is *not* the sentence but the issuing of an utterance in a speech-situation, there can hardly be any longer a possibility of not seeing that stating is performing an act' (139).

Thirdly, Austin's putative discussion of different types of illocutionary force brings together the above two points. Performatives and constatives can be viewed as similar in that they are both speech acts. They can be viewed as different in that they are speech acts with differing illocutionary force.

Finally Austin's approach recovers the notion of agency in understanding an utterance, without polarising between what is intended in the uttering of a sentence and what is achieved by uttering it. This middle way is of particular relevance in cases of written texts viewed as speech acts.

§3 John Searle's Theory of Speech Acts

Although there are many writers who still appeal directly and solely to Austin when discussing speech acts, it is best to see Austin's work as laying a foundation which invited development. This has been achieved most notably in the work of John Searle, who studied under Austin himself. In a series of books and articles Searle has provided by far the most comprehensive account of speech act theory.[40] As his work has developed he

---

[40] His major contributions to the subject are John R. Searle, *Speech Acts: An Essay in the Philosophy of Language*, Cambridge: Cambridge University Press, 1969; idem (ed.), *The Philosophy of Language*, Oxford: Oxford University Press, 1971; idem, *Expression and Meaning*; idem, *Intentionality: An Essay in the Philosophy of Mind*, Cambridge, Cambridge University Press, 1983; and with Daniel Vanderveken, *Foundations of Illocutionary Logic*, Cambridge: Cambridge University Press, 1985. He also contributed to and co-edited John R. Searle, Ferenc Kiefer and Manfred Bierwisch (eds), *Speech Act Theory and Pragmatics*, Dordrecht, Boston and London:

has sought increasingly to ground his philosophy of language in an intentionality-based approach to the philosophy of mind.[41]

Searle's major contributions to speech act theory may be considered here in four main categories:

1) his clarification of Austin's locutionary-illocutionary distinction;
2) his classification of different types of illocutionary acts;
3) his distinction between brute and institutional facts; and between regulative and constitutive rules; and
4) his development of the idea of the Background.

The first three of these, in various ways, provide valuable criteria for the notion of the illocutionary act. The fourth category, that of the Background, is his controversial but powerful contribution to the philosophy of mind which has most direct bearing on his speech act theory.

§3.1 Isolating the illocution

Austin predicted that 'it is the distinction between illocutions and perlocutions which seems likeliest to give trouble',[42] but in fact the bulk of the initial response to his work concerned the question of how to separate the illocution from the locution. This is a direct result of his problematic definition of the locutionary act, and is an area where Searle's approach is much to be preferred.

As early as 1963 Max Black was wondering whether Austin's notion of illocutionary force was any more stable a distinction than his abandoned performative/constative classification.[43]

D. Reidel, 1980; developed aspects of speech act theory further in his *The Construction of Social Reality*, London: Penguin, 1995; and offered various responses to critics in Ernest Lepore and Robert Van Gulick (eds), *John Searle and His Critics*, Cambridge, MA, and Oxford: Blackwell, 1991.

[41] He offers an overview of his 'systematic philosophy' in John Searle, *Mind, Language and Society: Philosophy in the Real World*, London: Weidenfeld & Nicolson, 1999, where, we may note, his account of 'how language works' (135–61) places speech act theory as his sixth and final chapter after discussions of the mind, intentionality and social reality.

[42] Austin, *HDTW*, 110.

[43] Max Black, 'Austin on Performatives', *Philosophy* 38 (1963), 217–26, reprinted in K. T. Fann (ed.), *Symposium on J. L. Austin*, London: Routledge & Kegan Paul, 1969, 401–11.

Perhaps the most serious challenge to his notion of illocutionary force was mounted by Jonathan Cohen in a 1964 article entitled 'Do Illocutionary Forces Exist?'[44] It is Searle's response to Cohen which has become the standard account.[45]

Black argued that Austin's conception of the locutionary act was incomplete as 'the normal sense' of saying something if it did not include illocutionary force, for what could it be to say something in the normal sense, fixing sense and reference, yet not also (i.e. thereby) asserting, questioning, ordering, or whatever the speaker was doing. For Black, this demonstrated the limitations of analysing ordinary language for theories of how language works. In short, Austin's dismissal of the performative–constative distinction would also cause his concept of locutionary act to fail. (Intriguingly Black actually thought that the performative–constative distinction was salvageable by careful definition of 'performative', but that ultimately since all locutions were illocutions there was no valuable sense of two types of utterances after all. This point is incidental to his major criticism, but in itself seems to lack coherence.)[46]

Black's article proved to set the scene for the ensuing debate. Jonathan Cohen, observing that Austin's account of *meaning* is particularly unclear, argued that 'the concept of illocutionary force developed [in *HDTW*] is empty'.[47] Cohen notes that in cases of explicit performatives, what Austin calls illocutionary force 'cannot be distinguished from the meaning', and in fact it simply *is* that part of an utterance's meaning which could be

[44] L. Jonathan Cohen, 'Do Illocutionary Forces Exist?', *PhQ* 14 (1964), 118–37, reprinted in Fann (ed.), *Symposium on J. L. Austin*, 420–44.

[45] John R. Searle, 'Austin on Locutionary and Illocutionary Acts', originally in *Philosophical Review* 77 (1968), and revised and reprinted in Isaiah Berlin et al., *Essays on J. L. Austin*, Oxford: Clarendon Press, 1973, 141–59. Responses to Searle include L. W. Forguson, 'Locutionary and Illocutionary Acts', in Berlin et al., *Essays*, 160–85, and David Holdcroft, 'Doubts about the Locutionary/Illocutionary Distinction', *International Studies in Philosophy* (1974), 3–16. An alternative response to Cohen is Mats Furberg's major redefinition of Austin's views in 1969: 'Meaning and Illocutionary Force, in Fann (ed.), *Symposium on J. L. Austin*, 445–67, with a one-page response by Cohen, 468. A helpful survey of these debates up to 1981 is provided by Graham Bird, 'Austin's Theory of Illocutionary Force', in Peter A. French, Theodore E. Uehling Jr and Howard K. Wettstein (eds), *Midwest Studies in Philosophy VI*, Minneapolis: University of Minnesota Press, 1981, 345–69.

[46] This is the gist of L. W. Forguson's reply to Black, 'In Pursuit of Performatives', *Philosophy* 41 (1966), 341–7, reprinted in Fann (ed.), *Symposium on J. L. Austin*, 412–19, especially 419.

[47] Cohen, 'Illocutionary Forces', 118.

(or is, if explicit) conveyed by the use of the utterance.[48] In short, Cohen proposed that it was more intuitive to see meaning as comprised of sense and force, both of which are intrinsic to the sentence, and then supplemented by reference on the occasion of utterance (and the reference may change every time). Austin, on the other hand, saw force as some extra component above and beyond sense and reference.[49] However, Cohen did not dispute the main thrust of Austin's analysis of performative meaning, indeed spending the majority of his article discussing eight reasons why Austin's overall framework is plausible even while arguing against the notion of illocutionary force.[50]

Thus we may say that the intuitive idea which Austin attempted to capture with his notion of illocutionary force is one with which Cohen had sympathy, but which to him did not require an additional category above and beyond meaning, which could be subsumed into the locutionary act in Austin's scheme. Once Cohen's point is put this way, it turns out to be methodologically similar to the reclassification proposed by Searle.

Searle also found Austin's distinction unhelpful, but recognised a difference between the utterance per se and the illocutionary force. This led him to attack the distinction the other way round, leaving illocutionary force in place as a category but consequently reducing the scope of Austin's locutionary act.[51] Unlike Cohen's view, Searle's has had a major impact on the subsequent development of speech act theory.

His basic contention is that although in theory one might see (Austin's) locutionary act as different from an illocutionary one, since they clearly represent different *concepts*, in practice they are never separate. This is because Austin's *rhetic* act is in fact illocutionary. Thus, as Cohen had argued, the locutionary act was always illocutionary in nature. Hence Searle proposed dropping the idea of the locutionary act, and instead insisted:

---

[48] Cohen, 'Illocutionary Forces', 122, 125.

[49] Cohen, 'Illocutionary Forces', 134.

[50] Cohen later produced a constructive and sympathetic, if non-standard, survey of speech act theory: L. Jonathan Cohen, 'Speech Acts', in Thomas A. Sebeok (ed.), *Current Trends in Linguistics*, vol. 12, *Linguistics and Adjacent Arts and Sciences*, The Hague: Mouton, 1974, 173–208.

[51] Searle, 'Austin on Locutionary and Illocutionary Acts'. Cf. also his 'What Is a Speech Act?', in Max Black (ed.), *Philosophy in America*, London: Allen & Unwin, 1965, 221–39. These earlier articles were essentially incorporated into his *Speech Acts*.

'We need to distinguish the illocutionary act from the propositional act – that is, the act of *expressing the proposition* (a phrase which is neutral as to illocutionary force).'[52] This modification has become the standard theory. It leaves Searle, when he restates it in his *Speech Acts*, with a framework of:

utterance acts: including Austin's phonetic and phatic acts
propositional acts: referring and predicating ('expressing the proposition')
illocutionary acts: stating, questioning, commanding, etc.
perlocutionary acts: persuading, convincing, etc.[53]

One should note, but many do not note, that the *locutionary act* has no place in Searle's scheme, and that, on the above account, it invites confusion to persist with the term if it is Austin's idea of 'locutionary' which is in view. Among non-philosophers appealing to speech act theory, I judge that Searle's 'propositional act' is viewed as a kind of limiting case of an illocution, and that his 'utterance act' is what is meant by talk of a 'locutionary act'. It is probably not necessary, for our purposes, to be more precise than this.[54]

Canonical notation and truth-functional semantics

A brief word is in order here about Searle's development of canonical notation for illocutionary acts, which follows directly from his above schema. By making the fundamental distinction that '*a proposition is to be sharply distinguished from an assertion or statement of it*',[55] Searle is led to a loose form of canonical notation for an illocutionary act:

---

[52] Searle, 'Locutionary and Illocutionary', 155.
[53] Searle, *Speech Acts*, 24–5; cf. 'Locutionary and Illocutionary', 159.
[54] Two helpful recent discussions of this issue are Jennifer Hornsby, 'Things Done with Words', in Jonathan Dancy, J. M. E. Moravcsik and C. C. W. Taylor (eds), *Human Agency: Language, Duty and Value: Philosophical Essays in Honor of J. O. Urmson*, Stanford, CA: Stanford University Press, 1988, 27–46 and 283–8, and François Recanati, *Meaning and Force: The Pragmatics of Performative Utterances*, Cambridge: Cambridge University Press, 1987, 236–66. Hornsby argues that Austin equivocated between 'rhetic' and 'locutionary' for the same thing (i.e. 'rhetic'), and that Searle uses 'locutionary' only in the phonetic + phatic + rhetic sense (285 n. 17). She concludes that 'locutionary' pertains to a particular language (English, French, . . .) while illocutionary will serve for a general account of language per se (36–7), and that *rhetic* remains the best option for what Austin was after. For Recanati's view, see n. 127 below.
[55] Searle, *Speech Acts*, 29.

$F(p)$ or $F(RP)$

with F being the indicator of illocutionary force, p the proposition in its most general form, and RP being his terms of reference and predication, that is, the non-illocutionary parts of the statement.[56]

This move, in retrospect, has been something of a Trojan horse, opening up speech act theory to a whole ontology of truth functions, completeness theorems, sentence radicals and logical forms.[57] At precisely this point, speech act theory is poised between the natural language arena from whence it came and the truth functional semantics into which it has, on occasion, headed.

One may grant that Austin's notion of locutionary act has proved unhelpful, since his rhetic act is already illocutionary. Searle, arguing the other way round from Cohen, has therefore isolated that part of the speech act which is not illocutionary, *by definition*. Where Cohen saw the illocutionary force irresistibly shifted over to the *meaning* of the utterance, Searle holds on to it by creating a new non-illocutionary entity: the propositional act. As with Austin's various acts this is an abstraction, and hence the question one must ask in evaluating it is not 'Is there such a thing?' because, on Searle's account there is not, but 'What use would such an abstraction be?', that is, what is its *function?*

In fact Searle equivocates between introducing his logical notation functionally: 'Symbolically, we might represent the sentence as containing an illocutionary force-indicating device and a propositional content indicator';[58] and not so functionally: 'The general form of (very many kinds of) illocutionary acts is $F(p)$ where the variable "F" takes the illocutionary force indicating devices as values and "p" takes expressions for propositions.'[59] This latter rides on the back of the following

[56] Searle, *Speech Acts*, 31–2; cf. 'Locutionary and Illocutionary', 156.

[57] The Trojan horse belongs, perhaps, to W. V. O. Quine, for whom 'to be is to be the value of a variable', 'On What There Is', *From a Logical Point of View*, Cambridge, MA: Harvard University Press, [2]1961, 1–19, here 15. For all their apparent similarities, the irreducible differences between Quine and 'ordinary language philosophy' (cf. n. 13 above) are brought out well by Hacker, *Wittgenstein's Place*, 183–227. Somewhat bizarrely, Quinean 'eliminative paraphrase' casts its long shadow over biblical interpretation, as we shall discover in ch. 4.

[58] Searle, 'Locutionary and Illocutionary', 156.

[59] Searle, *Speech Acts*, 31.

assertion: 'In the deep structure we can often identify those elements that correspond to the indicator of illocutionary force quite separately from those that correspond to the indicator of propositional content.'[60] He grants that on the 'surface' this is not quite so clear, but the 'thereness' (the 'ontological backing', we might say) of such elements in the language is unmistakeable.

The potential problem is then that these abstract entities assume a life of their own, and start to dictate terms in future theoretical considerations.[61] I suggest that it is just such an agenda which operates in Searle's (and Vanderveken's) subsequent work on classifying illocutionary acts, which will be considered below.

This need not be a major problem with Searle's work, but it is relevant. What appears to happen is that Searle wants to use Wittgenstein's radically different notion of philosophy (a philosophy which 'leaves everything as it is' and 'only states what everyone admits')[62] to get away from the mistaken *methods* of syntactic-semantic approaches but without necessarily eschewing the *goals* of such theories.[63] Such a view is suggested by a comment in Bede Rundle's *Wittgenstein & Contemporary Philosophy of Language*, which charts a course between what he calls formal semantics (following Frege) and Wittgenstein's 'meaning as use' paradigm.[64] For Rundle the goals of a theory may be worth pursuing without accepting the methodologies in use for reaching them. Searle's view of Wittgenstein also seems to suggest this dual-level approach to abstract theory construction.[65]

[60] Searle, *Speech Acts*, 30–1.

[61] A term for this kind of problem would be helpful. Perhaps, in the spirit of James Barr, one could call it 'illegitimately transferred abstraction'.

[62] Wittgenstein, *Philosophical Investigations*, §124; §599.

[63] Searle, *Construction of Social Reality*, 140, and perhaps as a subtext to much of *Speech Acts* (especially 146–9) and *Expression and Meaning* (e.g. 29).

[64] Bede Rundle, *Wittgenstein & Contemporary Philosophy of Language*, Oxford: Blackwell, 1990, ix–x, 265–6 and *passim*.

[65] Rundle, *Wittgenstein*, x; for Searle on Wittgenstein, see John R. Searle, 'Wittgenstein', in dialogue with Bryan Magee in Bryan Magee, *The Great Philosophers: An Introduction to Western Philosophy*, London: BBC Books, 1987, 320–47. This more nuanced view mitigates some, though not all, of the punishing criticisms directed at speech act theory by G. P. Baker and P. M. S. Hacker, *Language, Sense and Nonsense*. See James Bogen, 'An Unfavourable Review of *Language, Sense and Nonsense*'. A collection of essays indicating on-going tension over this issue is Searle, Kiefer and Bierwisch (eds), *Speech Act Theory and Pragmatics*.

§3.2 Classifying Illocutionary Acts

Searle's work on classifying illocutionary acts takes up Austin's last chapter in *HDTW*, and is a significant advance on it which, again, has become the standard theory.[66] In this he seeks to show that there are basically five (possibly six) types of speech act, arranged around the organising categories of directions of fit between word and world.[67] The direction of fit distinguishes between, for instance, assertives where an attempt is made to match one's words to the world (e.g. 'We ate fish for dinner') and directives which attempt to match the world to the words spoken ('Please could you open the window'). The idea, as we saw, goes back to a 1953 Austin paper, and Searle draws on Elisabeth Anscombe's elucidation of it.[68] Based on the observation that there are fundamentally only four possible directions of fit (word-to-world, world-to-word, mutual fit or no fit) he argues that the Wittgensteinian notion of limitless uses of language must be mistaken since:

> If we adopt illocutionary point as the basic notion on which to classify uses of language, then there are a rather limited number of basic things we do with language: we tell people how things are, we try to get them to do things, we commit ourselves to doing things, we express our feelings and attitudes and we bring about changes through our utterances. Often, we do more than one of these at once in the same utterance.[69]

Aside from direction of fit, the other major categories which facilitate his analysis are illocutionary point and psychological state (e.g. a belief or an intention), which correspond to the essential and sincerity conditions of speech act analysis respectively.[70] For the sake of convenience, and since it remains such an influential categorisation, I include a tabulated summary of Searle's full discussion.

---

[66] John R. Searle, 'A Taxonomy of Illocutionary Acts', in Keith Gunderson (ed.), *Language, Mind and Knowledge: Minnesota Studies in the Philosophy of Science*, Minneapolis: University of Minnesota Press, 1975; reprinted in Searle, *Expression and Meaning*, 1–29.

[67] Searle, *Expression and Meaning*, 3–4. Direction of fit is mentioned once, briefly, in *Speech Acts*, 124 n. 1, but is not developed there.

[68] G. E. M. Anscombe, *Intentions*, Oxford: Blackwell, 1957.

[69] Searle, *Expression and Meaning*, 29, with reference to Wittgenstein, *Philosophical Investigations*, §23.

[70] Searle, *Expression and Meaning*, 2–5.

A Taxonomy of Illocutionary Acts[a]

Type of act	Assertives	Directives	Commissives	Expressives	Declarations	Assertive Declarations
Logical Notation	$\vdash\downarrow B(p)$	$!\uparrow W(\text{H does A})$	$C\uparrow I(\text{S does A})$	$E\varnothing(P)(S\mid H+\text{property})$	$D\updownarrow\varnothing(p)$	$D_a\downarrow\updownarrow B(p)$
Illocutionary Point	Commits S to something being the case	S attempts to get H to do something	Commits S to some future course of action	Expresses the psychological state specified in the sincerity condition	Brings about correspondence between prop. content and reality (when successful)	An assertive with the force of a declaration
Direction of fit	word to world	world to word	world to word	none	both word to world and world to word	assertive is word to world; declarative is both ways
Sincerity Condition	Belief (that p)	Want (wish or desire)	Intention	varies in each case	none: $\varnothing$	Belief (that p)
Propositional Content	any p	H does some future action A	S does some future action A	ascription of some property to S or H	any p	any p
Example sentence	It is raining.	Open the door.	I will come at 6.00.	I thank you for coming.	Tony Blair is hereby elected.	You are guilty as charged.
Typical cases	suggest, put forward, insist, boast, deduce, hypothesize	ask, order, beg, entreat, command, request, plead, pray, invite, defy	promise, vow, pledge, covenant, contract, swear, guarantee	thank, congratulate, apologize, condole, deplore, welcome	[linguistic markers depend on institutional rules]	[linguistic markers depend on institutional rules]

[a] Source: Searle, *Expression and Meaning*, Ch. 1 'A Taxonomy of Illocutionary Acts', 1–29, especially 12–20; with some clarificatory notes from Austin, *HDTW*, 8–12. Key to symbols used: S = speaker; H = hearer; A = an action; p = a proposition; (P) = Psychological state; $\varnothing$ = the empty set (null); arrows = direction of fit. Note: the sincerity condition for a successful speech act specifies a psychological state.

Five points, of varying significance, may be made here about this classification, which has attained something of a canonical status in speech act theory. The first of these five points will suggest a different approach to this topic, which I shall explore briefly at the end of this section.

First, it is worth pausing to underline the final sentence in the quote from Searle's article above: 'Often, we do more than one of these at once in the same utterance.'[71] This is undoubtedly true, and yet the all-too-common impression given by Searle's taxonomy is that different speech acts fall into disjunctive categories. However, as is clear from the classification, the final category, of assertive declarations, is a hybrid one: for example, a judge who says, 'You are guilty', is both asserting and declaring. Other writers have suggested that other such hybrids may be possible, including, indeed, Searle himself in later work.[72] In fact, Searle's original article should lead us to *expect* hybrids as the normal occurrence. Rather than a taxonomy of illocutionary acts, we do better to read Searle as providing a classification of major illocutionary points. I shall consider other aspects of Searle's approach before returning to this theme below.

Secondly, such a consideration raises again the issue of the link between a working scheme and its canonical notation. Direction of fit, like illocutionary force, is again an abstraction, which must be judged to be useful in terms of whether it provides any analytical help. To observe that there are only four fundamental directions of fit does not say anything about the kinds of speech acts one might be performing within any one of them. Indeed, the existence of both directives and commissives in Searle's list indicates that direction of fit is not fully determinative of illocutionary point. What has been achieved is a certain form of notational classification, and there should be no surprises that there are 'blurred edges' to some of Searle's four fundamental categories.[73]

The point is that such a 'taxonomy' must of necessity be of functional use, and cannot, *contra* Searle, claim to be definitive.

---

[71] Searle, *Expression and Meaning*, 29, as quoted in n. 69 above.

[72] E.g. Terrence W. Tilley, *The Evils of Theodicy*, Washington DC: Georgetown University Press, 1991, 10–15, 29, n. 4, where he draws attention to Searle and Vanderveken, *Foundations of Illocutionary Logic*, 175, which allows all types of illocutionary act to have hybrid declarative forms.

[73] On the link between blurred edges and categories which are nevertheless distinguishable, see Wittgenstein, *Philosophical Investigations*, §71.

This is partly anticipated by Dieter Wunderlich's claim that 'There is no clear classification of speech acts. Neither Austin's, nor Searle's, nor anybody else's attempts are really convincing'.[74] He further observes that the question of which speech-act classification is given priority will depend on the purpose of the theory,[75] and he offers various possible functional criteria of organisation. What he does not make explicit, though, is the reason why this kind of classification must be dependent on purpose (or function): it is simply because we are dealing with abstractions made only for a particular purpose, and not with entities which can invite classification on their own (or objective) terms.

Thirdly, this challenge to the privileged position claimed for Searle's classification will also challenge his assertion that, *contra* Wittgenstein, there are a small number of uses of language. The number of uses one envisages can only be assessed *relative to* some conceptual scheme. I incline to the view that Wittgenstein is right on this point, but that the issues at stake are more terminological than substantive.[76]

Fourthly, we need to consider the reasons put forward by Searle to explain his claim that his categories are privileged, and this necessitates a brief detour into his philosophy of mind. He draws on the idea of 'intentionality', loosely defined as 'that property of many mental states and events by which they are directed at or about or of objects and states of affairs in the world'.[77] This notion of 'directedness' leads him on to say that the ability of the speaking subject to perform speech acts is 'an extension of the more biologically fundamental capacities of the mind (or brain) to relate the organism to the world by way

---

[74] Dieter Wunderlich, 'Methodological Remarks on Speech Act Theory', in Searle, Kiefer and Bierwisch (eds), *Speech Act Theory and Pragmatics*, 291–312, here 297.

[75] Wunderlich, 'Methodological Remarks', 297.

[76] As Recanati notes, classifications depend on prioritising certain features of utterances, and thus 'if we refuse to favor particular criteria, we must conclude, with Wittgenstein, that any treelike classification of illocutionary acts is illusory', Recanati, *Meaning and Force*, 152. In other words: actual classifications presuppose the favoring of particular criteria. For a critique of Wittgenstein's view here, see P. F. Strawson, 'Critical Notice of Wittgenstein's *Philosophical Investigations*', in Harold Morick (ed.), *Wittgenstein and the Problem of Other Minds*, New York: McGraw-Hill, 1967, 3–42, especially 6–7.

[77] Searle, *Intentionality*, 1; cf. William Lyons, *Approaches to Intentionality*, Oxford: Clarendon Press, 1995, 1, who defines it in terms of mental activities with a perspectival content and attitude.

of such mental states as belief and desire'.[78] Once mental states
are held to underlie speech acts in this way then a variety of
mental processes needs to be hypothesised and then explained
in order to account for how we can 'do' such things as 'move'
from a literal to a non-literal meaning of an utterance, or understand a metaphor, or even, most basically, perform a speech act
with a certain intention.[79]

The intentionality-based, 'mental states' philosophy of mind
which Searle develops is not, however, the only possible approach
to such questions. Consider, for example, the supposed problem
of how we are able to understand sentences that we have never
heard before.[80] This 'problem' presupposes that understanding
is something like a mental state that is attained through some
processing of data, and hence that one must account for how
this mental state is reached. Once accepted, this picture is likely
to hold us captive.[81]

A different picture suggests a different approach. Understanding is less a mental state than something like an ability, or
a competency.[82] The 'problem' of understanding new sentences
turns out to be exactly analogous to the 'problem' of how it is
that a painter can paint a totally new picture: that is, no problem
at all.[83]

Not only does this account find its expression in Wittgenstein's
work, including the very aspects of it which we analysed earlier
(§1.1 above), but also the same conception of speech acts as
actions which are not inherently tied to mental states is made

---

[78] Searle, *Intentionality*, vii.

[79] All of these examples are discussed at length by Searle, e.g. *Expression and
Meaning*, 30–57 (on 'indirect speech acts' and moving from literal to non-literal
meaning), 76–116 (on 'metaphor').

[80] This account draws on Baker and Hacker, *Language, Sense and Nonsense*, 316–
21, 345–56.

[81] Cf. Wittgenstein, *Philosophical Investigations*, §115.

[82] Baker and Hacker, *Language, Sense and Nonsense*, 349. They develop their
Wittgensteinian account of understanding in idem, *Wittgenstein: Understanding and
Meaning, Volume 1 of an Analytical Commentary on the Philosophical Investigations*,
Oxford: Blackwell, 1980, 595–620 in a section entitled 'Understanding and Ability'
on *Philosophical Investigations* §143–84, see especially 617–20. For some empirical
support for such a thesis, see Hans Ramge, 'Language Acquisition as the Acquisition
of Speech Act Competence', *JPrag* 1 (1977), 155–64. Competency has proved a
fruitful category in literary theory, cf. Jonathan Culler, *Structuralist Poetics:
Structuralism, Linguistics and the Study of Literature*, Ithaca: Cornell University Press,
1975, 113–30, on 'Literary Competence'.

[83] Baker and Hacker, *Language, Sense and Nonsense*, 354.

explicit by Austin in a brisk but significant passage at the beginning of *HDTW*:

> we are apt to have a feeling that [words being spoken seriously] consists in their being uttered as (merely) the outward and visible sign, for convenience or other record or for information, of an inward and spiritual act.[84]

This invites, of course, a version of the descriptive fallacy: utterances are true or false in that they either do or do not accurately report a state of (internal) affairs. Austin dismisses one who holds such a theory as 'surveying the invisible depths of ethical space, with all the distinction of a specialist in the *sui generis*' (!)[85]

Searle's philosophy of mind continues to remain controversial.[86] In my judgment it is possible to utilise the insights of his philosophy of language without necessarily adopting his framework of intentionality and mental states, even accepting that this directly contradicts Searle's own view: 'If there really are the five basic types [of speech acts], there must be some deeper reason for that ... these five must derive from some fundamental features of the mind.'[87] The logical connection here is elusive. In fact, his claim rests on his own theory that the conditions of satisfaction for speech acts and intentional states are identical by virtue of the requirements of direction of

---

[84] Austin, *HDTW*, 9.

[85] Austin, *HDTW*, 10. Stanley Cavell underlines the significance of these brief comments in his helpful reading of the passage, in his *Philosophical Passages: Wittgenstein, Emerson, Austin, Derrida*, Cambridge, MA, and Oxford: Blackwell, 1995, 52–65.

[86] He develops his views in John R. Searle, *Minds, Brains and Science: The 1984 Reith Lectures*, London: Penguin, 1991 (1984); *The Rediscovery of the Mind*, Cambridge, MA, and London: MIT Press, 1992; *The Mystery of Consciousness*, London: Granta Books, 1997; and he explores their role as basic to his overall approach in *Mind, Language and Society*, 39–110. It is fair to say that his position on intentionality is not widely followed. For surveys, see William Lyons, *Approaches to Intentionality*, Oxford: Clarendon Press, 1995, and, briefer but more entertaining, John Haugeland, 'The Intentionality All-Stars', in James E. Tomberlin (ed.), *Philosophical Perspectives 4: Action Theory and Philosophy of Mind*, Atascadero, CA: Ridgeview Publishing Company, 1990, 383–427. Both writers locate Searle at one end of the spectrum (or, in Haugeland's case, deep in the outfield). For critique, see Daniel C. Dennett, *The Intentional Stance*, Cambridge, MA, and London: MIT Press, 1987; and on whether Searle's view reduces to behaviourism: Ilham Dilman, *Mind, Brain and Behaviour: Discussions of B. F. Skinner and J. R. Searle*, London: Routledge, 1988.

[87] Searle, *Intentionality*, 166.

fit.[88] In response, Karl Otto Apel has argued that it is Searle's own earlier philosophy of language which offers a critique of his theory of intentionality.[89] We shall need to consider a further aspect of Searle's philosophy of mind in the discussion below of his theory of Background.

A fifth, and final, point arising from Searle's classification is the nature of the link between illocutionary acts and vocabulary markers for them. I defer discussion of this point until chapter 3, in the context of applying speech act theory to texts, and of Searle and Vanderveken's further work on classification.

An alternative approach

Before leaving this much-contested subject, I wish to draw out the implications of the first of these five points of critique, that in general more than one illocutionary point is operative in a speech act. Several writers have noted this, as indeed I have shown that Searle himself notes it.[90] In my judgment, the most compelling alternative is provided in a short review of Austin's and Searle's taxonomies and their theoretical rationales offered by Jerrold Sadock.[91]

Sadock takes a step back from the standard picture, and considers Searle's three important dimensions (namely illocutionary point, direction of fit and expressed psychological state) with their five, four and five possible values respectively, and observes that it is odd that only 5 of the possible 100 combinations of these parameters are adduced as actual illocutionary categories.[92] Further, the various accounts provided by Searle differ in terms of details about which dimensions of analysis are significant for demarcating types of illocutionary utterance. Thus Sadock suggests that in fact the major motivation of Searle's final fivefold listing is a desire to remain close to the tentative

---

[88] Searle, *Intentionality*, 10–11.

[89] Karl Otto Apel, 'Is Intentionality More Basic than Linguistic Meaning?', in Lepore and Van Gulick (eds), *John Searle and His Critics*, 31–55. Apel develops a view of the 'intersubjective validity of meaning', rather than intentionality, as grounding pragmatics (i.e. speech acts).

[90] See in particular the approach of Brümmer, *Theology and Philosophical Inquiry*, 16 and 26–31.

[91] Jerrold M. Sadock, 'Toward a Grammatically Realistic Typology of Speech Acts', in Tsohatzidis (ed.), *Foundations of Speech Act Theory*, 393–406.

[92] Sadock, 'Toward a Grammatically Realistic Typology', 395.

taxonomy provided by Austin at the end of *HDTW*, which also had 5 categories. There are detail problems too: declarations are not a different sentence type but have to be carried out by means of assertives, hence Searle's hybrid sixth category; while equally some common distinctions such as that between making statements and asking questions are not captured by the classification.[93]

Sadock's proposal, instead, is to deduce the basic dimensions of analysis from investigating how languages do in fact mark the significant differences between types of speech act, and the ground work for this approach is laid out in an earlier article in which twenty-three languages are surveyed and natural distinctions noted.[94] Sadock's conclusion from this study, and his programmatic proposal, is as follows:

> Acts of speech, I suggest, ordinarily have three separate communicative aspects, namely:
>
> 1 an informational, representational aspect . . .
>
> 2 an effective, social aspect . . .
>
> 3 an affective, emotive aspect.[95]

He labels these INF, AF and EF, and proceeds to demonstrate how various of Austin's insights into the peculiarities of performative utterance work out in this schema, as well as providing sample analyses of stating, requesting, promising, apologising, asking, accusing and criticising.[96] Each speech act can be primarily any one of these three types of act, with aspects of the other dimensions also possibly present. In considering any particular speech act, therefore, a key question is: which dimension is primary?

Although Sadock's proposal seems to me to be a helpful one which has the particular merit of being built on a broad basis of observed languages, I do not propose to follow it in detail in

---

[93] Sadock, 'Toward a Grammatically Realistic Typology', 404.

[94] Jerold M. Sadock and Arnold M. Zwicky, 'Speech Act Distinctions in Syntax', in Timothy Shopen (ed.), *Language Typology and Syntactic Description*. vol. 1, *Clause Structure*, Cambridge: Cambridge University Press, 1985, 155–96. This article is helpfully reviewed by William Croft, 'Speech Act Classification, Language Typology and Cognition', in Tsohatzidis (ed.), *Foundations of Speech Act Theory*, 460–77, especially 465–70.

[95] Sadock, 'Toward a Grammatically Realistic Typology', 397.

[96] Sadock, 'Toward a Grammatically Realistic Typology', 401.

this work, for the simple reason that it effectively requires a reorganisation of all the established terminology of speech act theory. However, I do propose to accept its demonstration of the point, widely mooted but rarely followed through with such rigour, that the different (illocutionary) points of a speech act are not mutually exclusive, but rather coexist with one point usually being primary. For practical reasons, therefore, I shall retain Searle's scheme of illocutionary points, but not some of the standard ways in which it has been used in the literature. Further justification for this move will become clear in the discussion of vocabulary markers in chapter 3.

§3.3 *Brute and institutional facts; regulative and constitutive rules*

One of the basic arguments of Searle's work is that

> the semantic structure of a language may be regarded as a conventional realization of a series of sets of underlying constitutive rules, and that speech acts are acts characteristically performed by uttering expressions in accordance with these sets of constitutive rules.[97]

Thus we come to his powerful distinction between *constitutive* and *regulative* rules: some rules *regulate* a pre-existing activity, for example, rules of etiquette; while other rules actually define the activity which they regulate, for example, what counts as checkmate in chess. We may say, therefore, that a constitutive rule 'creates the possibility of new forms of behaviour' by saying that a certain activity X will (*as a result of this rule*) count as activity Y in a context C or, to use Searle's concise formulation, 'X counts as Y in context C'.[98]

This distinction in turn enables another one. Searle draws on Elisabeth Anscombe's notion of 'brute fact', which comes in essence from the natural sciences and concerns facts about physical states of affairs, regardless of what anyone thinks about them.[99] In contrast to this, Searle proposes the notion of *institutional* facts, which 'are indeed facts; but their existence, unlike the existence of brute facts, presupposes the existence of certain human institutions' (e.g. marriage, or the rules of

---

[97] Searle, *Speech Acts*, 37.
[98] Searle, *Speech Acts*, 33–5.
[99] G. E. M. Anscombe, 'On Brute Facts', *Analysis* 18 (1958), 69–72.

baseball).[100] The particular sense of 'institution' which Searle has in mind here is 'system of constitutive rules', and it follows from this that 'the fact that a man performed a certain speech act, e.g., made a promise, is an institutional fact'.[101]

This feature of Searle's account is both powerful and, at times, problematic. It underlies his subsequent work on the construction of social reality, and is certainly in itself a helpful analytical tool for assessing the extent to which certain facts may be 'objective' (brute) while others can be subjective and yet not, therefore, devoid of criteria of assessment. The significance of this distinction will become apparent in later chapters where I shall appeal to it for help in various interpretive issues.

However, it is fair to say that Searle does not clearly explain *why it is* that 'X counts as Y in context C'. We shall have cause to return to this issue more than once. For now it suffices to notice that the question devolves quickly on to questions of morality, or ethical obligation. For instance Wolterstorff proposes that 'The relation [between uttering a sentence and counting it as a speech action] is that speaker and audience *ought* to count it as that – *ought* to acknowledge it as that in their relations with each other . . . To institute an arrangement for the performance of speech actions is to institute a way of acquiring rights and responsibilities.'[102]

Searle's more recent extended account of institutional facts also allows for rights and responsibilities to be conferred by X counting as Y. He speaks of the imposition of status functions on humans, and argues that institutional facts create and regulate deontic powers: 'The point of having deontic powers is to regulate relations between people. In this category, we impose rights, responsibilities, obligations, duties, privileges. . . .'[103] Symbolic powers, honour and procedural steps towards power are also, for Searle, functions of institutional rules.

---

[100] Searle, *Speech Acts*, 51.

[101] Searle, *Speech Acts*, 52. By 'speech act' here Searle means what he later calls 'illocutionary act'.

[102] Wolterstorff, *Divine Discourse*, 84; see also idem, *Works and Worlds of Art*, Oxford: Clarendon Press, 1980, 205–11. Recanati's work, discussed below in §5, is also relevant to the question of grounds for saying that x is counted as y in any particular case.

[103] Searle, *Construction of Social Reality*, 100.

Nevertheless, the view that the counting of X as Y is inevitably some bid for power, and that X is better seen as Z, is a familiar one, and questions of the criteria for counting, or for construal as it may be better termed, shall occupy us in chapter 4. In the meantime it is important not to let that discussion obscure the significance of Searle's clarification of 'institutional fact'. An alternative view of illocutionary acts which allows this question to be settled in some, but emphatically not all, cases by way of a look at *meaning* will be considered in §4 below.

§3.4 The Background

Searle's idea of the Background has developed through his various writings until it is now a full-scale contribution to a theory about the physiology of the human mind. I draw on it in particular for its role in explaining speech acts and institutional facts.[104]

The Background first appears as 'a set of background assumptions about the contexts in which [a] sentence could be appropriately uttered'.[105] This becomes more than just a theory about language when Searle goes on to develop a view of meaning as derived intentionality: different assumptions behind an utterance give different truth conditions for the utterance, and hence the meaning of a sentence is a function of the speaker's intentionality.[106]

In *Intentionality*, and in later works, this develops into a full theory of mind. The Background is the unspoken, even unarticulatable, support framework for one's mental states. It does not contain mental states itself and is non-representational. The Background supports a 'Network' of intentional mental states where it *does* make sense to talk of rule following. But as rules are followed, and behaviour learned, so the body 'takes over', developing *abilities* which it did not previously possess. It is *not* the case that skills are a matter of rules being followed

---

[104] The major sources in Searle's writings are 'Literal Meaning', now reprinted in *Expression and Meaning*, 117–36; 'The Background of Meaning', in Searle, Kiefer and Bierwisch (eds), *Speech-Act Theory and Pragmatics*, 221–32; *Intentionality*, ch. 5, 'The Background', 141–59; and *Construction of Social Reality*, ch. 6, 'Background Abilities and the Explanation of Social Phenomena', 127–47.

[105] Searle, *Expression and Meaning*, 117.

[106] Searle, 'Background of Meaning', 230–1.

unconsciously. Rather, says Searle, the body learns an alternative way of achieving those goals for which the rule following was initially designed. For Searle, this is ultimately a matter of developing physical capacities along neurological pathways.[107]

In *The Construction of Social Reality* Searle locates this approach between the two more established avenues of rule-governed understandings of intentionality (and mind in general) and behaviourism.[108] In the former, to speak a language is to engage in a highly complex rule-governed form of behaviour (as Searle's own speech act theory has it); in the latter, humans work on a behaviouristic model where 'brute physical causation' is the only explanation we have for what takes place.[109] Neither alternative is satisfactory, because although we follow principles which can be articulated as rules, we do not do so *as rule-following*. Thus:

> we should not say that the man who is at home in his society . . . is at home because he has mastered the rules of the society, but rather that the man has developed a set of capacities and abilities that render him at home in the society; and he has developed those abilities because those are the rules of his society.[110]

Searle sees that 'much of Wittgenstein's later work is about what I call the Background', in particular Wittgenstein's attempt to elucidate the necessary conditions for meaningful statements in *On Certainty*.[111] Indeed this account tallies with our earlier comments about understanding as an ability. For Searle, the Background is the essential facilitator of all intentional states: linguistic and perceptual interpretation take place against it; consciousness is structured by it; certain kinds of readiness are facilitated by it; and certain sorts of behaviour are made more or less likely by it.[112] The model is clearly a Wittgensteinian one of *competencies*: 'One develops skills and abilities that are, so to speak, functionally equivalent to the system of rules, without actually containing any representations or internalizations of

---

[107] This account is summarised from Searle, *Intentionality*, 141–53.

[108] Searle, *Construction of Social Reality*, 127–47.

[109] Searle, *Construction of Social Reality*, 141.

[110] Searle, *Construction of Social Reality*, 147. The label offered by Searle for his position is 'biological naturalism': Searle, *Mind, Language and Society*, 54.

[111] Searle, *Construction of Social Reality*, 132; idem, *Mind, Language and Society*, 169.

[112] These are the distinguishing characteristics noted in Searle, *Construction of Social Reality*, 132–7.

those rules.'[113] But in the 'Network', the foregrounded intentionalities and rules which we follow, then competency is no longer an adequate model.

Critics have argued that there is insufficient justification for this divide in Searle's scheme.[114] In the course of a comparison between Searle's theory and Gricean pragmatics, Marcelo Dascal claims that 'Those aspects of use that do not readily fit the institutional mould, the rule-based treatment, are either left to be handled by a complementary theory of use *à la* Grice, or else dumped in the ever present Background', thus rendering speech act theory incomplete as a theory of use.[115] Barry Stroud argues that there is a dilemma concerning how to speak of the Background: it is non-intentional, but must explain intentional states, and thus there is no language left in which to describe it. On the one hand, if we use intentional language, then we are talking about something that is not in it but, on the other hand, if we use non-intentional language we appear to be unable to explain the enabling of mental states.[116] But for Searle the mental and the intentional are not the same, and the distinction is justified by his argument about competencies taking over from rules at a certain point.[117]

Pursuing Searle's idea of the Background requires us to revise Searle's pivotal early text, 'Speaking a language is engaging in a (highly complex) rule-governed form of behavior',[118] to rather saying that speaking a language is engaging in highly complex behaviour which can *in general* be described by rules, and which on occasion is not just governed by but *constituted* by rules.

With Austin and Searle's work in hand, we are now in a position to offer a general overview of the key ideas of speech act theory. In fact, I propose that a helpful point of departure

---

[113] Searle, *Construction of Social Reality*, 142.

[114] See the earlier criticisms of Searle's views on intentionality, although the argument here is less concerned with basing speech act theory on a view of mind.

[115] Marcelo Dascal, 'Speech Act Theory and Gricean Pragmatics: Some Differences of Detail That Make a Difference', in Tsohatzidis (ed.), *Foundations of Speech Act Theory*, 323–34, especially 330, 333.

[116] This is one of the points raised by Barry Stroud, 'The Background of Thought', in Lepore and Van Gulick (eds), *John Searle and His Critics*, 245–58.

[117] Searle, 'Response: The Background of Intentionality and Action', in Lepore and Van Gulick (eds), *John Searle and His Critics*, 289–99. Searle addresses here explicitly the extent to which he follows Wittgenstein (292–3).

[118] Searle, *Speech Acts*, 12.

for such an overview is provided by just this issue: the question of the varying degrees of strength which such a constituting rule for language use might possess.

§4 The Key Ideas of Speech Act Theory

§4.1 *Strong and weak illocutions*

With the work of Searle, Austin's performative-constative distinction recedes further into the background, and all utterances are viewed as illocutionary acts. The inevitable question arising is thus whether we have lost the initial significance of the idea of an illocutionary act by broadening it out so much that everything is included. One might ask: are all illocutionary acts equal, or are some more significant than others? Furthermore: what criteria would one have for such a judgment?

My claim here is that it is helpful to consider illocutionary acts (or forces) in a spectrum ranging from strong to weak. In the weak sense we may say that almost any utterance is an illocutionary act. However, we shall want to reserve most of our attention for 'strong' acts, where the illocutionary force plays a significant role in the utterance. Something close to this view is proposed by one of Austin's 'co-workers', Geoffrey Warnock.[119]

Warnock observes that when Austin proposed his notion of *performative utterance*, it referred to the way in which saying something is sometimes to do something, and that 'Austin . . . was not at first thinking particularly, or even at all, of (as one might say, Searlean) *linguistic* acts'.[120]

Warnock allows that one can change the topic to 'speech acts' (general) by noting that there is indeed a sense in which all utterances are performative, but he insists that the original delineation of performatives need not be lost by admitting this wider class. Performative utterances were originally the cases where to issue them 'is to do something, in virtue of *conventions* to the effect that to say those things counts as, or constitutes, doing whatever it may be'.[121] There is no such convention in the general case of speech acts. Warnock's example of a general

[119] G. J. Warnock, 'Some Types of Performative Utterance', in Berlin et al., *Essays on J. L. Austin*, 69–89.
[120] Warnock, 'Performative Utterance', 70.
[121] Warnock, 'Performative Utterance', 71.

speech act is of warning you that the train will leave at three, and hence you should eat lunch quickly. There is no *convention* which *makes* this utterance an act of warning.

We may thus conclude that 'illocutionary forces ... are not in general convention-constituted'.[122] This point allows Warnock to disentangle what he perceives as two kinds of special case which occupy Austin: the original 'performative' sense (convention-based) which Austin came to reject on the basis that all utterances are performative; and the explicit-performative (e.g. 'I warn you not to come') which has at times wrongly been taken as the same special case. Warnock argues that in this latter case it is not convention at all, but in fact the *meaning* of the sentence which makes the warning a warning.[123]

We may grant that all linguistic meanings are in a sense conventional, but this is a different, weaker use of the word 'conventional' compared to that envisaged by Austin for the original performative utterance. Although Warnock does not use this terminology, it invites a distinction between strong and weak senses of 'illocutionary force'. I wish to make that distinction, and in so doing suggest that illocutionary force operates across a spectrum of strengths. This idea will play a central role in what follows. It is, I suggest, a refinement which allows us to capture a broad range of positions in speech act theory as permissible variations on the spectrum, and, most importantly of all, allows us to avoid the problematic tendency to polarise options and insist that, if one apparently common-sense position is mistaken, its opposite, typically extravagant, position must be right.

To reiterate, I shall call a strong illocution one which relies on a non-linguistic convention. This class, following Warnock, overlaps with but is not identical to Austin's explicit performative, and will include the Queen's saying 'I name this ship ...' not because it is an explicit performative, although it is, but because the conventions in place are not simply linguistic

---

[122] Warnock, 'Performative Utterance', 76.

[123] As indeed does P. F. Strawson, 'Intention and Convention in Speech Acts', *Philosophical Review* 73 (1964), 439–60, reprinted in Searle (ed.), *Philosophy of Language*, 23–38. He argues that 'there are many cases in which the illocutionary force of an utterance, though not exhausted by its meaning, is not owed to any *conventions* other than those which help to give it meaning' (26).

ones. I shall call a weak illocution one where the linguistic meaning itself is the only or only significant convention in view. 'The lamp is on the table' is a weak illocution, as is the explicit 'I state that the lamp is on the table'. Austin's performative–constative distinction is thus retained on one level (strong against weak illocutions) while collapsed in Austin's own manner on another level (both are illocutions). Two examples of how this idea relates to other discussions of speech acts may be briefly considered.

§4.2 *Performative utterances*

One of the basic confusions which arises in any attempt to articulate a speech act theory which draws on both Austin and Searle is that commentators find themselves discussing the significance of 'the performative' and illustrate this with reference to the illocutionary act. It is fair to say that the relation between the two ideas is a point of debate.

Searle and Vanderveken define a *performative utterance* as the utterance of a sentence consisting of 'a performative verb used in the first person present tense of the indicative mood with an appropriate complement cause'.[124] For them, Austin's examples such as 'I promise to attend the meeting' or – in the context of a wedding ceremony – 'I do' are indeed performative utterances. J. O. Urmson, in contrast, urged that performatives should not be classed as speech acts at all,[125] since he regarded the proper study of speech acts to be the field of inquiry of language use alone, and performatives clearly rely on non-linguistic conventions. Either view may have its merits, but Warnock's approach seems to provide a middle ground. We note that Searle and Vanderveken's solution is to define performative utterances as 'declarations whose propositional content is that the speaker performs the illocutionary act named by the performative verb' and thus as having the illocutionary force of a declarative and, derivatively, of whatever the performative verb is.[126] This indicates how a strong-weak approach might be taken up, if required,

---

[124] Searle and Vanderveken, *Foundations of Illocutionary Logic*, 2–3.

[125] J. O. Urmson, 'Performative Utterances', *Midwest Studies in Philosophy* 2 (1977), 120–7, reprinted in P. A. French, T. E. Uehling Jr, and H. K. Wettstein (eds), *Contemporary Perspectives in the Philosophy of Language*, Minneapolis: University of Minnesota Press, 1979, 260–7, here 267.

[126] Searle and Vanderveken, *Foundations of Illocutionary Logic*, 3.

into Searle's taxonomical approach.

Thus we may still talk of performatives and illocutions. In the former case, we are talking about illocutions which are primarily concerned with the performance of other illocutions. 'Strong' and 'weak' are more complex categories in this case, but they still apply.[127]

§4.3 Illocution defined

Jennifer Hornsby uses something like our above account to provide a more focused study of illocution, arguing that 'the division between illocutionary and perlocutionary marks a distinction between speech acts which are of proprietary concern to an account of language and speech acts which are not'.[128] She follows Strawson and Warnock in arguing that Austin thought that convention basically served as a covering term to distinguish illocutions, and that as a result of this he 'had nothing to say about illocution as such'.[129]

Hornsby's basic idea is that an illocutionary act is one which is successfully performed regardless of what response it evokes. It can, in this sense, be considered independently of any response. The only refinement to this basic idea required to make it work is to accept that the act must be performed in a context where it is *understood*. For this she uses the notion of 'reciprocity':

> It seems that the speaker relies only on a certain receptiveness on her audience's part for her utterance to work for her as illocutionarily meant: the audience takes her to have done what she meant to . . . When reciprocity obtains between people, they are such as to recognize one another's speech as it is meant to be taken.[130]

---

[127] Recanati makes a similar claim, also agreeing with Warnock, but rather than talking of strong and weak illocutions he suggests that in the case of performative utterances the locution 'stages' the illocution, and that this is precisely the distinction Austin originally had in mind between locution and illocution. Recanati, *Meaning and Force*, 236–66. Note his anticipation of this claim in 'Some Remarks on Explicit Performatives, Indirect Speech Acts, Locutionary Meaning and Truth-Value', in Searle, Kiefer and Bierwisch (eds), *Speech-Act Theory and Pragmatics*, 205–20. See also my own n. 54 above.

[128] Jennifer Hornsby, 'Illocution and Its Significance' in Tsohatzidis (ed.), *Foundations of Speech Act Theory*, 187–207, here 189.

[129] Hornsby, 'Illocution', 192. This might also explain why Austin's initial example of an illocutionary act, 'He urged me to shoot her' (*HDTW*, 102), is a 'weak' one.

[130] Hornsby, 'Illocution', 192.

Beyond this, an illocutionary act is effective regardless of response. In contrast, perlocutionary acts require more than just reciprocity to have their proper consequences.

Hornsby criticises Austin, and Searle and Vanderveken, for their attempt to locate the defining characteristics of illocution in convention. As we have seen with Warnock, such an attempt is ultimately insufficiently precise. Further, examples such as 'He urged her' or 'He warned her' make it clear that the notion of intended effect is not in itself a sharp enough tool to distinguish between illocution and perlocution, as is reflected in whether we choose to say 'She warned him but he never realized the danger' or 'She tried in vain to warn him'.[131]

In terms of our discussion, Hornsby indicates that conventions operate across both illocutions and perlocutions, but that the notion of reciprocity underlies the type of convention which is invoked when weak illocutions are in view. To put the point the other way around: where the non-linguistic conventions are in place (e.g. it is in fact the Queen naming the ship and not me), then the further convention required for a successful illocution simply is that of reciprocity.

The significance of her study may be illustrated by her own example. Focusing on the social conditions surrounding the speech act leads her to conclude: 'Just as it is more or less automatic that an attempt at an illocutionary act is fully successful when certain socially defined conditions obtain; so, when certain conditions do not obtain, there cannot be a fully successful performance.'[132] These socially defined conditions include the question of whose voices are authorised by any given community in terms of what can or cannot be 'heard' by members of that community. Thus, in a celebrated case, a man accused of raping a woman who had said 'No' is acquitted because, as the judge expressed it, 'it is not just a question of saying no'. The social conditions determine which illocutionary acts may be possible.[133]

§4.4 Summary

In this section I have argued for an idea of 'illocution' which includes a spectrum ranging from strong to weak illocutionary

---

[131] Hornsby, 'Illocution', 197.
[132] Hornsby, 'Illocution', 198.
[133] Hornsby, 'Illocution', 199–200.

acts depending on the extent to which the operative conventions are either non-linguistic or linguistic. A performative utterance is a certain kind of 'multiple' illocutionary act, and explicit performatives are not the same special case in Austin's original thinking as strong illocutions. An illocutionary act is successfully performed regardless of the response it provokes if its non-linguistic conventions are in place, and with the single further requirement of 'reciprocity': mutual understanding of the utterance.

§5 Further Developments in Speech Act Theory

In this chapter I have developed an account of speech act theory which seeks to understand its key ideas and terms in their appropriate contexts, as a necessary preliminary to my study of speech act theory and its role in interpretation, and specifically biblical interpretation. I have based my account around the major works of J. L. Austin and John Searle, which could hardly be called a controversial choice.[134] However, it is appropriate at least to acknowledge the various other prominent strands of thought in speech act theory, as well as offering the briefest of overviews of more recent developments.

The most obvious figure omitted thus far is H. P. Grice, whose articles 'Logic and Conversation' and 'Utterer's Meaning, Sentence Meaning, and Word Meaning' were significant early contributions to the whole topic.[135] His emphasis on intention in contrast to Searle's emphasis on convention led to a lively

---

[134] I have not had space to consider the various wholesale critiques of speech act theory, usually as part of blanket condemnations of 'ordinary language' concerns. For an excellent introduction to this kind of debate, see Rée, 'English Philosophy in the Fifties'. The angry denunciations of Ernest Gellner, *Words and Things: A Critical Account of Linguistic Philosophy and a Study in Ideology* (with an introduction by Bertrand Russell), London: Gollancz, 1959; Herbert Marcuse, *One Dimensional Man: Studies in the Ideology of Advanced Industrial Society*, London: Routledge & Kegan Paul, 1964, 170–99; and Perry Anderson, 'Components of the National Culture', *NLR* 50 (July–August 1968), 3–57, especially 21–5 and 43–6, tell us more, it seems to me, about their authors than about the philosophy concerned. On the refusal of Ryle to review Gellner's book, and the remarkable fuss it created, particularly with Russell, see the suitably deflationary account of Mehta, *Fly and the Fly-Bottle*, 11–21.

[135] H. P. Grice, 'Utterer's Meaning, Sentence Meaning and Word Meaning', *Foundations of Language* 4 (1968), 225–42; and reprinted in Searle (ed.), *Philosophy of Language*, 54–70; idem, 'Logic and Conversation', in P. Cole and J. L. Morgan (eds), *Syntax and Semantics*, vol. 3, *Speech Acts*, New York: Academic Press, 1975, 41–58. See next note.

debate in the 1960s which, in my judgment, is now subsumed into the broader frameworks of speech act theory described above, as for instance in the recent work of Recanati. Grice's overall approach to pragmatics, his 1967 Harvard lectures on 'Logic and Conversation' which, like *HDTW*, were given as William James lectures, were not finally published until the year after his death,[136] but the piecemeal earlier versions of his work have been widely followed. His focus on so-called 'conversational implicature' leads to a variety of insights concerning the style and structure of discourse, and I shall refer briefly to this approach in chapter 3, on speech act theory and texts, where it seems most appropriately treated.

Another fundamental issue which is to some extent prejudged in my presentation is the debate between those who, like Searle, see speech act theory as sytematising sentence meaning into an overall theory of language use without remainder,[137] and those for whom there remains an irreducibly pragmatic element which renders such a programme impossible.[138] The former emphasis, implicit in much of Searle's work, becomes explicit with the developments of it made by Daniel Vanderveken, who seeks as the rationale for his own two-volume work, to

> construct a general formal semantics for natural languages capable of characterizing the conditions of success as well as the truth conditions of literal utterances. This is necessary in order to interpret adequately sentences of any syntactic type (whether declarative or not) which express elementary speech acts with any possible force.[139]

Although Vanderveken has provided several helpful studies of particular types of logical relation between speakers' commit-

---

[136] Paul Grice, *Studies in the Way of Words*, Cambridge, MA: Harvard University Press, 1989. The articles from the above note are included at 117–37 and 22–40 respectively. For helpful overviews of the key differences between Grice's approach and that of Austin and Searle, see Dascal, 'Speech Act Theory and Gricean Pragmatics'; and more generally Anita Avramides, *Meaning and Mind: An Examination of a Gricean Account of Language*, Cambridge, MA, and London: MIT Press, 1989.

[137] See, for example, Jerrold J. Katz, *Propositional Structure and Illocutionary Force: A Study of the Contribution of Sentence Meaning to Speech Acts*, New York: Crowell, and Sussex: Harvester Press, 1977.

[138] At the risk of over-simplification, one may cite here K. Bach and R. M. Harnish, *Linguistic Communication and Speech Acts*, Cambridge, MA: MIT Press, 1979; D. Sperber and D. Wilson, *Relevance: Communication and Cognition*, Oxford: Blackwell, 1986.

[139] Daniel Vanderveken, *Meaning and Speech Acts*, vol. 1, *Principles of Language Use*, Cambridge: Cambridge University Press, 1990, 2.

ments and self-involving speech acts,[140] his attempt to extend such formal considerations to the whole of language must be considered as a different kind of enterprise with limited interest for those who remain unconvinced by his claim that 'there is no important theoretical difference between natural and formal languages'.[141] Further, despite the different agendas, it remains debatable just how far the approach of Vanderveken diverges in practice from the more pragmatic concerns of writers like Sperber and Wilson,[142] and in the work of François Recanati there is something of an attempt to draw together both traditions in the interests of finding a way forward for speech act theory.

François Recanati's *Meaning and Force* is a major contribution to the subject which is especially valuable for its thorough analysis of Austin and Searle's work in the light of more pragmatically inclined perspectives. He begins the book with a discussion of the difference between semantics and pragmatics, and contrasts his own approach with that of Searle, in that he does *not* see that utterance interpretation potentially reduces to sentence interpretation because there is an irreducible pragmatic content to meaning. Thus, 'it is impossible to make a sharp separation between the meaning of a sentence and the illocutionary force conveyed by an utterance of the sentence in a given context'.[143] Holding a view similar to William Alston's well-known idea of 'illocutionary act potential', he argues that the meaning of an utterance 'includes a "projection" of the utterance's illocutionary force, not the force itself, which must be inferred by the hearer on the basis of the supposed intentions of the speaker'.[144] Thus

---

[140] In particular his 'Illocutionary Logic and Self-Defeating Speech Acts', in Searle, Kiefer and Bierwisch (eds), *Speech Act Theory and Pragmatics*, 247–72.

[141] Daniel Vanderveken, *Meaning and Speech Acts*, vol. 2, *Formal Semantics of Success and Satisfaction*, Cambridge: Cambridge University Press, 1991, 2. One notes, for instance, that he finds natural language inadequate for his purposes, and feels compelled to replace the 'defects' of natural expression with '*an ideal unambiguous and perspicuous object-language* L'; Vanderveken, *Meaning and Speech Acts*, vol. 1, 35–6. In ch. 3, however, I shall draw extensively on his thorough work in this volume concerning the illocutionary logic of particular verbs, which again escapes criticisms levelled at his insistent formalist agenda.

[142] See the mediating survey of Graham H. Bird, 'Relevance Theory and Speech Acts', in Tsohatzidis (ed.), *Foundations of Speech Act Theory*, 292–311.

[143] Recanati, *Meaning and Force*, 14 (and see also 17).

[144] Recanati, *Meaning and Force*, 25–7; here 27; cf. William P. Alston, *Philosophy of Language*, Englewood Cliffs, NJ: Prentice-Hall, 1964, 36–9.

even explicit performatives may be misleading as to their illocutionary force, if, for instance, they are insincere.

Recanati also argues, similarly to Warnock, that Austin was mistaken to collapse the performative–constative distinction. He notes other ways, in addition to that demonstrated by Warnock, in which the distinction may be maintained: for instance in terms of demarcation between word to world and world to word directions of fit.[145]

Meaning and Force touches on many other issues which I have covered in this chapter. I have already discussed his comments about classification of illocutions being functional, and noted his argument about double-level illocutions in the case of explicit performative utterances: if I say, 'I state that the earth is flat', then I assert that the earth is flat, but I also record the fact that that is my assertion. This, for Recanati, is the heart of what Austin had in mind with his illocutionary/locutionary distinction.[146] What happens in (Austin's sense of) an illocutionary act is that a speaker who performs some locutionary act *x* '*presents himself as performing* the illocutionary act *x*'.[147] In other words an illocutionary act is staged by the locutionary act. Recanati concludes that 'one had better look behind the scenes' of this staging for a real understanding of the pragmatics of an utterance, which again is his thesis that intention must be as much a factor as convention in a full speech act theory.[148]

The publication, in 1994, of a major collection of papers on speech act theory, *Foundations of Speech Act Theory: Philosophical and Linguistic Perspectives*,[149] represents the latest major development of new directions in the subject. Several of its papers have been referred to in this chapter, and although there are many

---

[145] Recanati, *Meaning and Force*, 70–2 (cf. 20 n. 9). Recanati's classification of illocutionary acts according to direction of fit is at 154–63. He also endorses G. J. Warnock's argument, 72–4.

[146] See note 127 above.

[147] Recanati, *Meaning and Force*, 259.

[148] Recanati, *Meaning and Force*, 266. He develops an important implication of this main thesis in his defence of 'contextualism' in 'Contextualism and Anticontextualism in the Philosophy of Language', in Tsohatzidis (ed.), *Foundations of Speech Act Theory*, 156–66.

[149] Tsohatzidis (ed.), *Foundations of Speech Act Theory*, running to 500 pages and including 22 papers from 21 different authors in three sections: 'Speech Acts and Semantic Theory', 'Speech Acts and Pragmatic Theory', and 'Speech Acts and Grammatical Structure.'

conflicting viewpoints in the book, taken together its contributions indicate both the ongoing creative investigations in speech act theory and at the same time the pervasive significance of the contributions of Austin and Searle in setting the agenda for the subject.[150] It has been the intention of this chapter to enable us to have a clear view of their work and of the speech act theory which finally emerges from it, in order that we may now progress to ask questions about how speech act theory may illuminate questions of textual interpretation.

[150] For a full critical review, see Edda Weigand, 'The State of the Art in Speech Act Theory (Review article of Savas L. Tsohatzidis (ed.), *Foundations of Speech Act Theory: Philosophical and Linguistic Perspectives*, London & New York: Routledge, 1994)', *Pragmatics & Cognition* 4 (1996), 367–406. Weigand is impatient with the book, and notes the predominance of specifically Anglo-American concerns to the exclusion of any awareness of German traditions of pragmatics, which is fair comment, although perhaps it risks judging the contributors by inappropriate standards.

3

Speech Acts and Texts

It appears to me that literary theorists are at present looking for philosophical foundations of their theories. Derrida offered something to them, which some literary theorists found attractive, while analytic philosophers have hitherto offered very little in this respect. Here lies an important challenge to us analytic philosophers.[1]

In the preceding chapter we have looked at many issues of criteria in speech act theory, surveying the development of different approaches to terminological and classificatory issues, with our focus remaining within the broad tradition of analytic philosophy. However, when all is said and done, or in this case done by being said, one may rightly ask whether a philosophy which concerns itself with acts of speech is appropriate to acts performed by texts. Are textual acts the same as, similar to, or different from speech acts, and in what ways? In taking up this subject, we enter the wider philosophical and literary-critical arena, encountering in particular two of the most significant voices to be raised in discussions of speech act theory, those of Jacques Derrida and Stanley Fish.

In his recent theological analysis of philosophical issues in interpretation theory, Kevin Vanhoozer distinguishes 'two kinds of "postmodern" thinker: the deconstructor or *Undoer* and the pragmatist or *User*'.[2] He suggests that they 'evince a common

---

[1] Dagfin Follesdal, 'Analytic Philosophy: What Is It and Why Should One Engage in It?', in Hans-Johann Glock (ed.), *The Rise of Analytic Philosophy*, Oxford: Blackwell, 1997, 1–16, here 14.

[2] Vanhoozer, *Is There a Meaning in This Text?*, 38.

distrust of modernity's faith in scientific objectivity, reason and morality': they are the 'unbelievers' who 'insist on the non-naturalness of all systems'.[3] Vanhoozer, as we have seen, appeals to speech act theory in his approach, and in this case he attempts to chart a middle way between the undoer and the user. Although his concerns lie with a 'theology of interpretation' rather than with biblical interpretation as such,[4] his framework certainly highlights the apparent oddity that it should be Derrida and Fish who have had such an impact on the reception of speech act theory in literary circles. Sandy Petrey's useful introductory text, *Speech Acts and Literary Theory*, for example, discusses them more than any other authors except Austin and Searle.[5]

Furthermore, if one of our long-term goals is to harness some of the insights of speech act theory for biblical interpretation, then it is worth asking to what extent speech act theory has been adopted in broader literary circles. Alternatively, if literary critics have tried speech act theory and found it wanting, then what might this say to biblical critics?

In this chapter, therefore, I intend to examine what happens when speech act theory is brought to bear on the task of reading texts. Derrida's point of entry here is the problematical issue of authorial 'presence' in the written case, and the implications of this absence for the spoken case. His exchange with Searle is thus an appropriate focus for a discussion of the issues raised by speech act theory in relation to texts, not least because of its remarkably high profile. After Derrida's challenge, it also seems appropriate to turn to that branch of general literary theory which concerns itself with speech act theory, and see what in fact has been done and is typically claimed. This will raise a variety of questions about so-called 'speech act criticism' and the differences between texts in general and 'literary' texts. Finally, since my overall interest is actually in biblical texts, this will in turn raise questions of how one may assess which biblical texts are likely to be interesting candidates for a speech act analysis, which I thus take up as the third section of this chapter. In the meantime, the appeal to Fish raises issues of the nature

---

[3] Vanhoozer, *Is There a Meaning in This Text?*, 38 and 40 n. 5, also citing Rorty's comment that 'Pragmatists and Derrideans are, indeed, natural allies'.

[4] Vanhoozer, *Is There a Meaning in This Text?*, 9.

[5] Sandy Petrey, *Speech Acts and Literary Theory*, New York and London: Routledge, 1990. Only Shoshana Felman gets comparable coverage.

of texts themselves, and what kind of activity reading a text might be. I will attempt to bring some speech act insights to bear on this in chapter 4.

§1 Speech and Writing: Derrida's Challenge

Text, speech and agency

'*Text* has become *the* terminological football of recent criticism', writes Valentine Cunningham, noting that preoccupation with textuality and the nature of texts has dominated recent critical discussion.[6] In theological circles, Werner Jeanrond has appealed to the need for a theory of text in developing any kind of theological hermeneutic. In this he hopes to escape from over-concentration on the verse or sentence as an out-of-context foundation for dogmatism, as well as make sense of what it could mean for Christian faith to be based on the textual phenomenon of the Bible.[7] He notes approvingly that Austin and Searle's work in pragmatics highlights 'the important role played by the communicative situation for the constitution of meaning and its transparency'.[8]

Jeanrond's comments highlight the issue of agency: text as communication presupposes an agent of communication, even if literary theory has repeatedly and successfully underlined the role of the readers of a text in regulating and/or, to whatever extent, constituting its significant features. Indeed, theories of textuality today span a wide range, from pre-critical views of the given-ness of the text as 'other' through to more postmodern (constructivist) views. The former invite a subject–object conceptualisation of the interpretive process.[9] The latter lend themselves to more or less radical forms of contextual relativism,

---

[6] Valentine Cunningham, *In the Reading Gaol: Postmodernity, Texts, and History*, Oxford: Blackwell, 1994, 4.

[7] Werner G. Jeanrond, *Text and Interpretation as Categories of Theological Thinking*, Dublin: Gill & Macmillan, 1988 (1986), 73–5.

[8] Jeanrond, *Text and Interpretation*, 76.

[9] Most famously E. D. Hirsch Jr, *Validity in Interpretation*, New Haven and London: Yale University Press, 1967, although see now the considerable nuancing of his position in idem, 'Meaning and Significance Reinterpreted', *Critical Inquiry* 11 (1984), 202–25; and his rejection of formalism, written in the context of literacy education but with implications for his interpretive theory, in idem, 'Reading, Writing, and Cultural Literacy', in Winifred Bryan Horner (ed.), *Composition and Literature: Bridging the Gap*, Chicago and London: University of Chicago Press, 1983, 141–7.

as adopted in the proliferation of reader-response theories developed in literary theory.[10]

The notion that reader and text *interact* in the interpretive process is an influential one which, once free from a pre-critical view of textual otherness and objectivity, appears to be something of a common-sense position. The question before us, then, is whether the criteria of speech act theory, which has its focus on communicative action between a speaker and a hearer, can be used in the case of communicative acts embodied in texts which pass from writer to reader. The locus of this discussion is widely acknowledged as being the so-called 'Derrida–Searle' debate, to which we now turn.

§1.1 *Derrida on Austin:* 'Signature Event Context'

At a 1971 conference Derrida gave a paper in which, in the course of reflecting on the nature of writing and its possible communicative dimensions, he drew on the work of Austin.[11] Translated into English in 1977, it came to the attention of Searle, who wrote a brief response concerning its use of Austin's ideas.[12] This in turn engendered a lengthy reply from Derrida,[13] later republished together with a substantial additional 'afterword'.[14] Much discussed and heavily analysed, this remarkable debate briefly thrust speech act theory centre stage in wider critical circles. Derrida has not followed it up apart from his 'afterword'; while Searle's subsequent contributions have been trenchant and piecemeal.[15]

[10] For an incisive survey, see Jane P. Tompkins, 'An Introduction to Reader-Response Criticism', in idem (ed.), *Reader-Response Criticism: From Formalism to Post-Structuralism*, Baltimore and London: Johns Hopkins University Press, 1980, ix-xxvi, as well as the various essays collected in the book.

[11] Published as Jacques Derrida, 'signature événement contexte', in Jacques Derrida, *Marges de la philosophie*, Paris: Les Editions de Minuit, 1972, 365–93.

[12] John R. Searle, 'Reiterating the Differences: A Reply to Derrida', *Glyph* 1 (1977), 198–208; responding to the translated article Jacques Derrida, 'Signature Event Context', *Glyph* 1 (1977), 172–97.

[13] Jacques Derrida, 'Limited Inc abc . . .', *Glyph* 2 (1977), 162–254.

[14] Jacques Derrida, *Limited Inc* (ed. Gerald Graff), Evanston, IL: Northwestern University Press, 1988, including Derrida's 'Afterword: Toward an Ethic of Discussion', 111–60. Page references to Derrida's first two articles are given from this reprint, 1–23 and 29–110 respectively. Searle's article is summarised (25–7) but I shall refer to its full version in *Glyph*.

[15] See John R. Searle, 'The World Turned Upside Down [A review of Jonathan Culler's *On Deconstruction*]', *New York Review of Books* 30.16 (October 1983), 74–9; idem, 'Literary Theory and Its Discontents', *NLH* 25 (1994), 637–67.

Derrida's basic theme in 'Signature Event Context' is *communication*, and its various senses, most generally, 'are the conditions [*les réquisits*] of a context ever absolutely determinable? . . . Is there a rigorous and scientific concept of *context?*'[16] In the first half of the article, 'Writing and Telecommunication', Derrida begins by pursuing the implications of the absence of a fully determined communicative context in the case of *writing*. He develops the key notion of 'iterability': 'A writing that is not structurally readable – iterable – beyond the death of the addressee would not be writing' (7). One of the consequences of this distancing of writing from the communicative (spoken) context is 'the disqualification or the limiting of the concept of context, whether "real" or "linguistic", inasmuch as its rigorous theoretical determination as well as its empirical saturation is rendered impossible or insufficient by writing' (9).

However, in typical Derridean fashion, the characteristics which thus mark off writing as an etiolated form of speech are now shown to inhere in the very nature of all language. In particular, written signs 'subsist' beyond their moment of inscription; they are 'ruptured' from their originating context; and they emerge as themselves in their 'spacing' both from other signs and from other attempts to fix their present reference. Subsistence, rupture and spacing, to paraphrase baldly, delineate the *iterability* which makes a mark a mark, in whatever code or system it operates. Derrida insists on this 'possibility of disengagement and citational graft which belongs to the structure of every mark, spoken or written, and which constitutes every mark in writing before and outside of every horizon of semio-linguistic communication' (12).

Thus far this is Derrida's oft-noted concern with the 'deconstructive' possibilities inherent in language, and in particular his desire to overturn an established hierarchy which structures, in this case, speech and writing. The particular interest of the article, and the cause of its subsequent high profile, is that in the second section of it he turns to Austin's *HDTW* and proceeds to examine Austin's performative–constative distinction as an attempt to order language by way of supplying 'total contexts' within which, and only within which, speech acts may be understood (13–19). Austin's category of 'performative', he

---

[16] Derrida, *Limited Inc*, 2–3. Further page references are in the text.

suggests, which seems to promise so much, ultimately fails to secure its own domain because the whole opposition of performative–constative presupposes the availability of the kind of saturated context which Derrida has considered earlier:

> Austin has not taken account of what – in the structure of *locution* (thus before any illocutory or perlocutory determination) – already entails that system of predicates I call *graphematic in general* and consequently blurs [*brouille*] all the oppositions which follow, oppositions whose pertinence, purity, and rigor Austin has unsuccessfully attempted to establish. (14)

The 'total context', be it in the form of consciousness, or the 'conscious presence of speakers', 'implies teleologically that no *residue* [*reste*] escapes the present totalization' (14). Austin acknowledges all the various possible infelicities of the performative, but immediately excludes them in the name of ideal regulation (15).[17] On Derrida's reading, this is 'all the more curious': Austin has come so close to seeing the untenability of such idealised regulation, and has lapsed back into it at the last minute. Stage utterances were excluded by Austin as parasitic upon the *serious* use of language. For Derrida, this is the problem of philosophical privileging in a nutshell: the quality of 'risk' admitted by (and then banished by) Austin is not a surrounding problem which careful usage can avoid, but rather it is 'its internal and positive condition of possibility'. Derrida's conclusion on Austin is therefore as follows:

> For, ultimately, isn't it true that what Austin excludes as anomaly, exception, 'non-serious', *citation* (on stage, in a poem, or a soliloquy) is the determined modification of a general citationality – or rather, a general iterability – without which there would not even be a 'successful' performative? So that – a paradoxical but unavoidable conclusion – a successful performative is necessarily an 'impure' performative. (17)

In other words, Austin notes the obvious cases (the 'determined modification') but fails to note the 'general citationality' which underlies it, and which would thus, by implication, be equally banished if Austin's exclusion clauses are allowed. Derrida's preferred name for this 'general citationality' is *iterability* (18),

---

[17] This is a key passage, referring to the second lecture of Austin, *HDTW*, particularly 20–4.

and it is iterability which is presupposed by any successful performative such as 'I open the meeting': the performative works because it conforms to an iterable model. He allows for successful performatives (indeed he claims to account for them) and even for relative degrees of their 'purity'. Even these most 'event-ridden' of utterances fall short of saturated context: *différance* prevails, and in so doing makes communication possible (19).

Derrida concludes with a brief discussion of the signature, an example noted by Austin in passing as a way of countering the absence of the author of a written text as against the presence of a speaker. Signatures too, says Derrida, only function because of their iterability. He closes with a printed signature, challenging the assumed idea that he was, at some point, present himself to write it, and underlining its iterable nature.

'Signature Event Context' is perhaps one of the clearest examples of Derrida's philosophical approach. His discussion of iterability sets out the framework within which deconstruction attains purchase. Writing is not simply a distant form of speech, and neither are the possible demarcations between serious and non-serious speech sufficiently unambiguous to allow the certainty of successful communication. Austin's appearance in this post-structuralist landscape is, in one sense at least, more as an example of a philosopher close to unmasking, but still ultimately inattentive to, *différance*, rather than as a support or foil. Derrida characterises Austin's *HDTW* as 'patient, open, aporetical, in constant transformation, often more fruitful in the acknowledgment of its impasses than in its positions' (14); and in his subsequent rejoinder also remarks: 'I consider myself to be in many respects quite close to Austin, both interested in and indebted to his problematic.'[18] Nevertheless, Derrida's goal in the article is neither to mimic the performative–constative synthesis of Austin nor to exegete Austin but rather to show that, despite Austin's best efforts, he failed to grasp the 'graphematic' requirement of iterability which grounds all successful performatives. A blurring of these distinctions characterises the subsequent debate. I shall suggest that one need not agree with Derrida's argument in order to evaluate the extent to which he is or is not right about Austin.

[18] Derrida, *Limited Inc*, 38.

§1.2 *The Searle–Derrida exchange*

What then is one to make of Searle's 'reply'? Of his three contributions to this would-be correspondence it is I think by far the weakest, and for all that one may agree with his frustration about the role played by Austin in Derrida's article, it is hard not to sympathise with Derrida's subsequent comment about it as 'something identifying itself so much with Austin that it can only read *Sec* feverishly, unable to support the fact that questions might be posed serenely concerning the limits or the presuppositions of Austin's theory'.[19] 'Reiterating the Differences' makes several valid points about such issues as the role of intentionality in speech acts, and the nature of iterability. Where it fails is in its attempt to describe and sustain a clear dividing line between Derrida on the one hand and Searle and Austin on the other. Such a demarcation is immediately complicated by Searle's own self-distancing from Austin,[20] but is most completely destroyed by his unusual predilection for making precisely the point Derrida has in mind while presenting it as a disagreement with Derrida.

First, evidence for such a claim should be presented, and is done so at somewhat inordinate length by Derrida himself in his reply.[21] One example must suffice: Searle looks at the criteria for distinguishing writing from speaking, and notes that neither iterability nor absence will do. This is done 'in order to get at what is wrong with these [Derrida's] arguments'. Of course, that neither iterability nor absence will demarcate writing from speaking is just one aspect of Derrida's whole point. Searle's conclusion is that it is *permanence* which will do the distinguishing work, and he charges Derrida with confusing permanence and iterability. However, one cannot doubt that the work Searle intends 'permanent' to do is not the same as the work envisaged by Derrida with 'iterable'. For one it is the on-going availability

[19] Derrida, *Limited Inc*, 42. '*Sec*' is Derrida's favoured abbreviation for 'Signature Event Context'.

[20] Searle, 'Reiterating the Differences', 204 and n. 3.

[21] Derrida, 'Limited Inc abc . . .'. Derrida famously cites almost the whole of Searle's reply in this article, a typical example of his energetic attempt to disrupt the confidence of Searle's views on citation, iterability and intention. With style and substance so patently inseparable, any summary of 'Limited Inc abc . . .' must necessarily be inadequate, even the unusually lengthy summary provided by erstwhile Derrida translator Gayatri Chakravorty Spivak, 'Revolutions That as Yet Have No Model: Derrida's *Limited Inc*', *Diacritics* 10.4 (1980), 29–49.

of a token of a communicative type, which in itself is not (as Searle would agree) a particularly interesting metaphysical claim. For the other, it is the irreducible immersion of any token in the interconnecting play of presence and absence, of trace and supplement, in short of *différance*, without which communication could not even get started. The conclusion is that Searle's discussion of permanence is not what is at issue in 'Signature Event Context', and it is hard therefore to take it as a pointed objection to Derrida's article.[22]

Secondly, I judge that Searle does not indeed read Derrida's text closely. His discussion of Derrida's remarks on *agrammaticality*, for all that Derrida typically outruns patient definition here, are simply mistaken.[23] Searle mistakenly talks of 'ungrammaticality' and (untypically) misreads Derrida's *signifie* as 'means', and ends up highlighting clear nonsense, but alas not any nonsense drawn from 'Signature Event Context'.

It would take too long to discuss the debate in detail, and not least to examine its potentially more interesting development into the wider field of the ethics of discussion, which grows out of the reflections of both Searle and Derrida on the 'tone' (for want of a better word) which it exhibits, as characterised in its various examples of uncharitable reading or obfuscation.[24] Searle should not be above criticism for his attempt to pass off speech act theory as unproblematic and implacably opposed to 'Signature Event Context', most notably in his urbane reference to 'a detailed answer to the question' of the status of parasitic (in this case fictional) discourse from a speech act perspective, wherein he notes his own 'The Logical Status of Fictional Discourse' which itself concludes with the disclaimer

---

[22] For Derrida's discussion of this very point, see *Limited Inc*, 50–4.

[23] Searle, 'Reiterating the Differences', 203; discussing Derrida, *Limited Inc*, 12.

[24] This develops particularly in Searle, 'The World Turned Upside Down', where, in his aggrieved analysis of Derrida's style, he betrays a somewhat brutal dismissiveness himself; taken up in detail by Derrida, 'Afterword: Toward an Ethic of Discussion'. Certainly the debate has focused a dispute about the logical standards inherent in Derrida's work. His 'Afterword' is one of his clearest protestations of the need for logical rigour in one's deconstructive claims, see, e.g. *Limited Inc*, 114–31. Christopher Norris repeatedly uses Derrida's various contributions to *Limited Inc* to defend just such a thesis concerning deconstruction: Christopher Norris, *Deconstruction: Theory and Practice*, London: Routledge & Kegan Paul, [2]1991 (1982), 143–58; idem, 'Limited Think: How Not to Read Derrida', *What's Wrong with Postmodernism: Critical Theory and the Ends of Philosophy*, New York and London: Harvester Wheatsheaf, 1990, 134–63.

that 'there is as yet no general theory of the mechanisms by which such serious illocutionary intentions are conveyed by pretended illocutions'.[25] Derrida is right to point this out, for all that he does so in the most extraordinary way.[26] At the same time, although in general Derrida substantiates his claim that he has been misread, there are occasions when this comes extremely close to special pleading.[27] There is a considerable literature discussing these and various other aspects of the debate.[28]

However, the particular issue which I suggest all this raises for our own concerns is less to do with the relative merits of the Derrida–Searle exchange and more concerned with the way in which either side of the exchange does or does not contribute to the possibility of using speech act theory in the context of addressing written texts.

§1.3 *Consequences of the Derrida–Searle debate*

The major point to make here is one that follows from the above discussion about the blurring of the boundary lines between Derrida on the one hand and Austin and Searle on the other.

[25] Searle, 'Reiterating the Differences', 205 and 208 n. 4; referring to his 'The Logical Status of Fictional Discourse', *NLH* 6 (1975), 319–32, reprinted in idem, *Expression and Meaning*, 58–75, here 75.

[26] Derrida, *Limited Inc*, 94–6.

[27] This might lead us into the vexed territory of why Derrida feels so *persistently* misread, and whether he may in some sense be responsible for this. This is part of the subject matter of the 'ethics' debate (see n. 25 above, and in particular *Limited Inc*, 146). I must content myself here with the observation that, for example, *Limited Inc*, section 'r', 60–77, appears to take Searle's disagreement with 'Signature Event Context' (or perhaps better, its grammatological project) as evidence of misreading; or that when Derrida clarifies his comments about Austin one can both see what he means but also why he was misunderstood (e.g. on whether he said that Austin thought parasitic discourse was not part of ordinary language: 'the parasite *is part* of so-called ordinary language, and it is part of it *as* parasite', *Limited Inc*, 97).

[28] In addition to Norris and Spivak, mentioned above, see Jonathan Culler, 'Meaning and Iterability', *On Deconstruction: Theory and Criticism after Structuralism*, London: Routledge & Kegan Paul, 1983, 110–34; the works of Stanley Cavell noted below; and Petrey, *Speech Acts and Literary Theory*, 131–46. Stanley Fish, 'With the Compliments of the Author', is a most remarkable tour de force which reduces both Derrida and Austin to mimicking the standard Fishian complaint that there is no such thing as transcontextual criteria because interpretive conventions are always revisable and local; while Gordon C. F. Bearn, 'Derrida Dry: Iterating Iterability Analytically', *Diacritics* 25.3 (1995), 3–25, is helpful on the outline of the debate, but pursues the unique thesis that Derrida's view is that 'no linguistic communication is ever successful' (3).

Commentators like to polarise this issue: either Derrida is a misreader and Searle vindicates Austin, or Searle is the villain of the piece and Derrida is the speech act prodigal now revealed as Austin's true heir.[29] However, this seems to be yet another case where a predilection for mapping out positions distorts the very issues at stake.

Stanley Cavell's discussion of the issue suggests various significant ways in which Derrida misreads Austin, or at least too quickly assimilates Austin's voice to his own, but at the same time he clearly does not portray Austin as simply a pale precursor of Searle's later philosophy.[30] In particular, Cavell addresses the central issue noted above about the status of Austin's 'exclusions': are they the metaphysical stumbling block which Derrida uncovers or the methodological reasonableness which Searle champions? Neither, says Cavell, for they are in fact references made by Austin to work published elsewhere on 'etiolations' (excuses) and 'pretending'.[31] Derrida, always one to suggest that critics should 'read a little further', falls foul of this advice with respect to Austin; Cavell's surmise is here perhaps vindicated by Derrida's comments on Austin's 'Three Ways of Spilling Ink' which in many ways does support Derrida's approach to various issues of classification, but which was clearly not known to Derrida when he wrote about Austin.[32] The significance of this is not to discuss who had read what, but to lay the foundation for Cavell's main claim, that Derrida did not let Austin's distinctive philosophical voice (or 'pitch') set its own agenda. Derrida comes so close to an appreciation of Austin, with his focus on the importance of signature, and the claim of the human voice. However, for Derrida, '*even* Austin succumbs to the lure of voice':

> That Derrida finds this claim [of the voice] to be something that pushes Austin back into the crowd of philosophers, ancient and

---

[29] Something of this latter perspective marks out the contributions of Fish, Bearn and Petrey (see above note). Petrey's opposing of Austin and Searle is a major theme of his book, with relevance to the literary concerns discussed later in this chapter.

[30] Cavell, *Philosophical Passages*, 42–90; idem, *A Pitch of Philosophy: Autobiographical Exercises*, Cambridge, MA: Harvard University Press, 1994, 53–127. These are parallel treatments. I cite from the first only.

[31] Cavell, *Philosophical Passages*, 52. The references are to works now gathered in Austin, *Philosophical Papers*.

[32] Cf. Derrida, *Limited Inc*, 109, n. 3.

modern, in his view of the economy of voice and writing, seems to me not to do Austin's originality justice.[33]

Rather, in Cavell's view, Austin's opening discussion of Hippolytus, where he inveighs against the inward survey of 'the invisible depths of ethical space', indicates that Austin is very much aware of the dangers of metaphysical abstraction. Cavell's discussion of the Hippolytus passage[34] draws out the significance of this all too brief Austinian flourish, which I had cause to suggest in chapter 2 above sits uneasily with many Searle-like suggestions about the links between speech acts and intentional states. Here Cavell brings it to bear on the distinct sense in which Austin's aversion to metaphysics both separates him from the standard tradition in Derrida's sights and also makes him very different from Derrida:

> I say that if Derrida had noticed the business about Hippolytus, it would have been harder for him to continue to insinuate that if, or when, we crave such a tie [to a metaphysically independent world], Austin would wish to satisfy that craving . . . Derrida . . . takes metaphysics to have institutional and linguistic bases which cannot vanish at the touch of the ordinary; on the contrary, it is bound to swamp the ordinary, to take it under its own protection, or interpretation. Whereas for Austin, metaphysics is from its origin, from each individual current origin of itself, unnecessary, monitorable, correctible.[35]

If this is correct, and Cavell's contribution seems to me to be uniquely well placed in separating *three* voices in the debate rather than *two*, then the question of the 'consequences' of the Derrida–Searle debate for the applicability of speech act categories to written texts can no longer be framed in terms of whether Derrida's criticisms of Searle are successful. The vindication of either Derrida or Searle would, in neither case, prejudge the Austinian concepts of speech act theory.

To be more specific, one practical result of the debate has been a certain re-emphasis on Searle's part of the necessary vagueness of various distinctions. His criticism of Derrida's philosophy as 'pre-Wittgensteinian', with the concomitant claim that he, Searle, takes the later works of Wittgenstein *for granted* in

[33] Cavell, *Philosophical Passages*, 73.
[34] Cavell, *Philosophical Passages*, 55–63.
[35] Cavell, *Philosophical Passages*, 75.

everything he writes (his emphasis), reflects on one level the bizarre on-going nature of the debate with its propensity for each writer to claim that they got there first while studiously opposing the other, but more significantly it brings out more clearly than has perhaps always been the case that Searle's taxonomic categories and 'logic of illocutionary acts' reserves its clarity and precision for the purposes of accurately labelling vague concepts, and not for redefining all concepts into precise ones.[36] Despite the endeavours of the participants, the debate appears to have brought into common focus a helpful point here.[37]

By way of conclusion, therefore, we may say that Derrida's analysis of Austin does not demonstrate that a theory of performative utterances and speech acts must ultimately be consigned to a tradition of presupposed metaphysical presence. The deconstructive possibilities of language sit alongside both written and spoken utterances, and neither in Derrida's critique nor in Searle's reply is there a fundamental difference between the two which must leave speech act categories in place for one but not the other. In terms of metaphysical commitment, Austin offers a third alternative beyond Derrida or Searle, and thus speech act theory per se can be seen to refuse reduction to either so-called 'logocentrism' or to deconstruction as its essential nature.

This discussion in itself could doubtless lead to many fruitful metaphysical developments, but it is debatable whether these must be settled prior to the process of interpreting any particular text.[38] My concerns here thus remain with specific questions of the applicability of speech act categories to written texts, and I have tried to deal with this question by way of a discussion of Derrida because of his pre-eminence in bringing into question

---

[36] See Searle, 'Literary Theory and Its Discontents', 663–4, on Derrida as pre-Wittgensteinian; and 637–9 on clear and fuzzy concepts. See also Searle, 'The World Turned Upside Down', 78: 'it is a condition of the adequacy of a precise theory of an indeterminate phenomenon that it should precisely characterize that phenomenon as indeterminate'.

[37] This is also the view of Petrey, *Speech Acts and Literary Theory*, 145, who provides other similar examples.

[38] Nicholas Wolterstorff, for one, debates it: 'I have not argued against the practice of Derrida's alternative . . . There are a few texts, and passages in a fair number of texts, which call for exactly Derrida's style of interpretation. One doesn't have to repudiate ontotheology to say that' (Nicholas Wolterstorff, *Divine Discourse*, 169; see his generous but circumspect appraisal of Derrida from the vantage point of a speech act approach to interpretation on 153–70).

the speech-writing hierarchy, and in particular his appeal to Austin in this very case.[39] In so doing I have attempted to grant many of the points Derrida makes without declaring my hand on deconstruction itself, which it seems to me need not be an issue forced upon a speech act theorist. Despite Petrey's claim that 'there's no compelling reason why speech-act theory can't integrate basic deconstructive principles',[40] I suggest that this is a path that need not be followed by those for whom an Austinian approach suffices,[41] and I also propose that this discussion has shown that one may continue to use Searle's work and thereby make use of an assumed post-Wittgensteinian framework sympathetic to Austin, which must, I submit, judge those comments of Searle and others which might reasonably be taken in other ways. In other words: Derrida's voice of caution serves as a constant reminder that systematic elaborations of speech act theory do not and cannot entirely leave behind them the precise vagueness of Austin's work.

§2 Speech Acts and Literary Theory

If speech act theory can apply to texts, the next step is to ask what has happened when this has been done. What have literary critics made of speech act theory? It is not my intention here to provide a full review of this topic,[42] which would take us far afield into debates concerning philosophical and other theoretical criteria for literariness.[43] Instead my goal is to determine whether a speech act approach to texts should result in some form or other of 'speech act criticism'. I shall argue that it should not.

---

[39] I am aware too that some attempts to incorporate speech act theory into theological concerns are rebuffed with a kind of 'but Derrida proved it couldn't be done' review, which I hope hereby to have rendered unsatisfactory. For a recent example, see H. S. Pyper, review of Vanhoozer, *Is There a Meaning in This Text?*, in Lester L. Grabbe (ed.), *Society for Old Testament Study Book List 1999*, Sheffield: Sheffield Academic Press, 1999, 119–20. Less specific but with a similar view is Stephen E. Fowl, review of Francis Watson, *Text and Truth: Redefining Biblical Theology*, Edinburgh: T&T Clark, 1997, in *MTh* 15 (1999), 94–6, especially 95.

[40] Petrey, *Speech Acts and Literary Theory*, 142.

[41] Wolterstorff's discussion (n. 38 above) reaches the same conclusion.

[42] For just such an overview see Petrey, *Speech Acts and Literary Theory*.

[43] See §2.3 below. For a survey of issues raised in this area see further Peter Lamarque and Stein Haugom Olsen, *Truth, Fiction, and Literature: A Philosophical Perspective*, Oxford: Clarendon Press, 1994. In particular they are concerned to demarcate fiction and literature, while acknowledging a considerable overlap of relevant philosophical questions (e.g. 268–88).

For this purpose I choose one particularly well-known exposition of the possibilities of a speech act approach to a text, from the early work of Stanley Fish, and then discuss some of the issues this raises both in terms of its place within Fish's kind of rhetorical 'reader-response' theory, and of the relevance or otherwise of the 'literariness' of the text in question.

§2.1 *Fish and speech act criticism*

Fish provides one of the clearest examples of how to use speech act theory in literary criticism in a 1976 article entitled 'How to Do Things with Austin and Searle'.[44] Here he analyses Shakespeare's *Coriolanus* with a focus on how the title character is required by the conventions of the day to ask the citizens for the right to be named consul. The tribunes Brutus and Sicinius predict, accurately, as it turns out, that in the very performance of this (speech) act Coriolanus will undermine it in such a way that he fails to be elected. Following Austin and Searle, Fish observes:

> Simply by paying attention to the hero's illocutionary behaviour and then referring to the full dress accounts of the acts he performs, it is possible to produce a speech act 'reading' of the play . . . To the extent that this reading is satisfying, it is because *Coriolanus* is a speech-act play. That is to say, it is *about* what the theory is 'about'.[45]

One example may serve to illustrate that Fish does indeed accomplish what he describes in this summary. Coriolanus believes that he deserves to be made consul because of his own merit, not because he should need to ask for it. To ask is to accept a form of dependence on those less worthy than himself. Indeed Brutus and Sicinius have heard him say more or less this: that he will not 'lower' himself to ask anything of the people who, according to tradition, he must ask in order to be chosen. Their strategy is thus to let Coriolanus go ahead and ask the people to choose him, predicting that in the performance of this speech act he will make it void.

Fish points out that, according to Searle's analysis of the act of requesting, one of the preparatory conditions is that the

[44] Fish, 'How to Do Things with Austin and Searle'; page references from its reprint in idem, *Is There a Text in This Class?*, 197–245.
[45] Fish, 'How to Do Things with Austin and Searle', 220–1.

speaker believes that the hearer is able to do the act requested.[46] But Coriolanus has only contempt for his hearers, not at all believing that they are capable of choosing him. Neither does he particularly want them to do so (the sincerity condition) and in particular, because he believes that he deserves the consulship, he assumes that the hearers *will* do the requested action of their own accord without his asking (thus failing in terms of the other preparatory condition listed by Searle).[47] The conclusion of the citizens, as 'they open their copy of *Speech Acts* and begin to analyze the infelicities of his performance', is that 'he did not ask, but mock' (Act II, scene iii, lines 163–8).[48]

Fish's own view of why his analysis works so well forms the conclusion to his article, and bears quoting in full:

> Speech-act theory is an account of the conditions of intelligibility, of what it means to mean in a community, of the procedures which must be instituted before one can even be said to be understood. In a great many texts those conditions and procedures are presupposed; they are not put before us for consideration, and the emphasis falls on what happens or can happen after they have been met and invoked. It follows that while a speech-act analysis of such texts will always be possible, it will also be trivial (a mere list of the occurrence or distribution of kinds of acts), because while it is the conditions of intelligibility that make all texts possible, not all texts are *about* those conditions.[49]

In short: the analysis works because the play is about what speech act theory is about. It is significant here to note that when talking in these terms Fish is working with what I have called a 'strong' idea of speech acts. He is concerned with illocutions whose successful functioning is at issue in the narrative itself. Where this strong criteria is lost, applications of speech act theory to literature may be little more than mundane. One further clarification: the point his analysis actually makes is that speech act theory will only shed light on (strong) speech acts and their workings. This is a little more broad than a text's being *about* 'the conditions of intelligibility that make all texts possible', but it is certainly still very much restricted to texts which *concern*

[46] See Searle, *Speech Acts*, 66, for a schematic analysis of requesting.
[47] Fish, 'How to Do Things with Austin and Searle', 201, listing Searle's conditions; with his analysis at 200–1 and 212.
[48] Fish, 'How to Do Things with Austin and Searle', 212.
[49] Fish, 'How to Do Things with Austin and Searle', 245.

themselves in some sense with the workings of strong speech acts. In later chapters I shall adopt precisely this criterion for selecting biblical texts for speech act analysis, and in §3 below I shall discuss the practical question of how such texts may be located.

§2.2 Speech act theory as literary criticism

The article of Fish discussed above has not, it must be said, been widely followed. It represents a minority opinion within the literary critical world, and indeed it has not been followed by Fish, whose personal pilgrimage 'down the anti-formalist road' requires that we label this piece as 'early Fish'.[50] What I have suggested will work as a prime criterion for speech act analysis of a written text is later called 'a large mistake' by Fish himself, who no longer believes that any text is (independently) *about* anything, but rather that certain interpretive conventions render certain interpretive categories applicable.[51] I shall return to this issue in chapter 4. If we bracket for the moment the so-called 'neopragmatism' of Fish's later work, the more pressing question is why literary critics have tended to opt for the view that texts about (strong) speech acts are not necessary for the successful deployment of what we might call 'speech act criticism'.

Petrey suggests that Fish, and one or two others who have advocated a similar line of argument, simply cannot believe that a method which yields such results but has so few practitioners can be a generally applicable one: 'there must be something unique to the object of analysis', they say, but, in Petrey's view, this is a false modesty and will be dissipated as more such studies appear.[52] What this misses, in my view, however, is that the broadening out of speech act categories to encompass all texts effects a key change in the nature of the analysis, corresponding to my differentiation between strong and weak speech acts.

Speech act criticism as a method necessarily presupposes that the object of inquiry, the text, can always be analysed in terms of illocution and perlocution: that there is what one might call

---

[50] See Stanley Fish, 'Introduction: Going Down the Anti-formalist Road', *Doing What Comes Naturally: Change, Rhetoric and the Practice of Theory in Literary and Legal Studies*, Oxford: Clarendon Press, 1989, 1–33.

[51] The essays collected in *Is There a Text in This Class?* are each prefaced by revisionary comments reflecting the later change. In this case see Fish, *Is There a Text in This Class?*, 197–200, especially 200.

[52] Petrey, *Speech Acts and Literary Theory*, 101.

a 'speech act structure' (or perhaps an 'illocutionary structure')
in every text. Typically this is viewed as reflecting the Austinian
insight that all would-be constatives are performative, and thus
that textual effect can always be represented via the framework
of illocution and perlocution.[53] Here I suggest that the careful
analysis of chapter 2 above pays dividends, since it suggests
that there is indeed a level on which this is true, but that it is not
the level on which the interesting results of speech act theory
follow.

Fish himself, in his earlier guise, defends his view against just
such attempts to broaden out the approach. Wolfgang Iser, he
charges, confuses the idea of an illocutionary act operating
by *convention* in the sense of the convention constituting the
performance, with the broader literary use of *convention* which
refers to the expectations one brings to a narrative rather than
anything which constitutes narrative.[54] Richard Ohmann, says
Fish, confuses the idea of 'felicity': where speech act theory wants
to say that an illocutionary act is felicitous if it 'secures uptake',
Ohmann uses the term in a *perlocutionary* sense, arguing that
whether an act is felicitous depends on the effects which it has.[55]
Fundamentally, such approaches become more a matter of
stylistics once every sentence is viewed as a (weak) speech act.
Although every text may consist of assertives, directives, commissives, expressives and declaratives, this information is
worth very little in terms of interpreting an average text. To go
through it and note how many assertives there are, or how
many commissives, is not an indicator of 'illocutionary style', as
Ohmann might suggest. In fact it tells us nothing of interest.

Speech act criticism, therefore, seen in this light, does indeed
tend to reduce to a form of stylistics, and in this guise it will not
be the focus of my attention here. In the field of biblical studies,
however, it must be noted that such an approach is relatively
prominent. In my judgment this is in particular a result of the

---

[53] Specific examples will be discussed in §2.3 below.

[54] Fish, 'How to Do Things with Austin and Searle', 221–3; cf. Wolfgang Iser,
'The Reality of Fiction', *NLH* 7 (1975), 7–38; reworked in idem, *The Act of Reading:
A Theory of Aesthetic Response*, Baltimore and London: Johns Hopkins University
Press, 1978.

[55] Fish, 'How to Do Things with Austin and Searle', 223–31; cf. Richard Ohmann,
'Literature as Act', in Seymour Chatman (ed.), *Approaches to Poetics*, New York:
Columbia University Press, 1973, 81–108.

wish to have to hand a 'method of criticism' under the rubric of speech act theory, but this is to misunderstand the point of the enterprise. One may note the prevalence of Gricean models of speech act theory in many of these works. This is a direct result of Grice's focus on 'conversational implicature', which lends itself readily to stylistic analysis of the shape of a text's discourse. It must suffice here simply to underline that this is not primarily what I have in mind when I talk of a speech act approach to biblical interpretation.

In this section, therefore, I appropriate an argument made by (the early) Stanley Fish, albeit rearticulated in terms of my categories of strong and weak speech acts. As well as laying a constructive foundation for what follows, this view demonstrates that speech act theory cannot be a panacea for all one's hermeneutical problems: 'If speech-act theory is itself an interpretation, then it cannot possibly serve as an all purpose interpretive key.'[56] Indeed, I have argued that speech act theory will have little of interest to say about some kinds of text. However, in texts which concern themselves with particular speech acts, especially performative acts and strong illocutions, even if they do not particularly concern themselves with the conditions of intelligibility of these acts, we may expect to find worthwhile insights from a speech act perspective.

§2.3 Other implications

Before proceeding to a discussion of how to decide which texts should thus be the focus of a speech act analysis, I wish briefly to note two other implications of this discussion of speech act theory and literary criticism in general which are of particular relevance to my concerns with the biblical text: those of the literariness of texts, and of rhetorical criticism.

Literary and non-literary texts

First, one may pose the question of the literariness of the text in question. Is it that speech act criticism is appropriate to literary texts but not to texts in general, for instance? The standard range of answers to this question is as broad as the discussion of just what it is that characterises a text as 'literary'. Attempts have

---

[56] Fish, 'How to Do Things with Austin and Searle', 244.

been made to ascribe 'literariness' to inherent properties of texts, which are thereby essentially marked out as distinct from non-literary texts.[57] Alternatively, critics have argued that the notion of 'poetic language' per se is fallacious, and that literature is simply a context within which language works in all its ordinary forms. This view is most clearly defended by Mary Louise Pratt in her significant discussion of speech act theory and literary questions:

> With a context-dependent linguistics, the essence of literariness or poeticality can be said to reside not in the message but in a particular disposition of speaker and audience with regard to the message, one that is characteristic of the literary speech situation.[58]

Pratt takes issue with the more common account which suggests that in literature the speech acts are in fact pretended speech acts; that it is pretended that sincerity conditions and relevant presuppositions and so forth are in place. This is the view made prevalent by Richard Ohmann's discussion of 'Speech Acts and the Definition of Literature': literature involves the *suspension* of illocutionary force and the performance of *quasi*-speech acts.[59] However, as Pratt notes, the idea that such functions as reference are suspended in literature appears to confuse being *literary* with being *fictional*, and these are not the same thing. Indeed, in some cases the dividing line between fictional and non-fictional may remain undefined without affecting the point of an utterance. She thus responds: 'The real lesson speech act theory has to offer is that *literature is a context, too*, not the absence of one.'[60] Pratt's discussion is perhaps the most thorough analysis of this whole area which explicitly addresses the question of 'literari-

---

[57] This is perhaps most well known in its various formalist guises, notably Russian formalism and the position of the 'Prague school'.

[58] Mary Louise Pratt, *Toward a Speech Act Theory of Literary Discourse*, Bloomington: Indiana University Press, 1977, 87.

[59] Richard Ohmann, 'Speech Acts and the Definition of Literature', *Philosophy and Rhetoric* 4 (1971), 1–19, especially 13–14 for his definition (where he suggests that the illocutionary force of literature is 'mimetic', i.e. 'purportedly imitative'). In a subsequent article Ohmann explores how this leads to a view that literature discloses imaginative worlds; and laments literary leanings in the media which distort all discourse into this imaginative mode; idem, 'Speech, Literature and the Space between', *NLH* 4 (1972), 47–63.

[60] Pratt, *Toward a Speech Act Theory of Literary Discourse*, 99 (cf. her discussion of Ohmann, 89–99). Similarly cautious about Ohmann's literature-fiction confusion are Lamarque and Olsen, *Truth, Fiction and Literature*, 71–3.

ness' in speech act terms.[61] Inevitably it has met with a mixed response. Petrey suggests that, while Pratt successfully emphasises the role of the author in using ordinary language within a speaker/hearer framework, it is Ohmann who successfully addresses what happens after the production of the text when the author has left the scene and the text continues to be appropriated by readers anyway. For Petrey, each of these is a valuable, albeit distinct, emphasis.[62]

In an article-length review of Pratt's book, Michael Hancher contrasts Pratt's approach with that of Searle.[63] Searle, especially in his 'Logical Status of Fictional Discourse', takes 'literature' as a 'family-resemblance notion' and addresses instead the question of fiction. Searle suggests that 'Roughly speaking, whether or not a work is literature is for the readers to decide, whether or not it is fiction is for the author to decide'.[64] As a result he ends up with an eclectic approach which considers a text utterance by utterance and is willing to allow real illocutions to be interspersed with fictional (and thus pretended) ones.[65] In Hancher's words, 'What Searle offers is not a theory of fictional discourse, but a theory of discrete fictional acts.'[66] He suggests that Pratt's broader emphasis here endears her approach to literary critics, who are looking for a less narrowly applicable criterion than that offered by Searle. However, he also suggests

[61] Her 1977 book remains her major statement of the issue. However, see also Mary Louise Pratt and Elizabeth Closs Traugott, 'Speech Acts and Speech Genres', *Linguistics for Students of Literature*, New York: Harcourt Brace Jovanovich, 1980, 226–71; and Mary Louise Pratt, 'The Ideology of Speech-Act Theory', *Centrum* NS 1.1 (1981), 5–18, where she offers some qualifications concerning how far a standard Gricean model may apply across varieties of social interaction, as well as suggesting that the picture is complicated by taking more seriously the ways in which speech acts construct and constitute reality. I do not consider here the significant treatment of Susan Snaider Lanser, *The Narrative Act: Point of View in Prose Fiction*, Princeton: Princeton University Press, 1981, which uses speech act theory to underline the interpretive moves necessary to link novelistic discourse with its context (see especially 7, 64–107, 226–45 and 277), and which agrees to a significant extent with Pratt concerning the role of ordinary language in literary works (280). Lanser has written in and been utilised in biblical studies; see especially Susan S. Lanser, '(Feminist) Criticism in the Garden: Inferring Genesis 2–3', *Semeia* 41 (1988), 67–84.

[62] Petrey, *Speech Acts and Literary Theory*, 85.

[63] Michael Hancher, 'Beyond a Speech Act Theory of Literary Discourse', *MLN* 92 (1977), 1081–98.

[64] Searle, 'The Logical Status of Fictional Discourse', 59.

[65] Searle, 'The Logical Status of Fictional Discourse', 73–4.

[66] Hancher, 'Beyond a Speech Act Theory of Literary Discourse', 1094.

that one of the reasons for the divergence between Pratt's and Searle's models is that Pratt makes some fairly standard literary-critical assumptions, such as that the narrator is a fiction (or at least a *persona*), and thus that the broader literary model developed by Pratt, as a result, 'carries a strong *a priori* flavor', and that, in making fewer assumptions, Searle's approach is less likely to engender distortions of the texts being analysed.[67]

Different writers have suggested different ways of characterising the issues involved in a speech act analysis of fictional texts. As noted, Searle thinks it is for the author to decide whether something is fiction. Nicholas Wolterstorff, in his discussion of 'world projection' particularly as it occurs through the medium of a written text, suggests that 'the stance characteristic of the fictioneer is that of *presenting*. The fictive stance consists of *presenting*, of *offering for consideration*, certain states of affairs', and that these are presented to edify us, delight us, or illumine us, for example, as we reflect on the presentation.[68] The 'fictive stance' therefore is, again, that of the author. An account which attempts to bridge the gap between author-orientated and reader-orientated approaches to the question is that of Robert Brown and Martin Steinmann, who suggest that 'A discourse *is* fictional because its speaker or writer intends it to be so. But it is *taken as* fictional only because the hearer or reader *decides* to take it so.'[69] This introduces an important aspect of the discussion which I shall take up fully in chapter 4 below, but which, suffice it to say here, is problematic in its bald opposing of what something is with what it is taken as. Brown and Steinmann's article, in fact, is an analysis of fiction in response to the question 'What is literature?' This may be one reason why their focus differs from that of Searle and Wolterstorff, since it is an attempt to account for two different things under one rubric. It seems preferable to follow Pratt in separating the question of literariness from that

[67] Hancher, 'Beyond a Speech Act Theory of Literary Discourse', 1094, 1095; see 1092–5 for the full discussion. Searle's dislike of standard literary-critical assumptions is noted particularly by Petrey, *Speech Acts and Literary Theory*, 69, who nevertheless thinks Searle is right about the importance of readers' attitudes. For an example of a philosophical account which find Searle's approach here too restrictive concerning fiction, see Lamarque and Olsen, *Truth, Fiction and Literature*, 62–9.

[68] Wolterstorff, *Works and Worlds of Art*, Oxford: Clarendon Press, 1980, 233.

[69] Robert L. Brown Jr and Martin Steinmann Jr, 'Native Readers of Fiction: A Speech-Act and Genre-Rule Approach to Defining Literature', in Paul Hernadi (ed.), *What Is Literature?*, Bloomington, Indiana University Press, 1978, 141–60, here 149; also quoted approvingly by Petrey, *Speech Acts and Literary Theory*, 68.

of fiction, and then to follow Searle and Wolterstorff in affirming that 'the fictive stance' is that of the author.

If we follow Pratt, then literary discourse is not a separate type of text from other texts but simply the deployment of ordinary language in a literary context. While the question of fiction has invited discussion of various degrees of the suspension of the illocutionary act, in my judgment Pratt is successful in demonstrating that no such suspension need be assumed for a text just because it is a literary text. In fact, since her entire argument is devoted to showing that literature works precisely through the mechanism of 'ordinary language',[70] it follows a fortiori that all of the considerations we have adduced for the analysis of literature in the preceding sections of this chapter will also apply to texts in general. Speech act analyses of fiction may profitably follow Searle and Wolterstorff, but with specific regard to biblical texts my interest will not lie in this area. In any case, the stronger conclusion, that biblical texts are in general as susceptible as any others to speech act consideration, follows from Pratt's analysis. It should also be said that, where I have myself qualified my interests in terms of strong and weak speech acts in ordinary language, this distinction will also carry over into the analysis of biblical texts.

Rhetorical criticism

Secondly, I suggest that, particularly with respect to biblical studies, the discussion of this chapter mitigates against a tendency to see speech act theory as a natural extension of rhetorical criticism. Rhetorical criticism in biblical studies operates upon the twin pillars of its historical appropriateness in terms of the prevalence of classical rhetoric in the New Testament world, and its literary appropriateness in terms of its particular congruence with the dynamic of a text seeking to effect certain responses in the reader.[71] It is this latter point

---

[70] She intends the phrase in its literary situatedness, but is content to appeal to its logico-linguistic resonances also; Pratt, *Toward a Speech Act Theory of Literary Discourse*, 80, n. 1.

[71] See G. A. Kennedy, *New Testament Interpretation through Rhetorical Criticism*, Chapel Hill: University of North Carolina, 1984. A helpful and circumspect recent account of this huge area is given by Ian H. Henderson, 'A Defence of Rhetoric against Its Admirers', *Jesus, Rhetoric and Law* (Bib Int Ser 20), Leiden: E. J. Brill, 1996, 37–71. See further Litfin (n. 79 below), and J. D. H. Amador, 'Where Could Rhetorical Criticism (Still) Take Us?', *CR:BS* 7 (1999), 195–222.

which seems to draw some writers into thinking that speech act theory is essentially the same approach simply recast in modern terminology.

In my judgment this is mistaken. It is true that rhetoric as such finds its place within speech act theory as part of a consideration of perlocutionary effect, but this is not the area in which speech act theory makes its most prominent contributions. Indeed, one recent article suggests that significant discussions of perlocution are minimal in number.[72] In particular, one only has to recall that a strong illocutionary force involves an utterance counting as a non-linguistic action by virtue of conventions which are both linguistic and extra-linguistic, to note that this is an altogether different emphasis from that of rhetorical criticism, with its focus on persuasive and argumentative function.

It seems inevitable that any attempt to subsume rhetorical interests into a speech act framework will involve some degree of distortion. One of the few attempts to do so in biblical studies is that of Lauri Thurén, who, focusing on the New Testament letters, makes the point that there are two kinds of context which need to be noted in understanding the author's ideological or theological system: the historical and the argumentative.[73] This latter is important because 'the author's goal has been to change or modify the addressees' attitudes and behaviour'.[74] For instance, 1 Peter 1:6–9 describes the addressees as persistent, and yet the rest of 1 Peter exhorts them to persistence. This, he argues, illustrates the need for the interpreter to look always to the rhetorical context.[75]

---

[72] Yueguo Gu, 'The Impasse of Perlocution', *JPrag* 20 (1993), 405–32, who calls for a new 'transactional' approach to perlocution, not yet represented in the literature at all. This literature, he avers, comprises all of four papers, the most notable of which, in my judgment (Ted Cohen, 'Illocutions and Perlocutions', *Foundations of Language* 9 (1973), 492–503, and Steven Davis, 'Perlocution', in Searle, Kiefer and Bierwisch (eds), *Speech-Act Theory and Pragmatics*, 37–55) clarify the importance of context for perlocution, but do not suggest that this can really be incorporated into illocutionary aspects of speech act theory.

[73] Lauri Thurén, 'On Studying Ethical Argumentation and Persuasion in the New Testament', in Stanley E. Porter and Thomas H. Olbricht (eds), *Rhetoric and the New Testament: Essays from the 1992 Heidelberg Conference* (JSNTS 90), Sheffield: Sheffield Academic Press, 1993, 464–78, here 465.

[74] Thurén, 'Ethical Argumentation', 465.

[75] Thurén, 'Ethical Argumentation', 466, n. 5 and 465.

Thurén's article develops a schema of different kinds of argument and persuasion, beginning from the observation that the rhetorical context needs to be held in balance alongside the actual statements and ideas used. He argues that since 'rhetorical features in the New Testament are seen as general human communication' they 'should be analysed with the best means available, whether ancient or modern'.[76] Having discussed possible rhetorical frameworks for the analysis of arguments, he then cites speech act theory in the Austin/Searle tradition as a way of illustrating his approach.[77] However he notes that Searle's focus on the communicative setting of speech acts resulted in his not paying attention to the argumentative and persuasive (or, in Thurén's terms, cognitive and volitional) contexts, with the result that although the article situates its approach within broad speech act concerns, and describes those concerns as 'most useful', it does not offer any examples of how speech act categories provide any practical clarification.[78] In fact this must necessarily be a result of Thurén's perlocutionary focus, with its corresponding dislocation (self-confessed, no less) of Searle's focus on *illocutionary* force. The issue of theological significance in all of this is whether the notion of illocutionary force actually offers a challenge to the categories of rhetorical analysis, especially in the light of such passages as 1 Corinthians 1:18–2:13.[79]

Finally, one further reason why speech act concerns and rhetorical criticism do not promise a happy marriage must be simply that speech act criticism itself, as I have argued above, does not relate in any strong sense to the major insights of speech act theory. It follows, evidently, that speech act theory, since it does not lend itself to speech act criticism, must remain at the very least one step removed from rhetorical criticism as it is generally practised.

---

[76] Thurén, 'Ethical Argumentation', 471.

[77] Thurén, 'Ethical Argumentation', 469.

[78] Thurén, 'Ethical Argumentation', 476.

[79] On this challenge, see Duane Litfin, *St. Paul's Theology of Proclamation: 1 Corinthians 1–4 and Greco-Roman Rhetoric* (SNTSMS 79), Cambridge: Cambridge University Press, 1994, 247–52. Litfin also offers a detailed characterisation of the rhetorical backgrounds to the New Testament epistles (21–134).

§3 Criteria for Illocutionary Acts in Texts: The Question of Vocabulary Markers

Having assessed the various ways in which speech act theory may or may not be insightful for different kinds of text, it is time to focus on the practical question of how to assess the suitability of any particular text (and specifically a biblical text) for a speech act analysis. I have defended the view that speech act theory provides certain kinds of insights for certain texts and does not offer us a method of speech act criticism. In this section I intend to clarify how to proceed in practical terms.

It is perhaps helpful here to pause and consider whether, in the process of reading a text, we think of ourselves as encountering a speech act inhering in a sentence; or rather whether we encounter a sentence and have to determine the speech act. This is an over-simplification, and I do not intend to suggest that any act of reading may be decomposed into these separable components. Nevertheless, particularly if we come across a difficult sentence where we do not simply comprehend and move on, I wish to ask which comes 'first': the speech act or the sentence? In such a case it seems clear that it is the sentence which is the given, and that it is the nature of the speech act which is to be determined. To put the matter in the way in which I shall be considering it in the next chapter: how shall we take the locution in illocutionary terms? This fact, that the illocution is not necessarily determined by knowing the locution, complicates the question of how to go about proposing some such criteria as a 'vocabulary marker' for any particular illocution. However, it is common for theorists to demonstrate a certain inconsistency here in both disavowing vocabulary criteria for illocutionary acts and then proceeding to offer them.[80]

We recall that one of the foundational insights of speech act theory is that sentences which on the surface look like assertives are in fact functioning in other ways. This is evident in the many discussions of such simple sentences as 'It's hot in here', which may be both an assertive about the temperature of the room, or equally a directive attempting to get someone to open a window. Theological examples raise the identical issue,

---

[80] My argument of this section is now substantially followed by Anthony C. Thiselton, 'Communicative Action and Promise in Interdisciplinary, Biblical, and Theological Hermeneutics', especially 223–4, 229 and 233–4.

such as Donald Evans's paradigmatic utterance 'God is my Creator', which he labels 'self-involving' (i.e. as containing a commissive element) at the same time as being an assertive.[81] In general, following Sadock's discussion noted in chapter 2, and recalling one particular emphasis of Searle, one speech act will operate with a variety of illocutionary points of various strengths.

It thus seems to be the case that unless we know what kind of speech act we are looking for, then the kind of sentence we are confronted with will not settle the matter for us. In this oversimplified sense, the line of reasoning must be from illocution to sentence and not the other way around.

This point does not appear to be widely noted in applications of speech act theory to texts, although it is anticipated in more recent theoretical work, notably by Daniel Vanderveken.[82] Here he observes that 'many speech act verbs have *several* uses and can name different illocutionary forces', giving the example of the verb 'swear'. Thus one can swear that a proposition is true (assertive) but one can also swear that one will perform some future deed (a commissive use).[83] Indeed, he adds, 'some performative verbs are *systematically ambiguous* between several illocutionary points', and here he gives the example of 'alert', which is assertive and directive at the same time, since to alert is to assert the imminence of danger and to suggest, directively, evasive action.[84]

In the light of these observations it is at the very least potentially misleading that Vanderveken goes on to list something in the region of 270 performative verbs according to their illocutionary point, even if he is aware of the problem by appealing to '*paradigmatic central illocutionary meanings* of speech act verbs' in 'idealized' form.[85] Searle too criticises Austin for a mistaken reliance on vocabulary in classifying illocutions but goes on to offer various vocabulary criteria for illocutions.[86]

[81] Evans, *Logic of Self-Involvement*, 11–15, 158–60, and *passim*. See the discussion of Evans in ch. 5 below.

[82] Vanderveken, 'Semantic Analysis of English Performative Verbs', in idem, *Meaning and Speech Acts*, vol. 1, 166–219.

[83] Vanderveken, *Meaning and Speech Acts*, vol. 1, 168; cf. also Searle and Vanderveken, *Foundations of Illocutionary Logic*, 179–82.

[84] Vanderveken, *Meaning and Speech Acts*, vol. 1, 168.

[85] Vanderveken, *Meaning and Speech Acts*, vol. 1, 169. See further ch. 2 n. 141 above.

[86] Searle, *Expression and Meaning*, 9; cf. 12–20.

Having said this, the point is not that there is no value in listing standard verbs of certain types of illocutionary force. If there were no value in such a practice then the notion of illocutionary force would seem to remain hopelessly vague. Rather, such listings indicate indirectly which kinds of possible illocutionary *acts* we are looking for in a text, regardless of whether the word itself appears in the text.[87]

To substantiate this claim, and to illustrate the difference between the two alternatives described here, let us consider a basic speech act verb such as 'commit', often taken as the paradigmatic commissive (rather than the more common 'promise') because 'promise' has some exceptional features.[88] Then if we wanted to examine a commissive illocutionary act *based on the occurrence of the word 'commit'*, we would have to locate a sentence such as

(1) 'I commit myself to helping at the hostel every Wednesday.'

(Let us ignore for a moment that this is, according to Searle and Vanderveken, a declarative with the additional force of a commissive.)[89] Evidently not every occurrence of 'commit' will be a commissive. Consider: 'John committed a basic error in his driving test.' This would be $commit_2$ as compared to our commissive $commit_1$ if we adopt the Searle–Vanderveken convention for noting different illocutionary points pertaining to apparently similar words.[90] This is not the substantive point at issue, however, and may be passed over.

This 'analysis' of (1), however, which is perhaps not too far removed from the way in which speech act theory sometimes gets a passing mention in commentaries, in fact achieves very little. One already had to know that (1) was a commissive in order to spot it: the occurrence even of the basic word 'commit' was not enough, since it might have been $commit_2$. Further, if

---

[87] This is close to the claim of Thiselton, *New Horizons in Hermeneutics*, 298–9; although his reference to a *concordance* for locating particular illocutions (299) strongly suggests that actual appearance of the word in the text is in mind.

[88] See Searle and Vanderveken, *Foundations of Illocutionary Logic*, 192.

[89] Note their decision that 'the illocutionary force of a performative sentence is always that of a declaration, and then, derivatively, the utterance has the additional force named by the performative verb'; Searle and Vanderveken, *Foundations of Illocutionary Logic*, 3.

[90] Searle and Vanderveken, *Foundations of Illocutionary Logic*, 181.

we now take back the permission to ignore that (1) is actually a declarative with additional commissive force, we must note that (1) is not a commissive, pure and simple, after all. Indeed, on reflection, a pure commissive will most likely not use the vocabulary marker of commissive performative verbs at all, if it occurs in a text. Consider

> (2) 'As I was with Moses, so I will be with you. I will not fail you or forsake you.'

This is Yahweh talking to Joshua in Joshua 1:5; and indeed performing a divine commissive. However, this much can only be said if one *first* understands the illocutionary force of the sentence: it *is* a promise, the particular promise that Yahweh will 'be with' Joshua, and it has no vocabulary marker. The content may be vague (divine presence, after all, turns out to be a problematic idea in the Old Testament) but the *act* performed by Yahweh here, in the narrative, is that he commits himself to a future course of action. Indeed many interpretive disputes in biblical interpretation are concerned with precisely this question of how to take an uncontested locution and read it as an illocution.

This small case study bears out my claim that what we are looking for in locating and analysing illocutionary acts is not the occurrence of any particular word markers, nor even the paradigmatic cases for each type of illocutionary point, but rather *we are looking for those acts which correspond to the verbs which can be used to indicate illocutionary point.* It is in this sense that the standard lists of illocutionary verbs according to illocutionary point help us in identifying illocutionary acts in a discourse. Some examples perhaps make this clearer:

> Standard assertive verbs include *suggest, hypothesize, assert, guess . . .* The illocutionary acts we are looking for are thus *suggestions, hypotheses, assertions, guesses . . .*

> Standard commissive verbs include *pledge, threaten, vow, swear, promise . . .*

> Thus we are looking for *pledges, threats, vows, oaths, promises . . .*

The same could be said for any of the illocutionary points. In general, therefore, we shall not expect the word corresponding to the act (in this loose sense of 'correspond') to occur in the text. In the particular case of *promises* in the Old Testament, to pursue the example above, this point is highlighted by the observation that the Hebrew word rendered 'promise' in English translation is either *'amar* or *dabar*, that is, someone said or spoke a word with a future orientation. Of course if God speaks such a word, and his word is dependable, then one may justifiably translate it 'promise', but need not do so, as a comparison of Jeremiah 34:4–5 in the NIV and NRSV indicates.[91]

The argument of this section might perhaps be represented as an updating of James Barr's *Semantics of Biblical Language*, or perhaps the modulating of its central argument into the new key of speech act theory. It would be ironic if the adoption of a detailed pragmatic philosophy of language were to go hand in hand with the reintroduction of the kind of interpretative confusion between words and ideas which Barr so ably critiqued.[92]

To summarise: in the sense elaborated in this section, it is the speech act which we are seeking in the text, and not the occurrence of particular words. However, a knowledge of standard performative verbs and their general illocutionary force is a major clue to what kind of acts we are looking for, although *not* necessarily where we might find them.[93]

§4 Conclusions

My discussion in this chapter has analysed several problems of criteria and developed a framework within which it will prove possible to read texts for illocutionary acts. This framework, I have suggested, invites us to utilise speech act theory for certain types of text, rather than to adopt it as a form of 'criticism' which should either take its place alongside the various other biblical criticisms, or be seen as simply a variety of rhetorical criticism. It is perhaps worth noting in this regard that many

[91] See, amongst others, P. S. Minear, 'Promise', *IDB* 3:893–6. 'It was axiomatic to OT writers that God is absolutely faithful to every word he speaks' (893). In the NIV we find 'Hear the promise of Yahweh ... This is what Yahweh says ... I myself make this promise, declares Yahweh'; whereas the NRSV offers 'Hear the word of Yahweh ... Thus says Yahweh ... I have spoken the word, says Yahweh'.

[92] Cf. James Barr, *The Semantics of Biblical Language*, Oxford: Oxford University Press, 1961.

[93] See further Thiselton, 'Communicative Action and Promise in Interdisciplinary, Biblical, and Theological Hermeneutics', 223–39.

of the more substantial recent treatments of speech act theory in theological-biblical perspective do concern themselves with precisely the question of how speech act theory can contribute to various aspects of the hermeneutical task rather than with speech act theory as a form of criticism.[94] In chapter 1 I discussed Martin Buss's comment that, in the context of biblical interpretation, we might have two different goals with speech act theory: using it to refine our exegetical procedures or stepping back to utilise it in the theoretical reconceptualisation of exegesis.[95] At the risk of over-simplification, my argument here tends towards the view that more progress has been made with the latter task than the former. Significant exceptions to this generalisation, notably the works of Donald Evans and Dietmar Neufeld, will be considered in chapter 5 below.[96]

However, in the course of discussing how a text is to be read in illocutionary terms, and not least in appealing to the work of Stanley Fish in the development of criteria for reading strong illocutions, I have consciously postponed a discussion of the nature of the 'counting as' operation by which a sentence is counted as an illocution. To what extent does such an operation place the work of textual interpretation at the mercy of those doing the counting? The questions of criteria which concern us in this first part of our inquiry must now be focused on this topic of construal.

---

[94] Works such as Thiselton, *New Horizons in Hermeneutics*; Vanhoozer, *Is There a Meaning in This Text?*; and Wolterstorff, *Divine Discourse*. To some extent this is true also of the essays collected in *Semeia* 41 (Hugh C. White (ed.), *Speech Act Theory and Biblical Criticism*, Decatur, GA: Scholars Press, 1988).

[95] Buss, 'Potential and Actual Interactions between Speech Act Theory and Biblical Studies', here 125.

[96] I have elsewhere attempted to survey in some detail the highly varied applications of speech act theory to biblical texts which have been made to date; Richard S. Briggs, 'The Uses of Speech Act Theory in Biblical Interpretation', *CR:BS*, 9 (2001).

4

Construal: Construction without Reduction

Open a copy of the New Testament, leaf through its pages. What do we see? . . . All that we *see* is a set of black marks on white paper. What does one do with a set of black marks on white paper? . . . a moment's reflection suggests that, for different kinds of text, different kinds of activity count as what we might call the primary or fundamental form of their interpretation.[1]

The key Searlean formula for the constitutive rule by which an illocutionary act creates an institutional fact is 'X counts as Y in context C'.[2] This simple analytical building block lies at the heart of Searle's whole account, and especially his account of social reality. As noted in chapter 2, however, the difficulty in being clear about precisely how to understand this formulation is directly proportional to the weight invested in it by Searle. An obvious response to it, and one which has gained remarkably wide currency in recent years, is to account for constitutive rules as entirely generated by the community of interpreters. I shall be calling this the 'neopragmatist' position, and its most articulate champions are Stanley Fish in the field of literary theory and Richard Rorty in philosophy. My aim in this chapter is to draw out the similarities between a speech act approach to texts and the neopragmatist view, with the aim of then going on to

---

[1] Nicholas Lash, 'Performing the Scriptures', *Theology on the Way to Emmaus*, London: SCM Press, 1986, 37–46, here 37.
[2] Searle, *Speech Acts*, 33–5. See ch. 2, §3.3 above for the background to this discussion.

clarify the differences. To do this I will develop an account of *construal*: the mechanism which I propose stands at the heart of reading a text for its illocutionary acts. I shall argue that construal operates across a variety of strengths which precludes appealing to it as a uniform phenomenon either in an objectivist or pragmatist manner. If construal is indeed so important in a speech act account, then it also seems appropriate to sketch out how I see such a constructively orientated epistemology in comparison with various other well-known construction-based approaches, in particular the extraordinarily influential social-construction models which have followed in the wake of Peter Berger's sociology of knowledge. Thus in the last section of this chapter I attempt to show how one may appropriate the idea of construal non-reductively, for which I propose the phrase, used as part of the chapter title, 'construction without reduction'. This will conclude the discussion of criteria which has occupied us during part 1 of this study.

§1 The Neopragmatist Challenge

§1.1 *Stanley Fish: the strange case of the disappearing text*

In his book *Is There A Text in This Class?*, Fish collects together his major critical essays from the period 1970–80, charting his shifting concerns from 'affective stylistics' (how the text constrains the reader by guiding her response to each successive word or line) to his concluding position that

> the text as an entity independent of interpretation and (ideally) responsible for its career drops out and is replaced by the texts that emerge as the consequence of our interpretive activities.[3]

The key change occurs in his 1976 article, 'Interpreting the *Variorum*',[4] written in response to the publication of the initial volumes of the Milton *Variorum*, which surveys the critical history of Milton's works and analyses textual variants. Here, as he reflects on how he had been characterising his own reading of disputed lines in the light of widely disparate critical views, Fish encounters his Damascus Road:

[3] Fish, *Is There A Text in This Class?*, 13. Further page references in the text.
[4] Fish, *Is There A Text in This Class?*, 147–73; originally in *Critical Inquiry* 2 (1976), 465–85.

I did what critics always do: I 'saw' what my interpretive principles permitted or directed me to see, and I then turned around and attributed what I had 'seen' to a text and an intention. (163)

As a result, Fish urges that 'formal units are always a function of the interpretative model one brings to bear'; that 'the critic who confidently rests his analyses on the bedrock of syntactic descriptions is resting on an interpretation'; and that 'meanings are not extracted but made and made not by encoded forms but by interpretive strategies that call forms into being' (164; 167; 172–3).

How else, Fish suggests, can one account for such wide agreement and yet at the same time such principled disagreement, between interpretations? Even such apparently formal features as line-endings, he argues, are the results of interpretive conventions whose significance only becomes apparent within certain communal assumptions (165–6). In short, Fish arrives at the view that all the phenomena of agreement and disagreement in interpretation can be traced to the basic issue of one's location in an interpretive community:

Interpretive communities are made up of those who share interpretive strategies not for reading (in the conventional sense) but for writing texts, for constituting their properties and assigning their intentions. (171)

'Once again', he concludes, 'I have made the text disappear' (173).

This position reaches full critical expression with the title essay of the book and its accompanying, infamous piece, 'How to Recognise a Poem When You See One'. His well-known opening example is of a colleague who was questioned by a student with the words 'Is there a text in this class?' This turned out to be capably understood in two mutually exclusive ways, each of which was apparent in itself: either as a question about a set text or about the teacher's position on Fish's own theory (305). 'Notice', he writes, 'that we do not have here a case of indeterminacy or undecidability but of a determinacy and decidability that do not always have the same shape and that can, and in this instance do, change' (306). Thus, further, 'the category of the normal . . . is not transcendental but institutional' (309), which also allows Fish to conclude that due to this institutional community which is always, though varyingly, present, the fears of solipsism and relativism are removed (321).

The accompanying illustrative example, of how a list of names for a reading assignment was read as a poem by a keen class, is offered as typical of how one's conclusion about the meaning of a text is entirely a function of one's interpretive procedures.

§1.2 Anti-foundationalism: **Doing What Comes Naturally**

In *Doing What Comes Naturally* Fish explores the same issues over a wider field, with particular reference to legal studies as well as broader philosophical issues, essentially doing little more than claiming that the same argument works in any situation one envisages.[5] This follows from his view that there is an 'intimate relationship between formalism as a thesis in the philosophy of language and foundationalism as a thesis about the core constituents of human life' (5). Combining this with his key-note statement in the significant introductory essay, 'once you start down the anti-formalist road, there is no place to stop' (2), provides the framework for his repeated anti-foundationalist insistence throughout the volume.

It is important to scrutinise this opening rhetorical flourish, since it contains almost the entire argument of the book. Clearly there are parallels between formalism and foundationalism, but it is too sweeping to suggest that any argument that works for one will work for the other. Fish offers 16 characterisations of this position in rapid fire list format (6), but unless one accepts that they amount to a seamless package then most of his succeeding rhetorical strategy is undermined immediately.

Briefly, I suggest that the thesis that 'anti-foundationalism' labels one coherent position with wide-ranging implications across the intellectual spectrum is a confused one. It trades on a Cartesian straw man: Western society since Descartes has thought that absolute certainty was the hallmark of knowledge, and that questions of rationality were always and everywhere the same. Find one chink in this armour, which is of course not difficult, and *voilà*: anti-foundationalism – the new world-view.[6]

---

[5] Fish, *Doing What Comes Naturally*. Further page references are in the text.

[6] Postmodernism, a species of anti-foundationalism, trades on the same confusion. For just one example of a more nuanced view of foundations, see the essays collected in Plantinga and Wolterstorff (eds), *Faith and Rationality*. See now also

The key problem with Fish's account, therefore, is its failure to distinguish between 'interesting' and 'non-interesting' cases of this phenomenon, as a direct result of the global scale of this opening rhetorical announcement. Thus one must note that Fish consistently and helpfully draws attention to some of the contingencies involved in the hermeneutical enterprise. He is unwilling to allow any theory to assume a supposed middle-ground, or should one say a moral high ground, without exposing it to rigourous analysis for its ideological and epistemological assumptions. Once uncovered, they are then characterised as local and yet inevitably in place. What is lacking is a willingness to question to what degree this insight is always an important one.

For example, we drive on the left in Britain. This is our local convention, in place before any new driver begins to learn. The claim that this is a local convention, and thus 'contingent', is entirely true, but not altogether startling. Even a British driver emerging from the Channel Tunnel and driving into France does not experience epistemological soul-searching about the sudden relativisation of her ingrained driving habits. The important balance to strike here is therefore this: Fish may be right, but no significant consequences necessarily follow in any particular case. Of course many of his examples *are* interesting. His more recent discussions of issues such as free speech and minority-sensitive legislation are perceptive and challenging. There are cases where his thesis that '"Free speech" is just the name we give to verbal behaviour that serves the substantive agendas we wish to advance' is a good way of uncovering conventions in disputes precisely where the protagonists thought there were none.[7] Further, there is an important sense in which Fish is right that, correctly understood, his is a position of neither the right nor the left, because his anti-foundationalism, as a theory, *goes nowhere*, that is, it has no consequences.[8] I would

---

the similar complaints about anti-foundationalism of Thiselton, 'Communicative Action and Promise in Interdisciplinary, Biblical, and Theological Hermeneutics', especially 209–14.

[7] Stanley Fish, *There's No Such Thing as Free Speech and It's a Good Thing Too*, New York and Oxford: Oxford University Press, 1994, 102 (drawn from the powerful title essay, 102–19).

[8] Most eloquently argued in 'Anti-Foundationalism, Theory Hope, and the Teaching of Composition', *Doing What Comes Naturally*, 342–55 (originally 1987); see especially 350, 355.

suggest that this follows from the fact that, once Fish's position is articulated in its acceptable form, it is best seen as providing an alternative vocabulary for simply describing what is the case. It changes nothing, except possibly it dissuades us from vain 'theory hope'.[9]

It is therefore a mistake to attempt to argue, as many are wont to do, that there is some kind of inherent logical implausibility concerning Fish's position.[10] Critics persistently charge that anti-foundationalism is the thesis that there are no foundations, and that this is self-contradictory since it is a foundation itself. In literary critical terms, the charge is the familiar one that Fish reserves the right to have his theory read correctly but denies such a possibility in his theory itself. Of course since Fish is only arguing that any foundation (or meaning or interpretation) is local and contingent, he has little difficulty in dispensing with this view.[11] In any case, as Stephen Moore has observed, Fish's view is in many ways best seen as a literary corollary of the broader philosophical position that so-called naive empiricism (sometimes simply naive realism) is untenable, and in philosophical terms this is a broadly accepted view.[12] The debate is not so much over whether it is correct, but rather in what sense it is best understood.

§1.3 Fish in the context of neopragmatism

This is not the place for a full discussion of neopragmatism, nor even an attempt to define it clearly. Its typically American blend

[9] This is a contested evaluation of Fish. It is Fish's own view (see above note) but most of those who follow him believe that the abandonment of theory hope is a substantive achievement with various political ramifications. See the discussion below.

[10] A recent article by Paul Noble attempts to show up various illogicalities in Fish's position, but achieves this by making explicit assumptions which prejudge the substantive issues raised; Paul R. Noble, 'Hermeneutics and Post-Modernism: Can We Have a Radical Reader-Response Theory?', *RelStud* 30 (1994), 419–36, and 31 (1995), 1–22, especially Part 1: 423–4.

[11] Fish, *Doing What Comes Naturally*, 29–30.

[12] Stephen D. Moore, *Literary Criticism and the Gospels: The Theoretical Challenge*, London and New Haven: Yale University Press, 1989, 116. See 113–28 for Moore's reflections on Fish vis-à-vis biblical studies. On 116 Moore quotes Frank Lentricchia's claim that it is telling that common-sense philosophical positions are asserted but not defended (Frank Lentricchia, *After the New Criticism*, Chicago: University of Chicago Press, 1980, 146). I suggest that Searle's work should now be seen as something of a counter-example to this.

of thinking, seeking to incorporate the pragmatic insights of
Peirce, James and Dewey, is characterised by Cornel West as
antifoundationalist without necessarily being anti-realist, as
anti-theory although not always to such Fish-like lengths,[13] and
as committed to epistemic pluralism without, as West has it,
'epistemic promiscuity', a reference to the besetting obsession
with how neopragmatism avoids the bogey of 'relativism' (whatever such a term might mean in an anti-foundational context).[14]
The predominance of neopragmatism today is probably fairly
attributed to the influence of Richard Rorty, whose *Philosophy
and the Mirror of Nature* represents something of a manifesto in
the form of a revisionist account of Western philosophy as 'an
episode in the history of European culture'.[15] Fish and Rorty do
not always agree,[16] but in setting Fish's interpretive approach
into a wider philosophical perspective Rorty's work provides a
helpful focus for discussion.

Rorty himself has more than once commended a Fish-ian
vision of interpretive understanding, making the connections
between textual interpretation and a wider philosophical perspective in his articles 'Texts and Lumps' and 'The Pragmatist's
Progress'.[17] For Rorty, pragmatism is all about making useful
distinctions which enable us to clarify issues and argue persua-
sively with one another. Discussion and persuasion are all we

[13] See the essays (including one by Fish) collected in W. J. T. Mitchell (ed.),
Against Theory: Literary Studies and the New Pragmatism, Chicago and London:
University of Chicago Press 1985.

[14] Cornel West, 'The Limits of Neopragmatism', in Michael Brint and William
Weaver (eds), *Pragmatism in Law & Society*, Boulder, CO, and Oxford: Westview
Press, 1991, 121–6. For a good discussion of the shape of the 'relativism' issue in
this context, see Bernstein, *Beyond Objectivism and Relativism*, 197–206 and *passim.*

[15] Richard Rorty, *Philosophy and the Mirror of Nature*, Princeton: Princeton
University Press, 1979, here 390. A statement of his intent appears as 'The World
Well Lost', *JP* 69 (1972), 649–65, reprinted in idem, *Consequences of Pragmatism:
Essays, 1972–1980*, Minneapolis: University of Minnesota Press, 1982, 3–18.

[16] In particular Fish is critical of Rorty's view that we are better off in any way for
laying bare contingency in social mechanisms. See Fish, 'Almost Pragmatism: The
Jurisprudence of Richard Posner, Richard Rorty, and Ronald Dworkin', originally
in Brint and Weaver, *Pragmatism in Law & Society*, 47–81; reprinted in Fish, *There's
No Such Thing as Free Speech*, 200–30, especially 214–19.

[17] Richard Rorty, 'Texts and Lumps', *NLH* 17 (1985), 1–16; idem, 'The Pragmatist's Progress', in Umberto Eco, *Interpretation and Over-Interpretation*, ed. Stefan
Collini, Cambridge: Cambridge University Press, 1992, 89–108. He is responding here to Umberto Eco's attempt to delimit valid interpretation from overinterpretation ('Overinterpreting Texts', *Interpretation and Over-Interpretation*, 45–
66).

have left since there is no court of appeal beyond our practices. Indeed, when examined in detail, language, personhood and society turn out to have no essential nature. In lieu of such essences, Rorty's vision is of a radically contingent world where liberal pluralism offers the best way forward yet discovered, and solidarity with one's fellow travellers the most helpful ethical and moral guideline for coping with life as we live it. To expect more from philosophy is to live in vain hope, according to Rorty.[18]

The particular point which concerns us here is the implications of this neopragmatic position for questions of interpretation. Rorty's non-essentialism results in a hermeneutic predicated upon the notion that 'all anybody ever does with anything is use it'.[19] Thus:

> the coherence of the text is not something it has before it is described . . . It's coherence is no more than the fact that somebody has found something interesting to say about a group of marks or noises . . . a text just has whatever coherence it happened to acquire during the last roll of the hermeneutic wheel.[20]

On this non-essentialist view, the interpreter must avoid trying 'to make an invidious distinction between getting it right and making it useful'.[21] This philosophical framework for textual interpretation finds its definitive statement in Jeffrey Stout's 'What Is the Meaning of a Text?'[22]

Stout urges that the root of our disputes over meaning is very simply that we are talking about different things when we discuss 'authorial intention', 'contextual significance' or the like. Which of our various enquiries should be classified as the investigation into 'the meaning' of a text is a matter of our interests and purposes, and, in the limiting case of a classic text, our interests are sustained indefinitely which is why no amount of commentary exhausts the classic. Stout takes his lead from Quine's view that 'explication is elimination', namely, that a problematic

---

[18] These implications of his *Philosophy and the Mirror of Nature* are expounded with what one might term passionate irony in Richard Rorty, *Contingency, Irony and Solidarity*, Cambridge: Cambridge University Press, 1989.

[19] Rorty, 'Pragmatist's Progress', 93.

[20] Rorty, 'Pragmatist's Progress', 97.

[21] Rorty, 'Pragmatist's Progress', 108.

[22] Jeffrey Stout, 'What Is the Meaning of a Text?', *NLH* 14 (1982), 1–12, cf. Rorty, 'Pragmatist's Progress', 93 n. 2.

term can be clarified by being replaced with a more clearly delimited term.[23] What happens with 'meaning', argues Stout, is that in general usage it is always in a sufficiently clear context, but we then lose that context in such questions as 'What is meaning?'. 'The meaning of a text' is likewise an abstraction to the point where 'meaning' is no longer necessarily univocal. Better, then, to talk of whatever it is that does interest us. Indeed, on this account, even if God should one day reveal that meaning is authorial intention after all, that still would not guarantee that it was the interesting thing about texts. It could then be the case that we knew exactly what meaning was and were no longer interested in it. Stout appeals to the work of Fish as the ablest exponent of this approach to interpretation, as indeed does Rorty.[24]

This then is the neopragmatist challenge as it pertains to my own thesis concerning speech act theory. Texts are interpreted with reference to the interpretive interest of the reader(s). These interests determine what counts as what in interpretation. Speech act theory, like any other approach to language, can be subsumed into this framework. Not only has it been, by Fish himself indeed,[25] but also it seems positively to invite itself in since it postulates 'counting as' as its fundamental mechanism for illocutionary acts. Later I shall seek to show that some writers who appeal to speech act theory fail to guard against this possibility, but in the next section I propose that a sufficiently nuanced approach to speech act theory does offer a way forward.

§1.4 Neopragmatism and speech act theory: a difference of criteria

In my judgment, the question raised by Fish's approach is not whether he is right, but, more subtly, what criteria are available for discerning the extent to which his thesis is interesting in any particular case. It is here that I shall suggest the surface

---

[23] Cf. W. V. O. Quine, *Word and Object*, Cambridge, MA: Harvard University Press, 1960, 260.

[24] Stout, 'What Is the Meaning', 8 (and n. 6); Rorty, 'Pragmatist's Progress', 106.

[25] Stanley Fish, 'Normal Circumstances, Literal Language, Direct Speech Acts, the Ordinary, the Everyday, the Obvious, What Goes without Saying, and Other Special Cases', originally in *Critical Inquiry* 4 (1978), 625–44; reprinted in Fish, *Is There a Text in This Class?*, 268–92.

similarities of a neopragmatist and a speech act account give
way to different approaches.

In the first place it should be clear that an appeal to speech
act theory to evaluate the work of Fish cannot lead to a simple
affirmation or repudiation of his views. This reflects not only on
the various degrees of contextual pragmatism admitted into
speech act theory by different authors, but also from the fact
that Fish himself, besides being a former colleague of Searle's,
has noted 'I've been very much influenced by J. L. Austin in my
thinking about a great many things'.[26] It is worth recalling also
that Austin has been thought by some to stand closer to Derrida
than to Searle.[27] Others have described Austin's philosophy of
language as 'post-modern';[28] while elsewhere there has been
considerable debate about the extent to which Wittgenstein's
later work may be appropriated both for and against the neopragmatist position. One major recent interpretation, that of
Saul Kripke, produced an almost Fish-like view of community
norms for understanding out of the so-called 'private language'
argument of the *Investigations*, and although now widely felt
to be a misreading of Wittgenstein it does indicate a certain
spectrum of views on the nature of interpretive constraints.[29]
Against this background, it is only to be expected that there is
no such thing as a 'speech act refutation' of the neopragmatic
position.

Fish and Searle

Fish and Searle were contemporaries at the University of
California in Berkeley in the 1960s, and it is illuminating to note
some congruences between their approaches.[30]

[26] Fish, *There's No Such Thing as Free Speech*, 292 (from a 1992 interview).
[27] See ch. 3, §1 above.
[28] See, for example, the assessment of Murphy and McClendon Jr, 'Distinguishing
Modern and Postmodern Theologies', especially 201–3.
[29] Saul Kripke, *Wittgenstein on Rules and Private Language*, Oxford: Blackwell, 1982,
presents a Wittgenstein who looks a lot like Stanley Fish. Vigorous responses include
G. P. Baker and P. M. S. Hacker, *Scepticism, Rules and Language*, Oxford: Blackwell,
1984, and Colin McGinn, *Wittgenstein on Meaning: An Interpretation and Evaluation*,
Oxford: Blackwell, 1984, widely thought to be conclusive. A recent survey is provided
by Marie McGinn, *Routledge Philosophy Guidebook to Wittgenstein and the Philosophical
Investigations*, London: Routledge, 1997, 73–112.
[30] Fish explicitly notes his debt to Searle in *Is There a Text in This Class?*, vii.
Perhaps Searle's bemused reference to 'a few whose opinions I respect' (Searle,
Construction of Social Reality, 2) includes Fish.

John Searle	Stanley Fish
the notion of the literal meaning of a sentence only has application relative to a set of contextual or background assumptions	all speech acts are understood by way of relying on mutually shared background information
there is no constant set of assumptions that determine the applicability of the notion of literal meaning	There will always be a normal context, but it will not always be the same one
the notion of absolutely context free literal meaning does not have general application to sentences . . . [but] Literal meaning, though relative, is still literal meaning	There always is a literal meaning because in any situation there is always a meaning that seems obvious in the sense that it is there independently of anything we might do. *But that only means that we have already done it.*

Despite the widely divergent end results of their respective theories, these quotations, drawn in each case from just one 1978 article, appear to indicate definite cross-fertilisation of ideas. In each case the quotations represent a substantial part of the point being made in the article, not withstanding which Searle and Fish are in fact in disagreement over some aspects of the idea of 'literal meaning'.[31]

In fact the Fish quotations here are largely in the context of his rejection of Searle's account of indirect speech acts, but clearly the articulation of any point of substantive disagreement between them will have to be cautious. It is thus worth under-lining the fact that, for Searle, speech act theory goes on to underpin a robust account of the institutional nature of our constructed social reality, while for Fish speech act theory illustrates the radically contingent nature of interpretation, by showing that all meaning is relative to some context: an inter-pretive convention held by some interpretive community.

---

[31] The quotations are from John R. Searle, 'Literal Meaning', originally in *Erkenntnis* 13 (1978), and reprinted in idem, *Expression and Meaning*, ch. 5, 117–36, quotes from 117, 125 and 132; and Fish, 'Normal Circumstances', *Is There a Text in This Class?*, 268–92, quotes from 291, 287 and 276.

Although Searle has never explicitly addressed Fish's point here, I suggest that he might respond as follows. Where Fish writes 'all speech acts are understood by way of relying on mutually shared background information', Searle would want to capitalise 'Background' and thus argue that for certain basic issues of linguistic competence there is a common 'Background' which exists as a set of pre-theoretic intentional states which are partly constitutive of what it means to be a human being and a member of the linguistic community. In any case, for neither Searle nor Fish does the contextual nature of meaning and the impossibility of literal meaning pose much of a threat to felicitous communication. It simply drives them to differing accounts of how such communication takes place.

If we may speak then of Searle's 'response' to Fish we might characterise it as follows: Searle would allow the idea that texts are understood against community assumptions, but would insist that for a significant proportion of cases the community is large enough to include anybody who speaks the language.[32]

In true Austininan style, then, I propose that here is 'the bit where you say it and the bit where you take it back':[33] Fish lays bare the role of the reader or of the reading community in counting a text as a certain type of speech act. However, he fails to provide any criteria for this 'counting as', and concludes that it is always uniformly rhetorical. Searle's approach holds out much greater hope of criteria, through his distinction between a Background and what he elsewhere calls the 'network'.[34] Nevertheless, it remains the case that in Searle's writings the criteria for 'counting as' are often unexplored. As Sandy Petrey notes, albeit with a different agenda:

---

[32] In this connection one might also note that Wittgenstein also frequently takes humankind as a reference point, but is also willing to 'imagine a form of life' where localised conventions are in place. Note, for example: 'What determines our judgment, our concepts and reactions, is not what *one* man is doing *now*, an individual action, but the whole hurly-burly of human actions' (Ludwig Wittgenstein, *Zettel*, Oxford: Blackwell, [2]1981 (1967), §567), as well as his well-known discussions of forms of life (*Philosophical Investigations*, §§7 and 19, and p. 226).

[33] J. L. Austin, *Sense and Sensibilia*, Oxford: Oxford University Press, 1962, 2. Or, as Eco put it to Rorty, 'OK, all interpreters are equal, but some of them are more equal than others', Umberto Eco, 'Reply', in Eco (ed. Collini), *Interpretation and Overinterpretation*, 139–51, here 139.

[34] For a full account see ch. 2, §3.4 above.

Searle's emphasis on what an utterance counts as over the conventions through which it comes to count has the effect of devaluing the Austinian dialectic between illocutionary force and social identity. This change in emphasis leads to curious instances of completely asocial performatives.[35]

It is time therefore to attempt to provide a fuller account of this operation of 'counting as' or, to use a slightly more elegant formulation, of construal.

Before turning to this, perhaps one final comment on Fish's approach is worth making. There is one line of thought in Fish which I think offers something of a counterargument to his more usual position. His view that there is no such entity as a 'text' clearly problematises the notion of 'interpretive constraint', and with it makes one wonder what it is that accounts for a change in interpretation.[36] Fish's response is to note that 'beliefs are not all held at the same level or operative at the same time'.[37] This suggests, however, the possibility that we can achieve critical distance, or perspective, on a text within Fish's model precisely because we are not people who have only one idea at a time and only exist within one interpretive community at a time. In the survey essay which introduces *Doing What Comes Naturally*, Fish offers the following refinements of this thesis:

each of us is a member of not one but innumerable interpretive communities in relation to which different kinds of belief are operating with different weight and force . . .

One is often 'conflictually' constrained, that is, held in place by a sense of a situation as requiring negotiation between conflicting demands that seem equally legitimate . . .

constraints are themselves relational and shifting and . . . in the act of organizing and assimilating contingent experience constraints are forever bringing about their own modification.[38]

---

[35] Petrey, *Speech Acts and Literary Theory*, 63.

[36] This charge is well made by Steven Rendall, 'Fish vs. Fish', *Diacritics* 12.4 (1982), 49–57, who observed that 'Changes in our beliefs about "what is out there" are for Fish always Kuhnian paradigm changes, never gradual or partial (with respect to the point at issue) but sudden and complete . . . he is forced to adopt this model largely because he refuses to allow for differences of level or degree' (54).

[37] Fish, 'Change', *Doing What Comes Naturally*, 141–60, here 146. This article is partly a response to Rendall.

[38] Fish, 'Going Down the Anti-formalist Road', *Doing What Comes Naturally*, 30, 31, 32.

These points are perhaps underrated in general in evaluations of Fish's stance, and certainly in appropriations of his work in biblical studies and theological discourse, whether in support of him or in dismissal of his 'relativism'. They lend themselves to the epithet 'inter-subjective' in contrast to either subjectivism or objectivism. What they still do not do, of course, is provide any actual criteria as to how one's inter-subjective community commitments can be constrained by texts, since Fish is denying that texts exist to do any such thing.[39] However, in these passages, Fish does seem to be moving away from a monolithic account of 'counting as' with all the problems which that entails, not least elsewhere in his own writings.[40]

§2 Different Degrees of Construal

If the neopragmatists are right, then it is illocutions which vary according to community conventions, while locutions remain more or less stable across community boundaries. However, the fact that illocutions are relative to a community's conventions (i.e. to what it is that makes x count as y) does not tell us anything about how widespread such conventions may be. In one sense, a text *may* indeed mean anything at all; but this observation is of neither interest nor import. In his discussion of literal meaning, Searle himself demonstrates that it will always be possible to articulate further imaginable construals of any utterance, without limit.[41] The appropriate question is rather to ask what it *does* in fact mean, that is, in what ways is the text taken, construed or read? To phrase this point differently: a given locution is counted as an illocution. The question to ask is then: what counting operations are in place which produce this construal?

[39] This is the point highlighted by Stefan Collini against Rorty in his 'Introduction: Interpretation Terminable and Interminable', in Eco (ed. Collini), *Interpretation and Overinterpretation*, 1–21, here 12.

[40] That this point itself has implications against much of what Fish writes is clear in that it was anticipated by a prominent line of criticism of his work. Mary Louise Pratt suggests that the multiple and variously formed nature of our community commitments complicates irredeemably Fish's model of the interpretive community as a community fundamentally predicated on interpretive predilection. See Mary Louise Pratt, 'Interpretive Strategies/Strategic Interpretations: On Anglo-American Reader Response Criticism', *Boundary* 2 11 (1982), 201–31, especially 228.

[41] Searle, 'Literal Meaning', 128.

The problem of criteria which occupies this chapter is thus simple to state: what makes a construal a good one? or, what is the same thing, when is a construal acceptable? This question is familiar enough in terms of political or ideological readings of texts. My proposal is that it is in fact the basic question which speech act theory forces upon us for all reading, and thus need not have any specific political or ideological motivation at all.

§2.1 A minimal position

If our view of language is representational, that is, the purpose of language is simply to represent states of affairs, or describe facts, or however we might wish to characterise Wittgenstein's idea of 'the Augustinian view of language', then the process of reading a text can be seen in very straightforward terms. Basically, on this view, we just *read X,* where *X* is a locution. If we are pressed to greater sophistication within this view, we might say that we *read X as meaning Y.* However, *Y* here will be another locution, or an alternative way of describing what *X* describes.

This view of language is widespread in discussions of biblical interpretation. Preoccupation with whether the states of affairs reported by *X* were in fact as stated is common across the theological spectrum. 'It didn't happen', says one critic, concluding that the Bible is unreliable or untrustworthy; whereas another replies that it did indeed happen, and hence the Bible is historically reliable and authoritative. The authority here, it must be said, derives from another source, traditionally a view of the status of the Bible as the Word of God, inspired by God himself. Hence, when Paul writes to the Corinthians that they should set aside money on the first day of the week for a collection for when he comes, this is read simply as a statement of what Paul instructed the Corinthians. Any relevance it may have to today's reader, or any *self-involvement* of the reader with this text, derives from elsewhere, such as from a belief that some kind of principle is enunciated here which the Christian believer *should* follow. The significance of the locution, following Hirsch, is not its meaning.

This view is best seen as a minimal position on construal. The construal is, we might say, empty, and although technically one might still say '*X* is construed as meaning *X* (or *Y*)', this is nothing more than an elaborate way of saying that X simply does mean such-and-such.

§2.2 *A different basic formulation*

Our discussion of speech act theory in chapter 2, however, gave us a different basic formulation:

in reading we *construe* locutions (X) *as* illocutions (Y)

If this is so then the minimal position described above must be capable of being articulated according to this different view, and of course it is. The minimal position can indeed be characterised thus: in reading, we *construe* a locution (X) as the illocution (Y) which simply is the asserting of X. This is in general not especially interesting, nor perhaps very helpful.[42] It casts all language into Donald Evans's 'flat constative' mode.[43] However, one must not lose sight of the fact that, in certain cases, and indeed quite common cases, fact-stating is a perfectly respectable illocution.

That our basic interpretive move is that of reading locutions as illocutions is a proposal which has only recently been taken up in theological circles. Francis Watson offers a speech act 'defence of some unfashionable concepts' which includes the following claim:

To be understood at all, a series of words must be construed as a communicative action which intends a determinate meaning together with its particular illocutionary and perlocutionary force.[44]

The way in which Watson develops this claim will be considered later,[45] but it does not lead him in the same direction as a similar way of articulating the interpretive task offered by Nicholas Wolterstorff. When Wolterstorff approaches his specific hermeneutical proposals in *Divine Discourse* we find him saying:

The essence of discourse lies not in the relation of *expression* holding between inner life and outer signs, but in the relation of *counting as* holding between a generating act performed in a certain situation,

---

[42] However, it might be possible to draw out the implications of such a formulation for the *status* of the speaker-author in the reader's community, which would be far from trivial. In biblical studies this could be relevant to the various kinds of canon or canonical criticism.

[43] Donald D. Evans, *Logic of Self-Involvement*, 56. For 'constative' we would more likely now read 'assertive'.

[44] Francis Watson, *Text and Truth*, 103.

[45] See ch. 8, §3.1 below.

and the speech act generat*ed by* that act performed in that situation. **The goal of interpretation, correspondingly, is to discover what counts as what.**[46]

Wolterstorff's discussion of what he terms 'count-generation', although helpful in its clarification of the public-domain issues involved, does not consider the issues raised by the 'neo-pragmatist challenge'.[47] He offers a discussion of what it is to speak in which he suggests that what it is for X to count as Y is that the 'speaker and audience *ought to* count it as that – *ought to* acknowledge it as that in their relations with each other'.[48] Counting is a question of the moral relationship between a speaker and a hearer: 'To institute an arrangement for the performance of speech actions is to institute a way of acquiring rights and responsibilities', and to speak is 'to take up a normative stance in the public domain'.[49]

This is clearly a more subtle framework than the 'flat-assertive view'. However, it is perhaps susceptible to being seen as equally monolithic, and thus equally problematic. As a polemical response to a world of fact-stating discourse Wolterstorff's view is successful. The problem is that it appears to move all discourse over to the constructivist position advocated by the likes of Fish: it leaves every illocution at the mercy of the interpretive community. In particular, if the Bible is to be interpreted for God's voice, which is Wolterstorff's governing thesis, then the proposal offered in *Divine Discourse* might give rather too much comfort to sectarian readings which will feel free to justify themselves with the argument that they are indeed counting textual locutions as various divine illocutions. The spectre of pietistic relativism, that most authoritarian of all relativisms, looms large. I wish to propose, as an alternative, a middle way.

§2.3 A mediating proposal

It is a mistake to recognise only two options: fact-stating flat assertives and locutions which are counted as illocutions. Rather these two options represent widely divergent and perhaps

---

[46] Wolterstorff, *Divine Discourse*, 183, bold emphasis added.
[47] In addition to the discussion in *Divine Discourse*, 75–94, see also Wolterstorff, *Works and Worlds of Art*, 202–15.
[48] Wolterstorff, *Divine Discourse*, 84.
[49] Wolterstorff, *Divine Discourse*, 84, 93.

extreme positions across a spectrum of interpretive construals. As an initial characterisation, we may say that the idea of *construal* varies across a spectrum of strengths. Consider the following varieties of construal:

we *read X* as *Y*	. . . in context *C*
we *see / look on X* as *Y*	. . . in context *C*
we *take / count X* as *Y*	. . . in context *C*
we *construe / interpret X* as *Y*	. . . in context *C*
we *consider X* as *Y*	. . . in context *C*
we *conclude* that *X* must be *Y*	. . . in context *C*
we *declare* (*arbitrarily?*) *X* to be *Y*	. . . in context *C*
we *read X as if* it were *Y*	. . . in context *C*

These possible formulations are not offered as a definitive list, nor even as being all mutually exclusive. The list moves approximately from what I shall call 'weak' construal, where the deliberative aspect involved in construing *X* as *Y* is minimal or non-existent, through to 'stronger', that is, more deliberative construals. Often, in the process of reading a familiar text, there is no deliberative element at all, and indeed we would, if pressed, probably adopt the minimal position of §2.1 above in saying that *X* simply is *Y*.

Acknowledging the idea that the notion of construal is not monolithic does raise certain questions for an interpreter. For instance, one may consider to what extent one's construal is an arbitrary choice, or a reasonable judgment, or required by the facts of the situation. That this varies in different situations does not mean that the question is in principle impossible to answer in any given situation, and it follows that admitting the idea of construal into the interpretive process does not in itself foreclose any particular interpretive position on how a textual locution is to be read.

Seen in these terms, the problem with choosing to articulate the notion of interpretive construal in the manner of Fish is that a confusion takes place between the idea that a text is construed and the degree of difference that this might make in any particular case. Evidence that locutions are construed as illocutions, which is not necessarily a problematic idea, may then be marshalled for the extreme position that there is no point of appeal above and beyond the reading community's decision to count *X* as *Y*. In other words, construal is seen (monolithically) as *counting as,* and counting as in turn is seen as a constructive operation, and it is then said to follow that the meaning of a text is purely a product of one's reading strategy. This argument fails at the first step: accepting that all reading involves construal does not foreclose the question of constructivism.

Two related observations may be made here. The first is that construal in this sense of reading *X* as *Y* has a long and honourable hermeneutical history, particularly in biblical interpretation. It is at the heart of Bultmann's hermeneutical programme for demythologising the New Testament. Language about the second coming of Christ, to take the obvious example, is construed as the language of existential address: be prepared! There is not a problem with this provided that it is recognised that the notion of construal operating here is a strong, constructive one. The παρουσία language is being *taken as* address, or *counted as* address, and in itself it is not address, but appears to present itself as fact-stating discourse. The fact that one must construe the language in order to read it does not in itself demonstrate that Bultmann is right. One can, and indeed perhaps should, accept his methodology without accepting his substantive exegetical conclusions, and whether one accepts his conclusions is ultimately a judgment about the propriety, or more pragmatically the usefulness, of locating the point of existential address in such language.[50]

Secondly, given the particular preoccupation with historical questions which has been so prominent in biblical studies, it is perhaps inevitable that a call to recognise the workings of construal in reading will sound, at first, like an anti-historical polemic. Thus it is, I would venture to suggest, that speech act theory is allied to postmodern concerns, or seen as vindicating an anti-foundationalist epistemology, or simply as one more variety of reader-response criticism. That one can envisage Wolterstorff and Bultmann standing at the same end of the hermeneutical spectrum should indicate that this would be a mistaken analysis. Again, to reiterate the point, admitting the notion of construal into one's interpretive investigation does not foreclose questions of historical commitment, fact-stating

---

[50] A thorough discussion of Bultmann's hermeneutical approach, with examples, and which also suggests that it is insufficiently nuanced, is given by Thiselton, *Two Horizons,* 205–92 and, with specific reference to the approach of Donald Evans by way of contrast, 268–9.

language, existential address or reception history. Rather it
foregrounds them and insists that illocutionary force must be
considered appropriately in each case.

§2.4 *A spectrum of construal*

I have suggested above that construal operates across a spectrum
of strengths. A preliminary characterisation of this spectrum
might be broadly as follows:

⟵ Strong	**Spectrum of construals**	Weak ⟶
Strong Construals		**Weak Construals**
constructive; constructivist; deliberative; (pragmatic)		impressed upon us; 'flat assertives'; universally held
taking X as Y	– Characteristically –	*seeing X as Y*
Fish, Rorty (arbitrary); Bultmann (existential)	– e.g. –	a more 'traditional' position (e.g. representational; conservative)

The notion of a spectrum of strengths of construal is not a
familiar one in the literature of speech act theory, nor in
appropriations of speech act theory in biblical and theological
work, but it does have some precedent in other discussions which
concern themselves with construal. In particular, in hermeneutical discussion, one encounters the notion of construal in
considerations of the role of imagination. I will touch briefly
on this area below,[51] but here I acknowledge the helpful
insight of Walter Brueggemann, attributed in turn to the work
of his former research student Tod Linafelt, that the notion of
construal operates across a range of criteria from constructivist
positions ('We choose to count X as Y simply because we do')
through to receptive (or passive) positions ('X simply is Y and it
is not a question of our choice').[52] I judge that this insight can

---

[51] See §3.1 below.
[52] Walter Brueggemann, *Texts under Negotiation: The Bible and Postmodern
Imagination*, Minneapolis: Fortress Press, 1993, 16.

be utilised in this different area of reading locutions for illocutions.

On one level it is not new to propose using the notion of construal in interpretation. Indeed the category plays a significant role in David Kelsey's discussion of 'the uses of scripture in recent theology', which begins its analysis of what it might mean to 'prove doctrine' from Scripture by observing that

> theologians ... do not appeal to some objective text-in-itself but rather to a text construed *as* a certain kind of whole having a certain kind of logical force.[53]

Using this insight as his framework, Kelsey spends the first half of his book analysing the work of seven different theologians, ranging from B. B. Warfield to Karl Barth, and including Tillich and Bultmann, to look at what kinds of construal of the text authorise their specific theological proposals.[54] It is, however, debatable whether Kelsey does succeed in offering particular criteria for assessing one's construal, or rather whether his own proposal will work without some such notion as varying degrees of construal.[55] I suggest in fact that speech act theory offers a way of refining the kind of account which Kelsey sought to provide.[56]

Thus, although construal is not a new category, it has not in general been a category used with sufficient precision. Perhaps because of the apparent polarisation between fact-stating approaches and self-involving approaches to biblical language, discussions of construal have not in general made use of the idea of a specifically institutional fact created by a constitutive

---

[53] David Kelsey, *The Uses of Scripture in Recent Theology*, Philadelphia: Fortress Press, 1975, 14.

[54] Kelsey, *Uses of Scripture*, 17–88, with the programme set out on 14–17.

[55] He seems to equivocate between saying that 'once the imaginative judgment is made, it is open to reasoned assessment' (171) and that exegesis 'depends on a prior decision about how to construe and use the texts' which 'is not itself corrigible by the results of any kind of biblical study' (197–201). Some steps towards looking for a theological demarcation of the merits of different construals are present in David H. Kelsey, 'The Bible and Christian Theology', *JAAR* 48 (1980), 385–402, which is more helpful in this regard but perhaps still hampered by its singular notion of construal.

[56] A similar view is expressed by Kevin J. Vanhoozer, 'God's Mighty Speech-Acts', here 161–2, describing Kelsey's book as 'magisterial'. Vanhoozer does not have the particular point about strength of construal in mind, but rather the broader appeal to speech act theory.

rule. It is in exploring the congruence between these two approaches that I shall suggest that we are enabled to answer such questions as how far such a rule can operate independently of the interpretive community's choice to adopt it.

Could one, in the limiting case, create a constitutive rule by fiat, for example? In certain institutional settings this is precisely what happens. The cricket umpire calls, 'no ball', and the illocution is the declaration that the batsman cannot be out this delivery. New situations require new rules: what, for instance, is to count as the declaration of '5 runs for the ball hitting a safety helmet' – an unforeseen occurrence when cricket's laws were originally composed. In such cases the locution is *counted as* a certain, specified illocution.

In many cases, and perhaps more interesting cases, there is no such deliberate rule put forward. Jonathan Culler, in the course of discussing how limit setting in language always leads to the possibility of those limits being (deconstructively) over-turned, notes that

> Wittgenstein's suggestion that one cannot say 'bububu' and mean 'if it does not rain I shall go out for a walk,' has, paradoxically, made it possible to do just that.[57]

In such a case, the remark is *taken as* a certain, assumed illocution. We say that a locution is *taken as* an illocution when there is still a certain amount of deliberative judgment involved, but when, in general, there has not been an explicit stipulation to this effect beforehand.

Thus a student's semi-literate grunts during a tutorial are taken as the illocution 'Please continue your explanation (since I'm following you so far)'. The locution 'I'm cold' may be taken as the illocution of requesting another person to open a window. 'I would love to buy this book off you but cannot afford it' is taken as a request to lower the price. These, of course, are some of the very examples often used to illustrate the point of introducing a category such as performative language. I am suggesting that we have arrived at them here by way of more precise criteria.

As the deliberative step involved in construal becomes smaller so it becomes more appropriate to say rather that a locution is

---

[57] Culler, *On Deconstruction*, 124, referring here to the remark of Wittgenstein, *Philosophical Investigations*, p. 18.

seen as (or *read as*) an illocution.[58] The dividing line, of course, is blurred, and I do not intend to suggest that there need be any straightforward linguistic delineation of strong and weak construals. Nevertheless, different construing phrases do give clues about different strengths of construal, in particular when we are confronted with a phrase which is clearly *in*-appropriate.

Wittgenstein's discussion of 'seeing as', in which he develops his idea of the dawning of an 'aspect', focuses at one point on how we talk about our experience of such objects as Jastrow's duck-rabbit.[59] What if, he asks, we only see it as a picture of a rabbit, unaware of any ambiguity? Then:

> I should not have answered the question 'What do you see here?' by saying: 'Now I am seeing it as a picture-rabbit.' I should simply have described my perception . . . It would have made as little sense for me to say 'Now I am seeing it as . . . ' as to say at the sight of a knife and fork 'Now I am seeing this as a knife and fork' . . . One doesn't '*take*' what one knows as the cutlery at a meal *for* cutlery.[60]

This captures my point about the deliberative step involved in more constructive approaches such as 'taking as', and allows that as, we come to the 'weak' end of the spectrum, the notion of construal finally becomes empty, even if one could in theory use it to explain the interpretive step: 'I construe your locution "I am going for a walk" as the assertion that you are going for a walk.' We find it more natural to say here that the meaning of the sentence is apparent, and no construal is necessary.

It is worth noting, briefly, that there is no obvious correlation between strong illocutions, in the sense I defined it in chapter 2, and strong construals. An explicit strong illocution such as 'I promise to be there' requires minimal construal. A weak illocution such as 'John sat down' may be read as an assertion, taken as an indication of John's protest, counted as the end of his speech and so on. Strength of construal is an additional variable to strength of illocution, not a correlated one.

---

[58] See Wittgenstein, *Philosophical Investigations*, Pt II, §11 (especially p. 193–208), for the classic discussion of 'seeing as'. A recent survey is provided by Marie McGinn, *Guidebook to Wittgenstein and the Philosophical Investigations*, 177–204.

[59] Wittgenstein, *Philosophical Investigations*, 194.

[60] Wittgenstein, *Philosophical Investigations*, 194–5. Wittgenstein and Heidegger agree here, although Heidegger emphasises *functionality* with his idea of something being ready-to-hand. See Stephen Mulhall, *On Being in the World: Wittgenstein and Heidegger on Seeing Aspects*, London: Routledge, 1990.

§2.5 Interpretive interests revisited

In the light of this discussion it is now possible to return to the Fish–Rorty–Stout argument about preferred vocabularies, and their claim that disputes about the meaning of sentences are really disguised arguments about reading conventions and their relative strength.

In cases of strong construal it would seem that this might be a sustainable thesis. However, as the degree of construal involved becomes weaker it becomes harder to argue that it can support the weight of being dubbed a 'reading strategy'. If a reading strategy is a conscious, foregrounded interpretive decision, such as the decision say to read the Song of Songs as an allegory about Christ and the church, then one can allow that differences of opinion about the 'meaning' of a particular text in the Song of Songs can all be expressed, without remainder, as differences between how one and the same locution (X) is being *taken as* or *counted as* different illocutions $(Y1, Y2 \ldots)$.

Weaker construals, however, do not draw upon any such interpretive 'strategy'. Rather they proceed in terms of *seeing X as Y*, and if two contesting voices are arguing about the relative merits of $Y1$ and $Y2$, then their debate is most likely about the meaning of X, rather than the construal of X as an illocution.

In short, we want to accept, with Stout, that disputes over meaning do indeed on occasion devolve on to disputes about interpretive interests; and we can accept, with Fish, that these interests are community-relative; and we can perhaps even agree with Rorty that much of the time what is most interesting in disputes about meaning and truth is the pragmatic question of what difference it makes in promoting certain values and courses of action today. But these arguments all rely at some crucial point on the notion of construal, and they all go on to assume that construal is uniformly strong; indeed that is strongly constructive.

We can now see clearly why this creates the tension noted above in Fish's later work, where he does allow that interpretive interests shift in intensity, and that one interest now upholds, now displaces another.[61] This amounts to the view that construal is a variable, but, once admitted, this will undermine the 'neopragmatist position'.

---

[61] See n. 40 above.

The neopragmatist assumption of uniformly strong construal is in fact a sustainable assumption if and only if the interpretive constraint on the *Y* term provided by the *X* term is uniform. Uniform constraint requires one of two positions: either construal is uniformly empty, which is the 'traditional' view of language as representation, where *X* simply is *Y*; or construal is everything. It seems to me that the rhetorical move made by Fish and others at this point is without merit. Fish et al. correctly reject the former, and indeed win friends in so doing. But the counter-intuitive position that construal is everything ultimately leads to the view that the act of *counting as* involved in the construal is *so* strong that the locution (*X*) involved plays no role at all in determining what the *Y* shall be. It then follows, of course, that there is really nothing essential (or enduring) in the *X* term, except the conventionally perceived interpretive construct. *X* has no essence; it is whatever we make it. Thus, should one want to defend the position that interpretive dispute is solely the product of competing reading strategies, one will find that textual constraint on interpretation has dropped out, and while this does indeed happen often (and sometimes interestingly), the claim that it happens always and everywhere simply is the claim that there is no text there to constrain us in the first place. Uniform construal and non-essentialism are, then, the same claim; the opposite sides of the same coin. It seems confused, therefore, to offer either one as evidence for the other, but this appears to be one of the gambits of the neopragmatist argument.

One other consideration should be brought to bear on the position articulated by Stout's 'What Is the Meaning of a Text?'. In an apparently neglected article, Austin himself argued, much as Stout seeks to do, that a question like 'What is the meaning of a word?' is hopelessly confused, since it involves unwarrantable generalisation away from perfectly good questions like 'What is the meaning of "rat"?'.[62] For Austin the generalisation leads to nonsense. For Stout, however, although he thinks 'What is the meaning of a text?' does not deserve an answer, this is not because it is nonsense but because, following Quine, we can paraphrase it eliminatively to reveal that it was really a question about something else, namely whatever interested us about the

---

[62] Austin, 'The Meaning of a Word', *Philosophical Papers*, 55–75, especially 56–62.

text.[63] But, as Austin might put it, 'What is the meaning of a text?' is not referring to *any* text, but rather to no text at all, and is therefore inevitably confused.[64] Nevertheless, on Austin's account, one can still ask the meaningful question 'What does "Love your neighbour" mean?', whereas on Stout's account the meaningful is dispensed with along with the nonsense. It seems to me that this is a particular case of the problems of following Quine down the road of logical paraphrase into what is sometimes called 'post-positivism'. It must suffice here to suggest that all sorts of counter-intuitive results lie down this path, and that despite protests to the contrary this should give one pause for thought before embarking upon it.[65]

Conclusions

On the one hand I have sought to demonstrate why an approach such as that of Fish can be seen to make so many telling points in particular cases. Fish's studies of particular interpretive issues can be illuminating because he generally focuses on cases of strong construal.[66] His argument is less strong where he extends without warrant the assumption of strong construal into cases where it is not at home.[67]

Thus, in order to encompass both the insights of such an approach, and to explain accurately its limitations, I have pursued a more broadly based and nuanced understanding of construal which attempts to do justice to the wide variety of ways in which we do in fact read and interpret texts. This has involved the idea of a spectrum of strengths of construals, which must be considered case by case. It is within such a framework that I

[63] Stout, 'What Is the Meaning of a Text?', 1–2.

[64] Austin, 'Meaning of a Word', 58.

[65] On Quine's subtle but far-reaching divergence from ordinary language or analytical philosophy, see Hacker, *Wittgenstein's Place*, 183–227; cf. ch. 2 n. 57 above. The most obvious example I have in mind in this paragraph is Donald Davidson, 'A Nice Derangement of Epitaphs', in Ernest Lepore (ed.), *Truth and Interpretation: Perspectives on the Philosophy of Donald Davidson*, Oxford: Blackwell, 1986, 433–46: 'I conclude that there is no such thing as a language' (446). This conclusion is, we should note, welcomed by Rorty, *Contingency, Irony, and Solidarity*, 14–20.

[66] Especially of various Milton passages, in his *Is There A Text in This Class?*

[67] As with 'How to Recognize a Poem When You See One' where he reports, 'I told them [the class] that what they saw on the blackboard was a religious poem'. In so saying he carries over a strong construal into a situation (a recommended reading list) which invites a weaker one; Fish, *Is There a Text in This Class?*, 323.

appeal to speech act theory in interpretation without thereby committing myself to a neopragmatist position, and I suggest that it is in such a way that other appeals to speech act theory should also be understood.

In the remainder of this chapter I explore briefly some issues arising from this account. First, I look at some of the ways in which this discussion of construal offers tools for evaluating various approaches to theology and biblical interpretation. Secondly, I try to clarify the way in which construal, which will go on to play an important role in part 2 of this study, can be seen as a constructive element of a hermeneutical or epistemological framework without being necessarily theologically reductive, that is, without reducing theology to mere constructivism. This will clear the way for the use of the various criteria developed thus far to be taken up in the actual practice of biblical interpretation in later chapters.

§3 Construal and Theological and Biblical Studies

§3.1 *The theology of the imagination*

I have already noted that the idea of construal may be found in discussions of the imagination.[68] Although often derided in the Western philosophical tradition as mere fantasy or speculation, imagination has a strong tradition as a serious mode of philosophical inquiry.[69] In particular, imaginative construal occupies a significant place in modern philosophical debate, particularly concerning the nature of perception. Peter Strawson expounds and defends the Kantian line that imagination is a fundamental part of perception.[70] In contrast Roger Scruton draws a distinction between imagination as mental representation on the one hand, or as creative thinking on the other, noting the confusion that arises when these two are not kept distinct.[71]

Here already is much the same contrast as I have drawn between strong and weak construal. To use the word 'imagina-

---

[68] See n. 51 above.

[69] See Mary Warnock, *Imagination*, Berkeley: University of California Press, 1976.

[70] P. F. Strawson, 'Imagination and Perception', *Freedom and Resentment and Other Essays*, London: Methuen, 1974, 45–65 (1970).

[71] Roger Scruton, *Modern Philosophy: A Survey*, London: Sinclair-Stevenson, 1994, 341–54.

tive' as an adjective appropriate to all perception does not prejudge the issue of how strong a construal is involved in the perception. It does not, to be precise, imply that perception involves a forceful creative interpretation which shapes our perceptions into hitherto non-existent configurations. What Scruton notes as imagination as mental representation would correspond to my idea of weak construal, while what he calls creative thinking would move to varying degrees across the spectrum towards strong construal.

A 'theology of the imagination' needs to take this spectrum into account. As noted above, Walter Brueggemann offers an analysis of several works in this area which relates them to each other precisely in these terms, while developing his own view that 'all knowing . . . is imaginative construal, even if disguised or thought to be something else'.[72] Brueggemann himself develops the category of imaginative construal in a variety of works, although one may feel that his own work does not always avoid a uniformly strong view of construal.[73]

Of the works surveyed by Brueggemann,[74] the most specific on the topic of construal is Garrett Green's *Imagining God*.[75] Green's book is a powerful account of how imagination can be harnessed to theological concerns, without adopting a constructivist position towards the reality which is being imaginatively construed. Of particular value is his discussion of the varying significances of 'as', 'as if' and 'is', and his explicit consideration of imagination in relation to interpretation.[76] There is, Green

---

[72] Brueggemann, *Texts under Negotiation*, 1–25, here 12.

[73] See in particular Walter Brueggemann, *Israel's Praise: Doxology against Idolatry and Ideology*, Philadelphia: Fortress Press, 1988, especially 12–26 on the constitutive or world-making power of praise; idem, 'The Third World of Evangelical Imagination', *HBTh* 8 (1986), 61–84; reprinted in his *Interpretation and Obedience: From Faithful Reading to Faithful Living*, Minneapolis: Fortress Press, 1991, 9–27; and idem, 'Imagination as a Mode of Fidelity', in James T. Butler, Edgar W. Conrad and Ben C. Ollenburger (eds), *Understanding the Word: Essays in Honor of Bernhard W. Anderson* (JSOTS 37), Sheffield: JSOT Press, 1985, 13–36.

[74] His spectrum ranges from the 'constructivist' position of Gordon Kaufmann, *The Theological Imagination*, Philadelphia: Westminster Press, 1981; through the active/constructive 'take as' view of construal present in David Bryant, *Faith and the Play of Imagination: On the Role of Imagination in Religion* (StABH 5), Macon, GA: Mercer University Press, 1989; to the 'receptive' view of Garrett Green (next note). The labels are Brueggemann's, *Texts under Negotiation*, 12–17.

[75] Garrett Green, *Imagining God: Theology and the Religious Imagination*, San Francisco: Harper & Row, 1989.

[76] Green, *Imagining God*, especially 70–4.

notes, frequently no *deliberate* act of imagination in the 'seeing'. Even to say 'I see it as . . .' is to note the possibility of alternative perception. Thus:

> The paradigmatic imagination is the ability to see one thing *as* another. Kant called 'is' the copula of judgement; I take 'as' to be the 'copula of imagination'.[77]

He contrasts his position with that of Hans Vaihinger, who argued that 'as if' is the key move in religious discourse.[78] Others have argued for 'useful fictions': we live as if such-and-such were true even though it is not.[79] But this downplays the reliability of imagination as a method for unlocking ways of seeing what is really there, not what we would like to think might be there. Thus 'as' is better than 'as if': it sees the possibility of looking at something another way but stakes its claim on this way.

Green's primary concern is to defend the priority of construal in terms of 'as' rather than more constructive positions ('take as') or views which downplay the truth-stating element of religious language ('as if'). He stops short of articulating the idea of a spectrum of positions, but in a sense his entire argument is that it is a mistake to suppose that a recognition of the significance of construal forecloses the strength of construal involved. This is therefore a strong parallel to my argument about construal in biblical interpretation.

§3.2 Construal in biblical studies

Stanley Porter has noted that it is all too easy for biblical critics to appropriate critical models or methods whose implications are not fully understood.[80] In my judgment, this has certainly happened with appeals to the later work of Fish to support the notion of a theological or ecclesiological reading of Scripture. Thus, for instance, one finds Scott Saye championing a Fishian

---

[77] Green, *Imagining God*, 73.

[78] Hans Vaihinger, *The Philosophy of 'As If': A System of the Theoretical, Practical, and Religious Fictions of Mankind*, trans C. K. Ogden, New York: Harcourt, Brace & Co., [2]1935; reprint: Boston: Routledge & Kegan Paul, 1965.

[79] Notably, for example, Richard B. Braithwaite, *An Empiricist's View of the Nature of Religious Belief*, Cambridge: Cambridge University Press, 1955.

[80] S. E. Porter, 'Why Hasn't Reader-Response Criticism Caught on in New Testament Studies?', *LT* 4 (1990), 278–92, here 290.

interpretive-community approach as the recovery of a long-lost ecclesiological insight: 'I am suggesting that we find in Fish, and especially in his readings of Augustine and Andrewes, a reminder of certain practices of the church that have been largely forgotten.'[81] For Saye, a Christian will understand Fish's general theory 'as an attempt to extend analogously that which has been found to be true of the paradigmatic interpretive community – the church'.[82] Saye even suggests that Barth is a special case of Fish: both are antifoundationalists and one happens to be a Christian.[83] Likewise, Stanley Hauerwas attempts to 'unleash the Scripture' in the context of today's American individualist society, and entitles a key chapter of his manifesto 'Stanley Fish, the Pope, and the Bible': 'While Fish's and Stout's views strike many as dangerous, their ideas in fact share much with traditional Christian presuppositions.'[84]

This is surely precisely the wrong way to articulate what is good about Fish's insights for those interested in interpreting the Bible as Christians. What Fish and Stout share with traditional Christian presuppositions is basically only that who we are makes a difference to how we read; but this point would be shared widely. What distinguishes Fish and Stout from all those who would accept this wider point is the denial of the text and the radical contingency of interpretation (or the uniform strength of construal). This offers only a bleak vision for Bible readers who would like to see themselves as in any sort of continuity with historic Christianity, a point which can be made regardless of one's own view of that historic position.[85]

Only slightly less willing to follow Fish is A. K. M. Adam's *Semeia* article on the sign of Jonah.[86] Adam traces the history of the interpretation of 'the sign of Jonah' in order to urge that historical criticism is mistaken in its desire to isolate the one correct meaning of the text. Fish, of course, would prove much

---

[81] Scott C. Saye, 'The Wild and Crooked Tree: Barth, Fish, and Interpretive Communities', *MTh* 12 (1996), 435–58, here 458, n. 56.

[82] Saye, 'The Wild and Crooked Tree', 442.

[83] Saye, 'The Wild and Crooked Tree', 451.

[84] Stanley Hauerwas, *Unleashing the Scripture: Freeing the Bible from Captivity to America*, Nashville: Abingdon Press, 1993, 19–28, here 21.

[85] A similar judgment on Hauerwas is made by Alan Jacobs, 'A Tale of Two Stanleys', *First Things* 44 (1994), 18–21.

[86] A. K. M. Adam, 'The Sign of Jonah: A Fish-Eye View', *Semeia* 51 (1990), 177–91.

more, and thus it is interesting that Adam makes a small attempt to distance himself from the full Fishian position:

> I would suggest, however, that a more useful approach would be to concede the (possible) objective existence of the text, while denying it any *functional* efficacy . . . while the text as objective entity presumably exists apart from interpretation, it cannot function as a restraint on interpretation.[87]

With regard to his treatment of the biblical text, it is perhaps relevant to note that he is concerned with a selection of very short passages which are certainly obscure enough to invite varied interpretive interests to engage fruitfully with them. The result is that, short of a strong construal of some kind, these *logia* would remain dead locutions on the page. We are thus unsurprised, but not perhaps much enlightened, to see a 'Fish-eye' approach pay dividends.

Adam has also produced a powerful plea for 'nonmodern' approaches to New Testament theology, which includes a Fish-like appeal to the idea that 'all interpretation is allegorical interpretation'.[88] His call for a nonmodern approach to New Testament theology is based around the idea that all reading is construal and hence interpretive interest is the guiding key to biblical theology.[89] Here he draws freely, and confidently, on Rorty and Stout, as well as Fish, and makes the link, which has rhetorical force even if it plays no formal role in his argument, that his nonmodern approach returns us to the kinds of approach characteristic of the early church. His position is well captured in this extended quotation, where we should remember that 'modern' is a polemical term:

> Modern readers will lament the anachronistic tendentiousness with which Matthew might be made into an evangelist of women's liberation, or the Revelation represented as an archetypal journey to individuation. They will accuse nonmodern interpreters of importing agendas that are alien to the disciplinary role of New Testament studies, especially if those interpreters have interests and purposes oriented toward dogmatic theology. They will warn that, if the constraints on interpretation are social rather than dis-

---

[87] Adam, 'Sign of Jonah', 179.
[88] A. K. M. Adam, *Making Sense of New Testament Theology: 'Modern' Problems and Prospects* (StABH 11), Macon, GA: Mercer University Press, 1995, 175.
[89] Adam, *Making Sense of New Testament Theology*, specifically 170–81.

ciplinary, then just *anyone* can propound legitimate New Testament theology. These ominous consequences do not, however, show the necessity of modern New Testament theology; instead they mark out the intellectual and social limits of the jurisdiction of the rules of modern New Testament theology. If – as I have argued here – there are not transcendent criteria for interpretation, but only local customs and guild rules, the reluctance modern New Testament theologians express about admitting the possible legitimacy of other appropriations of the New Testament is an expression of cultural imperialism and intellectual xenophobia.[90]

I quote Adam at length because his case is powerful, well articulated and increasingly gaining ground among disaffected biblical interpreters tired of modernism dominating the discipline through historical critical method. This approach finds something of a manifesto in a recent collection of essays (themselves not all recent) edited by Stephen Fowl, who has himself been a prominent voice in the call to appropriate for biblical studies, apparently without qualms, Jeffrey Stout's position on interpretation.[91] What distinguishes Fowl and Adam from the more extreme position of Hauerwas is that they want to appeal to the 'interpretive interests' argument without following it all the way through to non-essentialism. Even to the extent that this may be right in principle, it requires a rather excessive amount of polemic against chimerical relativism precisely because it does not appeal to a sufficiently nuanced notion of construal. This would explain the two-pronged polemic of Adam's quoted passage (and elsewhere): first, those who disagree are imperialist and xenophobic; and, secondly, this non-modern option simply is traditional Christianity. Neither of these claims is sustainable; and nor is Fowl's desire to use such a non-essentialist view of meaning if he would also like to believe that as a Christian he might hear from a God who

[90] Adam, *Making Sense of New Testament Theology*, 179.

[91] See Stephen E. Fowl (ed.), *The Theological Interpretation of Scripture: Classic and Contemporary Readings* (Blackwell Readings in Modern Theology), Oxford: Blackwell, 1997, including his own 'Introduction' as a survey (xii–xxx). On appropriating Stout, see also Stephen E. Fowl, 'The Ethics of Interpretation; or, What's Left Over after the Elimination of Meaning?', in David J. A. Clines, Stephen E. Fowl and Stanley E. Porter (eds), *The Bible in Three Dimensions: Essays in Celebration of the Fortieth Anniversary of the Department of Biblical Studies, University of Sheffield* (JSOTS 87), Sheffield: JSOT Press, 1990, 379–98; and now taken up, somewhat problematically, into his *Engaging Scripture: A Model for Theological Interpretation*, Oxford: Blackwell, 1998, 32–61.

dwells beyond the text.[92] This is not to say that the concerns of this 'theological reading' are not valid, or important. Rather it is to say that disaffection with modernity is not itself a coherent interpretive position.

It can be seen, therefore, that a better understanding of what construal is, and the various ways in which it might operate as we read the Bible with an awareness of its various illocutionary acts, will lead us away from such broad attempts to locate the performative force of the text entirely in the domain of the reader. Construal has its key role to play, but it is one role in a wider picture.

§3.3 Are construction-based approaches necessarily theologically reductive?

There is not space here to compare the way in which my speech act account of construal compares with other construction-orientated approaches to epistemological and hermeneutical issues. In particular, the work of sociologist of religion Peter Berger is relevant here, as he has sought to explore how socially constructed models of reality inhabit a 'sacred canopy': 'religion has been the historically most widespread and effective instrumentality of legitimation . . . it relates the precarious reality constructions of empirical societies with ultimate reality'.[93] Berger's work draws on the remarkably influential book he co-authored with Thomas Luckmann, *The Social Construction of Reality*,[94] and it is worth noting that Berger himself does not see his approach as theologically reductive. In *A Rumor of Angels* he argues that the relativising perspective of sociology can itself be relativised, and that appeal to the ever-present possibility of transcendence (the rumoured 'angels' of the title) reminds us that 'secularized consciousness is not the absolute it presents itself as'.[95]

---

[92] Fowl does appear to believe this, which makes *Engaging Scripture* a somewhat uneven book.

[93] See Peter Berger, *The Social Reality of Religion*, London: Penguin, 1973, 41 (= *The Sacred Canopy*, New York: Doubleday, 1967). See also idem, *A Rumor of Angels: Modern Society and the Rediscovery of the Supernatural*, New York: Doubleday, expanded edition, 1990 (1969); idem, *The Heretical Imperative: Contemporary Possibilities of Religious Affirmation*, London: Collins, 1980.

[94] Peter Berger and Thomas Luckmann, *The Social Construction of Reality: A Treatise in the Sociology of Knowledge*, London: Penguin, 1967 (originally 1966 in the USA, with different page numbering).

[95] Berger, *Rumor of Angels*, 180.

Berger's work has been discussed and utilised across a wide range of disciplines.[96] However, the only point I wish to make here is that 'social construction' is not the same as the kind of project envisaged by Searle, that of laying bare the logical building blocks with which social reality is constructed. In a recent survey of theories of 'social reality', Finn Collin pursues essentially a Searlean critique of Berger and Luckmann's work along the lines of challenging the notion that social reality can be constructed without reference to basic/brute facts.[97] He notes that Berger and Luckmann attempt to set up their discussion in broadly phenomenological terms where their concern is simply what *passes for* knowledge,[98] but goes on to note that in the development of their argument they subscribe to the far more interesting and controversial position that it is actually social fact and not just 'fact' which is their topic: that is, real facts are created by societal consent.[99] Berger and Luckmann are thus reduced to a kind of Quinean 'ontological relativism' and Collin explores how it might be that the laws of sociology of knowledge themselves escape from this constructivist claim. Short of arbitrary decree, he notes, they do not, and thus, in almost Searlean terms, Collin concludes that 'no brute social facts would exist to set in train the process of social construction'.[100]

Somewhat disarmingly, Searle himself disposes of any possible direct links between his own work and that of Berger and Luckmann as follows:

> I was not in fact responding to nor was I inspired by Berger and Luckmann's book *The Social Construction of Reality*. In fact I never heard of their book until the first draft of my book was done. After my Kant lectures in Stanford, various people pointed out to me that there already was a book with a related title. I looked at that

[96] Of particular relevance are the comments of John Milbank, *Theology and Social Theory: Beyond Secular Reason*, Oxford: Blackwell, 1990, 133–6, in a section entitled 'Policing the Sublime: A Critique of the Sociology of Religion'. There is also a massive literature in biblical studies, ever since Wayne A. Meeks, 'The Man from Heaven in Johannine Sectarianism', *JBL* 91 (1972), 44–72; see especially 69–72.

[97] Finn Collin, *Social Reality* (The Problems of Philosophy), London and New York: Routledge, 1997, 64–79.

[98] Berger and Luckmann, *Social Construction of Reality*, 13; cited also by Collin, *Social Reality*, 67.

[99] Berger and Luckmann, *Social Construction of Reality*, 197–8; with commentary by Collin, *Social Reality*, 68.

[100] Collin, *Social Reality*, 75.

book, but found it so totally different from what I was attempting to do that I neither made use of it nor referred to it.[101]

In so saying Searle is not averse to a 'philosophy of society' or 'culture', and indeed suggests in the same article that this would be a profitable line of inquiry for academic philosophy.[102] (Although I have been unable to trace any link in the literature, I suggest further that the kinds of concern in Searle's view here are consonant with his analysis of student unrest on university campuses in the late 1960s wherein he provided an 'anatomy of student revolts' which included a logical decomposition of the stages of 'creation of the issue', 'creation of a rhetorical climate' and 'the collapse of authority', amongst other things. Here would be philosophical analysis in the service of understanding social structures, with the benefit that the issue is a recent and testable field of events.)[103] Searle's well-known antipathy towards the tradition of continental philosophy perhaps helps to clarify just what is in view here: not a hermeneutical or phenomenological approach to issues such as truth, but rather the laying bare of logical mechanisms such as those of 'institutions' in their various broad manifestations in the modern (and analytical) world.[104]

With 'construction' being such a broad and controversial academic category across a wide range of disciplines, it is helpful to have to hand the concise survey of its various forms from a philosophical perspective very much akin to Searle's, in Finn Collin's book on *Social Reality*. Collin's argument is simple to state, and has already been sampled above in his treatment of Berger and Luckmann: social construction arguments may be grouped heuristically into two distinct categories, the 'broad' and the 'narrow'. The broad ones which attempt a form of global constructivism fail logically since they lack the means to begin the process of fact creation while the narrow ones, which limit their constructivist sights to certain kinds of well-defined social facts, are both sustainable and useful analytical tools (*à la* Searle)

---

[101] John R. Searle, 'Replies to Critics of *The Construction of Social Reality*', *HHS* 10.4 (1997), 103–10, here 106–7. Searle's book developed out of the Kant lectures of 1992.

[102] Searle, 'Replies to Critics', 103.

[103] John Searle, *The Campus War: A Sympathetic Look at the University in Agony*, Harmondsworth: Pelican Books, 1972, especially 11–43.

[104] Searle, 'Replies to Critics', 110.

for examining the nature and function of concepts of Social Reality.[105]

Thus, following Searle and Collin, it is clear that one may adopt the language of construction and explore models of constructed reality (in certain aspects) without being committed to any form of *philosophical* reductionism. I want to suggest that it is only a short step from here to showing that one need also not be committed to *theological* reductionism.

It would be disingenuous not to allow that the reductive use of 'construction' terminology is widespread and indeed perhaps even the most prominent way in which it is used. A recent work which makes explicit appeal to speech act theory as one of its construction mechanisms, and which is reductive through and through, is Jonathan Potter's *Representing Reality*.[106] Appealing to both Austin and Berger and Luckmann as precursors, Potter's fundamental move is to take discourse not as representational but as rhetorical (the influence of Rorty being both evident and acknowledged here).[107] Thus through a careful examination of the tropes of ordinary discourse one may learn to appreciate how it is that 'real' objects have their reality constructed. Potter's view of Austin is that he began the process of isolating the rhetorically constructed nature of reality but restricted himself to artificial example sentences.[108] It was thus left to Derrida's critique of Searle to broaden out the implications to the whole area of written and oral discourse without any artificial 'serious/playful' divide (or 'hierarchy' as Derrida has it).[109] In the previous chapter I suggested that such a view misunderstands the relevance of the Derrida–Searle exchange to speech act concerns.

---

[105] The structure of Collin's book follows this argument: part 1 on 'Broad Arguments' (23–99) and part 2 on 'Narrow Arguments' (101–219).

[106] Jonathan Potter, *Representing Reality: Discourse, Rhetoric and Social Construction*, London: Sage Publications, 1996, 11–12, 202–4. I take this work as a particularly clear example of social *constructivism*, or, as Collin describes it by way of contrast, 'science constructivism' (cf. Collin, *Social Reality*, 13–14). Representative works in this area include Bruno Latour and Steve Woolgar, *Laboratory Life: The Social Construction of Scientific Facts*, Beverly Hills: Sage Publications, 1979, and the remarkable work of Malcolm Ashmore, *The Reflexive Thesis: Wrighting Sociology of Scientific Knowledge*, Chicago: University of Chicago Press, 1989.

[107] Potter, *Representing Reality*, 6.

[108] Potter, *Representing Reality*, 11.

[109] Potter, *Representing Reality*, 80–5.

Potter's account is on the one hand willing to adopt the idea of a spectrum of different strengths of construal (although he phrases his discussion less as '*X* construed as *Y*' and more as the degrees of modalisation of some *X* such as 'I know that *X*' or 'I think that *X*' or 'I guess that *X*').[110] However, the conclusion he draws from this is that, while the mechanisms of construction vary, the reality being represented is always rhetorically constructed. The way is open to him, therefore, to criticise Austin (or perhaps Austin's followers) for not following through on the initial insight that descriptions are not mere descriptions but are always established in some context by some procedure.[111]

It is important to recognise here that one can agree in broad outline with this view but still raise questions concerning the scope of its significance. I have argued that even if this 'rhetorical construction' can be universalised, it will in some cases be a trivial phenomenon. Again, as with Fish, there are all kinds of interesting examples where it is a good and valuable thesis, but examples must be taken case by case.[112]

Constructivist authors clearly tend to believe that theology is to be taken as simply a somewhat dim-witted rhetorical ploy, namely the protection of religious truths by safeguarding them from inquiry.[113] But this does not follow in any necessarily interesting sense from their approach, precisely because the all-inclusive view of speech acts here must of necessity be including weak (and trivial) speech acts as well as strong ones. Since not all illocutionary acts are equally strong, and therefore not all constructed reality is constructed in the same sense, one may not make a substantive point simply by describing all reality as constructed, even if technically one may be entitled to do so. It follows, I suggest, that construction-based epistemologies need not be theologically reductive, regardless of the depressing extent to which they are regularly pressed into anti-theological service.

---

[110] Potter, *Representing Reality*, 112.

[111] Potter, *Representing Reality*, 204.

[112] Some particularly good examples are found in Derek Edwards, Malcolm Ashmore and Jonathan Potter, 'Death and Furniture: The Rhetoric, Politics and Theology of Bottom Line Arguments against Relativism', *HHS* 8.2 (1995), 25–49. Even death and furniture, they avow, are always introduced into the discourse in some specific way to some particular end.

[113] Edwards, Ashmore and Potter, 'Death and Furniture', 40.

The unique and unjustly neglected joint work of Michael Arbib and Mary Hesse, based on their 1983 joint Gifford lectures, offers a perspective on precisely the issue of how construction may be utilised without being theologically reductive.[114] They develop a sophisticated schema-theory approach within the context of a ubiquitous theory of metaphor (drawing respectively on Arbib and Hesse's individual work) to argue that there may be links between the type of construction processes involved in apprehending spatio-temporal reality and those involved in the irreducibly symbolic world of religious faith. Most simply, they observe that 'cosmological theories about the beginning and end of the universe are distant extrapolations from the evidence, and they contain a high proportion of theoretical construction of unobservable entities and processes'.[115] They develop the way in which 'construction' is thus at work in both science and religion, and carefully break down supposed barriers between them. A key step in their argument is to develop schema theory as a non-reductive response to mind–brain questions (63–72), predicated on the observation that the old dualisms of mind/body, mind/brain, subject/object and others are all challenged by the notion of the 'essentially embodied subject' (38). A schema is 'a unit of representation of a person's world' and schema theory argues that 'all human mental phenomena reduce to (complex) patterns of schema activation' (12). Schemas are 'in heads and in the social relations between heads' (130). They then generalise schema theory from an individual to society as a whole by way of a 'network model of language' (where metaphor operates throughout to varying degrees) and of the socio-cultural hermeneutical approach of Gadamer (chapters 8 and 9 respectively). This allows a subtle approach to the question of 'reality': one can characterise a grand schema by analysing what it is that people assent to while accepting that the question of criteria for judging schemas will differ depending on what kind of extra-spatio-temporal claims they make.[116]

[114] Michael A. Arbib and Mary B. Hesse, *The Construction of Reality*, Cambridge: Cambridge University Press, 1986.

[115] Arbib and Hesse, *Construction of Reality*, 17. Further page references are in the text,

[116] Hesse is an Anglican and Arbib an atheist (cf. ix–xii), and they each conclude with a chapter on overall schemas which give shape to life: Hesse on the Bible as 'The Great Schema' partly following Northrop Frye's *The Great Code* (ch. 11); and Arbib on 'Secular Schemas' (ch. 12).

Partly because the book comes from the Gifford lectures, it stops short at the point of addressing the reliability of Christianity's actual claims about the transcendent, and its need for a revelation from beyond the spatio-temporal world, suggesting only a Kantian argument along the lines of 'What must reality be like for a God schema to have developed in human minds?' (243). Nevertheless, it is undeniable that Arbib and Hesse have demonstrated that there is no philosophical reason why construction-based epistemologies should settle theological questions in favour of adopting non-realist or projectionist (e.g. Feuerbachian) theological positions.

§3.4 Conclusion: the logical space for a hermeneutic of self-involvement

Within the scope of a construction-based epistemology which need not be theologically reductionist, we may be free to pursue a hermeneutic of self-involvement with respect to the biblical text. Strong illocutions create social reality which is thus sustained above and beyond the power of the individual to make arbitrary declarations about the world around him or her. The 'institutions' thus created and maintained, in Searle's sense of constructed institution, are thus accessed only via a hermeneutic of self-involvement. Our discussion to this point has demonstrated that locating the idea of construal at the heart of speech act theory need not invite reductionism, whether philosophical or theological. This is, I shall now go on to argue, a vindication of Donald Evans's work on self-involvement, and offers suggestions towards clarifying aspects of the logical grammar of Christian belief. The next step will then be to demonstrate actual examples of how self-involvement operates as a speech act category in the reading of the New Testament.

PART 2

Aspects of Self-Involvement in Interpreting New Testament Speech Acts

5

Exploring a Hermeneutic of Self-Involvement: The Work of Donald Evans

> In all discussions in the philosophy of language and the philosophy of mind, it is absolutely essential at some point to remind oneself of the first-person case.[1]

§1 Introduction

Having set out the stall of speech act theory in part 1 of this study, it is now time to harness its resources towards the development of a hermeneutic for reading the Bible in this second, and more overtly theological, part 2. Although I have touched briefly at various points on the work done in this area, I have left until now an examination of the work of Donald Evans, widely acknowledged as the single most important contribution in the field, in order that we may consider it with a full range of critical tools to hand. Where Evans writes of the 'logic of self-involvement', my purpose here is to draw on his work, combine it with my own discussion of speech act theory, and thus develop a 'hermeneutic of self-involvement'. The remaining chapters in part 2 will then explore the ways in which this hermeneutic may help us in the task of interpreting certain types of New Testament text.

The purpose of this chapter is therefore threefold: to clarify the concept of 'self-involvement', as discussed by Donald Evans;

---

[1] John R. Searle, 'Indeterminacy, Empiricism, and the First Person', *JP* 84 (1987), 123–46, here 126.

to examine significant uses of this concept in biblical studies; and to establish the guidelines for my subsequent use of 'self-involvement' as a hermeneutical tool in specific examples of biblical interpretation. This task is simplified by the observation that the insights of Evans's work have not been overly exploited in the field. Indeed, in my judgment, while several commentators have expounded it sympathetically and provided indications of new directions for it,[2] there are only two major studies which have made comparable approaches to the exegetical task, those of Timothy Polk on Jeremiah and of Dietmar Neufeld on 1 John, which we shall consider below.[3] Similarly, work in biblical studies has rarely utilised Evans's approach to anything like its full potential. Perhaps the one major area where some significant work has been done on the question of self-involvement is that of creeds and confessions. Not only has there been detailed investigation of the so-called *homologia* (or confessions) of the New Testament, such as 'Jesus is Lord' (attested for example in Romans 10:9) but also the investigation has moved beyond the elucidation of historical setting and considered the significance of the confessional form per se.[4] In most other respects, however, self-involvement remains an under-explored aspect of biblical language.

§2 Self-Involvement as a Speech Act Category: An Introduction

The basic point about self-involvement is that the speaking subject invests him or herself in a state of affairs by adopting a stance towards that state of affairs. Where self-involvement is most interesting and significant is in cases where the stance is logically (or 'grammatically')[5] entailed by the utterance itself. This is most obvious in cases where the language is present-tense first person language, although this is not a guarantee of an interesting case, but rather highlights the issues most clearly.

[2] Most notably G. B. Caird, *The Language and Imagery of the Bible*, London: Duckworth, 1980, 7–36, and Thiselton, *New Horizons*, 272–312.

[3] See §4 below.

[4] See ch. 6 for a full discussion.

[5] I use 'grammar' here in Wittgenstein's sense of the *logic* of the use of a word, phrase or proposition, as a way of drawing attention to the rules and implications involved in language use; cf. 'Grammar', in Glock, *A Wittgenstein Dictionary*, 150–5.

Thus in one of Wittgenstein's well-known examples, 'I am in pain' carries a different kind of logical implication from 'I love you': the first may fade away in a moment, but if one claimed that the love had faded away similarly it would call into question the original utterance.[6] Equally, 'I assure you, I have a pain there now' functions quite differently from 'I assure you, I know that's a tree'.[7] An example which brings out the particular relevance of first person utterances having logical implications is 'If there were a verb meaning "to believe falsely", it would not have any significant first person present indicative'.[8] That someone else believes falsely is not logically remarkable; but if I believe something then the grammar of 'believe' implies (among other things) that I am convinced about it, or of its truth, and hence it makes no sense to commit myself equally to its falsehood.

Since many biblical expressions are functionally equivalent to first person utterance, as indeed are many language uses in any case, this grammar of self-involvement suggests itself as a useful hermeneutical option. In later chapters we shall go on to explore how simple utterances such as 'Jesus is Lord' or 'I forgive you' stand equally as self-involving in certain respects. One could say that it makes no sense to say 'I confess Christ as Lord but I don't believe that he is'. At the heart of self-involvement as a hermeneutical tool is the observation that

> the speaker 'stands behind' the words giving *a pledge and personal backing* that he or she is prepared to undertake commitments and responsibilities that are entailed in extra-linguistic terms by the proposition which is asserted.[9]

This fundamental point has not been widely understood, nor, where understood, widely utilised, in biblical interpretation.[10] To demonstrate its wider applicability will be one of my recurring

---

[6] Wittgenstein, *Zettel*, §504.

[7] Wittgenstein, *On Certainty*, Oxford: Blackwell, 1969, §389.

[8] Wittgenstein, *Philosophical Investigations*, p. 190.

[9] Thiselton, *New Horizons*, 617, drawing here on both Wittgenstein and on the work of Dallas High, who was one of the first to explore the possibilities of Wittgensteinian analysis for biblical language. I discuss High's work in ch. 6 below.

[10] The main exception is the work of Anthony Thiselton, who has often advocated the use of logical grammar to aid biblical exegesis, although his work using speech act theory does not always focus on this precise area. For two good examples where he does make specific use of the idea, see his 'Supposed Power of Words' and 'Liar Paradox'.

themes in the following chapters. However, I immediately wish to go further, and to suggest that, in line with my proposals about strong and weak illocutions in earlier chapters, it is profitable to see self-involvement as operating across a spectrum of strengths ranging from strong to weak. As with any conceptual scheme, the justification for this is not in appealing to some property of the language, but the felicity or otherwise of this distinction in clarifying points of interest. Thus, to offer a simple introductory example:

(1) 'I am six feet four inches tall.'

is self-involving only in a weak (trivial) sense, corresponding to the way in which 'flat assertions' are classed as illocutionary. If I utter (1), then it is in fact true, and one could say that I enter into a commitment in the public domain to stand by the truth of this statement. One could of course imagine cases where this would be non-trivial: (1) may be more than a simple statement and have some further performative force, if, for example, I am applying for a job in the police force which has a certain height requirement of being over six feet, and I am hereby affirming that I qualify in this regard. Nevertheless, in general, in the same way that (1) is a weak illocution, it is not self-involving in a very interesting sense. Contrast:

(2) 'I am a Christian.'

Although this looks grammatically similar to (1), its logical grammar is quite different, and is a function of the stance-commitment entailed by the self-description 'Christian' in the public domain. Thus this is grammatically identical to an utterance such as 'I am a Liverpool fan', which brings with it its own commitments (such as cheering when Liverpool score a goal and restraining oneself when their opponents do) with the difference being entirely a matter of the scope of the entailments. Indeed, to utter (2) brings with it a variety of entailments, varying according to context. Sample entailments could easily be:

(2a) 'I am a regular church attender.'
(2b) 'I read the Bible for personal instruction.'
(2c) 'I take a stand against apartheid.'
(2d) 'I oppose the public ridiculing or cursing of Jesus.'

Of course one can supply instances of an enormous variety of entailments which have been understood to follow from (2), including

(2c') 'I support apartheid.'[11]

or commitments both for and against slavery,[12] and so forth, and this variety need not detain us here. The point is a methodological one: in uttering (2) I take a stance in the public domain which commits me to certain forms of (positive and negative) behaviour. In the language I wish to use (2) is strongly self-involving.

The form of (2) as a first person present tense verb highlights on the surface the level of personal investment in the utterance. However, as we shall see in a moment, for his discussion of self-involvement Donald Evans chose as his paradigmatic self-involving utterance

(3) 'The Creator made the world.'

On the face of it this does not look self-involving at all, but Evans analysed the differences between this and statements such as

(4) 'Jones built the house.'

to indicate that while their surface grammar is identical their logical grammar is very different.

The belief that speech act theory has much to contribute to biblical interpretation is, in my judgment, largely a consequence of this kind of investigation into logical grammar. Speech act theory is in particular helpful in clarifying the presuppositions, commitments and entailments of certain types of language game.[13] Among those language games which feature prominently in the biblical text, one could consider:

[11] Not always as bluntly as this, of course, but this claim can be substantiated with reference to, for example, the publication of the report of the Synod of the Dutch Reformed Church in South Africa: *Human Relations and the South African Scene in the Light of Scripture*, Pretoria: Dutch Reformed Church Publishers, 1976).

[12] See Willard M. Swartley, *Slavery, Sabbath, War and Women: Case Issues in Biblical Interpretation*, Scottdale: Herald Press, 1983, especially 31–64.

[13] It is important to remember to use this phrase in Wittgenstein's specific sense: processes consisting of language and actions woven together (*Philosophical Investigations*, §7) such as 'giving orders', 'describing the appearance of an object', 'asking, thanking, cursing, greeting, praying' (§23). The later, broader, inherently fideistic application of 'language game' to entire traditions unfortunately remains a major obstacle to understanding the significance of Wittgenstein for religious language. See Kerr, *Theology after Wittgenstein*, 28–31.

confessing; forgiving; pardoning; repenting; proclaiming; teaching; preaching; praying; interceding; lamenting; rejoicing . . .

To understand the language used in all these circumstances is to elucidate the nature of the speech act involved and, in strongly self-involving cases, is to draw the speaking subject (or agent) into the text as an irreducible aspect of the process of understanding. In passing, one may note that this approach offers a very different perspective on ways of highlighting reader involvement in the interpretive process from that offered by postmodern varieties of reader-response theory.

In this chapter I explore the possibility of such a hermeneutic of self-involvement. The next three chapters will investigate particular New Testament language games from this perspective. The final chapter will reflect briefly on some of the hermeneutical implications of a speech-act approach.

§3 Donald Evans and *The Logic of Self-Involvement*

Donald Evans was both a lecturer in theology in Montreal and later a professor of philosophy in Toronto. He began research under J. L. Austin in Oxford and completed it, after Austin's death, under I. T. Ramsey. Thus situated squarely at the birth of speech act theory as a discipline, and at the interdisciplinary divide between philosophy and theology (and in particular religious and biblical language), he was well placed to produce the foundational work on the use of speech act theory in biblical interpretation: *The Logic of Self-Involvement*, published in 1963. Evans's subsequent work is less well known, although this has not stopped that most common of debates: did a key thinker (in this case the 'early Evans') change his mind?[14] Certainly the emphasis of his later work is different, and perhaps one can say that it is widely taken as constituting something of a noncognitive disavowal of his *Logic of Self-Involvement* position. The complications of following Evans's own line of thought, allied to the lack of detailed interaction with the original book itself,

---

[14] See Stanley Hauerwas and Richard Bondi, 'Language, Experience and the Life Well-Lived: A Review of the Work of Donald Evans', *RelSRev* 9.1 (1983), 33–7, who argue that 'the change from the early to the later Evans is not as great as many assume' (33).

have not helped recognition of his important work on self-involvement.[15]

§3.1 The Logic of Self-Involvement

The Logic of Self-Involvement is a subtle and difficult book with a far-reaching agenda. In it Evans attempts to show that when one uses language such as 'God is my creator' in the biblical context, then, logically speaking, one makes certain self-involving commitments with respect to one's acknowledgement of status and role, as well as feelings and attitudes. Thus the use of biblical language draws the speaker logically into a relationship of a certain kind with God and the speaker's fellow humans. This is an ambitious argument, and I shall have cause to argue that it is in fact only partially successful, but it merits close attention since it remains the most detailed attempt to articulate a speech-act view of construal in biblical interpretation, which is all the more remarkable since the book pre-dates almost all the post-Austin development of speech act theory.

Evans's main focus is set out in his introduction:

> In saying, 'The Creator made the world', does a man commit himself to any future conduct, or imply that he has a particular attitude or intention, or express a feeling or attitude? Or is the utterance a neutral, impersonal statement of fact, like saying, 'Jones built the house'? (11)[16]

In the course of the book he defends the first of these two alternatives, and in this sense the language concerned is *self-involving*.

In the first of three chapters of philosophy he offers a re-casting of Austin's analysis of performative utterances. He uses

[15] Aside from Caird and Thiselton (see n. 2 above), and the Hauerwas-Bondi review article (n. 14 above), works drawing on or substantially reviewing Evans's work include J. Gordon Campbell, 'Are All Speech-Acts Self-Involving?', *RelStud* 8 (1972), 161–4; P. Masterson, 'Self-Involvement and the Affirmation of God', in J. Walgrave, A. Vergote and B. Willaert (eds), *Miscellanea Albert Dondeyne: Godsdienstfilosofie; Philosophie de la Religion*, Gembloux: Leuven University Press, 1974, 263–77; David Stagaman SJ, '"God" in Analytic Philosophy', in Sebastian A. Matczak (ed.), *God in Contemporary Thought: A Philosophical Perspective* (Philosophical Questions Series 10), New York: Learned Publications, 1977, 813–49, especially 826–38; Jacques Poulain, 'Pragmatique de la Communication et Dynamique de la Verité. La fidélite théorique de D. Evans à la révélation chrétienne', *RSR* 69 (1981), 545–72; Neufeld, *Reconceiving Texts as Speech Acts*, 37–60.

[16] Further references to Evans, *Logic of Self-Involvement*, are given in the text.

Austin's categories, save for replacing 'expositives' with 'constatives', a move which draws on Austin's rejection of the performative/constative distinction, even if it results in a less comprehensive classification (38 n.1). His twin aims here are an analysis of different types of implication and, more significantly, a discussion of institutional and causal words. He defines 'flat constatives' as constatives which lack behabitive or commissive force (56), thus paving the way for his main argument: that 'God is my Creator' is not a flat constative in the biblical context (64–6).

This raises particularly the question of the nature of the institutional settings within which words gain their currency. Evans asserts that 'institutional-relation words include as part of their meaning some indication of conduct which is thought to be appropriate' (67) since social life depends on certain expectations. For the key force distinction which Austin characterised as illocutionary/perlocutionary, Evans uses the terms *performative* and *causal* (70–1). Causal force, he says, is not a part of utterance meaning. 'When words are used performatively, institutional relations are sometimes established and sometimes invoked' (68).

Chapters 2 and 3 analyse expressions of attitude and feeling respectively. Two significant points are made, which will eventually turn out to be incompatible. First he flags the significance of 'rapportive' language, where imaginative sympathy with the utterer is required if the utterance is to be understood (110–13). The implications of this observation remain unexplored in the book, and are only picked up in his later work. Secondly, he analyses attitudes as fundamentally relational: they involve a judgment of whether or not one is for or against something. Having an attitude about *x* thus involves taking up a position in relation to *x* (123), which Evans calls an 'onlook': 'I have coined the word "onlook" as a substantive for what it is to "look on x as y"' (125).

Onlooks

Onlooks typically involve a commissive element (a personal involvement with the *x* which motivates the seeing of *x* as *y*), a verdictive element (which places *x* within some structure or scheme) and other elements such as autobiographical or expressive ones (126–7). Of the different kinds of onlooks considered by Evans (including literal and metaphorical where the *x is* in some sense *y*) the two he concentrates on are parabolic and analogical. The former concern cases where the appropriate attitudes for *x* are similar to those for *y* (e.g. 'I look on Henry as a brother'). The latter are similar but invite some independent point of comparison between *x* and *y* above and beyond the attitude suggested (e.g. 'I look on music as a language').

Evans later calls onlooks 'the most important and most novel item in *The Logic of Self-Involvement*',[17] and the following observations may be made at this point. First, there is a slight ambiguity about Evans's use of the word 'logic' in the first half of the book. If he has in mind the Wittgensteinian sense of 'logical grammar' then it is unobjectionable, but at times one is left wondering if a claim such as 'some attitude-words . . . have an intrinsic logical connection with feelings' (87) can be substantiated, or indeed whether it needs to be. The discussion of onlooks does not seem to depend entirely on the preceding analyses of feelings and attitudes, which appear more as ground-clearing exercises for the section on onlooks, perhaps to avoid the charge that 'seeing *x* as *y*' is *merely* a feeling or groundless opinion (perhaps reducible to attitude). In view of his later discussion, Evans's point is probably that attitude-words gain their currency only through experiencing ('rapportively') the attitudes involved; but this is not the same as saying that whenever one uses such a word the connection with the Mood concerned is a matter of logical grammar, still less of logical deduction. Rather, it is the context of the utterance which is the primary indication of how well the word is ever linked with the mood. My point is that the apparent ambiguity of the idea of 'logic' might give the appearance of a specifically *logical* weight behind an argument which actually stands or falls on other grounds, namely, the correct delineation of the *context* of the utterance. (It is in view of this, also, that I prefer the phrase 'a *hermeneutic* of self-involvement' in the title of this chapter.)

This leads to a second observation, that the lack of a context in view during his philosophical discussion leaves Evans's claims

---

[17] Donald D. Evans, *Faith, Authenticity and Morality*, Edinburgh: The Handsel Press, 1980, 10.

in his chapter 3 lacking in any clear idea of the nature of or the rationale for (to use Searle's phrase) the 'institutional backing' which is invoked in any particular case of construal, or onlook.[18] Instead, his context is revealed piecemeal at points in this chapter where some such appeal is obviously needed. For instance, 'I accept the authoritative words of Jesus' is the reason why he believes God is like a Father (134). There is also the strong indication that he believes that after death the parabolic onlooks will give way to literal ones. To make sense of these claims one must postulate something like the 'biblical context' which comes later: we look on people/events/actions in the context of biblical revelation, validated by Jesus' own authority in all he taught, and one day to be vindicated (after death) in literal terms.

This *onlook* is certainly foundational to Christianity. Evans addresses briefly the different question of whether it is in some sense 'correct':

> Religious belief is the conviction (or hope) that one's onlook conforms to an authoritative onlook, a divine onlook . . . Christians believe that there is a divine onlook . . . an onlook which is authoritative: human onlooks are 'true' in so far as they approximate to the divine onlook. (140)

One can never be sure, he admits, that one's onlook conforms to the divine one, and indeed a page earlier he writes

> Onlooks are sometimes self-verifying. That is, in so far as I actually look on x as y in my daily life, it becomes true that x is y. For example, if I look on my suffering as a means to moral growth, it is likely that my suffering will *be* a means of moral growth . . . In general, people tend to conform to the roles which they see themselves as playing. (139)

Whereas the first of these quotes invites us to see some kind of objective behind-the-scenes divine vindication of a particular world-view, the second is willing to be far more modest. For Evans, the second operates within the framework of the first, but it is not clear that he has, at this stage, any reasons for this. Indicating the path he would later take, he concludes the book with the far from logically self-involving claim: whether or not

---

[18] A related point is made by Stagaman in the only one of his criticisms of Evans with which I agree: 'we must inquire why we should accept the word of Jesus', '"God" in Analytic Philosophy', 835–6.

we accept the 'complex pattern of biblical onlooks' is a 'decision of faith' (267).

In fact, at this point in his argument something like an analysis of strong and weak onlooks in the manner we have described earlier for construals would appear to be exactly what Evans needs to account for these varying types of self-involvement. Strong construals are self-verifying (Evans's term) precisely because they create the institutional facts concerned. Weaker construals can be discussed in different terms, such as the success or otherwise of their correspondence to some pre-institutional ('brute') fact.

However, at least in outline, the idea of parabolic onlooks in religious language is a helpful one. Evans gives the example of 'looking on God as a Father' which, speaking parabolically, is a question of inculcating the same human attitudes toward God as we would have towards a human father (133–4). It may be that Evans is actually being inconsistent in his terminology here: he appears to have no qualms about saying that after death we will understand God's revelation in literal terms (134) which would seem to imply that he sees some kind of independent point of contact between God and the human father which goes beyond just the attitude, and therefore on his own terms he should see this as an analogical onlook and not a parabolic one. He is adamant that 'it is not a matter of acting *as if* I believed that God is like a father' (133) but rather 'God *is* like a father, but the nature of the likeness is obscure' (134). The difficulty in articulating this point convincingly leads Evans in his later work towards a more comprehensive theory of analogy which, in turn, calls into question this earlier account of onlooks as purely public-domain forms of linguistic self-involvement.[19]

Creation language

The second part of the book brings his linguistic analysis to bear on the biblical language of creation. Evans argues that the biblical idea of world-creation is inseparable from Israel's idea of nation-creation: they each involve the exercise of Yahweh's supernatural causal (i.e. perlocutionary) power at the same time as his institutional authority. For Israel this was seen in the

---

[19] See Evans, *Faith, Authenticity and Morality*, 10–24 and *passim.* (I discuss this in §3.2 below.)

miracle of the Exodus, and in the covenant whereby Yahweh ordained Israel into a subordinate role with a positive value. In this case it is clear that the covenant is the institution within which Yahweh's authority operates.

In the case of world-creation, Evans perceives the same combination of perlocutionary force (God's creative word which speaks the world into being) and institutional authority: appointing humankind to its role on the earth, with a positive assessment of human value and work; and a clear command to continue to uphold the creation. Thus:

> The efficacious word of God in Creation has not only supernatural causal power but also Exercitive, Verdictive and Commissive force; and man's word concerning the Creator who is Lord, Appointer, Evaluator and Guarantor is a self-involving acknowledgement. In the biblical context, if I say, 'God is my Creator', I acknowledge my status as God's obedient servant and possession, I acknowledge my role as God's steward and worshipper, I acknowledge God's gift of existence, and I acknowledge God's self-commitment to me. This act of acknowledgement includes both Behabitive and Commissive elements. (158)

Evans continues: 'biblical man . . . *looks on* Creation *as* a performative action . . . In the biblical context, the utterance "God is my Creator" is profoundly self-involving' (159–60). This is his central example of the main thesis of his book.

The crucial issue here, I suggest, is to determine what is meant by 'in the biblical context'. Evans argues that to speak in this context is to adopt the traditional-contextual implications of words which build up their meaning as the Bible is interpreted according to some theological tradition (161). He accepts that this might be better stated as '*a* biblical context', since obviously different traditions invest words with different meanings, but insists that he will continue to speak of *the* biblical context, meaning 'the biblical context which *I* am expounding'. It would seem that what Evans is doing here is actually speaking of an *ideal* biblical context, or what would today be called the *implied reader's* understanding of the text.[20] In other words, there is an

---

[20] For this term see, for example, Wayne C. Booth, *The Rhetoric of Fiction*, London: Penguin Books, [2]1983 (1961), especially 67–77; and Iser, *Act of Reading*. For a clear example of the idea in biblical studies see R. Alan Culpepper, *Anatomy of the Fourth Gospel: A Study in Literary Design*, Philadelphia: Fortress Press, 1983, 204–27.

understanding of a term like 'Creator' which comes from care-fully investigating its uses across the whole witness of biblical language.[21] We can put Evans's point as a conditional: *if* one uses the word 'Creator' in an utterance like 'God is my Creator' in such a way that all the biblical connotations are intended, *then* one is actually doing much more than making a statement (uttering a flat constative) because one is thereby involved in a whole series of attitudinal and other self-involving speech acts.

This differs from Evans in only one respect: his formulation of the conditional leaves the context outside, as an apparently simple condition of the rest of the conditional, that is 'assuming the biblical context, *if* one uses the word "Creator" . . . *then* one is performing a self-involving utterance'. But to my mind Evans's version gives a false impression, for it is at least possibly true that the majority of speakers who utter the words 'God is my Creator' do not acknowledge all that Evans says they do, simply because they do not speak 'in the biblical context'.

This difference appears small at first sight, but it lies at the root of why Evans changes his mind in later books. The funda-mental question raised is: how may we demarcate genuine self-involvement? Is it guaranteed by an idea of context which is as simple as saying 'when in the biblical context'? Or is it more problematic for his analysis, in terms of an investigation of non-linguistic criteria located in the speaker? Evans takes this latter route in his later work, but in fact we shall see later that *The Logic of Self-Involvement* itself offers hints that this is the way he would go. In its conclusion Evans notes: 'What is it to "mean what one says"? And what is it to intend that the utterance have its meaning in the biblical context rather than some other context? These are questions which I have not answered' (262). It is his later attempts to answer them which we must now consider.[22]

[21] In passing we should note that some of the ways in which Evans expresses himself about 'biblical context' are open to misunderstanding. For instance, do words build up meanings in the Bible as a whole? He makes the perhaps incautious assumption, outlined at the beginning of the book, that words have *essential* meanings, which seems to be a view he borrows uncritically from the then-prevalent biblical theology movement. Indeed he avers that a philosopher 'can only approach the words of the Bible *via* a biblical theology which is prescriptive and selective' (20) but this is far from self-evident.

[22] Other earlier works from Evans which correspond in large measure to his 1963 position include Donald D. Evans, 'Differences between Scientific and Religious Assertions', in Ian G. Barbour (ed.), *Science and Religion: New Perspectives*

§3.2 Evans's later work: critique, retraction and reaffirmation

Evans's later works clearly evince a personal pilgrimage away from the logical analysis of his first book and towards a multi-faceted position which seeks to combine and correlate philosophical and psychological insights on language and experience.[23] Although the changes of direction are evident, there are various ways of marking the continuities also. Hauerwas and Bondi note primarily the prominent strain of theological liberalism throughout his work: religious language interests him because it witnesses in whatever approximate ways to transformative religious experience, and his concern is always to locate some universal dimension of that experience, be it logically/linguistically necessary or psychologically fundamental.[24] Evans himself hints at this kind of agenda with his scattered remarks about his attempt to grapple with transcendence, from onlooks as the rudiments of a theory of analogy through to the existentialist sympathies of his later philosophical anthropology,[25] and perhaps most baldly with the statement: 'My own personal conviction is that a great deal of what Christians regard as revelation provides insight mainly concerning human nature and only indirectly and secondarily concerning the nature of God.'[26] I will attempt to strike an appropriate balance between emphasising the differences and the continuities in Evans's thought here.

---

on the Dialogue, London: SCM Press, 1968, 101–33; 'Barth on Talk about God', *Canadian Journal of Theology* 16 (1970), 175–92; and 'Reply to J. Gordon Campbell', *RelStud* 9 (1973), 469–72.

[23] The essays which chart the heart of this pilgrimage are gathered together and substantially reworked in Donald D. Evans, *Faith, Authenticity and Morality*, which is best read in conjunction with its companion volume, *Struggle and Fulfillment: The Inner Dynamics of Religion and Morality*, Cleveland: Collins, 1979 (UK 1980), where the later position is more fully articulated. He also authored the published version of the United Church of Canada report on communism as *Communist Faith and Christian Faith*, London: SCM Press, 1965, which includes some early personal thoughts on self-involvement as a broader than philosophical category (139–47); and his later papers are helpfully collected together in *Spirituality and Human Nature* (Suny Series in Religious Studies), Albany: SUNY Press, 1993.

[24] Hauerwas and Bondi, 'Language, Experience and the Life Well-Lived', 35.

[25] See especially Donald D. Evans, *Faith, Authenticity and Morality*, 10–24: 'in *The Logic of Self-Involvement* I sketched the beginnings of an approach to the problem of divine transcendence' (11). Note also his unpublished University of Chicago lectures of 1967 under the title 'Religious Language and Divine Transcendence' (265, n. 2)

[26] Evans, *Struggle and Fulfillment*, 211, n. 25.

Contexts: linguistic and prelinguistic?

The primary issue to be considered, as suggested above, is whether philosophical concerns are adequate for demarcating significant forms of self-involvement, or whether they need supplementing with psychologically-orientated models. In particular, Evans contrasts his idea that self-involvement can be characterised as a logical entailment of linguistic usage with the implications, originally unexplored, of his point about rapportive language. He develops this latter idea into a theory of 'existential belief': 'a belief where what is believed can only be understood to the extent that one has fulfilled certain existential conditions'.[27] Drawing in part on his own experience of psychotherapy which uncovered prelinguistic experience,[28] he concludes that 'personal self-involvement is epistemologically (and to some extent temporally) prior to linguistic self-involvement'.[29] In so saying he does not go back to a pre-Austin view of the performative utterance as reporting on an inner state, but rather urges that the public meaning of language is insufficient *on its own* for evaluating genuine self-involvement. Linguistic analysis must be supplemented by 'normative anthropology' and 'existentialist epistemology'.[30]

Thus although Evans still sees covenant as important, for instance, it now holds only a secondary importance.[31] The foundation of Evans's work has instead shifted away from verbal self-involvement. By 1980 he characterises his 1963 book as a form of 'modified empiricism' too impressed by what was observable and public, and instead defends his own foundation as 'a modified natural-law concerning human nature'.[32] Linguistic analysis can only judge between onlooks by fiat, but instead 'onlooks should be appraised primarily by reference to whether they facilitate discernments of the divine and contribute to human fulfilment'.[33] In short, Evans finally locates a demarcation between strong and weak construal in terms of the level

---

[27] Evans, *Faith, Authenticity and Morality*, 250.
[28] Noted in Evans, *Struggle and Fulfillment*, 1.
[29] Evans, *Faith, Authenticity and Morality*, 253.
[30] Evans, *Faith, Authenticity and Morality*, 251, 13.
[31] Evans, *Faith, Authenticity and Morality*, 193.
[32] Evans, *Faith, Authenticity and Morality*, 64, 195.
[33] Evans, *Faith, Authenticity and Morality*, 247, 242.

of the degree of existential authenticity. In certain key respects, and particularly in its appeal to the prelinguistic, this represents a different path from the one I have taken in earlier chapters, where I have suggested that we have a spectrum of construals which remain in the public (inter-subjective) arena.

With this subsequent shift in emphasis in view it becomes possible to notice the tension between the avowedly logical analysis and an incipient existentialism already in *The Logic of Self-Involvement*. Evans himself traces the tension to his appeal to the idea of 'rapportive language', as we have seen.[34] There is further evidence of it in his 1963 work in chapter 6 on 'Creation as a Causal Action' (218–52). Thus, again on how statements about creation can be self-involving, particularly parabolic statements:

> To accept a parable is to *adopt an attitude,* an attitude by which one lives so as to be in rapport with God and thus be enabled to *understand* the parable better in one's own experience. That is, the language of parables is self-involving and rapportive. (223)

Even if Evans is avoiding being motivated here by what one can and cannot believe today, but is rather aiming for the theological (attitudinal) point of the biblical text, it is clear that a demythologisation of the creation narratives is but a short step from this point. For example: 'breath of God' language invites us 'to take up an attitude, a parabolic onlook' (240) of continual dependence on God, rather than being a reference, in whatever attenuated form, to some actual characteristic of God. Likewise, he concludes his discussion by arguing that 'World-Creation is distinguished only in terms of onlook-attitudes' (251), since everything is created and therefore there is no separable 'core' factual element about which world-creation language is talking. This is clearly a change of tack from the rest of the book, and if one were to press this line of argument in isolation then the resulting position would be in large measure that of Willem

---

[34] Evans, *Faith, Authenticity and Morality*, 249. This is not to say that 'rapportive language' cannot be a helpful idea when used appropriately. Evans, for example, makes successful use of it in *Logic of Self-Involvement* in showing how God's work as Creator is closely linked to his glory and holiness, which terms can only be understood as the 'impressive observables' of an inner divine quality, which means that they evoke 'a correlative *human feeling-Response and acknowledgement*' (174). 'In short, God's glory and holiness are impressive qualities, which I understand in so far as I am impressed' (184–5). See the similar approach here of O. R. Jones, *The Concept of Holiness*, London: Allen & Unwin, 1961.

Zurdeeg's idea of convictional language which is not subject to tests for veridical reference:

> It is not the analytical philosopher's business to decide whether the reality meant in a certain language is 'really' there or not. The only thing he can do is to notice that if human beings speak either indicative or convictional language they refer to something which is 'real' for them.[35]

Helpful in what it affirms, this view turns its back precisely on the benefits of a speech act analysis in what it denies.

Adjustment or over-compensation?

Evans's later work stands in a complex relation to *The Logic of Self-Involvement*,[36] and I propose that it is indeed too simplistic to see his subsequent writings as representing a disavowal of his early concerns. The particular point which needs to be established here is whether his subsequent critique and retraction of certain elements of his early work substantially compromises its basic insights concerning the logical grammar of self-involvement.

The framework for his later inquiries which he develops out of his work on onlooks is that of analogy, and this may serve as a clear example of the position I wish to argue: that in broadening his work from its philosophical basis Evans over-compensates for aspects omitted from his earlier work.

Evans suggests that an analysis of the specific ways in which thinkers navigate between the human and the divine lends itself to a characterisation in terms of three different kinds of analogy:

1. Analogy of *activity*: divine activity is analogous to human activity
2. Analogy of *attitude*: an attitude of worship is appropriate to God, and corresponds to interpersonal attitudes (in particular 'basic trust', rather than worship)
3. Analogy of *relation*: the divine-human relation is analogous to human relations.[37]

---

[35] Willem F. Zurdeeg, *An Analytical Philosophy of Religion*, Nashville: Abingdon Press, 1958, 45.

[36] See in particular Evans, *Faith, Authenticity and Morality*, 3–24, 193–6, 223–7 and 247–63.

[37] Evans, *Faith, Authenticity and Morality*, 14. On 'basic trust', see Evans, *Struggle and Fulfillment*, 19–107. This paragraph draws from and summarises *Faith, Authenticity and Morality*, 10–24.

The second and third of these (although Evans does not
rule out the first also) are explicitly existential in orientation.
Evans comes to the conclusion that it is the *inward* attitude
which is most significant, and in particular that his earlier
work has neglected the idea of a 'person', treating this concept
as a somewhat thin 'attitudinal description of a metaphysical
entity'.

The concomitant change in his view of self-involvement is
clear in the next chapter, a reprint of a 1971 article with an updated postscript, discussing Ian Ramsey's idea of how qualifiers
shift the meaning of terms applied to God, which refer
analogically on different levels.[38] He now argues that there is an
irreducibly existential component to understanding 'cosmic
disclosures' which remains inaccessible to the viewpoint of
simply a logic of self-involvement, and in a footnote he criticises
his earlier view as relying on a fundamentally empiricist
epistemology of 'flat constatives' such as scientific statements.[39]
Elsewhere he allows his own approach to be characterised as
one which has 'great difficulty in accepting God's redemptive
presence in historical movements except as the sum of God's
presence in the hearts of . . . people'.[40]

There are many other indicators of Evans's desire to attach
greater significance to existential depth of involvement than
linguistic self-involvement.[41] However, reorientated and rein-
vigorated as he undoubtedly is in these later works, there remain
signs that this signals primarily a change of agenda rather than
a complete disavowal of his earlier position. For example, in his
advocacy of pre-linguistic meaning he does allow that 'Private
meaning can . . . be broadly shared by people who fulfil the
requisite existentialist conditions for understanding. And the
conditions are usually accessible, though in varying degrees, to
all human beings.'[42] He also reserves specific roles for speech
act analysis, as an 'illuminating reminder' of the mechanics of
construal in any human judgment, and as a way of highlighting
the difference between what convictions either should follow

---

[38] Evans, *Faith, Authenticity and Morality*, 25–72 ('Ian Ramsey on Talk about God').
[39] Evans, *Faith, Authenticity and Morality*, 64, and 272 n. 28. See also Evans,
'Differences between Scientific and Religious Assertions'.
[40] Evans, *Faith, Authenticity and Morality*, 277, n. 13.
[41] See especially Evans, *Faith, Authenticity and Morality*, 193–6 and 235–46.
[42] Evans, *Faith, Authenticity and Morality*, 251–2.

or must follow from any self-involving utterance.[43] Thus, his conclusion:

> Speech-act analysis is a way of groping towards a way of using language to get at what lies behind language in one's own most profound personal experience.[44]

As a reaffirmation this falls far short of all that one might wish to see embraced.[45] At best it serves to demonstrate that Evans's later work does not completely retract his earlier work. However, at heart, it appears to confuse the discovery of new agendas and new areas of inquiry with a re-evaluation of old agendas.

I suggest that at least part of the problem facing Evans was the confused nature of the illocution in Austin's work, which left Evans with inadequate means for isolating the illocutionary act from the perlocutionary in his original work. As a result, the way in which illocutions mark out self-involvement in a Wittgensteinian 'logical' sense becomes blurred with effective self-involvement in a perlocutionary sense. Wanting to stress the successful effect of a speech act as more important than its logical grammar, Evans may thus have mistakenly concluded that psychological concerns must overrule linguistic ones rather than acknowledging their different spheres of relevance in the hermeneutical task.

Finally Evans concedes too much, perhaps in part because he wishes to make his 'modified empiricism' carry a hermeneutical burden it was not designed to bear. The kinds of clarification and explanation provided by self-involvement as a speech-act mechanism in the public domain remain significant and helpful even if they do not resolve all existential concerns, valid or invalid. Since in fact I do not think that the turn to the pre-linguistic in Evans's work represents a sustainable step forward, for the various reasons discussed in earlier chapters concerning the nature of mental dispositions, a stronger conclusion may be maintained: that self-involvement as a hermeneutical category operating in intersubjective illocutionary acts is not significantly compromised by Evans's advocacy of existentialist anthropology as a better way.

[43] Evans, *Faith, Authenticity and Morality*, 261.
[44] Evans, *Faith, Authenticity and Morality*, 262.
[45] Although, ironically, it is close to the changes urged by Stagaman in his review of Evans's earlier work, who wanted a more Heideggerian-style mysticism in his self-involvement; Stagaman, '"God" in Analytic Philosophy', 835–8.

§3.3 Conclusion: the elements of a hermeneutic of self-involvement

The Logic of Self-Involvement remains remarkable for the extent to which Evans was able to work with the new concepts of speech act theory and attempt a broad application of them to significant aspects of biblical language. Handicapped as he was by the fact that most of what would now be regarded as received wisdom in speech act theory was unavailable to him, in particular Searle's reorganisation of the illocutionary-perlocutionary distinction, he nevertheless grasped the nettle of providing an account of biblical language which was both cognitive *and* functional. The conceptual difficulties of articulating such a position are manifest in the various tensions running through his account, as I have shown. It is perhaps not entirely surprising then that his awareness of the problems of articulating a *logical* form of self-involvement finally drew him away from the idea that linguistic analysis really explains anything at all.[46]

However, I have argued that while Evans's later work cannot be seen simply as a disavowal of his earlier position, it does represent an over-compensation for his earlier reliance on forms of self-involvement which could be demarcated entirely and adequately in logico-linguistic terms. Without suggesting that existential concerns are unimportant, I do argue that taking them on board represents a broadening of the inquiry which does not jeopardise the original idea of self-involvement as it arises in the performance of speech acts. If we read Evans's insights while keeping in view a spectrum of strong and weak construals, we can escape the potential polarisation between fact-stating and rapportive language.

With this in mind, I judge that Evans's work on self-involvement can still be pursued with profit today, independently of his own later modifications and changes of emphasis. In particular, its elucidation of self-involvement as a speech act category, which draws on the multifaceted nature of the speaking agent's investment in extra-linguistic states of affairs, models a non-reductive form of self-involvement which occurs in the interpersonal/public domain. In short, Evans provides us with the elements of a hermeneutic of self-involvement.

---

[46] It would doubtless be of little interest to him to think that his approach could make some useful points about implied readers.

§4 After Evans: Self-Involvement as a Hermeneutical Tool in Biblical Interpretation

Donald Evans's work has been more honoured in the breach than in the observance. G. B. Caird was convinced that it had the potential to be an enormously fruitful analytical tool for tackling the essentially hermeneutical problem of unlocking central biblical ideas in a way which *involves* the Bible in the life of the reader, but he did not live long enough to do more than sketch out this view in his last complete book, *The Language and Imagery of the Bible*.[47] I have also noted above Anthony Thiselton's use of Evans's ideas. To the limited extent that speech act theory has been utilised in biblical interpretation, *The Logic of Self-Involvement* has at least been noted, but frequently with no substantial engagement with its ideas.

Some recognition of self-involvement has been present in more general discussions of religious language;[48] and the idea of onlooks, or its later development into a full theory of analogy, finds obvious points of contact between self-involvement and works which self-consciously use the idea of construal, as noted in chapter 4 above. Here it is not my intention to provide a full catalogue of writers who have made use in some way of an idea of self-involvement. Rather I choose to focus on perhaps the only two book-length studies to have made significant use of the concept in biblical interpretation, in each case along with a broader appeal to speech act theory and its concerns: Timothy Polk on Jeremiah and Dietmar Neufeld on 1 John.

---

[47] Cf. Caird, *Language and Imagery of the Bible*, ch. 1 (7–36). Caird's oral comments explicitly to this effect, and dating back to his teaching in the late 1960s, are recorded in Thiselton, *New Horizons*, 16, but it must be noted that his posthumously published *New Testament Theology* (ed. L. D. Hurst), Oxford: Clarendon Press, 1994, is striking in its lack of any mention at all of such an approach. Evans shared with Caird both a Canada and an Oxford connection; credits him on *Logic of Self-Involvement*, 9; and contributed an article to the Caird Festschrift: 'Academic Scepticism, Spiritual Reality and Transfiguration', in L. D. Hurst and N. T. Wright (eds), *The Glory of Christ in the New Testament: Studies in Christology in Memory of George Bradford Caird*, Oxford: Clarendon Press, 1987, 175–86; reprinted as 'Spiritual Reality, Academic Skepticism, and Transfiguration', in Evans, *Spirituality and Human Nature*, 253–66.

[48] See, for instance, Dallas M. High, *Language, Persons, and Belief: Studies in Wittgenstein's* Philosophical Investigations *and Religious Uses of Language*, New York: Oxford University Press, 1967, which I discuss in ch. 6.

§4.1 Timothy Polk: self-involvement and self-constitution

Polk has authored two very different works, both of which make conscious use of a hermeneutic of self-involvement: his Yale Ph.D. thesis, published in 1984 as *The Prophetic Persona*,[49] and his more recent *The Biblical Kierkegaard*.[50] The former is more exegetical, while the latter, although very different in disciplinary orientation, retains a strong exegetical interest.[51]

The particular contribution of Polk's study of Jeremiah's 'language of the self' is in its attention to what I shall term the 'non-referential "I" of self-involvement'. Reflecting the book's origins as a Yale thesis, and in particular the influence of Paul Holmer, Polk seeks to demonstrate how the self which is constructed by Jeremiah's first-person language serves hermeneutically to mediate between the text and the reader, as a personal enactment of a corporate relationship between God and his people. Speaking of the textual self as a 'persona', Polk argues that

> The analysis of the persona's first-person speech will show that 'personal religion', in the sense of 'individual fellowship with God', is *assumed* by the text, not argued or justified as something new and unheard of, and moreover . . . the prophet's person is always depicted in terms of his vocation, which is fully corporate in orientation.[52]

The key to Polk's hermeneutic is in successive chapters with titles including the phrases 'The Language of the Self' and 'The Enactment of Identity'. In the former he discusses the metaphor of the heart, and takes to task exegetes who have proposed a literally orientated treatment of such language as reflecting contemporary thought of the physical 'heart' which literally grounds metaphors of the self. Rather, he argues for a sensitivity

---

[49] Timothy Polk, *The Prophetic Persona: Jeremiah and the Language of the Self* (JSOTS 32), Sheffield: JSOT Press, 1984.

[50] Timothy Houston Polk, *The Biblical Kierkegaard: Reading by the Rule of Faith*, Macon, GA: Mercer University Press, 1997.

[51] Polk's Kierkegaard draws together many of the themes of my own study: 'His is a speech-act hermeneutic that grounds itself non-foundationally in the canon', with more than a passing nod to the work of Stanley Fish (Polk, *Biblical Kierkegaard*, 4, 7–10). It is perhaps debatable just how far Polk does justice to Kierkegaard theologically, and, in so far as the book is relevant to my own argument, my critique would be along the same lines as with his Jeremiah book, discussed above.

[52] Polk, *Prophetic Persona*, 13.

to 'the logic of certain kinds of self-referential language', by which he means that the 'I' in many significant first-person utterances is a subject which emerges out of commanding its responsible use and 'does not refer to, name, or identify something'.[53] He then puts this concept to work in an analysis of 'heart' language in Jeremiah 4. The appeal of 4:4, for instance, he represents as the appeal for the people to return to Yhwh, make a fresh beginning with him, and 'thereby participate in his purpose and promise, or . . . leave their hearts unaltered, permitting their humanity to wither and losing themselves in divine judgment'.[54] Language games such as pledging and lamenting 'do not describe a condition so much as enact one'.[55] In Polk's words, the text 'shows the self to be the achievement of the responsible, first-person use of the language of the heart' and suggests that the biblical text, 'by delineating a range of behaviour regarded as essential to a proper relation to God . . . illustrates what it means to have a self'.[56]

Polk pursues this line of approach through lengthy exegeses of the so-called confessions of Jeremiah, and various other significant autobiographical passages, in order to show that the book of Jeremiah, by way of this prophetic self-involvement in the language of prayer and lament, 'intends its representation of the prophetic self "be used as an indirect route of insight for others" and that it eventuates in the rendering of a persona "molded by God"'.[57] In a concluding chapter he offers suggestions for how his approach fits with a more general account of the role of Scripture in the formation of identity.[58]

The Prophetic Persona is a helpful analysis of first-person language in biblical texts, and clearly demonstrates the difference it makes to interpret such texts within a coherent under-

---

[53] Polk, *Prophetic Persona*, 26 and 184 n. 12. He is following here Wittgenstein, *Philosophical Investigations*, §138, and in particular the illuminating essay of Paul Holmer, 'Wittgenstein and the Self', in Richard H. Bell and Ronald E. Hustwit, *Essays on Kierkegaard & Wittgenstein: On Understanding the Self*, Wooster, OH: College of Wooster, 1978, 10–31, who writes 'the "self" is a logical concept; it plays a role in the logic of language and of world . . . It is there necessarily, not in virtue of observation' (18).

[54] Polk, *Prophetic Persona*, 45.

[55] Polk, *Prophetic Persona*, 46.

[56] Polk, *Prophetic Persona*, 47, 57.

[57] Polk, *Prophetic Persona*, 169, quoting here Sallie McFague TeSelle, *Speaking in Parables: A Study in Metaphor and Theology*, Philadelphia: Fortress Press, 1975, 169.

[58] These concerns are taken up more fully in his *Biblical Kierkegaard*.

standing of the self and self-involvement. Polk provides many useful insights concerning the way in which speech act texts such as oaths, and performative utterances such as 'Correct me, O Lord' and 'We set our hope in thee' operate on a self-involving level with lifestyle implications which underwrite the non-referential self of such texts.[59] Indeed his focus on the 'non-referential "I" of self-involvement' is perhaps the major hermeneutical contribution of the book.

My reservation concerning his proposal derives from its eclectic philosophical orientation. Polk's account of the self is strongly Wittgensteinian, and he clearly combines this with a sure grasp of the relevant speech-act dynamics of performative utterances, making brief reference to both Austin and Evans in the process.[60] Nevertheless, his reading of Wittgenstein, perhaps reflecting something of the Yale provenance of the thesis, sees the non-referential 'self' as constructed through successful performance of the speech acts: 'People come to be who they are through their actions, and by their actions they are known.'[61] The Jeremiah of the text is therefore constructed as a 'persona', a 'literary-theological construct' who exists in the text's 'explicative sense' rather than its 'historical reference'.[62] From a speech act point of view, it does not seem to me necessary to go down this route, and the concept of Jeremiah's *persona* being a mediating presence between an actual Yhwh and actual readers may be one subtlety too many. Assuming, then, that one does not let this point detain us, Polk's work on self-*constitution* may profitably be transposed to the speech-act key of self-*involvement* and taken as a particularly clear example of the possibilities inherent in such a hermeneutic.

The final speech act approach to exegesis which we shall consider raises similar questions. The prevalence of this issue in

[59] Polk, *Prophetic Persona*, 39–40 on oaths (cf. 191 n. 13: 'The persistence into our own day of oath-taking in various non-Semitic cultures would be evidence in favor of the temporally and culturally *un*bound quality of this conception of the self'); and 167–9 on 'Self-Constitution and the Language of the Heart'.

[60] Polk, *Prophetic Persona*, 22–4, 26, 30 and 184 n. 12 on Wittgensteinian ideas; Austin and Evans are noted at 179, n. 28, but 'performative' is a major category throughout.

[61] Polk, *Prophetic Persona*, 38, with reference to Hans W. Frei, *The Identity of Jesus Christ: The Hermeneutical Bases of Dogmatic Theology*, Philadelphia: Fortress Press, 1975, 42–4, 91–4.

[62] Polk, *Prophetic Persona*, 8–10. Frei's influence is of course in, with and under such a claim.

the available literature is just one indication of why I have devoted so much attention to the implications of speech act theory for construction-orientated approaches in earlier chapters.

§4.2 *Dietmar Neufeld:* Reconceiving Texts as Speech Acts

Dietmar Neufeld's work on 1 John represents the most thorough integration to date of exegetical questions with speech act insights, although as we shall see he views speech act theory, problematically, as providing a way of avoiding insoluble historical-critical questions.[63] Although his book may at first glance look like precisely the kind of 'speech act criticism' which I have suggested should be avoided, in fact he only reads certain passages of 1 John in terms of speech act theory (in particular the prologue, the 'slogans of the opponents', the warnings about antichrists, and the 'confessions and denials'), and thus in practice he does restrict his focus to strong illocutions.[64] Indeed, *Reconceiving Texts as Speech Acts* is in particular an exemplary display of the significance of self-involvement as a hermeneutical category. Even so, he makes the same move as Polk in blurring the line between self-involvement and self-constitution, although this time it is Derrida rather than any Yale intratextualist who is offered as support.

Neufeld begins by noting that the traditional questions put to the text of 1 John have been historical, theological and literary-critical, all assuming that the text gains its currency from its historical setting. The problem with this, he argues, has been that so little is known about that historical setting that understanding of the book has been considerably handicapped, remaining at best 'tentative' (36). In a survey of various views of the author and his opponents as they have been characterised in past research, he demonstrates that 'Commentators are preoccupied with the material extrinsic to the text' (6), from Brooke who believed that 1 John was not primarily polemical, but was rather written to edify and teach adherents,[65] through Bultmann's influential view that the text was combating

---

[63] Neufeld, *Reconceiving Texts as Speech Acts.*
[64] Neufeld, *Reconceiving Texts as Speech Acts,* 61–132. Further page references are given in the text.
[65] A. E. Brooke, *The Johannine Epistles* (ICC), Edinburgh: T&T Clark, 1912.

gnosticism, with its Christology that denied that Jesus had come in the flesh,[66] and on to R. E. Brown's major work which saw the book as confronting the result of a schism brought about by a misunderstanding in the Johannine community of the Christology and ethical thrust of the Fourth Gospel.[67] As Neufeld concludes, historical reconstruction has been unable to agree on the nature of the supposed conflict, the identity of the opponents, or what they believed (30). In contrast, he proposes to take seriously both the anonymity and the universal character of 1 John (32). It is against this background that he develops his idea that speech act theory offers an alternative to the need to rely on historical reconstruction, while still doing justice to the directedness of the discourse.

Neufeld's methodology

Neufeld argues that speech and writing are both ways in which people produce meaning and exist in a meaningful universe: 'This connection between linguistic activity (speech) and written discourse embodied in "text", permits viewing "text" as representative of one aspect of embodied communication' (41). In particular, in the case of 1 John: 'The christological confessions and ethical exhortations may be viewed as *written effective acts* intended to change the content of the readers' confessions in order to bring about a proper alignment of speech and conduct' (41). However, the specifics of his appeal to speech act theory, particularly in the work of Austin and Evans, are broadened out by way of the generalised hermeneutical considerations of Ricoeur (whom he follows in seeing the language of the text as 'more than the sum total of the historical processes that brought it into existence' (43)) and, in particular, by his appeal to Derrida for help in 'exploring the constitutive function of language on the writing subject' (50).

Derrida appears to appeal to Neufeld because, at least if read selectively, he 'permits the perception of text as language and at the same time to recognize the act of writing as constitutive'

---

[66] Rudolf Bultmann, *The Johannine Epistles* (Hermeneia), Philadelphia: Fortress Press, 1973 (1967).

[67] Raymond E. Brown SS, *The Epistles of John* (AB 30), London: Geoffrey Chapman, 1982.

(52, *sic*). However this appeal is confessedly a selective use of Derrida, whose broader deconstructive agenda it is to challenge the very possibilities of hearing from any 'author' at all, or at least to challenge any supposed stability in the constituting of a present self. If Derrida's self is constituted in the text it is because for him textuality suffuses existence, and thus, in a certain sense, 'il n'y a pas d'hors text'.[68] Neufeld claims to be fully aware of the dangers of appealing to Derrida at this point (51–2) but in my judgment his appeal still sits uneasily with his own intention of reading 1 John.

It seems that Neufeld already has in his sights the conclusion he wants to reach: namely, that Austin's speech act theory will work well on 1 John if it can be adapted to allow for a text where the author is historically hidden; and Derrida has a view of textuality which fits hand-in-glove with a hidden author; and therefore he chooses to appeal to them both under the rubric of 'new understandings of textuality'. I have argued at length in earlier chapters that this is mistaken. Speech act theory is appropriate to certain kinds of self-involving texts. At the risk of over-simplification: it does not offer a new understanding of textuality, but clarifies what textuality always was. Where illocutions necessarily draw their currency from the extra-linguistic world, anonymity is actually a problem for Neufeld. However, I have my doubts that Neufeld's method is all that he claims it to be for, on turning to a careful reading of the exegesis of 1 John later in the book, one discovers the unavoidable postulation of some kind of (admittedly vague) historical context as a necessary presupposition of articulating just what illocutions are rendered in the text in the first place. In fact, since he does focus on precisely such texts as first-person pledges of witness or testifying, and does not in practice propose a speech act reading as a form of stylistics or 'criticism', his claim to have appropriated a new understanding of textuality appears to play no actual role in his

---

[68] Jacques Derrida, *Of Grammatology* (trans. Gayatri C. Spivak), Baltimore: Johns Hopkins University Press, 1975, 55; translated, perhaps misleadingly, as 'there is nothing outside the text'. I am aware of the complexity of pressing this one phrase into service as any kind of summary of Derrida's thought (the 'slogans in search of an author' approach rightly criticised by Christopher Norris, 'Of the Apopleptic Tone Recently Adopted in Philosophy', in idem, *Reclaiming Truth: Contributions to a Critique of Cultural Relativism*, Durham: Duke University Press, 1996, 222–53; especially 222–30) but whether it is read with or without sympathy it will serve to clarify the commitments of Neufeld's appeal to Derrida here.

study. I therefore propose to leave it to its idle ways and offer a positive evaluation of Neufeld's work.[69]

The prologue (1 John 1:1–4)

Neufeld's study of the prologue to 1 John reveals something of the gap between what he achieves and what he claims to achieve with speech act theory. Discussing the complex grammar and obscure terminology of the prologue, he concludes:

> The evocative language of the preface invites the reader to consider the complete work, including the apparently context-specific passages . . . from an aural, visual, and tactile perspective that is to engage the mouth and bring about appropriate confession and action. The language of the *incipit* with its profusion of sensory verbs shifts the focus away from the task of defining the specific content of the message proclaimed to determining the illocutionary forces involved in the act of proclaiming the message. (65)

This argument occurs in the context of suggesting that 'it is not necessary to determine the historical referent before proceeding with interpretation' (65). However, Neufeld is not arguing against historical reconstruction in general, but against 'particularized reconstructions' (65) as they are proposed in the secondary literature; and he does so on the basis of the nature of the text before us, not the nature of texts per se. It is, in the above quote, *the evocative language of the preface* which invites us into a speech act approach. Further, having argued that the introduction to 1 John serves not as a negative reaction (e.g. against Gnostics) but rather as a positive invitation 'to engage the reader in thoughtful action' (71), Neufeld goes on to show that the issue of authority lies at the heart of 1 John, noting that the writer does not possess authority already, but that the writing 'reflects the need to establish authority' (73). This consideration follows from, among other things, the use of 'we' in 1 John,

---

[69] A further issue which could be discussed along similar lines (cf. ch. 3 §2.3 above) is whether Neufeld subsumes speech act theory under the rubric of rhetorical criticism. For instance, he states that 'at the heart of this approach is the insight of the rhetorical character of historiography and the view that language is a form of action and power' (vii). I do think that he could have more helpfully distinguished between illocutionary uptake as it produces linguistically demarcated forms of self-involvement, and perlocutionary effect, but in his actual exegesis I would say again that rhetoric does not turn out to be his primary category, and that therefore he does not in practice conflate the two approaches.

which he sees as drawing the readers into association with the author's religious and ethical views (73). Here Neufeld has in fact observed something about the historical context of 1 John, something supported by the self-involving nature of the speech acts which the prologue contains. The particular speech acts in question are the historical ones which John (for the sake of argument) has performed: illocutionary acts directed to his original, real listeners (or readers). Establishing authority in the text like this is only an issue in the historical setting. Implied readers, or indeed today's real readers, have the issue of authority recast in terms of, for example, 1 John appearing as part of the biblical canon. It is only on historical grounds that we need to ask how it would have seemed as a document in its own right. Neufeld's analysis of the prologue of 1 John is successful in demonstrating that the author's aim is 'to create a world view wherein the cash value of theology is seen in the ethical conduct of the reader in the *kosmos*' (80) precisely because he is successful in showing what kinds of speech act the author actually performed. Indeed, one of the great merits of his study is to demonstrate how ethical issues are tied to lifestyle issues by using the speech act categories of stance and entailment to look at non-linguistic backing for successful speech acts.

Other sections of 1 John

The general approach to the so-called 'slogans of the opponents' (1 John 1:6, 8, 10; 2:4, 6, 9; 4:20) is to see them as actual 'boasts' of identifiable opponents, even given that John does not identify them. Neufeld argues that they are hypothetical: that they are speech acts depicted in a literary context of shocking disjunction – claiming fellowship with God and yet matching this with a context of darkness (chapter 5; 82–95). Only in such a situation would such speech acts be possible, and hence it is best to see the author as inviting a certain response in terms of behaviour (85). 'Expressed as hypothetical speech acts, the author engages the audience, committing them to a confessional and ethical stance common to them both' (82). This view is supported, for Neufeld, by the considerations of speech act theory: 'The force of the antithetical assertions suggests that in the very act of writing, the author, rather than reporting something is attempting to bring about a state of affairs that represents his own religious and ethical stance' (89).

In suggesting that the antithetical slogans represent the views of the author, and that his point is to draw out the ethical consequences involved in each, rather than to confront any sayings of his opponents, Neufeld is able to deal adequately with the fact that these sayings themselves are hardly objectionable. Since 'the slogans enabled the author to make the world rather than simply mirror it' (95), the only option left for readers unconvinced by the argument is to be out of fellowship with the author (cf. 1 John 1:3). Far from being a debate about doctrine alone, the issue is shown to be one of lifestyle and ethical stance.

1 John 2:18–24 is considered by Neufeld under the heading 'The Last Hour and the Antichrist' (chapter 6; 96–112). The basic thrust of his analysis is similar to the foregoing: the language is general, hypothetical (in this case couched in apocalyptic terms); and the historical questions are not of prime importance. This last point here involves quite a considerable challenge to the received way of reading 1 John, since 2:19 is the key verse in any reconstruction which sees the Johannine community persisting after the departure of the 'secessionists'. Neufeld argues instead that neither the error nor the secessionists are clearly defined, and that it is more to the point to notice the language of denial in 2:22. It could hardly have been the case that the belief that Jesus was not the Christ was a confusing heresy which needed opposing. Rather, we should ask after the nature of the self-involvement required from the passage.

Whereas 1 John 1:1–4 offered a picture of involvement in the witnessing tradition, here the potential error is to separate from that tradition. 'The last hour' indicates 'the beginning of the end during which contradictions in speech and conduct appear acceptable' (104). In this apocalyptic setting: 'even though the enemies of God were to be present everywhere, it should not be difficult for Christians everywhere to recognize them on the basis of their speech' (103). In 2:20 there seems to be a reference to an anointing which gives knowledge to be able to distinguish between truth and evil. A speech act reading suggests 'that the phrase simply sets apart two groups of people where what they confess and know stems from two different sources' (108). In conclusion, Neufeld urges that

The main purpose of 2:18–24 is to alert the reader to the dangerous theological and ethical consequences inherent in rejecting the apocalyptic speech circumstance the author delineates . . . the author reminds and encourages his audience that they cannot be part of a last hour as antichrists if indeed they have been re-constituted by a successful understanding of his speech acts. (110)

Again, it seems to me possible to follow this account without accepting that 2:19 does not refer to a historical event (a historical 'going out from us'). Speech act theory should suggest precisely that the function of the passage can be viewed in its historical context, not that the two should be set in opposition to each other. In a final study, Neufeld looks at the confessions and denials of 1 John 4:1–4, 16 and 5:6 (chapter 7; 113–32), which I shall mention briefly in chapter 6 below on the subject of confession as a speech act.

Concluding reflections

In his conclusion, Neufeld writes:

The power of the written word to transform the orientation of the readers does not lie in carefully argued theological propositions, but in acts of speech with the power to change the self of the speaker . . . 1 John is a communicative event that is written with dramatic sensitivity to reveal the author's religious and ethical stance, and his desire to bring about a change of world view in the reader. (134)

Despite the fact that just a page before this he has reiterated his belief that it is a new approach to textuality which has opened up his analysis, I suggest that the success of what he does is secured otherwise. As he himself notes, the author's intention to produce a change in lifestyle (as indicated, that is, by this speech act analysis) coheres with the content of 1 John in terms of walking in the light, and this is, in the final analysis, more significant than Neufeld allows. The various passages considered benefit from a speech act approach precisely because it is not that false doctrine has been successfully refuted and exposed, but that readers, in the revealed light of God, have been challenged to live in a way that is suitable to being in that light (136).

As with the work of Polk on Jeremiah above, Neufeld offers ample demonstration of a hermeneutic of self-involvement at work, even allowing that he himself would argue for a stronger form of self-constitution than appears to me to be required. Both writers have produced works of methodological complexity, and again it must be said that in terms of book-length studies there is little else that makes sustained use of speech act theory as a framework for a hermeneutic of self-involvement. The studies in this chapter on Evans, Polk and Neufeld have moved the discussion beyond the level of clarifying speech act theory itself, and towards the task of utilising it in the interpretation of biblical texts. I now attempt to draw together their various emphases, before proceeding to further speech-act studies of New Testament texts.

§5 Toward a Hermeneutic of Self-Involvement

The discussion thus far suggests the following key elements of a hermeneutic of self-involvement: first, the usefulness of being able to distinguish between illocution and perlocution, with the resulting distinction between brute and institutional fact and its implications for constructive models of reality; secondly, the significance of construal and its mediating role between the subjective and the objective; thirdly, the nature of text as communicative act; fourthly the locating of significant personal characteristics such as 'mental states' as accessible by public criteria in terms of stance and entailed commitment in the public domain; and fifthly, linked to this, the value of understanding the 'I' of self-involvement in various non-referential ways, without at the same time adopting a view of the self as simply constructed. All of these will recur in subsequent chapters.

§5.1 Aspects of self-involvement in interpreting New Testament speech acts

The remainder of our study will be given over to the task of utilising the conceptual apparatus of speech act theory and self-involvement in addressing various issues of New Testament interpretation. In particular, I choose three different kinds of speech act for detailed consideration: the confessing of one's faith; the forgiving of another's sin; and the multi-valent speech act of teaching, which will raise in miniature many of the broader concerns of how speech act theory sheds light on the workings of religious language. Indeed I focus on teaching precisely in order to address some of the issues concerning institutional facts, and their creation and maintenance, as significant aspects of New Testament interpretation. Teaching proves to be one of the clearest speech acts for illuminating this approach to the construction of reality and its significance. It remains here to add a few words about the choice of confession and forgiveness for the other studies.

It is Terrence Tilley who characterises confession and forgiveness as 'institutionally free' declarative speech acts.[70] We have seen that it is the declarative nature of certain speech acts which makes them particularly interesting for the biblical interpreter. While the self may not be *constituted* by the performance of declarative speech acts, I shall endeavour to show how the self (the speaking subject) is, to use Ricoeur's word, *refigured* in the process of performing such acts. The dynamics of self-involvement are therefore particularly in evidence in the cases of texts of confession and forgiveness. Where confession is one of the few topics to have been considered from such an angle, albeit largely independently of the expectations aroused by speech act theory, forgiveness remains relatively unexplored from this angle. Before turning to these two topics, both aspects of Tilley's characterisation require brief comment.

Declarative speech acts

In part 1 of this study I argued that we do well to follow Jerrold Sadock's approach to classification where 'declarative' speech acts are concerned.[71] Tilley's classification of confession as a 'declarative' rests on his use of the term to characterise the speech act of declaring one's own identity by way of declaring certain shaping autobiographical utterances (statements and commitments) particularly exemplified by Augustine's *Confessions*.[72] In contrast, my focus will be narrower, looking at specific utterances in the New Testament (such as 'Jesus is Lord') which, perhaps precisely because of their more specific nature, serve as much as commissive speech acts of public commitment as they do as declarative speech acts of self-definition. Whichever

---

[70] Tilley, *Evils of Theodicy*, 72.
[71] See ch. 2, §3.2 above.
[72] Tilley, *Evils of Theodicy*, 72–6: 'Augustine is *declaring himself to be who he is*' (72).

emphasis is chosen, the point here is that, following Sadock, the so-called 'declarative illocutionary point' is of a different kind to Searle's other illocutionary points, and in fact what we find in these confessional speech acts is declarative aspects of commissive and assertive speech acts. Thus, in his 'doxological' work of systematics, Geoffrey Wainwright notes that creeds and hymns in the New Testament, which we shall explore as commissives, do indeed serve a similar 'confessional' purpose to that of Augustine's confessions: 'As long as the believer goes on recapitulating his confession, he may be assured of his own identity in the identity of the Christian people.'[73] As we shall see, this declarative purpose of confession need not be set against its commissive aspects.

Thus while Tilley's remarks shape my discussion, I shall not hesitate to call confession and forgiveness commissive speech acts, without thereby intending to obscure their declarative nature.

By way of clarification, I should also add that this broad sense of confession as 'declaring one's own identity in the public domain' can encompass as a special case the act of confessing one's sin, whereby one takes a public stand of responsibility for sin in order to effect a change of identity with respect to it. Although I shall have occasion to mention this in what follows, it is not my primary interest, and the incidental juxtaposition of the terms 'confession' and 'forgiveness' in this study should not be taken to be implying simply the 'confession of sin' in contexts where forgiveness is also at issue.

Institutionally free speech acts

In Tilley's terms, an institutionally free speech act is one which 'can be performed without regard to the person's institutional status or role', in contrast to some status or role requirement within an institution which is necessary for the performance of institutionally bound speech acts.[74] Tilley notes that within his own Catholic context only the pope is authorised to declare official dogma, which is a particularly clear case of an institutionally bound declaration. He analyses baptism as a

---

[73] Geoffrey Wainwright, *Doxology: The Praise of God in Worship, Doctrine and Life*, London: Epworth Press, 1980, 190 (cf. the section entitled 'Creeds and Hymns', 182–217).

[74] Tilley, *Evils of Theodicy*, 33.

slightly more widespread example of an institutionally bound performative.[75]

A 'declarative' which has its world-creating or world-remaking capacity thrown open to all is evidently going to be a speech act of unusual interest: 'Not many of you should become teachers', cautions James (James 3:1), perhaps envisaging the chaos that inevitably follows when social (church) reality is opened up to private reconstruction. But while not all are teachers, all are invited to be confessors: confessing the Christian faith in self-involving acts of confession. Likewise, all are called to mutual forgiveness: declaring the sins of others forgiven and at the same time refiguring the forgiving self.

These chapters are concerned, therefore, with the interpretation of those New Testament texts which indicate the occurrence of just such institutionally free speech acts of self-involvement. In the case of confession the self is situated in a worshipping form of life. With forgiveness, the occasion of the act is harder to define, although it would seem to correspond to an attitude of hope (indeed an eschatological hope, where our present forgiveness draws on the anticipation of future forgiveness), and we perhaps do well to remember that 'hoping' is the only form of life explicitly named as such by Wittgenstein.[76] Teaching, as just suggested, explicitly concerns itself with the constituting and reconstituting of the public domain itself, and presupposes to some (variable) extent the according of some measure of authority to perform such speech acts.

My contention throughout is that the point of such New Testament language as confessing, forgiving or teaching may only be understood with reference to its self-involving nature. The point of such a study, again following Wittgenstein, is not to put forward a *theory* about confession or forgiveness, nor even to *explain* these practices, but rather to get into a position where we can see what it is that actually happens in such cases: 'Nothing is so difficult as doing justice to the facts.'[77] Austin, we recall,

---

[75] Tilley, *Evils of Theodicy*, 47–50; cf. also A. P. Martinich, 'Sacraments and Speech Acts', *Heythrop Journal* 16 (1975), 289–303, 405–17.

[76] Wittgenstein, *Philosophical Investigations*, p. 174.

[77] Ludwig Wittgenstein, 'Remarks on Frazer's *Golden Bough*', now reprinted in idem, *Philosophical Occasions 1912–1951* (eds James Klagge and Alfred Nordmann), Indianapolis and Cambridge: Hackett Publishing Company, 1993, 115–55, here 129 (cf. also 119 on theory and explanation).

described himself as a 'linguistic phenomenologist',[78] and it is my intention to use speech act theory in the same spirit in the chapters which follow.

[78] Cf. Austin, *Philosophical Papers*, 182.

6

The Confession of Faith

§1 Introduction

Confession is one of the few topics to have been explored as a self-involving use of religious language. However, with very few exceptions, such studies have omitted specific consideration of speech act theory.[1] One recent article entitled 'The Hermeneutics of Confessing Jesus as Lord' appeared to understand 'confess' as simply an alternative way of saying 'believe in', and focused entirely on the theological implications of confessional faith for biblical studies.[2] It thus seems fair to say that even if confession has been discussed as a self-involving speech act, this is still not necessarily the natural understanding of it which occurs to readers of the New Testament. Indeed, one of the incidental purposes of this chapter will be to highlight the differing extents to which the speech-act dimension of confession has been understood in the literature.

---

[1] One exception is Colin Brown, 'The Hermeneutics of Confession and Accusation', *CTJ* 30 (1995), 460–71. Confession is also discussed as an aspect of religious language in the speech-act orientated account of James Wm McClendon Jr and James M. Smith, *Convictions*, 62–74. See the brief discussion in ch. 1 above.

[2] Scot McKnight, 'The Hermeneutics of Confessing Jesus as Lord', *Ex Auditu* 14 (1998), 1–17. Likewise the essays gathered in John H. Skilton (ed.), *Scripture and Confession: A Book about Confessions Old and New*, Nutley, NJ: Presbyterian and Reformed Publishing Co., 1973, treat 'confessing' in terms of adhering to a doctrinal standard.

I propose to look at three major aspects of confession as a speech act in the New Testament. First, the need to locate the New Testament examples of confessional speech acts will involve considering the question of the link between the form and the function of confessional utterances, and hence the link between confessional speech acts and credal statements which may be used confessionally. Secondly, I shall examine the dynamics of self-involvement in confessional speech acts. Thirdly, it will then be appropriate to discuss the question of how this speech-act approach bears on the question of the truth of what is confessed. Before turning to these topics, I begin the chapter with the particular example of the confession in 1 Corinthians 12:1–3, in order to highlight the kinds of issues involved in a speech-act analysis.

§1.1 An introductory example: 1 Corinthians 12:1–3

1 Corinthians 12:3 provides us with an example of what is often called the earliest Christian confession: 'Jesus is Lord.'[3] This verse may serve here as an introductory example of the practical application of a hermeneutic of self-involvement to the task of biblical interpretation.[4] Paul writes:

> I want you to understand that no one speaking by the Spirit of God ever says 'Let Jesus be cursed!' and no one can say 'Jesus is Lord' except by the Holy Spirit. (1 Cor. 12:3, NRSV)

Debate around this verse has often focused on the possible situations in which such an utterance as 'Let Jesus be cursed' could have been made. Fee highlights the oddity of the situation: it is hard to imagine that a Christian would actually have cursed Jesus in a public Christian context, and yet, if they had done so, it seems odd that Paul's 'response' here should be so casual and 'totally noncombative'.[5]

---

[3] Cf. Romans 10:9–10; Philippians 2:11 and Acts 2:36. For brief introductions to early confessions, see Ethelbert Stauffer, *New Testament Theology* (trans. John Marsh), London: SCM Press, 1955 (1941), 233–57 on 'The Creeds of the Primitive Church'; John H. Leith, 'Creeds, Early Christian', in *ABD*, 1:1203–6; and Ralph P. Martin, *New Testament Foundations*. Vol. 2, Grand Rapids: Eerdmans, and Carlisle: Paternoster Press, revised edition, 1986 (1978), 268–75.

[4] See the introductory use of this verse also in Thiselton, *New Horizons*, 283 (cf. 283–91).

[5] Gordon D. Fee, *The First Epistle to the Corinthians* (NICNT), Grand Rapids: Eerdmans, 1987, 579.

Despite the postulation of various historical contexts in which Paul's addressees might conceivably have cursed Jesus, including a Gnostic separation between worshipping Christ and cursing the earthly Jesus,[6] or the view that the curse was uttered under duress in face of persecution and could be recanted later,[7] it seems right to follow the majority of commentators who urge that the context is that of Christian worship, and that the reference is either hypothetical, or is to curses uttered in the readers' pre-Christian pasts, with the point being that 'ecstasy alone is no criterion for the working of the spirit'.[8]

Of course other historical reconstructions lead to slightly different views of the issue.[9] Thus Bassler, for instance, makes a case for saying that the historical inquiry, while valuable, is unable to settle the issues of primary interest, which revolve instead around the role of this verse in the literary and logical flow of the argument in 1 Corinthians 12–14.[10] She views verse 3 not as a test for genuine Christian confession, which might appear to remove it from the flow of the argument, but as an analogy to verse 2 which speaks of the pagans being led astray: here in verse 3, says Bassler, Paul makes the analogous point that the Christian confession of faith is the work of the controlling presence of the Spirit, in contrast perhaps to Paul's own experience that the cursing of Jesus was

---

[6] Notably W. Schmithals, *Gnosticism in Corinth: An Investigation of the Letters to the Corinthians*, Nashville: Abingdon Press, 1971 (1956). See the refutation of B. A. Pearson, *The Pneumatikos-Psychikos Terminology in 1 Corinthians: A Study in the Theology of the Corinthian Opponents of Paul and Its Relation to Gnosticism* (SBLDS 12), Missoula, MT: Scholars Press, 1973, 47–50; and his background work on Gnosticism itself in idem, 'Did the Gnostic Curse Jesus?', *JBL* 86 (1967), 301–5.

[7] See here the works of Vernon Neufeld and Oscar Cullmann, both entitled *The Earliest Christian Confessions*, discussed later in the chapter (see n. 36 below).

[8] Hans Conzelmann, *1 Corinthians* (Hermeneia), Philadelphia: Fortress Press, 1975 (1969), 206; similarly Fee, *First Epistle to the Corinthians*, 581; C. K. Barrett, *A Commentary on the First Epistle to the Corinthians* (BNTC), London: A&C Black, ²1971 (1968), 279.

[9] Or indeed to wholly different views, such as Van Unnik's idea that *anathema* in v. 3 draws its meaning from passages like Romans 9:3 and Deuteronomy 13:13–18, and refers to the complete destruction of a cursed one in order to blot out the wrath of God; thus with a positive meaning when applied to Jesus. This must finally be judged intriguing but with insufficient evidence; W. C. Van Unnik, 'Jesus: Anathema or Kyrios (1 Cor. 12:3)', in Barnabas Lindars and Stephen Smalley (eds), *Christ and Spirit in the New Testament (FS C. F. D. Moule)*, Cambridge: Cambridge University Press 1973, 113–26.

[10] Jouette M. Bassler, '1 Cor 12:3 – Curse and Confession in Context', *JBL* 101 (1982), 415–18, here 415.

a part of his pre-conversion life. Commentators divide on this possibility.[11]

Nevertheless, although one may overplay the point, Bassler's suggestion that historical reconstruction is not the whole story is relevant, but not because it needs to be contrasted with a literary approach, but rather because the key point in the passage is the difference between *saying* 'Jesus is Lord' and *confessing* 'Jesus is Lord'. That confession is a strongly self-involving speech act and thus must be understood differently from the weaker 'saying' is the key point at issue. Not all commentators observe this distinction, and even among those who do so its significance is not necessarily noted. Thus Witherington, for instance, mentions this contrast but discusses it only long enough to demarcate confession as requiring 'the prompting of the Holy Spirit in the human heart'.[12] True as this may be, it misses the speech act concerned.

The speech act of confession grounds the utterance of the words in the lifestyle which gives them backing. To confess Jesus is therefore to stake one's claim in the public domain as a follower of Jesus. Its criteria are public: 'Jesus is Lord' said by someone who never makes reference to Jesus in any other instance is an infelicitous confession. It is thinking along this line which leads Holtz to suggest that the idea represented by 'cursing Jesus' is that of living a life which rejects Jesus: the utterance is indicative of the lifestyle.[13] Helpful as this is, it perhaps goes too far in replacing entirely the speech act with its lifestyle implications. The notion that the utterance is self-involving was brought out by Weiss around the turn of the century, discussing the early development of 'The Christ-Faith'. His discussion of what it means to confess with one's mouth that Jesus is Lord suggests that 'What it means in a practical religious sense will best be made clear through the correlative concept of "servant" or "slave" of Christ.'[14] Weiss notes that

---

[11] 'More ingenious than realistic', says Fee (*First Epistle to the Corinthians*, 581, n. 51 (e)); while Ben Witherington III, *Conflict and Community in Corinth: A Socio-Rhetorical Commentary on 1 and 2 Corinthians*, Carlisle: Paternoster Press, 1995, 256, finds it 'quite plausible'.

[12] Witherington, *Conflict and Community in Corinth*, 257.

[13] T. Holtz, 'Das Kennzeichen des Geistes (1 Kor. xii. 1-3)', *NTS* 18 (1971/2), 365-76.

[14] Johannes Weiss, *Earliest Christianity: A History of the Period A.D. 30-150. Volume II*, New York: Harper & Brothers, 1959 (1937), 458.

such a confession of faith does not rely on any special 'Christian language': Paul 'takes over the language of the Hellenistic community' but it is the use to which it is put which marks out the speech act of Christian confession.[15] Although scholars do not necessarily follow Weiss concerning the specific background of κύριος language, the point that normal language is taken over into a particular self-involving confession is well made, and the idea that confessing 'Jesus is Lord' carries with it the idea of attributing servanthood or slavehood to oneself is made by writers as diverse as Bultmann and Fitzmyer.[16]

The key question suggested by a speech act approach is whether such a confession is more than this. Does the point made by Weiss and Bultmann exhaust the significance of confessing Jesus as Lord? Here Fitzmyer is more helpful. On the one hand, as he notes, confessing Jesus as Lord (Romans 10:9) is a part of the ὑπακοὴ πίστεως (Romans 1:5; 16:26) which stands as the goal of God's work in the individual, and which Fitzmyer suggests is best translated as 'the commitment of faith'. Thus, 'Involved in the affirmation that the Christian makes, Jesus is Lord, is the entire concept of Christian faith, as Paul sees it.'[17] On the other hand, Fitzmyer makes several points concerning the attribution of κύριος to Jesus as a result of the early Christian understanding that Jesus was risen from the dead, noting for instance that in Philippians 2:6–11, where Lordship language is explicitly set in parallel with δοῦλος language, the attribution of the exalted name κύριος to Jesus follows on from certain events which have occurred concerning Jesus' death and resurrection.[18] Although Fitzmyer does not put the point this way, at issue are the non-linguistic states of affairs which under-write the strong illocutionary act of confession. The self is *involved* with states of affairs, and not simply *constituted* by the adoption of some particular attitude.

---

[15] Weiss, *Earliest Christianity*, 458.

[16] Rudolf Bultmann, *Theology of the New Testament*, vol. 1, London: SCM Press, 1965 (1952), 330–3; Joseph A. Fitzmyer SJ, 'The Semitic Background of the New Testament *Kyrios*-Title', *A Wandering Aramean: Collected Aramaic Essays* (SBLMS 25), Missoula, MT: Scholars Press, 1979, 115–42, especially 130–2.

[17] Fitzmyer, 'Semitic Background of the New Testament *Kyrios*-Title', 132. See also Joseph A. Fitzmyer SJ, *Romans* (AB 33), London: Chapman, 1993, 112–13.

[18] Fitzmyer, 'Semitic Background of the New Testament *Kyrios*-Title', 127–32. The Philippians 2 passage is considered more fully below.

The grammar of confession, therefore, indicates that the self-involving commitment of confession cannot be denied under the influence of 'the Spirit of God', and indeed Paul's point in 1 Corinthians 12:3 is precisely that one cannot make such a self-involving commitment 'except by the Holy Spirit'. Noting that the confession is a speech act combines an understanding of the content of the utterance with both the lifestyle implications of uttering it and the states of affairs which it presupposes. This is the dual focus of a hermeneutic of self-involvement which we shall be considering repeatedly in this and succeeding chapters, and the task of clarifying the kinds of states of affairs which are relevant for the speech act of confession will be one of the goals of this chapter.

§2 Confession and Confessional Forms: Form and Function

Norman Shepherd notes correctly that 'While it is necessary to distinguish between confession as confession of faith and as confessional document, it is at the same time true that confession of faith points the way to confessional documents.'[19] Indeed, from New Testament times onwards, confession has often been, as a matter of contingent historical fact, the adoption of a set form of words. Confession has often, therefore, taken the form of reciting a 'creed' or more generally a song or hymn, addressed to God or Christ. It is important to be clear about terminology here. Leith makes the point that 'Generally the word "creed" is given to the short and brief statements of the ancient catholic church . . . The comprehensive Reformed statements of faith are usually labelled confessions. However, there is no established terminology.'[20] As we shall see, confession as a speech act must be kept distinct from confession as a set form of words, not because there is no link between them, but because otherwise one risks blurring the important distinction between the *form* and the *function* of any particular passage. I shall attempt to demonstrate here that the criteria for identifying any particular

[19] Norman Shepherd, 'Scripture and Confession', in Skilton (ed.), *Scripture and Confession*, 1–30, here 13.

[20] Leith, 'Creeds, Early Christian', 1204; cf. Philip Schaff, *The Creeds of Christendom, with a History and Critical Notes: Vol. 1 The History of the Creeds*, Grand Rapids: Baker, 1983 (1931), 3–7.

literary form (creed, hymn . . .) in the biblical text will overlap with, but not necessarily match, those for identifying confessional statements.

In general terms this observation cuts at the root of form criticism with its preoccupation with locating literary forms in short segments of text, whether they be preliterary (i.e. oral tradition) or simply taken over from earlier written sources. Form criticism has often seemed to suppose that knowing the form of a text settles the question of its function. In contrast, speech act theory suggests that the link, which it affirms to some extent, is more flexible.[21]

On precisely this issue, Stephen Fowl has addressed the problems of assuming a direct link between form and function with respect to the so-called christological hymns in Philippians 2, Colossians 1 and 1 Timothy 3. The function of these passages is not simply settled by describing them as hymns, both because the literary category of 'New Testament hymn' might not be equated with our contemporary idea of 'hymn', and because an analysis of the content of these passages reveals their particular function as providing exemplars of the ethical life modelled in Jesus. In New Testament times, in contrast, the standard function of a ὕμνος was as an expression of praise to a god, and this is clearly not the purpose of these Pauline passages.[22]

On the second of these two points, Fowl follows Thomas Kuhn's idea of an exemplar ('a concrete formulation or experiment which is recognized and shared by all scientists') and applies it to the use made by Paul of the figure of Christ:

> Paul's aim is to present each community with a story of its founder – a story to which they are committed by virtue of their community membership – and then to spell out the implications of this story for their everyday faith and practice.[23]

---

[21] Studies of form criticism now generally recognise that it needs nuancing; e.g. John Muddiman, 'Form Criticism', in *DBI*, 240–3. The literature on the need to move beyond form criticism is vast; cf. the scepticism about scholarly confidence in form-critical conclusions evinced by M. D. Hooker, 'On Using the Wrong Tool', *Theology* 75 (1972), 570–81, and G. N. Stanton, 'Form Criticism Revisited', in Morna Hooker and Colin Hickling (eds), *What about the New Testament? Essays in Honour of Christopher Evans*, London: SCM Press, 1975, 13–27.

[22] Stephen E. Fowl, *The Story of Christ in the Ethics of Paul: An Analysis of the Function of the Hymnic Material in the Pauline Corpus* (JSNTS 36), Sheffield: JSOT Press, 1990, 31–2.

[23] Fowl, *Story of Christ*, 93, 199.

That one should choose to call such passages *hymns* is therefore a matter of convenience, but such a term may be misleading if it calls to mind our contemporary idea of a 'hymn'.

Thus regarding the first of his major claims, Fowl delimits his own study of the three Pauline passages mentioned not by a reconstruction of some supposedly pre-existent hymn, but by the recognition of common characteristics of the passages which justify taking them collectively. In each of these three cases he locates 'a distinctive passage poetically describing certain aspects of Christ's work',[24] but denies that this entitles one to go beyond the formal observation to a characterisation of the passage as a hymn.[25]

Fowl's distinction between form and function, made with a passing appeal to precisely the consideration of speech act theory,[26] is successful in clarifying what is at issue in looking for confessional statements in the biblical text. Although his own interests lie elsewhere, his analysis raises the question of much of the *purpose* of work on hymnic and credal passages in the New Testament, to which we now turn.

§2.1 The significance of confessional forms

Several writers have considered the question of the literary form of confessional materials in the New Testament, and all appear to have struggled with questions of preliterary existence and criteria for identifying literary forms. W. H. Gloer provides a survey of major writers who have given explicit criteria for their work on identifying hymnic forms.[27] He identifies up to 16 possible criteria for hymns and homologies, including amongst others:

- the presence of a quotation particle (e.g. ὅτι, as at 1 Corinthians 15:3–5)

---

[24] Fowl, *Story of Christ*, 25.
[25] Fowl, *Story of Christ*, 16, and ch. 2, 'What Is a Hymn?', 31–45.
[26] Fowl, *Story of Christ*, 42.
[27] Cf. J. T. Sanders, *The New Testament Christological Hymns* (SNTSMS 15), Cambridge: Cambridge University Press 1971; Ralph P. Martin, *A Hymn of Christ: Philippians 2:5–11 in Recent Interpretation and in the Setting of Early Christian Worship*, Downers Grove: IL., 1997 (= revised edition of idem, *Carmen Christi: Philippians ii.5–11 in . . .*, Grand Rapids: Eerdmans, 1983 (1967)); idem, *Worship in the Early Church*, Grand Rapids: Eerdmans, 1974 (1964); Stauffer, *New Testament Theology*, 233–57; R. H. Fuller, *The Christology of the New Testament*, London: Collins, 1965.

- the presence of certain introductory formulae (e.g. καθώς γέγραπται at Romans 8:36)
- syntactical disturbance (e.g. at 1 Timothy 3:16)
- stylistic and linguistic differences (e.g. rare language, as at Romans 1:3)
- parallelism (e.g. Ephesians 2:14–16)
- arrangement in strophes (e.g. Philippians 2:5–11)[28]

However, for all the value of Gloer's perceptive summary of different scholarly criteria, it is not at all apparent that one can reasonably talk about criteria for two quite different categories all at one level. If homologies and hymns overlap, as Gloer suggests they do, it is not because they have certain criteria in common and others not, but because hymns may be used confessionally, and confessions may be hymnic, but the criteria for each are operative on distinct levels.

This confusion has various implications. Gloer begins his article by stating that the preliterary forms of Christian tradition provide valuable material for reconstruction of the worship of the early church, but it is evident that none of his criteria delineate *preliterary* tradition as such.[29] In a rather unfortunate but perhaps significant turn of phrase he actually suggests that his criteria are tools to help 'scholars wishing to *remove* the homologies and hymns . . . found in the literature of the NT'.[30] Discussion of the use to which Paul puts what may or may not be pre-Pauline traditions continues, but its significance must lie more in the realm of assessing how Paul argues and makes his case in the light of prior traditions, rather than any insight into the pre-Pauline settings of those prior traditions.[31]

While the *Sitz im Leben* of an early Christian confession is a matter of some interest, which I take up below, it does not

---

[28] W. Hullitt Gloer, 'Homologies and Hymns in the New Testament: Form, Content and Criteria for Identification', *PRS* 11 (1984), 115–32, here 124–9. See the similar list gleaned from similar sources by Markus Barth, *Ephesians 1–3* (AB 34), New York: Doubleday, 1974, 7–8, in his section on 'Hymns and Traditional Material' (6–10).

[29] Gloer, 'Homologies and Hymns', 115; and thus rejecting his claim on 130.

[30] Gloer, 'Homologies and Hymns', 130, emphasis added. He surely meant 'isolate' or 'locate'.

[31] See the recent work of Anders Eriksson, *Traditions as Rhetorical Proof: Pauline Argumentation in 1 Corinthians* (Coniectanea Biblica NT 29), Stockholm: Almqvist & Wiksell, 1998; with particular reference to 1 Cor. 15:3–5 (86–96); 8:11 and 11:23–25 (97–106); 12:3 and the background of *kyrios* (110–14) and 8:6 (120–6).

follow that the *Sitz im Leben* of a hymn is either illuminating or ever recoverable. This is true especially where we grant Fowl's distinction between ancient and modern senses of 'hymn.' In fact, I want to argue that hymns are significant precisely where they are confessional, because it is the stance of worship with its connotations of testimony and endorsement which bespeaks self-involvement on the part of the author or the 'users' of the text. This is a point about the function of the language and not about its aesthetic quality as hymnic or poetic.

However, even a brief review of the literature suggests that the form/content confusion reduces writers on the New Testament hymns to such bland observations as 'hymns are more easily remembered than abstract statements of truth',[32] or, in one recent survey article, 'Since it is hymnic material, its message would make a greater impact upon the readers.'[33] One has to say that the significance of confessional forms is here entirely eclipsed as a direct result of mistaking the hymnic form itself for evidence of self-involvement. If one eschews the reconstructionist path but stops short of a philosophy of self-involvement then it is not at all clear what point there is to the classification of hymns in the New Testament.

The argument of this section may be viewed as a particular demonstration of my contention in chapter 3 above that speech acts cannot be demarcated reliably by vocabulary considerations and the like. Thus while a dictionary article on ὁμολογέω is of definite use in locating confessional speech acts in the New Testament,[34] we shall find ourselves considering many other texts in the next sections which do not use the word.[35]

§3 Confession as Self-Involvement: Stance and Entailment

In the light of the above discussion, our chosen path must be to look at how the earliest Christian confessions, in the New Testament, are self-involving; that is, how they bring together

---

[32] Cited with approval by Gloer, 'Homologies and Hymns', 121, n. 33, as coming from Donald Guthrie, *New Testament Introduction*, Downers Grove, IL: IVP ³1970, 551, but I can find no trace of this quotation in Guthrie's work or its later edition.

[33] Julie L. Wu in J. L. Wu and S. C. Pearson, 'Hymns, Songs', in *DLNTD*, 520–7, here 522, drawing on Eugene Nida et al., *Style and Discourse*, New York: United Bible Societies, 1983.

[34] For example, Otto Michel, 'ὁμολογέω κτλ', in *TDNT* V (1967), 199–220.

[35] As noted similarly by Norman Shepherd, 'Scripture and Confession', 10.

both the content (what is confessed) and the force or stance with which it is confessed. Two books with the same title, *The Earliest Christian Confessions*, present us with the various strands of historical evidence for how some of these credal affirmations were made,[36] and my thesis is that in so doing such investigations demonstrate precisely the speech act issues involved in 'the language game of confessing one's belief'.[37]

Vernon Neufeld, in his study of the *homologia*, concludes that 'The confession of Jesus as the Christ was in the first instance a personal declaration of faith', as with Peter in Mark 8:29 and more widely in the early church (John 20:31; 1 John 5:1, 5). More broadly, he highlights several likely functions of the confession of faith:

- promoting and preserving faithfulness in times of difficulty (Heb. 4:15; 10:23)
- serving as the basis for the *didache* of the church (Col. 2:6–7; 2 John 7–9)
- serving as a baptismal assent to faith (Acts 8:37;[38] Rom. 10:9; 1 Tim. 6:12; 2 Tim. 2:2; 1 Peter 3:18–22)
- expressing worship in liturgy or hymnody (e.g. Phil. 2:5–11)
- proclaiming the *kerygma* of the early church (Rom. 10:8–9; 2 Cor. 4:5; the *Christos-homologia* with its Jewish relevance in Acts 9:20–22; and the *kyrios-homologia* with its Hellenistic applicability in Acts 11:20)
- polemically combating false ideas (1 Cor. 15:3–5)
- responding to persecution (Matt. 10:32–33)[39]

In many cases, we may note, more than one of these speech acts may be performed at the same time (e.g. worship which is also

---

[36] Vernon H. Neufeld, *The Earliest Christian Confessions* (New Testament Tools and Studies V), Leiden: E. J. Brill, 1963; and Oscar Cullmann, *The Earliest Christian Confessions*, London: Lutterworth Press, 1949 (1943).

[37] To use the title of the study of Sr Mary-John Mananzan OSB, *The 'Language Game' of Confessing One's Belief: A Wittgensteinian-Austinian Approach to the Linguistic Analysis of Creedal Statements* (Linguistische Arbeiten 16), Tübingen: Max Niemeyer Verlag, 1974; cf. also High, *Language, Persons, and Belief*, ch. 6, '"I Believe in . . . ": Creedal and Doctrinal Understanding', 164–84.

[38] We may say here with Kelly that for these purposes it does not matter whether this verse is original or an interpolation; J. N. D. Kelly, *Early Christian Creeds*, London: Longman, ³1972 (1950), 16.

[39] Neufeld, *Earliest Christian Confessions*, 144–6.

proclamatory, or even polemical). In similar vein, Oscar Cullmann's discussion of the 'Circumstances of the Appearance and Employment of the Rules of Faith' argues that it is a mistake to isolate any one external cause as the explanation for particular confessional developments in the earliest days of the Church, but instead proposes 'five simultaneous causes' which 'made necessary the use of a rule of faith':

- baptism and catechumenism
- regular worship (liturgy and preaching)
- exorcism
- persecution
- polemic against heretics

Cullmann allows that while there is no simple link between particular instances of a confessional formula in the New Testament and one of these situations, it is still possible to demonstrate approximate correspondences.[40]

The similarities in these findings match the identical titles of the two books. Neufeld's work is more detailed, in particular tracing the distinctive confessions in the Pauline and Johannine literature (*Kyrios Jesus* and *Christos Jesus* respectively), as well as providing comprehensive surveys of research into the creeds and of the various nuances and differing contexts of the use of the word *homologia* in ancient literature.[41] However, his conclusions are strikingly close to Cullmann's, allowing that he criticises Cullmann for viewing *Kyrios Christos* as the primitive confession without noting the importance of *Kyrios Jesus* for Paul, and of *Christos Jesus* in general.[42]

The key insight of both these studies is that performing an utterance such as 'Jesus is Lord', as it became a standardised formula, counted as the act of committing oneself both to a certain standard (or content) of belief and also to certain future actions. In speech act terms: it counted as the illocutionary act of committing oneself to some future course of action (Searle's definition of a commissive). This self-involving dimension is precisely what is significant about confession.

---

[40] Cullmann, *Earliest Christian Confessions*, 18–19.
[41] Neufeld, *Earliest Christian Confessions*, 13–33; cf. Michel, 'ὁμολογέω κτλ', 200–7.
[42] Neufeld, *Earliest Christian Confessions*, 10.

The variety of life-settings which these studies suggest for the *homologia* indicate a particular utterance serving to *perform* speech acts which are embedded in the non-linguistic world (be it a baptismal setting, or in the face of persecution, and so forth). Credal and confessional statements, therefore, which seem at first sight to be clear examples of statements of truth designed to uphold a particular theological standard, turn out to be prime examples of commissive speech acts. This contrast should not be misunderstood as a simple opposition: it does not indicate that such confessions lack cognitive content, that they are simply statements of existential conviction, for instance, about the value one places on Jesus. The question of 'truth' raised here is important (and we consider it in §5 below) but it should not be allowed to take precedence over the understanding of particular commissive speech acts in the New Testament, as if at the end of the day a speech act approach collapsed back into questions of truth and correspondence after all.

§4 Specific Examples of Confession in Different Forms of Life

In investigating specific examples of confessional affirmations in the New Testament, we must consider the *forms of life* within which these self-involving speech acts find their home. Two considerations urge caution here: the first is the observation of Cullmann's noted above that the causes of particular confessions did not operate in isolation. Secondly, it is worth noting that the majority of elements of the later creeds go back in oral tradition to before the production of most of the New Testament documents. As Cullmann has suggested, the creeds emerge out of a more general attempt to maintain coherence and integrity in the proclamation (in various contexts) of the Christian message (whether it be preaching the *kerygma* or any of the other considerations listed above), and hence it is appropriate that Cullmann's study begins by looking at the emergence of the 'rule of faith':

> The Church had not yet made a choice among Christian works; it had not yet accorded to a small number of them the dignity of Holy Scripture and set them beside the Old Testament. For this reason a *summa fidei* was indispensable.[43]

[43] Cullmann, *Earliest Christian Confessions*, 11.

Of course the very notion of a 'canon' of Holy Scripture is precisely that of a 'rule' or way of measuring what is to be accorded status and what is not. The 'rule of faith' as it developed in the second and third centuries may thus be seen as a transition between the early confessional statements and the later creeds.[44] In itself the rule of faith was never a fixed form of words, and indeed as one traces back the confessions to earlier times there is a clear absence of the characteristic fixed confessions of the later creeds.[45] However, overly precise developmental hypotheses, such as the one proffered by Cullmann himself where a single christological confession becomes bipartite and then tripartite in response to the particular exigencies of Gentile mission or baptismal formulae, tend to overlook the fact that all (or almost all) the elements of the loose oral tradition predate the production of any of the relevant New Testament texts.[46]

With these caveats in mind, we look briefly at some specific examples of confessional speech acts in the New Testament by taking in turn some of the different forms of life evident in the New Testament.

§4.1 *Responses to persecution and heterodoxy*

Adversarial contexts underline clearly the self-involving grammar of confession. It is one thing to discuss what does and does not constitute orthodoxy, and quite another to offer one's personal backing to a statement which will incur consequences of suffering and perhaps even death. Cullmann notes that it is thus essential to consider how the context of persecution shaped the use of the *homologia*.[47] He cites 1 Timothy 6:12 as an example of Timothy being commended for 'making the good confession' in a judicial setting (perhaps even a courtroom), although commentators are by no means agreed about the reference here. While verse 13 appears to compare Timothy's confession with that of Christ under Pilate, prompting Cullmann to support the

---

[44] Frances Young, *The Making of the Creeds*, London: SCM Press, 1991, 8–9.

[45] See especially Kelly, *Early Christian Creeds*, 1–29.

[46] Thus Kelly, *Early Christian Creeds*, 23–9; in response to Cullmann, *Earliest Christian Confessions*, 35–47.

[47] Cullmann, *Earliest Christian Confessions*, 25–30, here 25.

judicial view, others have suggested that the reference is to Timothy's baptism or ordination vows.[48]

Even if the Timothy reference does not refer to persecution, Cullmann does succeed in pointing out that 'Jesus Christ is Lord' represents a particularly bold stance in the context of the Roman state's demand for the civic confession 'Κύριος Καῖσαρ'. Perhaps, as he says, 'persecution fixed this confession in its stereotyped form':

> For the sake of this brief formula Christians suffered martyrdom. The heathen could not comprehend how Christians could show themselves so narrow-minded.[49]

The obvious question, posed as far back as the *Martyrdom of Polycarp*, was 'What harm is there to say "Lord Caesar", and to offer incense and all that sort of thing, and to save yourself?'[50] But in performing the utterance required by the Romans one would in fact be performing the *act* of denying Christ's lordship, and not just uttering the words, that is, performing an illocutionary act and not just a locutionary one. The speech act is not, as we have seen before, a report on an inner mental state which could simply be falsified to save one's skin, but rather the confession of 'Caesar is Lord' is, whether one intends it or not, a denial of the self-involving claim of Christian confession. The point is not, therefore, that one would be lying (reporting falsely on a mental state), but rather that one would be denying Christ simply by virtue of performing the speech act. It is precisely this absence of any 'distance' between the locution and the illocution in confessional speech acts which also underlies the thinking of Romans 10:9–10.

In a recent brief study, Hugh Williamson has suggested that a wide variety of the New Testament uses of 'Jesus is Lord' are best understood in this polemical manner: Jesus' lordship is particularly to be understood as a response to a rival claim of lordship, whether it be of death (cf. Acts 2:36), of 'dumb idols' (1 Cor. 12:3), or of Caesar, or whatever is dominating the

---

[48] Cullmann, *Earliest Christian Confessions*, 26–7; cf. J. N. D. Kelly, *The Pastoral Epistles* (BNTC), London: A&C Black, 1963, 141–44 (arguing for baptism), and George W. Knight III, *The Pastoral Epistles* (NIGTC), Grand Rapids: Eerdmans, 1992, 264–5 (arguing for ordination).

[49] Cullmann, *Earliest Christian Confessions*, 28.

[50] *Mart. Pol.* 8.2. (in LCC 1, *Early Christian Fathers*, 152).

believer's life.[51] In all these various cases, the utterance 'Jesus is Lord' is a confessional speech act of self-involvement in response to a rival claim.

Polemical confessions of orthodoxy noted by Cullmann include 1 Corinthians 15:3–8 (which as he notes is thus a good example of a confession not occasioned by only one circumstance) and 1 John 4:2: 'every spirit that confesses that Jesus Christ has come in the flesh is from God'.[52]

The confessions of 1 John have been studied from a speech act perspective by Dietmar Neufeld, who argues that the author is putting forward his Christology in a climate of heterodoxy, and not against any particular (e.g. docetic) claim: 'The confessions function as tests by which to determine who is indwelt by the Spirit of deceit or the Spirit of truth or deemed worthy to have fellowship with the author, God, and his son Jesus Christ (1:1–4).'[53] In particular he notes a large number of apparently unexplained christological statements (2:22, 23; 3:23; 4:2, 14, 15; 5:1, 5, 6, 10, 13) which 'function as catch slogans' to mark out those willing to count themselves as 'in' (in the Johannine world of two spheres, those who believe and those who do not):

> Significantly, each of the christological slogans is prefaced by a verb which indicates the action of believing, confessing or denying. The focus is not on the content of what is believed, confessed or denied, although the substantive content of each statement is nonetheless significant.[54]

Although Neufeld himself is reluctant to draw conclusions about any speech acts performed in historical situations 'behind' the text, I have indicated earlier why such scepticism is not obligatory. Thus, in responses to heterodoxy as well as in responses to persecution, we may say that the early Christians confessed their faith with self-involving confessions both of content and commitment. We shall now explore the less adversarial nature of confession in various forms of life which may be gathered together under the rubric of 'worship'.

---

[51] Hugh Williamson, *Jesus Is Lord: A Personal Rediscovery*, Nottingham: Crossway Books, 1993.

[52] Cullmann, *Earliest Christian Confessions*, 30–2.

[53] Dietmar Neufeld, *Reconceiving Texts as Speech Acts*, 119. See ch. 5 §4.2 above on Neufeld.

[54] Neufeld, *Reconceiving Texts as Speech Acts*, 126.

§4.2 *Worship*

The context of the church as a worshipping body has been proposed as an obvious setting for the emergence of the New Testament documents, as well as being a major theme running through them,[55] and while it would be an over-simplification to suggest that worship as a form of life is the overarching category within which confessional speech acts find their natural home certainly various of the emphases of Cullmann's and Neufeld's work can be brought together under this heading.

David Peterson suggests that the worship of God is best described as essentially 'an engagement with him on the terms that he proposes and in the way that he alone makes possible'.[56] At the end of his lengthy exegetical study he offers the following summary:

> Fundamentally ... worship in the New Testament means believing the gospel and responding with one's whole life and being to the person and work of God's Son, in the power of the Holy Spirit.[57]

Such a view balances the divine and human interaction involved in worship rather than focusing on worship simply as a response to God, even if it is the response which is our interest here.[58]

Indeed, in Wittgensteinian terms, Christian worship as a form of life is perhaps best understood as a disposition to engage with God (or more narrowly to respond to God) characterised by such attitudes as praise and expectant trust. In his general study of the topic, Ninian Smart suggests that the truth 'a god is to be worshipped' is analytic in that the concepts of worship and of god are internally related. However, the concept of worship, understood as relational, ritualistic and itself sustaining (or a part of) the power of the worshipped god, becomes a helpful way of understanding the purpose of language about

---

[55] Thus C. F. D. Moule, *The Birth of the New Testament* (BNTC), London: A&C Black, ³1981 (1962), 19–43; and note the study of idem, *Worship in the New Testament* (Grove Liturgical Study 12/13), Bramcote: Grove Books, 1983 (1961).

[56] David Peterson, *Engaging with God: A Biblical Theology of Worship*, Leicester: Apollos, 1992, 20.

[57] Peterson, *Engaging with God*, 286; cf. also Wainwright, *Doxology*.

[58] See also C. E. B. Cranfield, 'Divine and Human Action: The Biblical Concept of Worship', *Int* 12 (1958), 387–98. A more 'responsive' definition characterises the various works of R. P. Martin (see below).

God.[59] Smart follows Donald Evans in noting 'the centrally performative role of language in worship' and urges that self-involvement in religious worship may run deep in ethical and political areas owing to the strong ethical dimension of religious views.[60] In short, worship is a self-involving activity which, when expressed through language, is achieved by way of self-involving speech acts which represent personal engagement (of various illocutionary forms) with God and with facts about God.[61]

Cullmann refers to Philippians 2:6–11 as an example of the hymns used in early corporate worship, and notes also its inclusion of the confessional formula 'Jesus Christ is Lord'.[62] For Cullmann, the development of fixed texts in worship arose from the desire for a corporate confession of what it was that united believers before God, but evidently there was no 'fixed and universal text for this christological confession'.[63] He suggests that the confession retained in 1 Corinthians 15:3–7 would have served well in worship and preaching.

Two points may be made here. First, there is an appropriate hesitancy in Cullmann's discussion about delineating certain contexts as 'worship' over against other proposed settings. Thus baptismal and catechetic settings for confessional statements clearly overlap with settings of gathered worship. In general, while 'worship' serves as a useful term for uniting several important aspects of the forms of life of Christian confession, it remains limited. This tallies with the proposal of Ralph Martin to apply J. C. Beker's framework of 'coherence' and 'contingency' to the attempt to recover doxological and liturgical forms and settings in the New Testament documents.[64] Martin proposes that, among the stable 'coherent' features which we find in New Testament worship, we might include the focus on the risen

---

[59] Ninian Smart, *The Concept of Worship*, London and Basingstoke: Macmillan, St Martin's Press, 1972, 51–2.

[60] Smart, *Concept of Worship*, 31.

[61] Smart suggests, vis-à-vis our own discussion, that Evans leaves the objective side of this performative account 'tenuous'; Smart, *Concept of Worship*, 31.

[62] Cullmann, *Earliest Christian Confessions*, 22–3. The status of the passage as a 'hymn', on which see §2 above, need not concern us here.

[63] Cullmann, *Earliest Christian Confessions*, 21–3.

[64] Ralph P. Martin, 'Patterns of Worship in New Testament Churches', *JSNT* 37 (1989), 59–85, here 64, referring to J. C. Beker, 'Contingency and Coherence in the Letters of Paul', *USQR* 33 (1978), 141–50; now expanded as a full thesis in idem, *Paul the Apostle: The Triumph of God in Life and Thought*, Philadelphia: Fortress Press, 1980.

and exalted Lord Jesus, the awareness of the role of the Spirit, and a concern for others and the upbuilding of the community.[65] Among the contingent factors he includes, for instance, the emphasis in the Pastorals on order and orthodoxy,[66] which would lead us to consider Cullmann's category of 'polemic' perhaps more than 'worship' per se.

A related second point is that the polarisation in views about the difference between the *kerygma* and the *didache* in early Christian church life again serves unhelpfully to over-demarcate proposed life-settings for confessional speech acts. In the tradition of Bultmann, it has been common to take some such line as that of C. H. Dodd in his study of apostolic preaching: 'The New Testament writers draw a clear distinction between preaching and teaching . . . It was by *kerygma*, says Paul, not by *didache*, that it pleased God to save men.'[67] In fact the 'hymn' of Philippians 2 has been one battleground of this very debate, between so-called 'kerygmatic' and 'ethical' interpretations.[68] Philippians 2:5 (literally: 'This think among you which also in Christ Jesus'), has been emended in a variety of ways, but the two major proposals have traditionally offered alternative characterisations of themselves:

the 'ethical' view: τοῦτο φρονεῖτε ἐν ἡμῖν ὃ καὶ [ἦν] ἐν Χριστῷ Ἰησοῦ[69]

the 'kerygmatic' view: τοῦτο φρονεῖτε ἐν ἡμῖν ὃ καὶ [φρονεῖτε] ἐν Χριστῷ Ἰησοῦ[70]

Martin correctly notes that the labelling of these views has led to an unfortunate polarisation between the view that the example of Christ in the hymn is an ethical model for how we should treat one another, and the view that a pre-existent hymn

---

[65] Martin, 'Patterns of Worship', 65–73.

[66] Martin, 'Patterns of Worship', 79–81.

[67] C. H. Dodd, *The Apostolic Preaching and Its Developments*, London: Hodder & Stoughton, 1936, 7–8.

[68] The enormous secondary literature on this passage is presented in the updated study of Martin, *A Hymn of Christ*.

[69] This, the 'traditional' view, is clearly defended by C. F. D. Moule, 'Further Reflexions on Philippians 2:5–11', in W. W. Gasque and R. P. Martin (eds), *Apostolic History and the Gospel: Biblical and Historical Essays Presented to F. F. Bruce*, Exeter: Paternoster Press, 1970, 264–76.

[70] See E. Käsemann, 'A Critical Analysis of Philippians 2:5–11', *JTC* 5 (1968), 45–88. This is also the view of Martin.

focusing on the primitive kerygma is serving to remind the Philippians of their own attitude toward Christ so that they might adopt it among themselves.[71]

Regardless of the best solution to this particular exegetical issue,[72] one does suspect that at least part of the problem is an unwarranted opposition between the two views, rooted in a belief that the summoning power of the *kerygma* must be set against the content of the *didache*. Such a polarisation has often been shown to be untenable, however, most comprehensively by James McDonald in his study entitled *Kerygma and Didache*, which notes the 'complementarity' and yet the 'peculiar inter-relatedness' of the two terms.[73] McDonald traces the ways in which different forms of Christian utterance combine elements of both *kerygma* and *didache*, with studies of *propheteia, paraclesis* and *homilia, paraenesis* and *catechesis*, and *paradosis*, the tradition which he sees as informing them all but which, for example explicitly in 1 Corinthians 15:1–11, combines expressly didactic functions with serving as the basis of the *kerygma*. To over-simplify: all teaching keeps summons in view; and all forms of summoning expect and hope to be explained and under-stood.[74]

The speech act of confession, operative in the setting of worship in its various contingent forms, is concerned both with content (locution) and response to divine address (illocution and self-involvement). The logical grammar of confession is the self-involving personal backing behind the truth confessed, and this link runs through all the various New Testament instances of *homologia*.[75]

---

[71] See Martin, *Carmen Christi*, xv, in the foreword to the second edition.

[72] For discussion, see the essays collected in Ralph P. Martin and Brian J. Dodd (eds), *Where Christology Began: Essays on Philippians 2*, Louisville, KY: Westminster John Knox Press, 1998. On the confessional use of the passage note particularly the chapter therein by Colin Brown, 'Ernst Lohmeyer's *Kyrios Jesus*', 6–42, especially 23–5.

[73] James I. H. McDonald, *Kerygma and Didache: The Articulation and Structure of the Earliest Christian Message* (SNTSMS 37), Cambridge: Cambridge University Press, 1980, 6.

[74] See the summary of his findings in McDonald, *Kerygma and Didache*, 126–7.

[75] In this regard one may note Paul's commendation of the Corinthians' generosity in the collection for Jerusalem, which represents 'obedience to the confession of the gospel of Christ' (2 Cor. 9:13). See also Hebrews 3:1; 13:15; John 12:42 (and 1:20) and, in the Old Testament, 1 Kings 8:33–35 and its parallel 2 Chronicles 6:24–26.

This study of the self-involving nature of confession has high-lighted the importance of understanding it as a strong speech act, which therefore invites consideration of the issues of stance and entailment, while also making clear that the content of what is confessed remains important. It is appropriate, therefore, to conclude this study of confession by asking how such a speech-act approach bears on the question of the truth of what is confessed.

§5 Confession and Truth: What Statements Have to Be True for a Performative Utterance to Be Happy?

This discussion of confession and truth is, I would suggest, at least in part necessitated by concerns drawn from elsewhere: concerns about truth and religious language rather than about the dynamics of speech acts as such. Nevertheless, I shall argue that speech act theory can address these concerns in a helpful manner.

§5.1 A false polarisation

The debate about the truthfulness of Christian confessional claims is well worn and over familiar, although the topic of confession offers a particularly simple way into it. At the beginning of his 1935 book *Creeds in the Making*, Alan Richardson introduced the historical Christian faith as based upon 'certain key facts':

> It is the business of Christian doctrine to interpret these facts . . . The Apostles' Creed, for example, strongly insists upon the historical facts . . . The facts about the historical Jesus are therefore the data of theology.[76]

When invited to write a replacement book some fifty years later, Frances Young began with a conscious distancing of herself from this position, and suggested that 'modern philosophies' no longer allowed this kind of approach, since all facts are accessible only through interpretation and narrative creates history (more or less responsibly), and hermeneutics (perhaps especially

---

[76] Alan Richardson, *Creeds in the Making: A Short Introduction to the History of Christian Doctrine*, London: SCM Press, 1935, 7, 9.

suspicious ones) invite us to a gentler view of doctrine as 'coping' with our historical narratives.[77]

The appearance of opposition between these two views rests, as so often, on an unhelpful generalisation about the way that language works. Is there only one type of fact and does all confessional language approximate to it in the same way? By no means, on either count. But we must be cautious about an over-hasty appeal to speech act theory as a way out of this dilemma.

§5.2 *A premature resolution*

It was Austin himself who observed, crucially, that 'for a certain performative utterance to be happy, certain statements have *to be true*'.[78] I want to argue, however, that this does not allow one to reduce the analysis of performative utterances to an enumeration of facilitating truths behind every felicitous performative. This would in fact lose sight of the very point of speech act theory.[79] Yet it is a route which beckons to theologians concerned to explicate the meaningfulness of statements of Christian faith, perhaps mindful of the largely positivist attitude which remains prevalent today even after the demise of *logical* positivism. In my judgment, the analysis of performatives along these lines would not allow one to proceed much beyond a phenomenalistic account of religious language.

Consider, for example, a point made by Anthony Thiselton against Bultmann's demythologising language, appealing to precisely the words of Austin just quoted:

> But can these statements [e.g. 'Christ is Lord'] be translated in this way [i.e. in a demythologised way] *without factual remainder*? In our example, the words 'this is poison' can function as a warning

---

[77] Young, *Making of the Creeds*, ix–xii. 'Coping' is Rorty's word and not Young's, but in my view the notion of 'coping' is one of the great analytical tools Rorty has offered the contemporary academic, and modern theologians sometimes seem particularly capable of being characterised as 'copers'. I should add that Young's book is a fine introduction to its chosen subject, namely, 'the *making* of the creeds'. I am simply interested in noting how she feels the need to locate her study away from Richardson's view of facts.

[78] Austin, *HDTW*, 45.

[79] I am not just arguing against a straw man here. See, for example, James W. Voelz, *What Does This Mean? Principles of Biblical Interpretation in the Post-Modern World*, St Louis, MO: Concordia Publishing House, 1995, 275–321, who appears to have precisely this view of the point of speech act theory.

or plea only because (either in fact or in belief) the poison was poison.[80]

This serves as part of a wider argument, critical even while sympathetic to Bultmann, that his existentialist conception of biblical language is reductive.[81] Here I wish only to point out that the success of this argument is *not* dependent on a simple appeal to the supporting truths of other statements which every performative requires, since, as the above quote makes abundantly clear, there are in general two alternative ways in which Austin's 'maxim' might be fulfilled. On the one hand the poison may in fact be poison, but on the other the performative succeeds (even if technically 'infelicitous' in Austin's terms) if it is simply *believed* to be poison. On its own, the point made by Austin is insufficient to ground the self-involving nature of such speech acts as confession in any *particular* state of affairs.

Thus it would follow, for example, that in 1 Corinthians 15 (particularly v. 14) Austin would have us insist that either it is the case that the resurrection is a brute fact, or that it is the case that Christians believe that the resurrection is a brute fact, and if neither of these holds then the faith of the Corinthians is in vain. At first sight, however, there is little in the language, nor even in the philosophy of language, which will determine which of these two conditions might obtain.

However, if one arrives on other grounds at the belief that the resurrection occurred (i.e. bodily in some sense) then speech act theory shows why this does not negate the existential dimension of uttering the creed, but that is to approach the problem from the other end. In general, it appears that the New Testament writers do approach the problem from the other end: Paul himself assumes that the fact backs up the credal affirmation in 1 Corinthians 15. However, as noted by Danker, Paul is 'utilizing established credal affirmations as his indicative base, [and] is able to move forward in his favorite manner to the imperative: the practical concern'.[82] In other words, Paul's

---

[80] Thiselton, 'Use of Philosophical Categories', 96, and quoting Austin's maxim in the next sentence. The same Austinian sentence is also appealed to in Thiselton, *Two Horizons*, 269, 355 and 437, but the particular formulation of the 1973 article is not repeated, and thus the further issues are not raised.

[81] Thiselton, *Two Horizons*, 205–92.

[82] F. W. Danker, *Creeds in the Bible*, St Louis, MO: Concordia Publishing House, 1966, 12.

argument about the significance of the resurrection presupposes the fact of the resurrection, and its status as fact is not at issue in the passage.

Partial resolution

This discussion should not be seen as the claim that, after all, speech act theory fails to offer substantive help in demarcating the truths which a successful performative utterance presupposes. I shall consider how to make positive progress with this question below. First, I wish to underline that what I have termed here a 'premature' resolution of this question does nevertheless make genuine if only partial progress towards looking at how facts are presupposed by performatives.

The point I wish to make is that the logic of certain forms of speech *presupposes* certain general assumptions about reality and the reliability of historical reconstructions. Such an argument is indeed part of Searle's defence of (external world) realism,[83] and is easily adapted to a defence of the normal reliability of historical statements of external world occurrences where, as C. A. J. Coady has argued, speech acts such as testimony play a crucial but neglected role in our assumed epistemology.[84]

In a related and somewhat celebrated argument, Terrence Tilley proposes that one need not believe in God in order to pray (and pray meaningfully) to him.[85] While he accepts that 'as a practice, petitionary prayer must presuppose that the intentional object to whom the prayer is directed is real, that is, that there is an addressee who can "answer" the prayer', he claims that the individual pray-er is required only to 'believe, hope or wish' that the addressee can do what the pray-er asks.[86] In short, Tilley suggests that if there is ultimately no addressee, which might perhaps never be known, the speech act of prayer is still coherent. This is a particularly clear example of an argument which would still satisfy Austin's requirement that certain statements have to be true for the performative to succeed, but

---

[83] Searle, *Construction of Social Reality*, 177–97.
[84] C. A. J. Coady, *Testimony: A Philosophical Study*, Oxford: Clarendon Press, 1992.
[85] Tilley, *Evils of Theodicy*, 58–63; cf. also idem, '"Lord, I believe: help my unbelief": Prayer without Belief', *MTh* 7 (1991), 239–47.
[86] Tilley, *Evils of Theodicy*, 58, 56.

which has clearly travelled a long way from ensuring that any particular statements are true.

Tilley's argument represents the most minimal position possible concerning how successful performatives presuppose truths, but he appears to underestimate the extent to which individual self-involvement must be operative. Vincent Brümmer, for instance, argues that the logic of *address* which necessarily characterises prayer is incoherent if the one praying actually believes there is no God.[87] The strength of Brümmer's position is that he also argues forcefully for the importance of the self-involving ('affective') aspect of prayer too. As Mananzan has put it: 'Christian religious discourse does not depend on a proved existence of God but on a serious belief of God's reality.'[88] This 'serious belief' must be held by the individual and not, *contra* Tilley, by the tradition.

I suggest, then, that there are requirements in the philosophy of language which do prescribe to some extent the range of possible 'facilitating truths' for a felicitous performative. Even if such requirements may in some cases fall short of being sufficient for the purposes of making substantive theological points regarding exegetical issues in particular New Testament texts, they do, to return to our 1 Corinthians 15 example, demonstrate precisely that one cannot maintain convictional language about the resurrection entirely divorced from questions concerning certain presupposed facts. This is the 'partial resolution' which can be offered to the question of confession and truth by considering simply the dynamics of speech act theory. To make further progress, we must refine what we mean by 'the question of truth'.

§5.3 Refining the question of truth

It is helpful to pursue the question of truth in the same manner as Austin, who noted that 'truth and falsity are . . . not names for relations, qualities, or what not, but for a dimension of assessment'.[89] The question thus arises: what is the most beneficial dimension of assessment for the particular confession(s) of the

---

[87] Vincent Brümmer, *What Are We Doing When We Pray? A Philosophical Inquiry*, London: SCM Press, 1984, 22–8.

[88] Mananzan, *'Language Game' of Confessing One's Belief*, 146.

[89] Austin, *HDTW* 140–7, with this summary statement at 149.

New Testament? To answer this one must consider the *home
language game* of confession, or the *form of life* which supports
confession, and in so doing we are drawn to the conclusions of
Mananzan's study of this very topic. She argues that the key issue
in analysing confessional utterances is to realise that they
challenge the very framework of non-performative assessments
of truth, and overturn the dichotomy between cognitive and
non-cognitive language, or between confirmable and non-
confirmable observation:

> Theistic propositions have essentially another function, namely, to
> articulate certain human experiences which are beyond the
> competence of empirical factual statements to express, because they
> involve those aspects of being human, which, although they manifest
> themselves within the concrete world, nevertheless escape an exact
> pinpointing within its coordinate system.[90]

Mananzan is avoiding a false polarising of alternatives here by
noting that confessional statements relate to truths which are
manifested in the 'concrete' world, but which are not reducible
to such concretised manifestations.

A similar, briefer discussion by Dallas High draws comparable
conclusions:

> There are good reasons why the traditional creeds (or even tradi-
> tional doctrinal utterances) make use, in some way, of the 'I believe
> in' formula.
>   By virtue of this antecedent, the utterances, including their
> attached phrases, are actions and linguistic performances of self-
> involvement.[91]

High explores this in particular by looking at credal affirmations
as responding to questions about the valuation of personhood
in such contexts as promises, covenants and interpersonal
loyalties. He notes that God's self-revelation in Exodus 3:14 ('I
AM WHO I AM') is in personal terms of a particular kind, that
is, not simply anthropomorphic concepts but a particular model
of 'I' as a self who acts as an 'other' with whom humans may
have inter*personal* dealings. Thus, 'like acts of self-involvement
with another person, creedal and doctrinal expressions are acts
of self-involvement with one who is like an "I" and whom I deem

---

[90] Mananzan, *'Language Game' of Confessing One's Belief*, 145.
[91] High, *Language, Persons, and Belief*, 175.

worthy of my trust and valuing'.[92] In short, we cannot identify ourselves except with reference to others, and God-talk works itself out within the framework of the logical grammar of God's being one of those others. Thus credal language is irreducibly self-involving.

What, in these accounts, has happened to the question of truth? It has not been bracketed out, as irrelevant, but rather it has been positioned, as one component of a performative utterance. Indeed, later in his book High goes on to discuss the necessity of avoiding a mistaken appeal to the idea of 'language game' as a way of escaping the need for providing reasons to support one's religious truth claims. He is rightly critical of those aspects of the work of modern theologians such as Tillich and Bultmann (and arguably also Barth) which attempt to salvage the validity of religious confession by removing it from the court of cognitive judgment. 'Giving reasons' is itself a language game which requires an appropriate form of life, and therefore is not a matter of impersonal criteria:

> 'justification' and 'reasons' are given by 'persons', not by rules, logical or otherwise, as if rules themselves derive the justification. 'Persons,' we must remember, are alone the ones who can and do fashion 'justifications,' 'reasons,' and 'rules,' count something as a 'justification' or 'reason' and make 'justifications' and 'reasons' count whether for or against some utterance or belief.[93]

High is arguing here against another form of the same problem with which we started, which divided Young from Richardson: the modern theologians he opposes have begun from the assumption that there is only one form of justification, have found exceptions to or problems with this monolithic conception, and have therefore concluded that cognitive justification cannot be the appropriate way of arguing theologically. By following High and Mananzan, however, we should instead conclude that the multifaceted nature of such terms as 'fact' and 'justification' calls for an altogether more cautious appraisal of the strengths and weaknesses of our traditional terminology. Likewise, this time *with* Tilley, the question of 'the cognitive nature of religious language' sets itself up for confusion wherever it presumes that it is always and everywhere equally cognitive.

---

[92] High, *Language, Persons, and Belief,* 181.
[93] High, *Language, Persons, and Belief,* 206–7.

Tilley's conclusion on this matter encapsulates the point we are also making with regard to truth, facts and all these other terms: 'there is no wholesale way to decide on the cognitivity of religious language because the speech acts performed in religious contexts are so varied'.[94]

At the same time this 'cautious' approach should not be confused with the reduction of 'truth' to 'true for a community', as for example in the recent work of Richard Rorty.[95] Although one may wish to refine William Placher's formulation of the matter, he is right to say that 'The way we can go about justifying a belief is always context dependent, but the truth claimed for that belief is not.'[96] As I have urged at length in earlier chapters, the apparatus of speech act theory allows us to adopt 'constructionist' terminology without any necessary concomitant reductionist implications.

§5.4 *Truth and fact*

My limited aim here (under such an all-encompassing title!) is to apply the above argument to particular examples concerning Christian confession in order to try and clarify the point being made. We recall also our earlier argument concerning the spectrum of facts ranging from brute to institutional, as well as Searle's observation that one of the distinctive features of illocutionary acts is that their continued use sustains and strengthens the institutional facts which they create.[97] In general it seems most likely that any set of religious speech acts will both be

[94] Tilley, *Evils of Theodicy*, 79.

[95] For a recent clear statement of Rorty's position, see his 'Is Truth a Goal of Inquiry? Donald Davidson versus Crispin Wright', *Truth and Progress: Philosophical Papers Volume 3*, Cambridge: Cambridge University Press 1997 (originally 1995), 19–42 .

[96] William C. Placher, *Unapologetic Theology: A Christian Voice in a Pluralistic Conversation*, Louisville, KY: Westminster/John Knox Press, 1989, 123, drawing in particular on Jeffrey Stout's distinction between truth (as a trans-communal property) and justification (as a community-relative one), in his *Ethics after Babel: The Languages of Morals and Their Discontents*, Cambridge: James Clarke & Co., 1988, 21–8 and *passim.* Stout believes that after one follows Austin in exploring the uses of 'true', there is nothing further on a theoretical level which will be more interesting in understanding truth (24), but he disputes Rorty's reductionist tendencies with regards to truth (especially ch. 11 'The Moral Consequences of Pragmatism', 243–65).

[97] Searle, *Construction of Social Reality*, 34 (on creation) and 117–19 (on maintenance).

founded upon certain brute facts and at the same time constitutive of certain institutional facts. If one may express it this way: there will always be a degree of social construction in religious faith, but one cannot tell in advance of the particularities of any situation what degree it will be.[98] Examples will clarify this important theoretical distinction between brute and institutional facts.

It is, in the context of this discussion, significant that the basic Christian confession was 'Jesus is Lord' (for Paul) or 'Christ is Lord' (more generally), as well as the 'primitive' confession of 'Christ Jesus'.[99] The words κύριος and, at least early on, Χριστός are not straightforward names of objects, or in this case names for the person, Jesus of Nazareth. These words are not available to be used with word-to-world direction of fit in assertive speech acts, as was noted in essence by G. B. Caird with respect to such passages as Mark 8:29.[100] Rather these words 'imply a certain *force* of commitment on the part of those who favor them' as Colin Brown expresses it in his study of confession as a speech act.[101] The commissive confession operates with world-to-word direction of fit,[102] and thus following Searle we would want to say that confessional statements of the form 'Jesus is the Christ' create institutional facts.

Even more so, 'Jesus is Lord' is anything but a 'flat constative'. It is, as we have seen, the personal confession of commitment and stance indicating a relationship to Jesus which is to be valued over and against, for example, commitment to Caesar. It is therefore significant that we do not in general find in the New Testament statements such as 'Jesus is Lord of all' which would

---

[98] One implication of this is that the adoption wholesale of any model whereby the sustaining power of illocutions is made to bear the whole weight of religious infrastructure is precisely the mistake of prejudging this variable. I have considered some aspects of such approaches in ch. 1 above.

[99] Neufeld, *Earliest Christian Confessions*, 10.

[100] Caird, *Language and Imagery of the Bible*, 10; cf. also idem, *New Testament Theology*, 338–40.

[101] Colin Brown, 'Hermeneutics of Confession', 463.

[102] Brown appears to take confession as an assertive speech act rather than a commissive one, with the result that he actually has the opposite view of the direction of fit in Mark 8:29, although I find that his argument seems to support that of Caird and would therefore best be seen as world to word at this point; Brown, 'Hermeneutics of Confession', 460–4. The terminology 'word to world' and vice versa is confusing and evidently often confused, but as yet there is no agreed alternative.

indicate a non-self-involving use of the word. Romans 10:12 and Acts 10:36, describing Jesus as 'Lord of all', are at least to some degree more interested in the Jew–Gentile issue; and verses where Jesus' supremacy is in view (e.g. John 1:1–18; Col. 1:15–20) do not in general use κύριος language. Noting the absence of 'our' in the confessions of Romans 10:9,. 1 Corinthians 12:3 and Philippians 2:11, which all have 'Jesus is Lord' rather than 'Jesus is our Lord', Werner Kramer suggests that 'only in a later period does it become necessary, for polemical purposes, to reflect whether the *Lord's* dominion embraces the whole world or only the Church'.[103]

To ask, therefore, whether it is true that Jesus is Lord seems in this particular sense to be a poorly defined question. Further, since we have seen that Christian confession typically concentrated on just such convictional statements as 'Jesus is Lord' and 'Jesus is the Christ', the general question of the relationship between what is confessed and what is true must be judged, in these important examples, to be an insufficiently precise question.[104]

Nevertheless, the question which stands as the subtitle of this section remains: what statements have to be true for a performative utterance to be happy? Where Austin's words quoted earlier might have led us astray to look for 'supporting truths' for every confession, Searle offers a different image: 'In order that some facts be institutional, there must be some other facts that are brute.'[105] Thus while the standard Christian confessions do not, on our account, admit easily of true/false characterisation, there remain nevertheless certain facts which are presupposed by significant confessional statements.

The longer creeds of later development include certain of these brute facts among their direct claims: that Jesus the Christ was in fact Jesus of Nazareth, and that he did in fact die (on the cross) and was buried. To follow High's analysis, the kind of justification to be made for offering such a confessional state-

[103] Werner Kramer, *Christ, Lord, Son of God* (SBT 50), London: SCM Press, 1966, 219–22, here 221.

[104] For a similar approach to the logic (or grammar) of convictional and especially religious language, see McClendon and Smith, *Convictions*, especially 47–109. I am, however, in some disagreement with their proposal, as indicated in ch. 1.

[105] Searle, *Construction of Social Reality*, 56. See also 120–5 on 'The Hierarchy of Facts: From Brute to Institutional'.

ment (such as the Apostles' Creed which includes these last two claims) must differ from that offered for confessing 'Jesus is Lord'. It is not my intention here to engage in a discussion about the truth-status of these claims, but I do wish to point out that the truth-issue at stake must necessarily be of a different order from that in the case of the earliest Christian confessions.[106] To simplify: following Searle opens up a greater potential 'distance' between the confession and any presupposed states of affairs, but as we examine various confessional statements down through the history of the church, some of these presupposed states of affairs do come into view, and thus the confession is tethered, if indirectly, to questions of truth.

Romans 1:3–4 may be an instructive example of the various levels of truth-claim involved in the case of Christian confession. Although there is general consensus that the verses are a pre-Pauline confession,[107] it is as well to recall that they need not be in order to be used confessionally. Thus, where Poythress for example urges that there is insufficient evidence to claim more than that Romans 1:3–4 'is a free composition using a number of traditional expressions and ideas',[108] the passage may still be considered in confessional terms as a self-involving speech act.

In making a specific claim about the interrelationship of Jesus' earthly descent (from David, κατὰ σάϱξ) and his divine sonship declared through the resurrection (κατὰ πνεῦμα), this passage combines statements of brute fact with institutional claims of self-involving significance.[109] Of particular note is the ascription of divine sonship *with power* to Jesus as attested in the resurrection. Although there is a debate as to whether 'in power' (ἐν δυνάμει) modifies 'declared' (as with the NIV rendering 'declared with power to be . . .') or modifies 'Son of God', so

---

[106] Which again is why I disagree with McClendon and Smith's discussion (see n. 104 above).

[107] Thus Käsemann, *Commentary on Romans*, 10–12; cf. Paul Beasley-Murray, 'Romans 1:3f: An Early Confession of Faith in the Lordship of Jesus', *TynB* 31 (1980), 147–54. For a survey of views as well as a proposal of a three-stage redaction, see R. Jewett, 'The Redaction and Use of an Early Christian Confession in Romans 1:3–4', in D. E. Groh and R. Jewett (eds), *The Living Text: Essays in Honor of Ernest W. Saunders*, Lanham, MD: University Press of America, 1985, 99–122.

[108] Vern S. Poythress, 'Is Romans 1³⁻⁴ a *Pauline* Confession after All?', *ExpT* 87 (1976), 180–3, 182.

[109] See J. D. G. Dunn, 'Jesus – Flesh and Spirit: An Exposition of Romans 1:3–4', *JTS* 24 (1973), 40–68, who sees Paul making a claim about two overlapping modes of existence in Jesus' earthly life (54).

that Jesus is declared to be 'Son of God with power', this latter reading seems the preferred sense.[110] The status of Jesus as 'Son of God with power' is an institutional fact, and to confess Jesus in this way is certainly to take a stance in the public domain. Yet the confession explicitly claims that this is the same Jesus who is descended from David, which is a brute fact. As a single confession, therefore, institutional and brute facts are brought together, and the self-involving speech act makes clear its claim to particular commitments to truthful statements. In short, one cannot reduce the confession of Jesus as 'the Son of God with power' to a question of fact, and yet one must insist also that the overall confession itself is explicitly linked to factual states of affairs.

§5.5 Summary

Searle's approach throws into precise relief the false polarisation of our opening discussion: to Richardson one wants to say, 'Not all facts are brute facts', and to Young, 'Not all facts are institutional facts'. Similarly, truth is a concept with blurred edges which is operative in relation to Christian confession in the various contexts of the different forms of life which we examined in §4 above. Speech act theory *does* shift the overall discussion of the meaning of religious language into the public domain, by showing that confessional (commissive) language depends on states of affairs. But there is no simple correspondence between a successful commissive such as a credal statement presupposing the resurrection and the fact of the resurrection in the extra-linguistic world. Rather, each speech act must be examined on its own merits in its own relevant form of life. It is in this context that the researches of Neufeld and Cullmann and others are of such value.

§6 Conclusions

In our study of confessional speech acts in the New Testament we have found that it is the self-involving nature of confession which is most significant. Confessions are strong illocutions with

---

[110] So Fitzmyer, *Romans*, 235; Douglas Moo, *The Epistle to the Romans* (NICNT), Grand Rapids: Eerdmans, 1996, 48.

commissive force but which are also declarative, and in particular in the New Testament they typically include a commitment to a certain definable content: 'Jesus is Lord' or 'Jesus is the Christ'. Credal forms in the New Testament are indications of likely self-involvement, but confessions did not need to be (and in fact were not) always credal. We have seen that confessional speech acts need to be understood in their particular forms of life, and that they do not negate, although they situate, the question of truth.

We will find a similar mix of commissive and declarative elements in the speech act of forgiveness in the next chapter. Although the act of forgiveness does not raise the question of truth in quite the same way as that of confession, it does require the same focus on its self-involving nature, and will raise related questions about brute and institutional facts (as we should expect) by way of forcing us to consider the nature of sin and its status in brute and institutional terms.

In this connection it is again appropriate to note, by way of a last word on confession, that to confess one's sins may also be seen as a self-involving speech act whereby the confessor *asserts* that he or she has committed particular acts (or perhaps has omitted to perform certain required acts) but, more significantly, performs the *expressive* act of distancing themselves from endorsing those acts. The clearest example of such a use in the New Testament is 1 John 1:9: 'If we confess (ὁμολογέω) our sins, he who is faithful and just will forgive us our sins.' Thus, this 'negative' sense of ὁμολογέω[111] might be seen as the public commitment *not* to take a stand behind a particular fact. The following discussion of forgiveness will bring us back to this idea of confession in due course.

---

[111] Only here with this sense in the New Testament; cf. BAGD, 568. This sense is more normally indicated by ἐξομολογέω, as at Matthew 3:6; Mark 1:5; James 5:16, etc. (cf. BAGD, 277).

7

The Forgiveness of Sin

§1 Introduction

Forgiveness is a subject which, rather surprisingly, has suffered from considerable neglect in philosophical and theological reflection. In the former case discussion of forgiveness has tended to gravitate around such questions as 'Is forgiveness a virtue?' and 'How do forgiveness and mercy interrelate?' based on the assumption that forgiveness may be cashed out in some such terms as the forswearing of resentment. In the latter case, the tendency has been to subsume forgiveness under the wider rubric of Christology or atonement, but this is problematic as we shall see.

Studies of forgiveness in theological terms have been few and far between.[1] If one may gauge anything from its appearance in dictionary articles, it is that the topic is of minor theological significance, or in the case of one major recent explicitly *ethical* and theological dictionary, no significance at all.[2] In a particularly interesting case, John McIntyre presents a thorough and penetrating study of atonement, concluding with a chapter on

---

[1] Older studies include H. R. Mackintosh, *The Christian Experience of Forgiveness*, London: Nisbet & Co, 1927, and Vincent Taylor, *Forgiveness and Reconciliation: A Study in New Testament Theology*, London: Macmillan & Co, 1946. For further post-War treatments see n. 76 below.

[2] There is no article on 'forgiveness' (i.e. the topic, let alone the word) in Paul Barry Clarke and Andrew Linzey (eds), *Dictionary of Ethics, Theology and Society*, London and New York: Routledge, 1996.

forgiveness in which he attempts to 'earth' the once-and-for-all crucifixion in our own lives in the practice of forgiveness.[3] He concludes the book with a brief description of forgiveness as it 'emerges' out of the very nature of God, noting various aspects such as the wiping out of sin and the restoring of fellowship with God. Then, in the very last paragraph of the book, he notes:

> What we have not so far taken account of, in all our deliberations, is the role which we as brothers and sisters play in the mediation of forgiveness to those about us . . . No account of the shape of soteriology, however otherwise impeccable, can afford to ignore the final finishing touch thus given to it by human agency.[4]

McIntyre cites here various stringent requirements from the Gospel of Matthew, such as that we shall not be forgiven if we do not forgive. However, it is hard to avoid the conclusion that in fact this 'final finishing touch' has been, if not ignored, then at least seriously underestimated.

Forgiveness thus remains elusive in theological reflection. I suggest that one of the reasons for this is that some significant aspects of forgiveness are difficult to grasp without something approaching a speech-act view of forgiveness.

In view of this, my discussion of forgiveness takes a slightly different course from that on confession in the previous chapter. Confession is often viewed as self-involving, with the result that the question of form and function could be addressed first before explicating the self-involving nature of the speech act and then pursuing the question of truth thus raised. In contrast, with forgiveness I judge that the primary need is to provide a speech-act account of forgiveness in the first place, and then to turn immediately to the question of 'truth' as it is raised in forgiveness in the New Testament, which, I shall argue, rests in turn on an understanding of the 'sin' which is to be forgiven. After this I shall conclude with a consideration of specific exegetical examples of texts concerned with forgiveness, where the issues of vocabulary markers and the link between form and function shall finally be examined.

---

[3] John McIntyre, *The Shape of Soteriology: Studies in the Doctrine of the Death of Christ*, Edinburgh: T&T Clark, 1992, 109, 120. The last chapter (109–29) is entitled 'The Nature of Forgiveness'.

[4] McIntyre, *Shape of Soteriology*, 129.

§2 Forgiveness and Self-Involvement: Stance and Entailment

Forgiveness as a speech act

It is clear that speech act theory has the potential to clarify certain aspects of forgiveness. Very simply: to forgive is to perform an act; to say 'I forgive you' is to perform a speech act.[5] I should say immediately that it is equally clear that there are aspects of forgiveness which will elude any speech act analysis. How, for instance, shall we *evaluate* the various contested criteria which are offered as good grounds for forgiveness? This key question cannot be settled simply by appealing to the workings of language. I thus agree with Gregory Jones when he notes 'the significant yet limited relevance of performative declarations such as "I forgive you"'.[6] In fact Jones's generally excellent theological discussion of forgiveness does not focus on this 'significant' area, in contrast to my own concerns.

§2.1 *What is it to forgive?*

Many modern discussions of forgiveness go back to Bishop Joseph Butler's early eighteenth-century sermons on the themes of resentment and forgiveness.[7] For Butler, forgiveness is the application of Jesus' command to love our enemies. Where 'resentment is not inconsistent with good-will', since it may still co-exist with love for our enemy, it may grow into revenge (when resentment 'entirely destroys our natural benevolence towards [our enemy]').[8] Thus for Butler, forgiveness is the forswearing of revenge, or, in comparable words, the limiting of resentment to its helpful roles.[9] Indeed one of the principal arguments of

---

[5] In fact very few treatments of forgiveness consider its speech act dimension. The notable exception, considered below, is Joram Graf Haber, *Forgiveness*, Savage, MD: Rowman & Littlefield, 1991.

[6] L. Gregory Jones, *Embodying Forgiveness: A Theological Analysis*, Grand Rapids: Eerdmans, 1995, 236.

[7] Joseph Butler, 'Sermon VIII: Upon Resentment' and 'Sermon IX: Upon Forgiveness of Injuries', *The Works of Joseph Butler, in two volumes. Vol II: Sermons, etc,* ed. W. E. Gladstone, Oxford: Clarendon Press, 1896, 136–49 and 150–67 respectively.

[8] Butler, *The Works of Joseph Butler*, 158.

[9] I thus find it puzzling that Jeffrie Murphy, one of the most prolific of modern writers on forgiveness, characterises Butler's view as 'the forswearing of resentment'; Jeffrie Murphy, 'Forgiveness and Resentment', in Jeffrie G. Murphy and Jean

the first of Butler's two relevant sermons is that resentment, when held in check, serves valuable roles in society: it is an inward witness to virtue, and it is a 'generous move of mind' which witnesses with indignation against injury and wickedness.[10] With regard both to resentment and forgiveness we find in Butler particular examples of the overarching theme of his moral thought: that humanity is possessed of an inherent benevolence which it is our duty to cultivate and extend; and that therefore the urge to do what is right is at bottom natural, and is mediated to us through our consciences, which are, in his view, rational, universal and authoritative.[11]

In Butler's world all things, even resentment, work together for the good, and it is not surprising that subsequent thinkers, often operating outside Butler's Christian convictions, have begged to differ. Nevertheless, his treatment of forgiveness sets the subject squarely on the path of its relation to resentment, a path which has dominated discussion of the topic.[12]

Joram Graf Haber's treatment of forgiveness as a speech act should thus be seen as something of a departure from the philosophical norm, one which in my view has a good deal to commend it in what it affirms, but which is perhaps overly dismissive of other emphases.[13] Haber offers us a model of 'I forgive you' as a performative utterance along the following lines.[14]

§2.2 A performative model

Haber begins by noting that, in line with one of Austin's major emphases, the locution 'I forgive you' does not primarily report

---

Hampton, *Forgiveness and Mercy* (Cambridge Studies in Philosophy and Law), Cambridge: Cambridge University Press, 1988, 14–34, here 15. The qualifications which Murphy then offers to this position are thus not, in my judgment, qualifications of Butler's position (15–16).

[10] Butler, *The Works of Joseph Butler*, 148–9.

[11] See Terence Penelhum, *Butler*, London, Boston and Henley: Routledge & Kegan Paul, 1985; T. A. Roberts, 'Editor's Introduction', in T. A. Roberts (ed.), *Butler's Fifteen Sermons Preached at the Rolls Chapel and A Dissertation of the Nature of Virtue*, London: SPCK, 1970, ix–xxiv (especially xv).

[12] Cf. P. F. Strawson's title essay in his *Freedom and Resentment and Other Essays*, London: Methuen, 1974, 1–25 (1962); and particularly the various treatments of Jeffrie Murphy.

[13] Haber traces other dissenting voices from the 'forgiveness is the overcoming of resentment' view; Haber, *Forgiveness*, 16–23.

[14] I draw here from his account in Haber, *Forgiveness*, 29–57.

on an inner mental or emotional state, such as the overcoming of resentment. If it did then one would be forced to introspect ever anew to discover if indeed there were no longer any resentment against the offending person. In fact to utter 'I forgive you' is to *express* the overcoming of resentment. Although Haber does not use these terms, it is a matter of sincerity and stance, by which the self is situated with respect to the other: for example, 'I now make the (cognitive) decision not to count your offence against you in our continuing relationship, at this present time'.

The notion that an emotional issue (such as resentment) is nevertheless founded on cognitive states is implicit here: 'in [this] view, emotions involve specific attitudes and certain ways of looking at the world', and Haber appeals to various voices in the philosophical tradition who have defended this idea.[15] This is an important point, one on which the entire speech act analysis of forgiveness depends, but in my judgment it is well taken. Murphy, for instance, notes that emotions involve stances towards things, people or events and thus can be changed or at least influenced by rational persuasion.[16] One can also appeal more widely than just the philosophical literature to defend the view that as well as obviously emotional or affective aspects, phenomena such as forgiveness and resentment have a definite cognitive component. Richard Fitzgibbons suggests that therapists rely precisely on the 'intellectual or emotional decision to part with anger' even while 'For most patients, forgiveness continues for some time as an intellectual process, assisted by the therapist, in which patients do not truly feel like forgiving'.[17]

Once freed from the model of seeing forgiveness as reporting on an inner mental state, Haber is able to propose the following model of the performative utterance of forgiveness, whereby a speaker S, expressing forgiveness of an agent X for his act A, represents as true all of the following:

[15] Haber, *Forgiveness*, 35, citing Bernard Williams, 'Morality and the Emotions', *Problems of the Self: Philosophical Papers 1956–1972*, Cambridge: Cambridge University Press, 1973, 207–29; William Lyons, *Emotions*, Cambridge: Cambridge University Press, 1980; and Strawson, 'Freedom and Resentment', 6–8.

[16] Jeffrie Murphy, 'Introduction. I. The Retributive Emotions', in Murphy and Hampton, *Forgiveness and Mercy*, 1–10, here 5, n. 7.

[17] Richard P. Fitzgibbons, 'The Cognitive and Emotive Uses of Forgiveness in the Treatment of Anger', *Psychotherapy* 23 (1986), 629–33, here 630.

(1) X did A;

(2) A was wrong;

(3) X was responsible for doing A;

(4) S was personally injured by X's doing A;

(5) S resented being injured by X's doing A; and

(6) S has overcome his resentment for X's doing A, or is at least willing to try to overcome it.[18]

Three implications of this analysis are worth noting. Haber points out that 'for particular persons to be appropriate for the invocation of the procedure, they must have standing both to forgive and be forgiven'.[19] Thus what he terms 'third-party forgiveness', whereby I may attempt to forgive A for a wrong committed against B, misfires, because I have not been wronged. The distinction here, if it can be sustained, is between the *resentment* which I feel in being wronged and the *indignation* which I may feel when B is wronged. For Haber, there is a 'non-arbitrary' distinction between the two, since the former is tied up with the maintenance of self-respect whereas the latter is not.[20] The notion that resentment is a protection of self-respect and that its absence is indicative of defective self-esteem is prominent especially in the work of Murphy, whose main argument that forgiveness is not always a virtue is predicated precisely on the notion that it may undercut a responsible self-respect.[21]

Secondly, the particular issues surrounding condition (6) serve to clarify the way in which forgiveness may misfire. Haber proposes that 'if S *sincerely intends* to will away his resentment, then he *does* succeed in expressing forgiveness. If he should give up his effort at a later time, then – and only then – can we say his forgiveness was infelicitous'.[22] This would seem to bear out

---

[18] Haber, *Forgiveness*, 40.

[19] Haber, *Forgiveness*, 44.

[20] Thus Haber arrives at the same conclusion as Piers Benn, 'Forgiveness and Loyalty', *Philosophy* 71 (1996), 369–83, who rather than utilising speech act categories develops his own of 'full' and 'quasi' forgiveness. What may be most interesting about this is that it demonstrates how speech act theory provides sharp analytical categories without which certain straightforward questions cannot be answered. For an opposite view of third-party forgiveness, drawing on psychological as well as philosophical insights, see Thomas Tryzna, 'The Social Construction of Forgiveness', *CSR* 27 (1997), 226–41, considered below.

[21] See especially Jeffrie Murphy, 'Forgiveness and Resentment', 16–19.

[22] Haber, *Forgiveness*, 51.

my suggestion that Haber's view can be expressed as a matter of sincerity and stance in the public domain: I have forgiven A precisely where I am willing to overcome resentment towards A. This invites us to say that the act of forgiving may be felicitous to differing degrees at different moments in time. In my judgment this accords with our own experiences of the difficulties involved in overcoming resentment in many serious cases.

Finally, Haber applies his model to the issues of overcoming resentment and addresses the question of when this overcoming is appropriate. He follows Murphy in arguing that forgiveness is appropriate only in cases where it preserves self-respect, but differs from him in maintaining that such cases are precisely those where the wrongdoer repents for the wrong done.[23] His analysis is Kantian: the repentant wrongdoer is in a sense reconstituted as a new person, and thus can be forgiven since there is no condoning of the offender as such (the offender now being 'replaced' by the 'repenter'). Forgiveness, on this model, remains the prerogative of the forgiver, and cannot be earned by repenting. Where Murphy allows five different types of situation where forgiveness may be offered, all loosely under the rubric of 'preserving self-respect', Haber allows only this one: forgiving the repentant wrongdoer.[24] Both writers are critical of Jesus' parable of the unforgiving servant (Matt. 18:21–35) with its view that one should forgive because one is in turn in need of forgiveness.[25]

§2.3 Evaluation of the performative model

The performative model of forgiveness as articulated by Haber has both strengths and weaknesses. First, it is successful in separating the issue of forgiveness from a supposed introspective examination of feelings. Its speech act apparatus enables it to navigate these various problems concerning the 'self', what I would term the 'non-referential "I" of self-involvement'.

---

[23] Haber, *Forgiveness*, 90.

[24] Contrast Haber, *Forgiveness*, 103–9, with Jeffrie Murphy, 'Forgiveness and Resentment', 24–30.

[25] Murphy, 'Forgiveness and Resentment', 30–4; Haber, *Forgiveness*, 109. Haber is particularly curt: 'I do not think this is a good reason to forgive, if only because, in the forgiveness situation, our own moral history is not at issue' (109).

Secondly it does indeed clarify why it is that forgiveness in difficult situations seems to be elusive even in cases where resentment had apparently been overcome. The resurfacing of resentment, perhaps as the self is disrupted out of its normal mode of being in the world and past hurts are foregrounded again, causes the misfiring of the illocution which had heretofore been felicitous.[26] Thirdly, as Haber acknowledges, all the benefits of his analysis are predicated on this paradigm case of the particular first-person present tense utterance 'I forgive you', but can *mutatis mutandis* be applied more generally.

A fourth and significant benefit of this approach, in my view, is its particular focus on the nature of the institutional facts involved in forgiveness, although this is not discussed by the writers cited. We remember that, on Searle's account, institutional facts are created by illocutions of the form 'x counts as y in context c'. Under the terms of his Kantian analysis, Haber's condition (6) in cases of a repentant wrongdoer may be expressed as

(6a) S is willing to *count* X *as* X' who did not perform A

but this *cannot* be cashed out as a statement such as

(6b) The offensive results of A are removed or destroyed

precisely because of the distinction between brute and institutional facts. Thus if you have burned down my house, and the house no longer stands, this is a brute fact unaffected by my forgiveness, whereas the institutional fact that you owe me £50,000 to rebuild the house may be forgiven, and, indeed, 'removed' from our social reality. More generally, in forgiving we may say that the forgiver adjusts his or her stances towards the various brute facts involved, and thus changes the institutional facts involved. Indeed Murphy notes that this point is at the heart of the legal systems which attempt to regulate the social operations of justice and retribution:

> Speaking very generally, we may say that the criminal law (among other things that it does) institutionalizes certain feelings of anger, resentment, and even hatred that we typically (and *perhaps* properly)

[26] This notion, that forgiveness remains always contingent upon the future continuance of the overcoming of resentment, clearly lays a philosophical foundation for the claim that forgiveness may best be viewed as an eschatological category.

direct toward wrongdoers, especially if we have been *victims* of those wrongdoers.[27]

One of the features of the book in which Murphy and Hampton go on to explore this institutionalisation is their engagement with the question of how our notions of 'forgiveness' and 'mercy' differ from these notions as traditionally understood within a Christian theological framework. This is a key issue for my discussion, and raises the following challenge which must be addressed at this point: does an analytical approach such as that of Haber have significant things to say to theological questions concerning forgiveness as it has been viewed in Christian tradition and in interpretation of the New Testament? As well as meeting this challenge by way of exegetical examples later in the chapter, I propose the following response at this stage.

First and foremost, I believe that we must lay to rest the persistent mischaracterisation of the analytical approach as working with a 'thin' conception of its key terms. The notion that moral and ethical categories are susceptible of 'thin' and 'thick' description may be useful in sorting out ways of evaluating discussions,[28] but this is a separate and separable question from that of whether an approach such as speech act theory is one which does or does not do justice to the life setting of particular illocutionary acts. Indeed, there is a significant irony about the mischaracterisation of the analytical approach as 'thin', which is that the genesis of the whole idea of 'thick' and 'thin' description occurs in some of the last papers of that archetypal analytic philosopher, Gilbert Ryle, in his discussions of the nature of thinking.[29] Ryle's well-known example is of two boys performing identical swift contractions of the eyelids, but only one of whom is winking: the 'thick' description operating on this more complex level than muscle-contraction description. But as Ryle develops this view, it becomes apparent that he has

---

[27] Jeffrie Murphy, 'The Retributive Emotions', 2.

[28] It is certainly well-enough established in this context, as adopted by Clifford Geertz, *The Interpretation of Cultures: Selected Essays,* New York: Basic Books, 1973, 3–30; and popularised by Lindbeck, *Nature of Doctrine,* 112–38. See now also Michael Walzer, *Thick and Thin: Moral Arguments at Home and Abroad,* Notre Dame: University of Notre Dame Press, 1994.

[29] Gilbert Ryle, 'Thinking and Reflecting' and 'The Thinking of Thoughts: What Is *Le Penseur* Doing?', reprinted in idem, *Collected Papers Vol. 2: Collected Essays 1929–68,* London: Hutchinson & Co., 1971, 465–79 and 480–96. Ryle is acknowledged as the source of the terminology by Geertz, *Interpretation of Cultures,* 6–7.

in mind precisely the same multi-layered phenomenon as Austin's idea of locutions, illocutions and perlocutions: thus the utterance of syllables may at the same time be 'telling someone something' and 'imparting a piece of wanted information' and so forth.[30] To set what Ryle calls here these 'thicker descriptions' *against* an approach such as that of speech act theory seems to miss entirely the point of speech act theory. As we have been arguing throughout, performative speech acts are significant precisely in that they do imply and entail habituated stances and commitments. Thus while one should allow that the notions such as 'wrong', 'personal injury' and 'resentment' which operate in Haber's analysis do not always operate with the same strength or force, it does not follow that the speech act analysis is compromised in any way by this.

Gregory Jones attacks modern philosophical (especially analytical) approaches on precisely these grounds: they fall short in abstracting the performative utterance from the on-going tradition. More specifically, 'they have tended to assume that a philosophical account of forgiveness can be offered independently of any theological convictions'.[31] For Jones, much of the significance of forgiveness derives not from the act but from the transformed practices which derive from it. He in turn develops a view of forgiveness as a craft which he sees as in line with an Aristotelian–Thomist view of the significance of the continuities of habits, crafts and traditions. It is thus particularly significant that his book is entitled *Embodying Forgiveness*.[32]

I suggest that Jones has not entirely succeeded in avoiding a false polarisation between an analytical approach and an 'embodied' approach. He criticises Haber for extracting incidents of forgiveness and treating them as concerned with 'isolated situations of wrongdoing or guilt',[33] but, although this may be a reasonable criticism of aspects of Haber's own presentation, two points may be made in response. First, such acts are not simply an insignificant part of the overall topic of forgiveness, since Jones himself uses the same focus precisely at

---

[30] Ryle, 'Thinking of Thoughts', 484.
[31] Jones, *Embodying Forgiveness*, 210; cf. his general discussion of this point, 210–19.
[32] Jones, *Embodying Forgiveness*, 225–39.
[33] Jones, *Embodying Forgiveness*, 213.

the point of summarising his 'embodied' approach, where the performative utterance marks a particular point (not always the same point) in the on-going process of forgiveness.[34] Secondly, a speech act analysis must in any case locate the speech act in the context of a stance and its commitments and entailments, and therefore need not be seen as setting a study of particular acts against ongoing traditions. It is doubtless true that analytical approaches are used reductively, but in this case it would not appear to be so. In short, it is not apparent why Jones's own valuable emphasis on communities and traditions need foreclose analytical questions in any particular case.

In general, then, there is no reason to rule out a priori that the restoration of a relationship may be a particularly powerful reason to forgive an offender in a certain case, such as in a marital relationship, for example. Likewise, the parable of the unforgiving servant does offer insight into our attitudes to forgiveness which rely on deepening (or 'thickening') our conception of it in a way in which Haber's brief dismissal of the parable fails to acknowledge. However, in both these cases, the point is not that a speech-act approach falls short of elucidating the issues, but that Haber's own treatment has not taken sufficient account of the relevance of habituated stances and commitments to evaluating the felicity of self-involving speech acts.[35]

Finally, Jones correctly locates a key issue in understanding forgiveness as being the confrontation which it invokes against sin and evil: 'In its broadest context, forgiveness is the way in which God's love moves to reconciliation in the face of sin.'[36] Here, at least, there is force to his argument that a philosophical approach risks ignoring the overarching context within which stance and entailment can be evaluated, the context of '*culpable* complicity' (sins) and 'a pervasive reality of always-already brokenness and diminution' (sin) which calls for the central role of forgiveness in Christian theology.[37] Certainly it is true that discussions of forgiveness divorced from any theological

---

[34] Jones, *Embodying Forgiveness*, 236–8.
[35] This I would judge to be particularly true of his discussion of Matthew 18 (Haber, *Forgiveness*, 109), where Jones is right that Haber is wrong, but mistakenly concludes that it is his model which has led him astray.
[36] Jones, *Embodying Forgiveness*, 5; cf. 59–64, 83–91 and *passim*.
[37] Jones, *Embodying Forgiveness*, 49.

moorings have a propensity to drift into an unbalanced focus on psychological effects alone.[38] Moreover, as we come to consider the New Testament, we shall have to look at the contrast which may be made between 'forgive' as an intransitive verb and 'forgive' as a transitive verb: how does a speech act approach relate to the specific context of forgiving sin? I suggest, in fact, that the conceptuality of speech act theory provides a very helpful way of understanding what it means to forgive sin because it allows us to understand what kind of reality is in view when we talk of 'sin'. This, once more, is the question of the link between successful performatives and truth, and hence our next section examines the question of truth, before proceeding to an analysis of specific New Testament instances of forgiveness.

§3 Forgiveness and Truth: Sin as an Institutional Fact

Again the question of truth is best approached via Searle's distinction between brute and institutional facts. I shall argue that a key question to ask in any particular situation is not 'Is such and such an attitude or action or disposition a sin?' but 'Which attitudes, actions or dispositions *count as* sin?' (and, implicitly, in which contexts?)

§3.1 The overcoming of resentment and the forgiveness of sin

Our performative account of forgiveness has led us to a view of forgiveness as the overcoming of resentment in certain types of situation. On turning to the theological literature from this perspective, one must immediately be struck by the regular assumption that the nature of forgiveness is unproblematic, and that it is inevitably focused on the question of sin:

> The existence of forgiveness takes for granted the fact of human sin as an offense against God's holy law or against another human

---

[38] As, for example, in the 'therapeutic' notion of forgiveness evident in M. J. Kurzynski, 'The Virtue of Forgiveness as a Human Resource Management Strategy', *Journal of Business Ethics* 17 (1998), 77–85. For an example of how psychological insights need not militate against theological categories, see Jared P. Pingleton, 'Why We Don't Forgive: A Biblical and Object Relations Theoretical Model for Understanding Failures in the Forgiving Process', *Journal of Psychology and Theology* 25 (1997), 403–13.

being . . . Forgiveness is not simply 'the remission of penalties; what is remitted is sin'.[39]

Thus the opening of the *ABD* article on New Testament forgiveness, possessed as it is of a somewhat forthright ontology. To complicate the picture yet further, 'sin' in the language games of New Testament studies, particularly in the Gospels, operates with still other nuances of logical grammar, as we shall see. Doubtless one could chart more than one path through this maze, but I propose to proceed by arguing that sin is an institutional fact created out of the act of counting acts or dispositions as evil. Evil, in turn, I take to be the mysterious brute fact the existence of which calls forth the vain task of theodicy: the attempt to *explain* evil. In a certain sense, evil impinges on the creation as brute facts which are the chaos from which we fashion our institutional facts, which are the sins.[40]

§3.2 Sin as an institutional fact

We start with the observation that almost any human action can be called a sin given the appropriate circumstances, and that equally almost anything that might easily be labelled as 'sin' can be condoned in other circumstances. Evidence for such a claim is to hand in the form of the broad brush strokes of such sociologically orientated studies as Oliver Thomson's *History of Sin*, or Jeffrey Burton Russell's studies on the history of perceptions of the devil.[41] Thomson notes, as examples of the latter, the Nazi ethic which condoned mass murder and torture, the fourteenth-century Catholic ethic which encouraged the slow burning of non-orthodox members of its own faith, the

---

[39] Gary S. Shogren, 'Forgiveness (NT)', in *ABD*, II:835–8, here 835, and citing Taylor, *Forgiveness and Reconciliation*, 3.

[40] Although my account does not depend on this image, the notion of evil as 'brute chaos' finds support in a certain tradition of readings of Genesis 1. See, for example, Walter Brueggemann, *Theology of the Old Testament: Testimony, Dispute, Advocacy*, Minneapolis: Fortress Press, 1997, 158–9, drawing in particular on the account of Jon D. Levenson, *Creation and the Persistence of Evil: The Jewish Drama of Divine Omnipotence*, San Francisco: Harper & Row, 1988.

[41] Oliver Thomson, *A History of Sin*, Edinburgh: Canongate Press, 1993; Jeffrey Burton Russell, *The Devil: Perceptions of Evil from Antiquity to Primitive Christianity*, Ithaca and London: Cornell University Press, 1977. See also, by the same author and publisher, the continuation of his survey in *Satan: The Early Christian Tradition* (1981); *Lucifer: The Devil in the Middle Ages* (1984); and *Mephistopheles: The Devil in the Modern World* (1986).

Puritans who regarded it as moral to drown muddled old women suspected of witchcraft, and, in the 1990s, the married women of Uzbekistan who felt impelled to set themselves on fire if accused of adultery.[42] His list deliberately ranges across the social and religious spectrum, without even including the obvious example of 'war', where the changed labelling of the social situation turns killing from morally bad to morally sanctioned. 'Labelling is everything', as pacifist theorists are wont to say, but, in the language of chapter 4 above, this trades implicitly on the presupposition of uniformly strong construal, and in what follows I shall seek a constructive but non-reductive way forward which nuances rather than abandons this judgment.

We may note also here Russell's view on the 'social construction' of the devil: 'I assert the reality of the Devil, but by this I do not intend a judgment as to the metaphysical reality of such a being.' Russell views the devil as 'the concept of the Devil', and while he may or may not be more than this we can never know. In short: 'The Devil is a real phenomenon; therefore, the Devil is real.'[43] In a personal afterword at the end of the book, he says that he does believe in the existence of a personification and principle of evil, '*call it what you will*'.[44] Within biblical studies it is well known that the figure of the devil undergoes development, and that in the Old Testament at least it is not a personification of evil, but rather a messenger whose job it is to accuse, or an 'adversary', but that 'in any event, there is no single celestial *satan*'.[45] The development of the personal concept of 'devil' out of these disparate beginnings, without any necessarily reductive conclusions, has been traced in the recent study of Elaine Pagels.[46]

Once again I propose to account for these understandings by appealing to the notion of an institutional fact. 'Sin' is a matter of naming, as is the choice to use the word 'devil' to refer to a particular view of personified evil. What is more significant than locating metaphysical realities behind these terms

---

[42] Thomson, *History of Sin*, 29–30.

[43] Russell, *The Devil*, 43.

[44] Russell, *The Devil*, 258–60. Italics added.

[45] Peggy L. Day, *An Adversary in Heaven: Satan in the Hebrew Bible* (HSM 43), Atlanta: Scholars Press, 1988, 147; cf. her summary of the evidence on 127–45.

[46] Elaine Pagels, *The Origin of Satan*, London: Allen Lane, 1995.

is to understand them dispositionally in relation to how they are experienced by human beings. As a potent example, Arthur Miller's *The Crucible*, his largely historical account of the seventeenth-century Salem witch trials, demonstrates the complexities of trying to reduce the language of evil (in this case of the devil and witchcraft) to statements of brute fact. Nevertheless, Miller draws out the genuine consequences of the effects of labelling certain people as witches, all the way to the ultimate brute fact of death. Not only so, but Miller's portrait of evil as it is characterised and institutionalised in the play was intended to demonstrate that the same processes were at work in his day in the McCarthyite desire to label and ostracise 'communists', again with real effects only made possible, and thus to some extent at least created, by the labelling.[47]

It is in the context of just such a 'dispositional' account that the particularities of Thomson's investigation are useful as a reminder to expect that 'sin' will always be defined in particular situations with reference to particular concerns. Indeed one recent philosophical account notes the distinction between those deeds considered wrong because they are immoral and those which are wrong because they offend against God, suggesting that one may adopt the terminology of 'objective' and 'subjective' sin in this regard.[48] Rather than using these labels 'objective' and 'subjective', I would say here that different institutional realities are in view.

Needless to say, this contextual approach to defining 'sin' is often not what is in mind when Christian theologians use the word, with the aim of characterising something more general. Attempts have been made to generalise across the contingencies of sinful acts in different times and places, such as, for example, Oliver Thomson's own list of 'five main characteristics, varying substantially in intensity and emphasis' which are 'common to almost all moral codes: reciprocity, altruism, obedience, absolutes and manners'.[49] Such characteristics move the discussion to the level of disposition, which is where it is best considered as a theological issue.

[47] Arthur Miller, *The Crucible: A Play in Four Acts*, Harmondsworth: Penguin, 1968 (1953).
[48] Philip L. Quinn, 'Sin', in *REP*, 8:791–6, here 792.
[49] Thomson, *History of Sin*, 6–11 and 35.

§3.3 *Disposition to sin*

This idea has been expounded most recently and clearly by Wolfhart Pannenberg, who takes up the theme as it has always been viewed in Christian theology, as a central part of understanding the human condition.[50] For Pannenberg, sin is best understood as an anthropological condition: 'the situation of the universal failure to achieve our human destiny that theology calls sin'.[51] His historical treatment of the doctrines of 'Sin and Original Sin' attempts to navigate a difficult path.[52] On the one hand, we have theology's self-conscious distancing of itself from a doctrine of original sin, the inevitable result of the assault on its presumed original 'act' (in Eden), its subsequent New Testament exegesis (in Rom. 5), and its idea that one could be held responsible for the act of another (Adam), all of which have gradually fallen away. On the other hand, the resultant reduction of 'sin' language to an individual notion of sinful acts loses completely the idea of the universal dimension of sin, and leads irreversibly to a moralism which turns against those ensnared by evil, a moralism which is hypocritical in the extreme, for Pannenberg, since it cuts against the whole point of the gospel. This marginalisation of sin language is a problem since 'Christian faith does not create the fact of sin but presupposes it'.[53]

In an effort to rehabilitate sin language in its universal dimension, Pannenberg returns to the Old Testament, and in particular to three of its words for 'sin', which, he suggests, emphasise different aspects of the New Testament use of ἁμαρτία:

ḥaṭṭāʾṯ	carelessness; missing the mark (possibly inadvertent)
ʿawon	wilful and therefore culpable failure to hit the mark; or violation of a norm or standard
peshaʿ	intentional revolt against the norm (e.g. apostasy); moral guilt or iniquity before God[54]

[50] Wolfhart Pannenberg, *Systematic Theology* (Vol. 2), Edinburgh: T&T Clark, 1994 (1991), 231–75.

[51] Pannenberg, *Systematic Theology*, 2:239, 252.

[52] Pannenberg, *Systematic Theology*, 2:231–65.

[53] Pannenberg, *Systematic Theology*, 2:236.

[54] Pannenberg, *Systematic Theology*, 2:239. In fact Pannenberg's rendering of these last two terms reverses the more common understanding, as found in R. Knierim, *Die Hauptbegriffe für Sünde im Alten Testament*, Gütersloh, 1965, and summarised by

The first two of these words relate specifically to particular acts (while the third focuses more on one's state), but all highlight the intention or motivation of the doer. One may say that they range from having virtually no institutional component (in the case of carelessness) through to strongly institutional characteristics depending on the nature of the violated norms, and that all of them are circumscribed within some institutional view of social reality.

Where Old Testament talk of sin always has transgression in view, however, with Paul, and particularly in Romans 7:7–11, sin is seen as coming before the commands, and is discovered by law. In subsequent Western tradition, taking its lead from Paul and through Augustine, sin is viewed not in terms of sinful acts but as a result of the perverted will which is manifested in pride and (later) anxiety. This sense of sin is universal, although it can be known fully only as we know God (which thus identifies 'unbelief' as a root of sin, rather than as sin) and can be *perceived* via (rather than identified with) anxiety and 'unbridled desire'.[55]

The doctrine of original sin has a profoundly anti-moralistic function: all are responsible for sin and there is therefore no ground for moral superiority over others. Pannenberg's particular contribution is to hold on to this anti-moralistic benefit of the doctrine without recourse to the actual doctrine itself, with its supposed universal human presence in the original Adam. Not all are persuaded by his account. Elsewhere Al McFadyen has argued that the doctrine itself is required, no matter how unfashionable (because anti-autonomous) it may be.[56] Nevertheless, Pannenberg's account adds a considered view of the development of Christian doctrine to those voices from other fields which argue that the Bible simply offers no explanation of sin, nor its provenance, but rather focuses on its universal corrupting power. For Pannenberg, the point of the

---

Robin C. Cover, 'Sin, Sinners (OT)', in *ABD*, VI:31–40 (especially 32), but this need not concern us here.

[55] Pannenberg, *Systematic Theology*, 2:252.

[56] Alistair I. McFadyen, 'Original Sin in Modern Theology', paper presented to the Nottingham Theological Society, Nottingham, 30 June 1998; and see now Alistair I. McFadyen, *Bound to Sin: Abuse, Holocaust and the Christian Doctrine of Sin* (Cambridge Studies in Christian Doctrine), Cambridge: Cambridge University Press, 2000.

Genesis 3 story is that sin increases even while God takes counter-measures.[57]

Thus while particular sins are varyingly characterised as brute or institutional facts, 'sin' as it is often used in theological discourse is best understood as a dispositional phenomenon. In forgiving, therefore, I suggest that the forgiver's disposition is refigured through an act of self-involvement. At the same time, a new stance is taken toward brute facts, which is in accord with Haber's condition (6) on overcoming resentment. It is true that resentment is equally a disposition rather than a mental state, and thus that forgiveness might equally well be characterised as the refiguring of dispositions, but, in what follows, I shall speak of the speech act itself refiguring the institutional realities concerned through an act of self-involvement. That brute facts are involved too highlights the non-reductive approach of speech act theory.

§3.4 *The construction of sin: two examples*

Specifically within this non-reductive framework, I propose that 'construction' is a helpful term for clarification when we use speech act theory to approach texts such as forgiveness texts. I discuss briefly two examples of particular relevance to our task of explicating New Testament texts of forgiveness in a speech act perspective; a third will occur in our actual exegesis itself with reference to understandings of 'sin' and 'sinners' in New Testament times.

Miroslav Volf's Exclusion and Embrace

The basic thesis of Miroslav Volf's 1996 work on reconciliation is that 'embrace' is a powerful metaphor for understanding how

---

[57] Pannenberg, *Systematic Theology*, 2:262–3, where he offers his reading of the fall narrative of Genesis 3. This anti-theodicy view characterises the work in other areas of Tilley, *Evils of Theodicy*, especially 221–55; and of Kenneth Surin, *Theology and the Problem of Evil*, Oxford: Blackwell, 1986, who prefers theodicies with a 'practical' emphasis to those which he labels 'theoretical'; cf. his remark 'The Christian who takes the atonement seriously has no real need for [theoretical] thinking' (142). See also the phenomenological account of Paul Ricoeur, *The Symbolism of Evil*, New York: Harper & Row, 1967; idem, 'Evil', in Mircea Eliade (ed.), *The Encyclopedia of Religion* (16 vols), New York: Macmillan, 1987, 5:199–208; and idem, 'Evil: A Challenge to Philosophy and Theology', *JAAR* 53 (1985), 635–48, now reprinted in his *Figuring the Sacred: Religion, Narrative, and Imagination* (ed. Mark I. Wallace), Minneapolis: Fortress Press, 1995, 249–61.

exclusion between oneself and another can be overcome in a way which acknowledges both otherness and sin.[58] Significantly, the background to his analysis is his own Croatian identity set against the Balkan conflict, and he mounts a compelling argument for seeing a four-stage 'drama of embrace' (opening the arms, waiting, closing the arms, opening the arms again) as a model of the reconciliatory process which is required of those who would overcome violence.[59]

Of significance for my account is Volf's use of evil as the violent and real backdrop to all theorising. Commenting on Rorty's ironic and contingent self, which weaves its identity in interaction with other beliefs and desires, Volf comes to the crux of the issue:

> 'Weaving' would be a rather innocent way to describe this production, possibly a fitting image for how Rorty's books are written but not for how human selves are shaped. 'Struggle' and 'violence' come closer to being an adequate description.[60]

The full sweep of Volf's argument is that non-violence is the Christian way, but not a non-violence predicated on a non-violent God, rather a non-violence which believes that justice is God's alone, and that it is therefore the divine prerogative to exact vengeance on evil. He explicitly suggests that the unpopularity of this thesis is because the theorist generally works against 'the quiet of a suburban home' rather than 'a scorched land, soaked in the blood of the innocent'. Some things only God can do: extracting vengeance, according to the New Testament, is one of them.[61]

I sketch out these broad contours of Volf's argument in order to demonstrate that it is within an entirely non-reductive framework that Volf does in fact adopt a construction-orientated approach concerning sin and evil. Arguing that sin is embodied in exclusionary practices (as a background to his 'embrace' metaphor for reconciliation), he notes that

> Most of the exclusionary practices would either not work at all or would work much less smoothly if it were not for the fact that they

---

[58] Miroslav Volf, *Exclusion & Embrace: A Theological Exploration of Identity, Otherness, and Reconciliation*, Nashville: Abingdon Press, 1996.
[59] Volf, *Exclusion & Embrace*, 140–7.
[60] Volf, *Exclusion & Embrace*, 67.
[61] Volf, *Exclusion & Embrace*, 301–4.

are supported by exclusionary language and cognition. Before excluding others from our social world, we drive them out, as it were, from our symbolic world.[62]

Volf shows how Jesus takes on social boundaries, typically of uncleanness, by a mission of 're-naming': no foods are unclean (Mark 7:14–23); the flow of blood from a woman's body is not unclean (cf. Mark 5:25–34); and the 'mission of re-naming' abolishes the 'system of exclusion', that is, it reconstitutes the institutional facts determinative of the social reality of the time.[63] Evil, referred to at times by Volf with the kind of 'chaotic land of exclusion' language I have used above,[64] is *not* ignorance, as if a corrected 'noetic stance' would overcome it. Rather, in a key image, Volf suggests that

> Symbolic exclusion is often a distortion of the other, not simply ignorance about the other; it is a willful misconstruction, not mere failure of knowledge.[65]

Sin as wilful misconstruction: Volf is sensitive to the reductive possibilities of such a formulation, but set against his unwavering insistence that inexplicable evil undergirds so much human endeavour he never does in fact collapse his account of forgiveness into a mutual reweaving of noetic stances.[66] The strong illocution of forgiveness is irreducibly bound up with the brute facts of embrace, with the 'other' who remains a separate agent. It is only in such a context that we may use Volf's suggestion: forgiveness as wilful reconstrual.

Thomas Tryzna's 'Social Construction of Forgiveness'

Explicitly adopting the image of 'social construction', Thomas Tryzna likewise shows how forgiveness must be set against the specifics of its socially-delineated situation in order to be understood as a boundary-establishing speech act.[67] The aim of Tryzna's study is to examine evidence for, and the coherence

---

[62] Volf, *Exclusion & Embrace*, 75.
[63] Volf, *Exclusion & Embrace*, 73.
[64] Cf. Volf, *Exclusion & Embrace*, 98.
[65] Volf, *Exclusion & Embrace*, 76.
[66] Volf, *Exclusion & Embrace*, 76, in the same paragraph as the previous quote.
[67] Tryzna, 'Social Construction of Forgiveness'. In general, for reasons explored in ch. 4 above, I prefer 'construction' to 'social construction' as a term well suited to a speech-act approach.

of, forgiveness as it occurs between groups, as well as the related issue of third-party forgiveness, but of interest to my own concerns are some of the uses he makes in the process of philosophical and psychological work on forgiveness.

He situates his study in the particular social contexts of assembly-line work in military aircraft manufacture, and of surgeons training for medical school. What these studies suggest is that, for example, while trainee surgeons may make errors of medical judgment, 'the most serious kind of error is . . . the violation of the social code . . . actions that threaten the "life" of the system'.[68] In these (social) circumstances, 'forgiveness is a mechanism for establishing boundaries that *includes* people, while punishment is a mechanism that excludes'.[69] In other words, the social role of forgiveness is to enable offenders to maintain their role within the community, through a process of 'forgiving and remembering' which seeks to minimise social distance at the point of forgiveness rather than prefacing it with distancing judgment.[70]

In conclusion, Tryzna suggests that forgiveness as a felicitous speech act presupposes social contexts of (group) membership,[71] where forgiving is limited not by philosophical restrictions on speech acts in dyadic relationships, but rather 'by the capacity of particular individuals and groups to comprehend and to act morally within communities of different sizes'.[72] Thus 'the limit on what is morally meaningful is socially constructed, not analytically determined by study of the meaning of forgiveness as a universal concept'. In closing, Tryzna notes some theological sides to his work, particularly in refusing to limit discussion of forgiveness to dyadic interpersonal relationships within the church.[73]

---

[68] Tryzna, 'Social Construction of Forgiveness', 231.

[69] Tryzna, 'Social Construction of Forgiveness', 234.

[70] Tryzna, 'Social Construction of Forgiveness', 232–3; and drawing on the sociological work of Charles L. Bosk, *Forgive and Remember: Managing Medical Failure*, Chicago: University of Chicago Press, 1979; and Nicholas Tavuchis, *Mea Culpa: A Sociology of Apology and Reconciliation*, Stanford, CA: Stanford University Press, 1991. Significantly, one of Tavuchis's most instructive examples of a delineated social system is a case of a church excluding one of its members; Tavuchis, *Mea Culpa*, 83–7.

[71] Tryzna draws on the speech act approach of Tavuchis, *Mea Culpa*, 22–32 and *passim*.

[72] Tryzna, 'Social Construction of Forgiveness', 239.

[73] Tryzna, 'Social Construction of Forgiveness', 240.

It must be noted that Tryzna's study focuses on situations where 'sin' occurs in a highly institutionalised manner owing to the particularly clearly defined heirarchical and institutional structures of his test cases. This is both a strength and a weakness: a strength in that it foregrounds precisely the 'social construction' aspect of forgiveness and makes the workings of count-generated institutional facts perspicuous; and a weakness in that it might lead one to conclude that this is an exhaustive account of forgiveness. My own view is that his article is useful precisely for illuminating the social mechanisms of forgiveness and the presupposed social setting which enables the speech act to work, but that this clarity is achieved precisely because the setting is strongly institutional. I thus conclude that what Tryzna has achieved is an analysis of that aspect of forgiveness which is indeed socially constructed, while leaving untouched the setting of brute facts (particularly evil) which, as we saw with Volf's work, constitutes the background against which acts of forgiveness are performed. However, I shall argue below that when forgiveness is viewed in church-related terms, the significant aspects of Tryzna's study prove to be directly applicable.

Thus equipped with a non-reductive view of forgiveness as a speech act concerned with refiguring institutional facts, we turn to particular texts of forgiveness in the New Testament.

§4 Forgiveness in the New Testament

Gregory Jones suggests that we need 'an eschatological under-standing of Christian forgiveness. Christian forgiveness is not simply a word of acquittal; nor is it something that merely refers backward', and he goes on to note that once Protestants had taken *justification* as *the* central theological category forgiveness was too easily reduced to a subcategory of it which referred backward only, that is, to acquittal. Not only was the eschatological aspect lost but also the 'personal' aspects of forgiveness were given undue prominence by being falsely detached from larger ecclesial, ethical and political issues.[74]

---

[74] L. Gregory Jones, *Embodying Forgiveness*, 66, and 66, n. 38. A similar concern is expressed by Alan Torrance: 'Forgiveness: The Essential Socio-political Structure of Personal Being', *JTSA* 56 (1986), 47–59.

Likewise Krister Stendahl, who also approaches the topic from outside that particular Protestant tradition, suggests that the priority of forgiveness is not compromised by Paul's particular need to focus on justification for his own reasons.[75] However, a survey of the literature quickly reveals that the idea of forgiveness within human relationships has *not* featured prominently in theological discussion, with only a handful of books addressed to the topic,[76] and the majority of treatments not in any case focusing on the actual (speech) act of forgiveness.[77]

In locating the appropriate texts for our study we face again the issue of vocabulary markers for illocutionary acts, and with this caveat in mind it is appropriate to begin with the word ἀφίημι (forgiveness). The vast majority of uses of ἀφίημι in the New Testament are in the synoptics (Matthew 47×, Mark 34×, Luke 34×, John 14× and only 13 other uses in the whole New Testament) although many of these are not uses in the sense of 'forgive'.[78] In contrast, ἄφεσις, which occurs 17 times, means 'forgiveness' always except in its jubilary uses ('release from captivity') in Luke 4:18. With the exception of Ephesians

---

[75] Krister Stendahl, 'Justification rather than Forgiveness', *Paul among Jews and Gentiles and Other Essays*, Philadelphia: Fortress Press, 1976, 23–40; as well as idem, 'Sin, Guilt, and Forgiveness in the New Testament', *Meanings: The Bible as Document and as Guide*, Philadelphia: Fortress Press, 1984, 127–36.

[76] Between Taylor in 1946 (n. 1 above) and Jones in 1995, there were very few book-length treatments of forgiveness. Most notable were W. Telfer's historical study, *The Forgiveness of Sins: An Essay in the History of Christian Doctrine and Practice*, London: SCM Press, 1959; Hartwig Thyen, *Studien zur Sündenvergebung im Neuen Testament und seinen alttestamentlichen und jüdischen Voraussetzungen* (FRLANT 96), Göttingen: Vandenhoeck & Ruprecht, 1970, which explored the various settings of and influences on the notion of forgiveness, tracing in particular its eschatological dimension and early non-sacramental uses; and Christof Gestrich, *The Return of Splendor in the World: The Christian Doctrine of Sin and Forgiveness* (trans. Daniel W. Bloesch), Grand Rapids: Eerdmans, 1997 (1989), which focused more on sin despite its dual title.

[77] Of particular note are Geiko Müller-Fahrenholz, *The Art of Forgiveness: Theological Reflections on Healing and Reconciliation*, Geneva: WCC Publications, 1996; issues of *Concilium* and *JRE* devoted to the topic: Casiano Florian and Christian Duquoc (eds), *Forgiveness* (*Concilium* 184), Edinburgh: T&T Clark, 1986; and articles by John P. Reeder Jr, 'Forgiveness: Tradition and Appropriation' (136–40), Paul Lauritzen, 'Forgiveness: Moral Prerogative or Religious Duty' (141–54), and Louis E. Newman, 'The Quality of Mercy: On the Duty to Forgive in the Judaic Tradition' (155–72), *JRE* 15 (1987), 136–72; as well as John S. Kselman, James H. Charlesworth and Gary S. Shogren, 'Forgiveness', in *ABD*, II:831–8; and Jonathan Baker, *How Forgiveness Works* (Grove Spirituality Series 53), Nottingham: Grove Books, 1995.

[78] For details in this paragraph, see H. Vorländer, 'Forgiveness,' *NIDNTT* 1:699–703.

1:7 and Colossians 1:14 the word does not occur in the Pauline letters, which perhaps signifies that it becomes widespread only later in the apostolic age, for reasons we shall consider below concerning the early church practice of binding and loosing. It is of course the case that forgiveness is the topic when the specific vocabulary is absent, as for instance with the image of 'erasing the record that stood against us' in Colossians 2:14.[79]

Although statistics can be at best only a rough guide to significance, the Gospels are indeed particularly relevant to our study. Texts of major importance include Matthew 6:14–15 (and v. 12) on forgiving others and being forgiven by God; Matthew 18 with its various discussions of community life, frequently on forgiving; and Matthew 16:18–19 and 28:16–20, with their commissions to forgive.

In my judgment, the major emphases which emerge from these various uses of ἀφίημι and ἄφεσις can best be understood by organising our discussion around the speech act categories of stance and entailment. I shall argue that, in line with the expectations aroused by the foregoing analysis of constructed forgiveness and institutional and social facts, forgiveness in the New Testament is concerned above all with issues of reciprocity (stance) and membership (entailment). Since forgiveness as a speech act primarily concerns interpersonal human forgiveness, this will be my focus, although I shall suggest some ways in which divine forgiveness can also be considered under these categories.

§4.1 Forgiveness and stance: reciprocity

One of the major emphases of the New Testament discussion of forgiveness is what I shall term 'reciprocity'. Matthew 6:14–15 (cf. also Mark 11:25), Luke 6:37, John 20:23, Colossians 3:13, Ephesians 4:32 and also 2 Corinthians 2:10, all highlight this aspect of forgiveness: 'forgive one another', urges the author of Ephesians; and 'Forgive, and you will be forgiven', records Luke. Key to understanding this idea, I suggest, is that we see it as using forgiveness in a dispositional sense. Matthew 6:14–15,

---

[79] So Roy Yates, 'Colossians 2,14: Metaphor of Forgiveness', *Biblica* 71 (1990), 248–59.

which follows the Lord's prayer in Matthew 6, may serve as a suitable representative formulation of this idea of reciprocity:

> For if you forgive others their trespasses,
>   your heavenly Father will also forgive you;
> but if you do not forgive others,
>   neither will your Father forgive your trespasses.
>
> (Matt. 6:14–15, NRSV)[80]

Significantly this passage comes soon after the line in the Lord's prayer 'forgive us our debts as we also have forgiven our debtors' (v. 12). Davies and Allison note that in both cases, 'The point has to do not with deserts but with desire: God's forgiveness, although it cannot be merited, must be received, and it cannot be received by those without the will to forgive others.'[81] This, to my mind, is a helpful comment in search of a framework for understanding its significance.

If we recast the point as being concerned with *stance* rather than 'desire', then we may grasp the significance of this approach. In these verses it is 'debts' or 'trespasses' which are being forgiven, but perhaps it is significant that monetary debts, at least, often thought to be particularly in view in Luke's version of the Lord's prayer (Luke 11:4), are in many respects paradigm examples of institutional facts, forming a major test case of Searle's own analysis in *The Construction of Social Reality*. Debts therefore are both count-generated, but also possess what we might term an 'interpersonal solidity'. This point may be extended, once we grant the fundamentally institutional nature of many of the most significant trespasses (as well as our preparatory discussion above of the institutional nature of sin). The legal profession today remains preoccupied with the kinds of reparation required when the trespass is precisely a reconstituting speech act which affects stance and standing. As two recent commentators have noted:

> while there are some injuries that cannot be repaired just by saying you are sorry, there are others that can *only* be repaired by an apology. Such injuries are the very ones that most trouble

---

[80] For a full treatment of historical and critical issues surrounding these verses, see W. D. Davies and Dale C. Allison Jr, *A Critical and Exegetical Commentary on the Gospel according to Saint Matthew* (ICC), 3 vols, Edinburgh: T&T Clark, 1988, 1991, 1997; here 1:615–17.

[81] Davies and Allison, *Matthew*, 1:610–11.

American law. They include defamation, insult, degradation, loss of status, and the emotional distress and dislocation that accompany conflict.[82]

Seen in this light, one might say that 'I forgive you your debt (to me)' is the speech act of 'overcoming resentment' in the particular sense that the expectation of repayment is abandoned: the speech act alters the institutional fact which is part of the social reality of the forgiver and the forgiven. This ability to construe the world as a place where heretofore reasonable expectations of being repaid are waived is precisely what is at stake in the text. By learning this ability, the speaking agent is moved from a world ruled by repayment and invested instead, through this self-involving speech act of forgiveness, in a different world. This different world, according to the text, is one in which one's heavenly Father will construe one's own deeds with the same reconfiguration of debt and pardon.

The logical grammar of this passage is therefore not that God's forgiveness is offered after human forgiveness has taken place, from a divine person to a human person who has already forgiven another human person, in a succession of trans-actions between independent persons. Rather it is that the human person involved is re-constituted (or refigured, to use Ricoeur's word) through performing the act of human forgive-ness in such a way that he or she becomes a recipient of God's forgiveness.[83]

This emphasis fits with the idea that Matthew's Gospel is written for Christians[84] and that as such it is indeed plausible that verses such as 6:14–15 are referring to practices known 'from the inside' as it were by the Gospel's readers, rather than being a teaching concerning a new practice of forgiveness.

---

[82] Hiroshi Wagatsuma and Arthur Rosett, 'The Implications of Apology: Law and Culture in Japan and the United States', *Law & Society Review* 20 (1986), 461–98, here 487–8; cited in Tavuchis, *Mea Culpa*, 95.

[83] There are similarities between this account and the view of prayer developed by D. Z. Phillips, *The Concept of Prayer*, London: Routledge & Kegan Paul, 1965, in which he attempts to clarify the 'grammar of worship' (24). Phillips urges a similar link to mine, but perceives its significance the other way round: 'Being able to see that one is forgiven by God entails being able to live with oneself' (63). His account has a different focus, namely that of exploring the ways in which prayer provides self-knowledge.

[84] Whether or not this might be a 'Matthean community', as recently contested in Richard Bauckham (ed.), *The Gospels for All Christians: Rethinking the Gospel Audiences*, Edinburgh: T&T Clark, 1998.

One may read Matthew 18:21–35 in a similar fashion, not least because of the obvious attention to the same subject matter. As noted by I. H. Jones, 'It is clear that 18:30–35 was written under the influence of Matthew 6:14–15.'[85] Here the emphasis is on the non-practice of forgiveness: the failure of the forgiven slave to forgive his debtor evidences his inability (or at least his failure) to make the requisite construal of the world in terms of divine and human stances and relationships. Thompson's comment on this passage highlights the link suggested above between institutional issues such as debts and forgiveness: 'Matthew understood the forgiveness of a personal offense as analogous to releasing a man from a financial obligation. The evangelist himself has created this interpretation by framing the parable (vv. 23–34) with expressions about forgiving a fellow-disciple (vv. 21, 35).'[86] I thus demur from the judgment of Haber and of Murphy that Jesus is offering a ground for forgiveness in these verses.[87] Rather the point is that the practice of forgiveness is a work of self-involvement: to invest in forgiving is to be refigured as one who is forgiven. As the parable of Matthew 18 serves, at least in its final context, as a response to the question of Matthew 18:1 ('Who is the greatest in the kingdom of heaven?'),[88] it is noteworthy that the main thrust of its answer to this question is in terms of stance. The stance of a disciple is to be that of a willingness to forgive, which in turn is precisely what allows the disciple to receive God's forgiveness. This stance is what secures the successful performance of illocutionary acts of forgiveness.

The issue of stance permeates Matthew 18. Richard Hays suggests that the chapter presents forgiveness as the mediation between rigour and mercy: the two poles of Matthew's ethical

---

[85] Ivor Harold Jones, *The Matthean Parables: A Literary & Historical Commentary* (NovTSup LXXX), Leiden: E. J. Brill, 1995, 211–26, here 223. See also William G. Thompson, *Matthew's Advice to a Divided Community. Mt. 17,22 – 18,35* (Analecta Biblica 44), Rome: Biblical Institute Press, 1970, 203–37, especially the comparison of the two passages on 223–5.

[86] Thompson, *Matthew's Advice*, 225.

[87] See n. 25 above.

[88] Ivor Harold Jones, *Matthean Parables*, 225–6. Thompson's view is that the unit of discourse begins with Jesus' prediction of the passion at 17:22, which in his view lends an eschatological slant to the application of Matthew 18, since it reflects on how the Christian community may await its final consummation and cope with internal dissension in the meantime (Thompson, *Matthew's Advice*, 267). Although this changes the context of the point made here about stance, it does not affect its content.

framework.[89] Even with the instruction to treat an offender who refuses to listen to correction 'as a Gentile and a tax collector' (18:17), Hays notes that this still requires the stance of aiming to regain the lost brother or sister: to be treated as a Gentile or a tax collector is to become a focus for the church's missionary efforts. Prominent in the background to the whole chapter is Leviticus 19:17, occurring in a passage which immediately went on to say 'you shall love your neighbour as yourself' (Lev. 19:18).[90] Significantly, Leviticus 19:17 concerns itself with both heart attitudes and external actions. James Kugel suggests that Matthew 18:15 is finally bringing together two divergent readings of the Leviticus passage: the 'externalising' and the 'judicial' approaches; the former of which involves open reproach to prevent anger 'in the heart', and the latter of which focuses on the prevention of taking reproach into the legal system.[91] Here then is a good example of an interpersonal speech act in the public domain being dependent on stance while still at the same time admitting of interpersonal criteria to assess its suitability.

Also helpful concerning stance is a 1978 article by C. F. D. Moule in which he contrasted the apparently conditional nature of forgiveness in the Lord's prayer (we are forgiven only as we forgive) with the more evidently unconditional forgiveness of both Paul and of Jewish liturgy.[92] Is there a conflict here? Moule responded:

> The key to an answer to this question lies in distinguishing between, on the one hand, earning or meriting forgiveness, and, on the other hand, adopting an attitude which makes forgiveness possible – the distinction, that is, between deserts and capacity.[93]

Forgiveness cannot be earned, grants Moule. However, it does not follow that it is not conditional: 'forgiveness, though not conditional on merit, is nevertheless conditional – conditional

---

[89] Richard B. Hays, *The Moral Vision of the New Testament: A Contemporary Introduction to New Testament Ethics*, Edinburgh: T&T Clark, 1996, 101.

[90] Hays, *Moral Vision of the New Testament*, 101–3.

[91] James L. Kugel, 'On Hidden Hatred and Open Reproach: Early Exegesis of Leviticus 19:17', *HTR* 80 (1987), 43–61.

[92] C. F. D. Moule, '" . . . As we forgive . . .": A Note on the Distinction between Deserts and Capacity in the Understanding of Forgiveness', *Essays in New Testament Interpretation*, Cambridge: Cambridge University Press, 1982 (1978), 278–86; referring to the work of Israel Abrahams, *Studies in Pharisaism and the Gospels*, Cambridge, 1924, 95–100, on Jewish liturgy.

[93] Moule, 'As we forgive', 281.

on response to the gift, conditional on the capacity to receive it'.[94] Armed with this distinction, Moule presses on to make sense of Luke 7:36–50 where the woman who falls at Jesus' feet with perfume is described as forgiven 'because' she has showed much love: or rather, as Moule has it, that her love is evidence of the capacity to receive forgiveness. He also uses it to clarify the parable in Matthew 18: the forgiven servant has demonstrated, by his failure to forgive, not that he had not done enough to earn God's forgiveness, but that he did not have the capacity to receive it.

Moule's exegetical approach here is in line with his own earlier work on 'The Theology of Forgiveness', where he rejected the idea that forgiveness can be 'measured' in credit/debit terms as if it were a transaction between persons, and suggested instead that in forgiveness both the offender and the offended are involved in satisfying the restoration of the personal relationship.[95]

What Moule has termed 'capacity' is, I would suggest, approximately what a speech act analysis will prefer to call 'stance', and is certainly dispositional in nature. Moule's analysis makes sense of the various biblical texts in their context of first-century Judaism. While I will go on to argue below that a speech act approach requires us to consider further essential aspects beyond just stance/capacity, and that therefore there is more that must be said, I first address briefly the issue raised by Moule's first-century focus concerning how Jesus' talk of forgiveness might have been viewed in its historical context.

The forgiveness of sin and the forgiveness of sinners: forgiveness in the context of covenant

ἄφεσις in the New Testament is always used in the context of the forgiveness of sins,[96] and we must consider whether our discussion of the 'construction' of sin may be applicable here.

---

[94] Moule, 'As we forgive', 284.

[95] C. F. D. Moule, 'The Theology of Forgiveness', *Essays in New Testament Interpretation*, 250–60. See now also the essays collected in idem, *Forgiveness and Reconciliation*, London: SPCK, 1998, especially part 1, 'The Theology of Forgiveness', 3–47.

[96] Allowing for the above noted exception of Luke 4:18, Ephesians 1:7 has τὴν ἄφεσιν τῶν παραπτωμάτων and Mark 3:29 clearly implies that sins are at issue. Elsewhere the phrase is always ἄφεσιν ἁμαρτιῶν.

In recent years there has been prominent debate, sparked by the work of E. P. Sanders, about the identity of 'sinners' in the Gospels, and concerning in what ways exactly Jesus' offer of forgiveness may have been remarkable (or at least controversial) in first-century Judaism.[97]

The precise details of this debate need not concern us here. What is relevant is the question of how far the various constructions of 'sinners' may be understood in the constructed but non-reductive terms I have proposed above. Sanders's basic point, in line with his earlier revisionist work on the nature of the Palestinian Judaism opposed by Paul,[98] is that the issue in the Gospels is not one of legalistic works-righteousness being confronted by an anachronistic Lutheran (whether Paul or Jesus). Jesus, rather, is a prophet of Jewish restoration, working within an accepted framework of covenantal nomism, whereby obedience to the Jewish law was a mechanism for remaining in the covenant community, wherein salvation was understood to be entirely a matter of grace. In particular, for our purposes, it follows that it is mistaken to argue that Jesus' offer of forgiveness to sinners would, by itself, have been remarkable, since forgiveness was available within the parameters of the law already.

What was offensive to normal piety about Jesus, in Sanders's view, was not the offer of forgiveness, but his willingness to embrace complete outsiders (e.g. tax collectors) without the stringent requirements of admission to Judaism. The 'sinners', in the synoptic Gospels, are the *resha'im*, 'virtually a technical term. It is best translated "the wicked", and it refers to those who sinned wilfully and heinously and who did not repent'.[99] The *resha'im* were not the 'common people' (the *'amme ha-arets*, or 'people of the land'), and Jesus' association with 'sinners' thus does not offend against narrow religious sensibilities, but rather threatens to undermine the very infrastructure of Judaism.

[97] Arising particularly from the work of E. P. Sanders, *Jesus and Judaism*, London: SCM Press, 1985, 174–211; idem, 'Jesus and the Sinners', *JSNT* 19 (1983), 5–36 (an earlier version of his 1985 material); and idem, 'Sin, Sinners (NT)', in *ABD*, VI:40–7, for a summary of his views. Cf. James H. Charlesworth, 'Forgiveness (Early Judaism)', in *ABD*, II:833–5; and N. T. Wright, *Jesus and the Victory of God*, London: SPCK, 1996, 264–78.

[98] E. P. Sanders, *Paul and Palestinian Judaism: A Comparison of Patterns of Religion*, London: SCM Press, 1977.

[99] Sanders, *Jesus and Judaism*, 177.

While the details of Sanders's claims remain debated, there is a general agreement that he has successfully altered the shape of the discipline of New Testament study with his focus on the historical Jesus within Judaism.[100] In my view, Sanders's focus on what 'sinners' would mean in the context of first-century Judaism provides a particularly clear example of how 'sin' must be understood in self-involving terms. To label something as 'sin', or a person as a 'sinner', is a self-involving act indicative of one's stance towards that sin or person. In Sanders's account, 'sinners' functions almost as a technical term, and forgiveness operates as part of the eschatological programme of Jewish restoration in Jesus' ministry: Jesus grounds his words of forgiveness in the lifestyle of eating with 'sinners'. I suggest that this account provides a particularly clear, and evidently non-reductive, example of the 'construction' of forgiveness.

Agreeing with Sanders on covenantal nomism, Roger Mohrlang notes that one finds in Matthew particularly:

> a strong demand for obedience to the law, set within the context of an underlying structure of grace and the framework of the new covenant of God's salvation and forgiveness in Jesus.[101]

The demand for human acts of forgiveness, relatively prominent in Matthew compared to the rest of the New Testament, is always grounded first in God's forgiveness, but, suggests Mohrlang, the theme of grace is generally presupposed rather than a subject in its own right.[102]

That forgiveness operates in the Gospels within a presupposed framework of covenant and grace leads us on to consider the second major aspect of a speech act analysis of forgiveness: that of entailment. In this respect we might cast Sanders's discussion in terms of *membership*: does one stand with the Pharisees, or with Jesus and his restorationist eschatology? This, I suggest, is

---

[100] Bruce D. Chilton, 'Jesus and the Repentance of E. P. Sanders', *TynB* 39 (1988), 1–18, here 1–2. On the so-called 'third quest' of the historical Jesus, see Wright, *Jesus and the Victory of God*, 83–124.

[101] Roger Mohrlang, *Matthew and Paul: A Comparison of Ethical Perspectives* (SNTSMS 48), Cambridge: Cambridge University Press, 1984, 17, referring in particular to Matthew 1:21 and 26:28

[102] Mohrlang, *Matthew and Paul*, 80. He goes on to suggest that Paul evinces a greater eschatological confidence and hence focuses more quickly on the salvific aspects of the cross, whereas Matthew does not draw out this angle (91).

again a particular example of the speech-act dynamic of forgiveness. Where the stance of forgiveness is marked in the
New Testament by reciprocity, its entailment is primarily an
issue of membership, whether this be understood in terms of
some specifically religious grouping ('church' membership, as
it might be today) or, more broadly, any socially delimited
grouping.

§4.2 Forgiveness and entailment: membership

The primary implication of forgiveness is, in individual terms,
a restored relationship. The second major aspect of forgiveness in the New Testament is indeed that of membership,
which in theological terms I suggest means fellowship, and is
rooted in seeing forgiveness as operative with respect to one's
social location in or out of the church (or perhaps, putatively,
the Matthean community, as the case may be). In other words,
the speech act of forgiveness is felicitous where it leads to the
restoration of fellowship.

This is clearly the emphasis of the parable in Matthew 18
considered above, and is equally the point at issue in Luke 15
with its famous parable of the two sons, where, we might note,
the speech act of forgiveness is achieved by the father without
using the particular words for forgiveness at all: Luke 15:22–24
has the father forgiving his returned son with words such as
'put a ring on his finger . . . let us eat and celebrate'. This is a
particularly clear example of an illocution without a clear
vocabulary marker.

I propose, therefore, that an adequate analysis of forgiveness
as an illocutionary act in the New Testament must involve an
analysis of its entailment in terms of admitting or re-admitting
the forgiven 'sinner' into fellowship. As Tavuchis has noted in
the related case of apology as a speech act, 'the offender's group
membership is at stake or called into question' and the offender,
socially or morally demoted, now requires a 'means for his return
to institutional grace' which the apology provides.[103] Put simply:
it is not possible to forgive felicitously and still exclude from
fellowship, and, conversely, it is not possible to maintain fellow-

---

[103] Tavuchis, *Mea Culpa*, 73, 76. Note again Tavuchis's example of church
exclusion, cf. n. 70 above.

ship unless sin is forgiven. The particular passages which discuss this very aspect of forgiveness are the 'binding' and 'loosing' verses in Matthew 16 and 18.

Binding and loosing

In Gregory Jones's words, the practice of binding and loosing is the 'sustaining of permeable boundaries'.[104] My limited concern here is to substantiate the claim that, in this practice, the speech act of binding (or loosing) serves to include or exclude one judged to be a sinner, precisely because the illocution involved is a self-involving one of community delineation: boundaries are sustained but the boundaries are permeable. In other words, the speech act of binding and loosing serves to mark the scope of the entailments of forgiveness by regulating community membership.

The secondary literature on binding and loosing is disproportionately vast, simply because of the Protestant–Catholic divide over the interpretation of Jesus' commission to Peter in Matthew 16:18.[105] Even amongst those works more inclined to commentary than to treatment of the partisan issue per se, there is a wide variety of proposals about the meaning and significance of binding and loosing. Davies and Allison list 13 different approaches to the terms, while Jones (referring to Matt. 18:18) suggests that there 'are eight possible interpretations' of binding and loosing.[106] Despite this variety, however, the essential functions with respect to which 'binding' and 'loosing' are appropriate terms may reasonably be reduced to two:

> (1) forgiveness: to bind is to withhold fellowship and to loose is to forgive

---

[104] L. Gregory Jones, *Embodying Forgiveness*, 182–97.

[105] For helpful summaries see: the ecumenical treatment of Raymond E. Brown, Karl P. Donfried and John Reumann (eds), *Peter in the New Testament*, Minneapolis: Augsburg Press, 1973, 83–101; the study of the debate as it occurred in Reformation times in Gillian R. Evans, *Problems of Authority in the Reformation Debates*, Cambridge: Cambridge University Press, 1992, 147–66; and the study of the history of effects (*Wirkungsgeschichte*) of Matthew 16 by Ulrich Luz in his *Matthew in History: Interpretation, Influence, and Effects*, Minneapolis: Fortress Press, 1994, 57–74. More thoroughly, see Joseph A. Burgess, *A History of the Exegesis of Matthew 16:17–19 from 1781 to 1965*, Ann Arbor: Edwards Brothers, 1976.

[106] Davies and Allison, *Matthew*, I:635–9; Ivor Harold Jones, *Matthean Parables*, 216, n. 140.

(2) moral discernment/teaching authority: to bind is to determine one way or the other (i.e. to either forbid or to enjoin) while to loose is to leave free.[107]

I take this particular formulation of the terms from a widely cited article by Mennonite theologian John Howard Yoder, and indeed it is significant that this penetrating study of the issue comes from such a thinker, in the Anabaptist tradition which has self-consciously had to wrestle with these issues of community self-definition and membership. As Yoder reflects on 'the centrality of binding and loosing in the life of free-church Protestantism', he comments that the juxtaposition of the binding and loosing passages in Matthew with Jesus' only attributed use of ἐκκλησία suggests that 'the church is, therefore, most centrally defined as the place where "binding and loosing" takes place'.[108]

In fact Yoder does not use the particular formulation 'teaching authority' and prefers 'moral discernment', a point which again may reflect ecclesiological commitments, although in his discussion he clearly talks about 'moral teachings and decision making' as practised by the rabbis.[109] However, both these two major emphases are fundamentally linked, precisely because the standard of 'truth' against which the sinner must be measured as requiring forgiveness (in sense (1)) is a standard determined by the one 'binding' or 'loosing' in sense (2). In Yoder's words, 'Forgiving presupposes prior discernment'.[110] 'Binding' in this constructive sense of declaring truth is well-expressed by Gestrich as follows:

> Whenever representatives of the church say in binding terms what is true and what is not true, they are not making statements about

[107] John Howard Yoder, 'Binding and Loosing', *The Royal Priesthood: Essays Ecclesiological and Ecumenical* (ed. Michael G. Cartwright), Grand Rapids: Eerdmans, 1994, 323–58.

[108] Yoder, 'Binding and Loosing', 336–7. Revealing also in this regard is the historical overview of W. Telfer, who discusses the practice of 'loosing' as it develops in the third century as part of the response to the problem of post-baptismal sin and the failure of believers to maintain their confession under persecution. What is significant is that binding and loosing is a prominent issue at *this* point in time, and largely fades from prominence with the conversion of Constantine as the problems involved in 'maintaining traditional standards of Christian initiation' (75) change in nature completely; cf. Telfer, *Forgiveness of Sins*, 61–74.

[109] Yoder, 'Binding and Loosing', 327–8.

[110] Yoder, 'Binding and Loosing', 328.

factual issues as defined by natural science; rather, they are interpreting the gospel and applying its contents ad hominem.[111]

In Matthew 16:19 the authority to bind and loose is given by Jesus to Peter. In Matthew 18:18 it is broadened to the whole group of disciples.[112] On an exegetical level considerable (perhaps disproportionate) attention has been given to the clarification of the tenses used in these verses in order to assess whether the human act of binding forces God's hand in heaven, or whether it is consequent on a binding already achieved in heaven.[113] Protestants, in particular, have been nervous in this area. Nevertheless, the dominant rabbinic usage behind the image supports the notion of real teaching authority being operative here, even if interpreters have had differing opinions about the relevance of rabbinic parallels owing to disputes about relative dating.[114]

I suggest that a speech-act approach helps here by clarifying the question of what it can mean to have teaching authority. We have seen that forgiveness involves the stance of reciprocity and the resultant ability to construe the world as a place where God forgives sin, and thus allows for the restoration of a relationship between reconciled parties. Evidently the speech act of forgiveness is felicitous (i.e. it secures illocutionary uptake) where the stance of resentment is overcome, and the institutional fact of

[111] Gestrich, *Return of Splendor in the World*, 312.

[112] A third relevant reference is John 20:23, where the emphasis appears to be more on forgiveness than on teaching authority; cf. Steven E. Hansen, 'Forgiving and Retaining Sin: A Study of the Text and Context of John 20:23', *HBTh* 19 (1997), 24–32.

[113] See J. R. Mantey, 'The Mistranslation of the Perfect Tense in John 20:23, Mt. 16:19, and Mt. 18:18', *JBL* 58 (1939), 243–9; idem, 'Evidence That the Perfect Tense in John 20:23 and Matthew 16:19 Is Mistranslated', *JETS* 16 (1973), 129–38; and the helpful response to Mantey's first article: Henry J. Cadbury, 'The Meaning of John 20:23, Matthew 16:19 and Matthew 18:18', *JBL* 58 (1939), 251–4. See now also S. E. Porter, 'Vague Verbs, Periphrastics, and Matt 16:19', *FNT* 1 (1988), 155–73.

[114] Davies and Allison, *Matthew*, II:639, citing Str-B I:738–41 for the rabbinic texts. See the rabbinic images of 'prohibiting' or 'permitting' entry into the kingdom through Torah-interpretation as relevant here, with J. D. M. Derrett, 'Binding and Loosing', *JBL* 102 (1983), 112–17. In contrast, those who see the rabbinic parallels as too late focus instead on the general 'key' imagery of verses like Isaiah 22:22 and take the binding and loosing to refer to the way in which Christians' witness, preaching and ministry make it either possible or impossible for people to enter into the kingdom; thus G. Korting, 'Binden oder lösen: Zu Verstockungs- und Befreiungstheologie in Mt 16,19; 18, 18.21–35 und Joh 15,1–17; 20, 23', *SNTU* 14 (1989), 39–91.

sin is successfully removed. As an *illocutionary* act, this need not imply perlocutionary success, that is, that the relationship be successfully restored, or that the community membership be successfully re-established.

It is important therefore to clarify that the authority at issue here to bind and loose is *illocutionary* and not *perlocutionary*. Indeed, if exegetical ingenuity has been expended on trying to demonstrate how verb tenses and so forth do not force God's hand in conforming to human decisions, it might have been better deployed in reflecting on the nature of the speech act concerned. Peter receives authority from Jesus not because he is persuaded by Jesus, or because Jesus is particularly assertive on this occasion, but because Jesus' commission in Matthew 16:17-19 is an *illocution*, and thus it brings into being the state of affairs it describes. The church, in this technical speech-act sense, is therefore an *institution*, and hence the authority which Peter (and then in Matt. 18 the disciples) may utilise is an institutional authority, that is, it is the accreditation to perform the speech acts of forgiveness and teaching which are circumscribed by the institutional facts of their setting, namely, the church as a constructed reality with 'permeable boundaries'. Illocutionary authority, one would have to insist, is not authoritarian, in contrast to perlocutionary authority, and perhaps the nervousness in the ecumenical debate concerning these verses may be thus addressed. On this account, forgiveness is a self-involving speech act not least because it requires the forgiver to embrace (in Volf's image, used here metaphorically) the forgiven in the same institutional reality. In my view, 'membership' is the appropriate description of this entailment of the successful illocution.

The important consequence of this analysis is that it clarifies the worried questions of 'But am I *really* forgiven?' or 'Does Peter (or today's church) *really* have authority to make this pronouncement?' The answer is yes on both counts, because the question is in fact concerned with institutional facts and not brute facts. These are created by the relevant illocutions when successfully performed, and the requirement for successful performance simply is the appropriate setting of the speaker's role combined with the appropriate stances as delineated above.

I suggest, briefly, that a similar analysis will reveal a comparable understanding of two related issues concerning forgiveness and sin in the New Testament, as found in Mark 3:29 and 1 John 5:16.

The unforgivable sin and the sin that leads to death

The unforgivable sin, 'blasphemy against the Holy Spirit', which is referred to by Jesus in Mark 3:29 (and parallels: Matt. 12:31 and Luke 12:10) has raised various problematic issues in the history of interpretation, although these have not been predominantly exegetical since in fact the passages concerned are relatively straightforward. Taken on its own, for instance, Mark 3:28–29 clearly suggests that blasphemy against the Holy Spirit, which can never be forgiven, is simply the persistent refusal to accept God's redemptive work, and thus is 'an eternal sin' (αἰωνίου ἁμαρτήματος). However, placed as it is within the larger story of the confrontation between Jesus and the scribes over attributing Jesus' work to Beelzebul, which concludes in verse 30 with 'for they said, "He has an unclean spirit"', Mark appears to present the 'unforgivable sin' as the attribution of God's work to Satan.[115]

More ambitious redaction-critical studies separate out two different sayings: the original preserved in Mark (on being forgiven every sin except blasphemy against the Holy Spirit), which is then conflated in Matthew with a secondary one, also recorded by Luke, which contrasts sinning against the Son of Man with this unforgivable sin.[116] O'Neill, taking such a line, suggests that the secondary saying is a corruption of the first, and that the 'spirit' referred to in the original saying is basically an 'attitude of mind': in fact precisely the attitude of being willing to forgive which does indeed stand as a prerequisite to receiving forgiveness, as we have seen above.[117] If this is right then the saying about the unforgivable sin is indeed a matter of stance and disposition.

However, even if such a redaction-critical approach should be mistaken, I suggest that the speech act categories of stance and entailment clarify what is at stake here. One must ask, first, what it could mean to call a sin unforgivable? While it is

[115] So R. A. Guelich, *Mark 1:8:26* (WBC 34a), Waco: Word, 1989, 180.
[116] E.g. J. C. O'Neill, 'The Unforgivable Sin', *JSNT* 19 (1983), 37–42; cf. Robert H. Gundry, *Matthew: A Commentary on His Handbook for a Mixed Church under Persecution*, Grand Rapids: Eerdmans, ²1994 (1982), 237–9.
[117] O'Neill, 'Unforgivable Sin', 41.

apparent that in any particular case forgiveness may misfire as an illocution, this is generally because the conditions for it are not met in the particularities concerned: for example, I am unable to bring myself to overcome resentment, or I fail to adopt the 'reciprocal' stance characterised above. But to say that a sin is unforgivable is prima facie to preclude such an illocution from taking place, and must therefore suggest that the required stance is not just unattained, but unattainable. It would appear, therefore, that some such solution as O'Neill's must be correct in its analysis of what unforgivability entails, regardless of the particular redaction one proposes about the saying: to commit the unforgivable sin is to maintain a stance irreconcilable with reciprocity, and hence to force the misfiring of any attempted illocution of forgiveness.

If stance is at issue with respect to the unforgivable sin, then it is membership that is to the fore in the case of 1 John 5:16–17 concerning the sin that leads to death (πρὸς θάνατον). In this somewhat under-defined phrase, doubtless left unclear because it needed no clarification in the original context, either John is suggesting that there is sin that can lead to expulsion from the community (the church) or that sin committed by those outside the church is sin that leads to death. A variety of approaches has been proposed here. Historically the most influential view, deriving from Tertullian, is that certain sins are worse than others, leading directly to a classification of 'mortal' and 'venial' sins.[118] Raymond Brown argues that the difference in view is not between different types of penalties or sins, but between different types of sinners, those within the community and the 'secessionists'.[119] In all probability, one need not circumscribe 'those outside the community' as narrowly as the 'secessionists',[120] since if we grant the foregoing speech act account of forgiveness then expulsion from the community is nothing less than the decision to disable the possibility of extending forgive-

[118] On the history of the interpretation of this passage see D. M. Scholer, 'Sins Within and Sins Without: An Interpretation of 1 John 5:16–17', in G. F. Hawthorne (ed.), *Current Issues in Biblical and Patristic Interpretation*, Grand Rapids: Eerdmans, 1975, 230–46, especially 236–8.

[119] Raymond E. Brown SS, *The Epistles of John* (AB 30), London: Geoffrey Chapman, 1982, 612–19.

[120] See Dietmar Neufeld, *Reconceiving Texts as Speech Acts*, 105, for the (disputable) view that a historical secession need not be in view here.

ness to the offender. Thus the sin leads to death, and 'death' in this context *is* exclusion from the community of forgiveness.

§5 Conclusions: The Community of Forgiveness

I have suggested that, as with confession, forgiveness is a speech act which can be understood more precisely by recognising it as a strongly self-involving illocutionary act. I have developed a performative model of forgiveness as a speech act, and as a part of analysing this model for strengths and weaknesses have been drawn to explore further the relationship between brute and institutional levels of fact and the successful performance of speech acts of forgiveness. I have defended the view that forgiveness works within the context of a non-reductive view of sin as (socially) constructed, serving as an illocutionary act which (re-)constitutes the institutional facts concerned. In my judgment, organising one's approach around the speech act categories of stance and entailment successfully highlights two of the prominent concerns of the various New Testament texts which concern forgiveness: those of reciprocity and membership.

My discussion is intended to highlight the speech act dynamics of self-involving speech acts. It is not intended, in its analysis of requirements and entailments, to suggest that by virtue of analysing the particular mechanisms of the speech act one has made the practice of forgiveness any more straightforward or easy to accomplish. Indeed, I hope that one of the benefits of this analysis is to lay to rest the misapprehension that an analytic approach such as this should in any way be offered as a counter to analyses which focus on emotional or embodied aspects of forgiveness. Rather, as I have argued, speech acts occur within habituated stances with entailments concerning future embodied commitments. Highlighting these does not simplify them. Nor, in my discussion of 'construction', is the analysis intended to suggest that recognising a fact as an institutional fact is a reductive move. In the case of forgiveness, recognising that God is one of the members of the Christian community of forgiveness is just one way of marking out this understanding of (socially) constructed community as non-reductive in the particular case of the church.

8

Teaching

§1 Introduction

Our third and final study of a speech act found in the New Testament is a study of teaching. I choose this because, since it is a different kind of speech act from confessing or forgiving, it draws out different aspects of speech act theory. In particular, it lends itself to an exploration of the relationship between brute and institutional facts: facts 'external' or prior to the speech act and facts created by the speech act. Although I do not claim that the nature of teaching cannot be understood without such a conceptual framework, I do argue that some aspects of the function of teaching in the New Testament are liable to be overlooked.

On the one hand, teaching is more obviously a speech act than forgiving: it is clearly an act achieved by speaking. On the other hand, it is less obviously interesting since at first glance it appears that 'to teach' is simply a variation of 'to assert'. My argument will be, however, that one cannot fully understand teaching without looking at its directive and declarative aspects as well as its content. In his survey of performative verbs, Vanderveken does not include 'teach'.[1] However, it is instructive that several performatives which touch on aspects of teaching *are* included, and that they are distributed across a variety of classifications: *assert* and *tell* as assertives; *assure* and *certify* as

[1] Vanderveken, *Meaning and Speech Acts*, vol. 1, 166–219.

commissives; *tell, instruct* and *prescribe* as directives; *declare, approve, stipulate, define* and so forth as declaratives; and perhaps even *acclaim* and *disapprove* as expressives. To teach, therefore, is to operate across a whole range of illocutionary acts.

We recall that in the first half of his developing argument about the possibility or otherwise of distinguishing performatives from statements (constatives), Austin paused to consider whether there might be a linguistic criterion of performativity such as the use of the word 'hereby': ' "Hereby" is a useful criterion that the utterance is performative' although only in 'highly formalized' utterances; and in any case one may go on to say 'I hereby state . . .' without intending a 'performative'.[2] The ensuing failure to demarcate performatives linguistically or grammatically leaves us with performative statements of just such a kind: 'I hereby state that x'.[3] Thus, 'to say' or 'to state' have their performative aspects: Austin succeeds in getting them on the illocutionary map, as it were, without clarifying what might be interesting about them as illocutions.

Likewise, when Jesus says, 'ἀμὴν λέγω ὑμῖν' in prefacing some remark,[4] it is something of an equivalent case. One could almost describe this phrase as a vocabulary marker for the illocutionary act of teaching, albeit not a necessary one. What this alerts us to is that in investigating a subject such as the teaching of Jesus, one is investigating an illocutionary act. This will also allow us to ask to what extent such teaching is self-involving.

After a characterisation of teaching as a speech act, I investigate in this chapter a spectrum of cases of teaching in the New Testament which demonstrate its self-involving character as it ranges from weak to strong cases. In particular, I conclude with a discussion of Jesus' teaching about the kingdom of God, where I suggest that the strength of illocution is one variable which it is helpful to bear in mind in considering the various contested interpretive issues.

---

[2] Austin, *HDTW*, 57–8, 61.

[3] For a clear and wide-ranging discussion of just such performatives in legal theory, see Dennis Kurzon, *It Is Hereby Performed . . . Explorations in Legal Speech Acts* (Pragmatics & Beyond VII:6), Amsterdam and Philadelphia: John Benjamins Publishing Company, 1986, especially 5–8.

[4] E.g. Matthew 5:18; 6:2, 5, 16, and many times through the synoptics. In John it is prefaced with a double ἀμὴν (John 1:51; 3:3, 5, 11, etc.).

§2 Teaching as a Speech Act: Then and Now

Teaching may be more than a speech act, but it is at least a speech act.[5] Once one has observed this basic fact, it is striking how many books occupy themselves with such topics as *The Kingdom of God in the Teaching of Jesus*, for example, without any discussion of what kind of an activity teaching is, and thus what implications this would have for the kinds of illocution being performed by Jesus in such cases.[6]

By way of contrast, modern discussions of the philosophy of education evince considerable attention being given to the nature of teaching. Clearly it will not be appropriate to assimilate the oral teaching of the Gospel traditions to contemporary practice in the classroom, but certain aspects of the discussion may prove helpful in clarifying the issues. I thus pursue this topic from both ends: investigating what sort of activity teaching was in the time of Jesus, but first pausing to see whether useful categories may arise from a look at the contemporary philosophy of education.

The act of teaching today

Thomas Green, in his book *The Activities of Teaching*, highlights the different types of act performed by a teacher: logical acts, strategic acts and institutional acts.[7] In this way he intends to separate out the basic teaching activities into three kinds: those relating primarily to thinking and reasoning; those concerning the organisation of material and the direction of students; and those which arise as a function of the teacher's membership in an educational institution rather than their particular role of teaching.

This distinction between what teaching is and what teachers do leads Green to propose that teaching itself can be understood as two different kinds of activity: either teaching someone

---

[5] But see n. 13 below.

[6] This particular title has heralded books by Norman Perrin (London: SCM Press, 1963); Gösta Lundström (Edinburgh: Oliver & Boyd, 1963); and Bruce Chilton (ed.) (Issues in Religion and Theology 5; London: SPCK, 1984); cf. Bruce Chilton, 'The Kingdom of God in Recent Discussion', in Bruce Chilton and Craig A. Evans (eds), *Studying the Historical Jesus: Evaluations of the Current State of Research* (New Testament Tools and Studies XIX), Leiden: E. J. Brill, 1994, 255–80, 255 n. 1.

[7] Thomas F. Green, *The Activities of Teaching*, New York: McGraw-Hill, 1971, 4–9.

how to do something and teaching someone that something is the case, or, respectively, 'shaping behavior' and 'shaping belief'.[8] The first of these he develops along Wittgensteinian lines as an account of 'training': learning, for instance, a series of numbers until one says, 'Now I know how to go on'. Wittgenstein's work has been a key resource in the philosophy of education.[9]

Green's second distinction leads us in the direction of 'teaching as teaching that': the imparting of information. Teaching in perhaps its most mundane sense might well include teaching someone that something is the case. The speech act here is assertion: the teacher tells the class that '2 + 2 = 4'. This is a truth and the teacher is asserting it. In line with our proposal concerning strong and weak illocutions, this is a weak illocutionary act. Indeed, one has to postulate basic situations in which the rehearsal of facts is the issue in order to discover such weak illocutions as the vehicle of teaching.

What is far more common is that even 'teaching that' is fundamentally a self-involving exercise in training someone to think in a certain way, to apprehend a situation with a certain construal, or to develop an ability to understand in a certain way.[10] In fact, as Gabriel Moran argues, Green has rightly posed the question of what teaching consists in over and above its institutional trappings, but then restricted his answer to the kinds of situation still constrained by a teacher–student classroom situation.[11]

Moran's contention is that the essence of teaching is in 'showing how'; indeed, that the idea of teaching is parasitic on a background of wider ethical and moral judgments which necessarily underwrite the practice. Thus: 'Teaching is showing

[8] Green, *Activities of Teaching*, 21–3.
[9] Green, *Activities of Teaching*, 23–7; cf. Wittgenstein, *Philosophical Investigations*, §151 (and §§5–6). On the so-called 'analytic revolution' in the philosophy of education, see S. J. B. Magee, *Philosophical Analysis in Education*, New York: Harper & Row, 1971, 3–18. For the influence of Wittgenstein see, most notably, P. Smeyers and J. D. Marshall, *Philosophy and Education: Accepting Wittgenstein's Challenge*, Dordrecht: Kluwer, 1995. I am indebted here to Hong-Hsin Lin, 'The Relevance of Hermeneutical Theory in Heidegger, Gadamer, Wittgenstein and Ricoeur for the Concept of Self in Adult Education', unpublished Ph.D. thesis, University of Nottingham, 1998, 2–19 and 154–88 (especially 157).
[10] See Lin, 'Relevance of Hermeneutical Theory', 222–9, on 'ways of thinking'.
[11] Gabriel Moran, *Showing How: The Act of Teaching*, Valley Forge, PA: Trinity Press International, 1997, 31–3.

someone how to live and how to die.'[12] His argument cuts across some of the traditional debates about whether teaching is necessarily a human activity (can the sea teach?)[13] as well as the distinction developed by Ryle, and much appealed to, between the 'task verb' of teaching and the 'achievement verb' of learning.[14] For Moran, teaching and learning interact in a variety of more or less formal situations.

It is important not to downplay the significance of teaching content: 'The world remains in need of occasions when someone who knows something stands up and says, "So and so is the case".'[15] At the same time, this must always be held in balance with the all-pervasive activity of showing people how to live.[16] What follows from this analysis of the teaching *act* is that, in all but the most elementary cases, the teaching–learning complex can only be understood by participation in the activity of 'showing how–learning how'. When we thus confine our interest to speech acts of teaching, we will find them generally to be self-involving, and hence, if we wish to interpret texts of teaching acts, we will be looking at self-involving illocutions.

Illocutionary teaching acts might range from the evaluative judgment which dictates an inquiry ('the most important event in the lead up to the first world war was the assassination of Archduke Ferdinand') to the authoritative illocution which establishes and thus determines the issue at hand ('It is wrong to tell lies'). In practice, as we would expect, most speech acts used in the process of teaching are declarative to some greater or lesser degree. As we saw in part 1, this is a different claim from the postmodern one that all speech acts are essentially

---

[12] Moran, *Showing How*, 41.

[13] Moran, *Showing How*, 43–6. See n. 5 above, where, technically, we should say that the teaching performed by a person who teaches, using words, is at least a speech act. Philosophy of education spent much of the 1960s and 1970s discussing the meaning of 'to teach' and debating whether the sea, or a mountain, for example, could teach. This is not my concern here. Moran follows broadly this approach. It is probably fair to say that, in the wake of Alasdair MacIntyre's work on moral traditions, the focus in philosophy of education has shifted to the contested nature of education rather than attempts to capture its commonly agreed essence by linguistic precision.

[14] Moran, *Showing How*, 40; cf. Gilbert Ryle, *The Concept of Mind*, London: Hutchinson, 1949, 149–52.

[15] Moran, *Showing How*, 33.

[16] Moran, *Showing How*, 219. A Wittgensteinian view of training is clearly at work here.

rhetorical acts and that constructed reality is simply whatever
we say it is. Rather, speech act theory suggests that a typical
teaching speech act will be a multi-dimensional speech act which
draws upon and interacts with non-linguistic states of affairs:
asserting; declaring; and perhaps at other times also being
directive or commissive. In short, the speech act of teaching
can rarely be reduced to simply informing someone that
something is the case.

Teaching in the time of Jesus

Having now established the various illocutionary dimensions of
teaching, we must also prepare the ground historically. As
Pheme Perkins notes at the beginning of her helpful survey of
Jesus as a teacher, 'In order to understand what the people who
heard Jesus expected from his teaching, we need to know about
the different types of teachers in the first century.'[17] Discussing
those teachers who might have had adult followers, Perkins
conveniently summarises the relevant evidence by noting that
there were four basic different types of teacher:

(1) Philosopher-teachers
(2) Sages and teachers of wisdom
(3) Teachers of the law: Scribes, Pharisees and Rabbis
(4) Prophets and visionaries[18]

She uses all of these to varying degrees to highlight different
types of teaching given by Jesus in the Gospels, although her
presentation falls short of suggesting that Jesus, either
consciously or unconsciously, sought to combine them all.[19]

---

[17] Pheme Perkins, *Jesus as Teacher* (Understanding Jesus Today), Cambridge:
Cambridge University Press, 1990, 2. Perkins's survey, as I shall note, places the
emphasis on categories of teaching. The more familiar emphasis in the literature
is on Jesus' pedagogy (and/or psychology) itself; notably in the extensive study of
Riesner, who focuses on the various aspects of oral tradition in Jesus' time in and
behind the Gospel accounts: Rainer Riesner, *Jesus als Lehrer: Eine Untersuchung zum
Ursprung der Evangelien-überlieferung* (WUNT II/7), Tübingen: J. C. B. Mohr (Paul
Siebeck), 1981; cf. idem, 'Jesus as Preacher and Teacher', in Henry Wansbrough
(ed.), *Jesus and the Oral Gospel Tradition* (JSNTS 64), Sheffield: Sheffield Academic
Press, 1991, 185–210, especially 201–8.

[18] Perkins, *Jesus as Teacher*, 1–22. She is drawing here on H. I. Marrou, *A History of
Education in Antiquity*, New York: New American Library, 1964.

[19] For the four emphases see, respectively, Perkins, *Jesus as Teacher*, 6 (sayings
characteristic of Cynic philosophy); 42–51 ('Jesus and the Wisdom Tradition');
51–4 ('Legal Sayings'); and 54–61 ('prophetic sayings and apocalyptic images',
discussing the kingdom of God).

Certainly, in the wider literature, these models of Jesus have had their champions, all seeking to show how, in orientating one's view of Jesus around a particular dimension of his teaching, one may correctly locate him in his first-century milieu.[20]

My point here is not to engage in the endless debates concerning the relative merits of these different emphases, which are too easily played off against each other in mutually exclusive ways, as is noted by Rainer Riesner when he comments that 'the example of Qumran shows how little an end-times orientation excludes methodical handling of Scripture'.[21] Rather I simply wish to put forward a somewhat straightforward corollary, suggested by the foregoing speech act analysis, that it is the illocutionary act and not just the content of Jesus' teaching which should occupy the interpreter, and which perhaps provides a useful step forward in understanding what Jesus is trying to *do* in any particular case. Again, I propose that this speech act approach is a more fruitful way into situating the content (i.e. locution) of a biblical text than the various 'social construction' models which have often characterised attempts to view teaching as more than informing.

As a further hypothesis it does not seem unreasonable to suppose that each of the various aspects of Jesus' role as teacher lends itself to a different characteristic type of illocution: the apocalyptic declarative-commissive; the philosophical expressive; the wise directive; the legal assertive becoming declarative as issues of authority concerning the Torah are broached. I intend this characterisation as illustrative only: the categories will not be unvarying.

It may be the case that speech act theory offers a way beyond the impasse of contrasting Jesus as a disembodied teacher on the one hand with Jesus as the embodied enactment of some

---

[20] Thus we have F. Gerald Downing, *Christ and the Cynics: Jesus and Other Radical Preachers in First-Century Tradition*, Sheffield: Sheffield Academic Press, 1988 (and idem, *Cynics and Christian Origins*, Edinburgh: T&T Clark, 1992); Ben Witherington III, *Jesus the Sage: The Pilgrimage of Wisdom*, Edinburgh: T&T Clark, 1994 (which includes a critical appraisal of the 'Cynic' view, 117–45); S. Westerholm, *Jesus and Scribal Authority* (Coniectanea Biblica NT 10), Lund: C. W. K. Gleerup, 1978, especially 53–132; and what is perhaps the predominant view from Schweitzer onward: the apocalyptic preacher announcing the end. These authors are sympathetic with other emphases to considerably varying extents.

[21] Rainer Riesner, 'Teacher', in *DJG*, 807–11, here 810.

symbolic or theological destiny on the other.[22] To call Jesus a teacher is to open up a link between these two characterisations, not to foreclose it. N. T. Wright, for example, writes of one commentator that he 'asks what the parable of the prodigal son is "intended to teach", and is surprised at how difficult this is to establish. Perhaps this is because the better question would be: what is the parable intended to *do*?' Indeed, but this does not demonstrate that it was a mistake 'to assume . . . that Jesus was basically a *teacher*'. Rather it shows that taking a teacher seriously involves asking what speech *acts* he/she was trying to perform.[23]

My discussion here has focused upon *Jesus* as a teacher, but with appropriate modifications it may be seen to apply to any teaching which can be read out of the New Testament text. An utterance of Paul, or one of the evangelists, or indeed an utterance placed on the lips of Jesus by one of the evangelists, may still be viewed as a speech act with similar interpretive possibilities concerning its assertive or declarative nature. Some of the examples considered in the next section will thus be drawn from the sayings of Jesus, others from the New Testament writers. The speech act issues raised are the same, even if the theological debates thus joined have tended to exist in their own separate worlds.

§3 Degrees of Self-Involvement in New Testament Teaching Acts

In this section I consider some New Testament examples of the speech act of teaching, whether cases of reported direct speech acts, or cases where the illocution in the text is a teaching one, across the spectrum of strengths from weak to strong speech

---

[22] Note the Jesus Seminar's move on from the sayings of Jesus to the acts of Jesus in their forthcoming work; and the two-volume work of C. A. Evans and B. D. Chilton (eds), *Authenticating the Words of Jesus* and *Authenticating the Activities of Jesus* (New Testament Tools and Studies 28/1 and 28/2), Leiden: E. J. Brill, 1999.

[23] Wright, *Jesus and the Victory of God*, 101, n. 63, and referring in the quote to Christopher F. Evans, *Saint Luke*, London: SCM Press, 1990, 589. To be fair to Wright, he often does work successfully with the notion of speech as act; e.g. 85 (and 85 n. 11), and indeed he is making this point precisely in the context of the predisposition of the 'Old Quest [for the Historical Jesus]' to fail to look for the acts performed by the words of Jesus. Nevertheless, the wording seems unfortunate.

acts. After commenting on the usual issue of vocabulary markers for illocutionary acts, I shall take, in turn, weakly self-involving speech acts such as assertions, strongly self-involving speech acts which focus our attention on issues such as construal, and finally a topic of Jesus' teaching where perhaps it is helpful to realise that the degree of self-involvement varies, as we look at the types of speech act at work in the 'kingdom of God' sayings in the Gospels.

The vocabulary of teaching

It is obvious that in terms of vocabulary, teaching acts may range over almost any form of language at all. The word 'teach' will occur only in the most formal of cases: 'I hereby teach . . .' springs to mind. In terms of biblical texts, as suggested at the beginning of this chapter, it is Jesus' 'ἀμὴν λέγω ὑμῖν' which comes closest to such a formal device. Perhaps one may generalise and say that there are two basic types of sentence which lend themselves for consideration.

First, we have first person present tense address, such as 'If the son makes you free, you will be free indeed': reported direct speech from Jesus, in John 6:36. Secondly, there will be cases of third person texts not in direct speech, but presented from the point of view of the author or narrator, as, for instance, almost all of an epistle would be, except for those parts of it which consciously engage other speech acts such as greeting or thanking. Even here Paul is not averse to teaching too: witness the theological content of the opening greeting in Romans 1:1–6. I shall draw on both these types of text in what follows.

§3.1 Teaching as an assertive speech act

As suggested above it is teaching as the rehearsal of certain basic facts which is in view here. To some extent, it is when the facts in question are brute facts that we will be considering teaching as an assertive speech act: this is teaching as primarily the imparting of information.

One knows instinctively where to turn for a consideration of this emphasis: to that stream of theologically conservative literature which has always wished to underline the propositional content of biblical texts, and in particular of the New Testament message.[24] This emphasis has been observed by Nancey Murphy in terms relevant to our discussion:

> In more conservative branches of the Christian tradition, propositional (referential) views of religious language abound ... These views have their own problems, one of which is to counter the charge that they overlook the element of self-involvement appropriate to all religious discourse.[25]

It is of course too easy to overreact against this relentlessly referential view of language which restricts teaching to the speech act of assertion, as the constant championing of 'rhetorical' approaches to biblical texts demonstrates. Acknowledging teaching as a speech act seems to me to offer the obvious solution: teaching is a performative action which is irreducibly involved with the assertion of states of affairs, while in the process capable of creating new states of affairs, or indeed acting in a variety of performative ways.[26]

A full study of this topic would be as broad as the Bible itself (since it is, in a sense, the question of the status of biblical language in general), but one aspect of it is worthy of particular exploration here. I have suggested that it is in fact difficult to observe cases where teaching is simply assertive: where the rehearsal of facts is all that is at issue. In fact, it is debatable whether an assertive, especially one which is passed down as a part of the biblical text, can ever be just an assertive.

A variety of passages are candidates for the role of 'rehearsing the facts'. 1 Corinthians 15:3–8 makes precisely this claim for itself ('I handed on to you as of first importance what I in turn had received') and yet, as we saw in considering this passage in chapter 6 above, this statement of faith is best classified as a *confessional* speech act which stakes one's stance in the public domain. Without in the least denying its assertive character, it is

[24] In the interests of completeness, and lest straw men are suspected, one may point to Wayne Grudem, 'Scripture's Self-Attestation and the Problem of Formulating a Doctrine of Scripture', in D. A. Carson and John D. Woodbridge (eds), *Scripture and Truth*, Leicester: IVP, 1983, 19–59 and 359–68; or indeed to most of the essays contained in this volume.

[25] Nancey Murphy, 'Textual Relativism, Philosophy of Language, and the Baptist Vision', in Stanley Hauerwas, Nancey Murphy and Mark Nation (eds), *Theology without Foundations: Religious Practice & the Future of Theological Truth*, Nashville: Abingdon Press, 1994, 245–70, here 248.

[26] For a similar view which still remains sympathetic to 'propositional' concerns, see Vanhoozer, 'Semantics of Biblical Literature'.

much more than assertive. The same consideration must apply to other similarly credal utterances, as well as to any passages where the facts are rehearsed with some further illocution in view (e.g. the list of Titus 3:3–7 which is followed by 'I desire that you insist on these things . . .').

A second type of candidate for this role, although this will require us to understand 'teaching' with some latitude, is a text which 'simply' reports the facts, such as the mundane elements of those narrative sections of various New Testament books or on occasion the historical narratives alluded to in the epistles. Even here, however, one must question the extent to which any assertive is an assertive pure and simple. A narrative such as Paul's narration of his travels in Galatians 1:13–24 is clearly a multiple speech act. His catalogue of places visited and not visited is part report and part commissive-declaration: he swears that his gospel is of God and not learned at the feet of Peter and the Jerusalem Apostles. Rhetorical studies of Galatians have little difficulty making this point, even if they do appear willing to sit lightly to the assertive role of a speech act in any particular case. In characterising Galatians 1:11–2:14 as the *narratio* of the letter, Ben Witherington observes that

> the *function* of the narrative material we find in Gal. 1–2 is to provide examples for the audience of what sort of behaviour to adopt or shun . . . Paul is providing *exempli* in his *narratio*.[27]

Nevertheless, Witherington, with his comment that 'the marshalling of facts could serve to correct mistaken impressions about the speaker',[28] keeps a stronger balance between declaration and assertion than does Hans Dieter Betz, whose approach indicates the key difference between a rhetorical approach and a speech act approach when he writes

> the facts themselves, as well as their delivery, are subjected to partisan interest . . . whether the 'facts' are true or fictitious, the effort required to make them believeable is the same.[29]

---

[27] Ben Witherington III, *Grace in Galatia: A Commentary on St. Paul's Letter to the Galatians*, Edinburgh: T&T Clark, 1998, 29.

[28] Witherington, *Grace in Galatia*, 95; cf. 94–164.

[29] Hans Dieter Betz, *Galatians: A Commentary on Paul's Letter to the Churches in Galatia* (Hermeneia), Philadelphia: Fortress Press, 1979, 60. In fact Betz does credit Paul here ('it would seem he follows the natural order of events in 1:13–2:14, since there is no indication that he does not', 61), but the *tone* of the approach is certainly different.

However, might it still be the case that less controversial, less significant texts, such as the background narrative which links episodes in the Gospels or Acts, can be viewed as straightforward assertion? In such cases is a writer such as Luke performing the speech act of assertion: simply telling us what happened? This question, while to some extent tangential to our particular concerns with 'teaching' (except that teaching be taken broadly), nevertheless enables us to clarify the speech act workings of biblical language in a way which does, I believe, address some general concerns about speech act theory and biblical interpretation. I discuss this question with reference to the recent work of Francis Watson, whose appeal to speech act theory concerns itself precisely with a verse such as Mark 1:9 ('In those days Jesus came from Nazareth in Galilee and was baptized by John in the Jordan').[30]

Watson, as the polemical title of his chapter indicates, is concerned to defend some definite and singular concepts against the encroaching tide of pervasive metaphor, textual autonomy and (radically) subjective interpretation; and he fastens upon this apparently unpromising narrative text in Mark in order to show that 'to be understood at all, a series of words must be construed as a communicative action which intends a determinate meaning together with its particular illocutionary and perlocutionary force'.[31] Watson asks, quite rightly, 'what takes place when a sentence such as [Mark 1:9] is understood?' and explores various conventions by/through which the author situates his narrative within a broader 'institutional context' (such as the time, the place, the person of Jesus as defined in the whole Gospel). He touches on precisely our issue when he addresses the nature of Mark's illocution at this point:

> If we ask what Mark is *doing* in writing as he does, the initial answer is that he is *informing* or *reminding* his readers of something . . . one does not inform or remind one's addressee of just anything at all, but of that which one takes to be significant within the context of utterance . . . What Mark is *doing* is not simply telling a story but *proclaiming the gospel.*[32]

---

[30] Watson, *Text and Truth*, 103–6. The title of the relevant chapter of this book is 'Literal Sense, Authorial Intention, Objective Interpretation: In Defence of Some Unfashionable Concepts' (95–126).

[31] Watson, *Text and Truth*, 103.

[32] Watson, *Text and Truth*, 105.

In this I think Watson is correct. He has perhaps chosen a relatively insignificant verse from Mark's narrative precisely to show how the informative function of *any* text must be seen as an aspect of its performative role in a wider institutional context: literal meaning inheres in the illocution which remains operative wherever the institutional context is preserved.[33] From this he concludes that a Christian reading of this text (and thus any Gospel text) is not justified by appealing to the partisan nature of all interpretation, which he would regard as a pyrrhic victory indeed, but is warranted objectively by its subject matter. This thesis is obviously more controversial than his basic speech act claims, and its precise fit with his broader advocacy of theological hermeneutics (or a 'redefined biblical theology' as the subtitle of the book has it) leads me to wonder whether his appeal to speech act theory here is more a matter of its perceived congruence with his wider aims than a result of any conviction about the irreducible speech act dynamic of all (textual) communication. Certainly he does not appeal to it elsewhere even when discussing 'the gospels as narrated history'.[34]

In my judgment, Watson's use of speech act theory here must be adjudged only partially successful, but in fact successful in precisely the area germane to my own inquiry at this point, that of the performative nature of assertion in even the most apparently unpromising of biblical texts. In other words: assertion can hardly be 'mere assertion', unless perhaps we were discussing some idling form of language, utterances 'said for no conceivable reason'.[35]

On the broader front, and although I am in sympathy with his desire to elaborate a non-partisan theological hermeneutic, I am unpersuaded that speech act theory does in fact guarantee a literal sense for a text, except that literal sense be *defined* as 'illocution construed in a fixed institutional context'. Watson does not quite say this; for him it is 'the sense intended by the author in so far as this authorial intention is objectively embodied in the words of the text'.[36] However, he does go on to add that 'If speech-acts are embodied in written texts, their

[33] Watson, *Text and Truth*, 106.

[34] Watson, *Text and Truth*, 33–69.

[35] These fundamental qualifications are from Wittgenstein, *Philosophical Investigations*, §132; and Austin, *HDTW*, 146; and cannot be stressed too often.

[36] Watson, *Text and Truth*, 115.

intended illocutionary and perlocutionary force as communicative actions requires institutional continuities extended through the space and time that they traverse' and he contends for 'the reality of institutional continuities that guarantee the identity of the God referred to [in the biblical text] with the God who is still the object of worship'.[37] As far as I can see, Watson has correctly laid bare the requirement of institutional continuity, and one must say that this is an important and all too rare achievement, but he has not demonstrated that this is guaranteed in a way that transcends precisely the community-relative partisan advocacy which he is seeking to avoid. He avers that 'to read a text is to construe it',[38] and thus seeks to orient the interpretive act towards the communicating agent. However, as I have suggested in part 1 of this study, while the communicating agent is indeed introduced by such a construal, against any textual autonomy view, the point of fixing on the mechanism of construal is that it *mediates* between the communicator and the reader, rather than handing over the final word to the communicator. Thus appealing here to speech act theory does not in itself demonstrate that 'reading communities' do not validate their own construals. Even if one hedges this conclusion about with phrases such as 'within limits', or 'as constrained by the meaning of the text', I suspect that the 'objectivity' to which Watson aspires here is intended as something more than the 'interpersonal objectivity' which I suggested in earlier chapters is actually what follows from this line of argument. I judge that in fact Watson has further good *theological* reasons for making his case,[39] but that speech act theory itself does not do quite the work he asks of it.

Nevertheless, on the more specific level of demonstrating that even the flattest of flat assertions, to develop Donald Evans's terminology, is more than an assertion, Watson's account is convincing. For the purposes of this section, therefore, we are justified in affirming that teaching as an assertive speech act is best viewed as a limiting case rarely if ever attained in practice.[40]

---

[37] Watson, *Text and Truth*, 117–18.

[38] Watson, *Text and Truth*, 97; in fact suggesting that this is 'overwhelmingly plausible'.

[39] See his trinitarian 'intratextual realist' account, most powerfully articulated in Francis Watson, *Text, Church and World: Biblical Interpretation in Theological Perspective*, Edinburgh: T&T Clark, 1994, 221–93.

[40] Cf. Austin, *HDTW*, 146.

Rather, the speech act of teaching is always operative in other illocutionary dimensions at the same time.

It is perhaps helpful to draw attention here to the related speech act of preaching. I would suggest that this could also be explored under some such rubric as the interpretation of brute fact and the resulting advocacy of institutional fact. The only speech act account of preaching which I have discovered, that of Michael McNulty, charts a helpful speech act path between 'academic' and 'emotivist' approaches to preaching, and uses it, for example, to explore the familiar contrast between Paul's Athens sermon in Acts 17 and his 'performative approach' at Corinth. McNulty is particularly clear about the role of self-involvement in grounding performativity in extra-linguistic fact, although he does not specifically consider the categories of brute and institutional fact.[41]

Before going on to attempt a study of a particular teaching theme where the variable nature of the speech act may help us, I first clarify the other end of the spectrum, where the teaching act is so strongly self-involving that the facts concerned are institutional, that is, created by the performance of the illocution.

§3.2 Teaching as a declarative speech act: the grammar of ἡγέομαι

In this section we look at the teaching of institutional facts: creating a fact by the successful performance of an illocutionary act. In chapter 4 I discussed the significance of construal in speech act theory, and its relevance to some theological aspects of interpretation, noting also that it is the key notion in the construction of social reality. Here I want to propose that close to the heart of the grammar of Christian belief is the notion of *reconstrual*, and that this grammar is inscribed in some of the main ways in which the New Testament sets about teaching.

Christian belief takes its stand on the advocacy of particular construals, on a variety of grounds (ethical and historical grounds; theological and faith commitments, in an interlocking variety of approaches). One of the clearest examples of reconstrual in the New Testament is the opening exhortation of James:

---

[41] T. Michael McNulty, 'Pauline Preaching: A Speech-Act Analysis', *Worship* 53 (1979), 207–14; comparing Acts 17 with Acts 18 in the light of 1 Corinthians 1–4.

'My brothers and sisters, whenever you face trials of any kind, consider it nothing but joy' (James 1:2, NRSV).

Luke Timothy Johnson notes that at the beginning of this letter, 'The theme is faith and its reaching a fullness or perfection through a variety of "testings" presented by an alternative understanding of the world.'[42] In the face of these possibilities, James advocates a particular conception of reality as the appropriate one for a Christian: a construal where God gives gifts to humanity and thus breaks open what might seem to be the closed system of trial and tribulation: 'This theological construal of reality is what makes the turn to prayer something other than an arbitrary piece of pious advice.'[43]

I suggest that *re*-construal captures what is at issue here better than 'construal'. James advocates wilful reconstrual, presupposing that construal may in such a case be a cognitive endeavour. Indeed in terms of our earlier discussion, it is also a non-mentalistic endeavour: reconstrual occurs in the public domain and the reality concerned is a social reality available only to those whose engagement with it is self-involving. This, then, is teaching of the most strongly self-involving type.

The word used in James 1:2 is ἡγέομαι (in fact the imperative here, ἡγήσασθε, which indicates the cognitive nature of re-construal). ἡγέομαι plays a significant role in the logic of Christian belief. It is used some 20 times in the New Testament, and is perhaps the key term for capturing the link between the 'X' and the 'Y' in Searle's 'X counts as Y' formula: thus the grammar of construing, considering, regarding, judging, counting, treating, esteeming or thinking of X as Y is particularly clear where ἡγέομαι is used. See, for example:

Acts 26:2	I *consider* myself [*as*] fortunate
2 Cor. 9:5	I *thought* it necessary [= I *judge* it *as* necessary]
Phil. 2:3	*regard* others *as* better than yourselves
Phil. 2:6	did not *regard* equality with God *as* something to be . . .
Phil. 3:7	whatever gain I had . . . I have come to *regard as* loss
1 Thess. 5:13	*esteem* [those who labour among you] very highly

[42] Luke Timothy Johnson, *The Letter of James* (AB 37A), Doubleday: Anchor, 1995, 182.

[43] Johnson, *James*, 184.

1 Tim. 6:1	[Let slaves] *regard* their masters *as* worthy of all honour
Heb. 11:11	[Abraham] *considered* him faithful who had promised ...
2 Peter 3:15	*regard* the patience of our Lord *as* salvation.[44]

Faith as the advocacy of a particular construal is also a prominent theme in the New Testament, as with Hebrews 11:1: 'Faith is the assurance of things hoped for, the conviction of things not seen.' This conviction, or faith, must be mediated through the mechanism of self-involvement: without the act of construal the 'reality' which is germane to faith is simply not there to be considered. Clearly there is a reality, an 'X term' which is there to be construed as a Y,[45] and it is in this well-defined and non-reductive sense that it is appropriate to pursue 'constructive' models of the world for theological purposes.

The grammar of ἡγέομαι as sketched out here provides a particularly clear example of the logic of Christian belief: clear for our purposes because it is fitted precisely to the logic of illocutionary acts. I would go further and argue that the notion of construal underwrites the idea of the Bible as Christian Scripture: what Moule calls the Bible's 'one proper and distinctive function . . . of confronting the readers with a portrait of Jesus Christ and with the events that show that he lives and is with them'.[46] That portrait is a construal of a reality which, while it cannot be accessed except by way of construal, can nevertheless be accessed by a variety of construals. Christian faith assumes the advocacy of a particular (range of) construal(s), and it is in this context that the Bible serves as Christian Scripture: 'A canon is a canon only in use; and it must be construed in a certain way before it can be used', as Charles Wood has it.[47] It is also I suggest in this connection that one may properly develop the irreducibly

[44] ἡγέομαι is used 20× in this sense: 1 in Acts; 8 in Paul (including 6 in Philippians); 3 in the deutero-Paulines; 3 in Hebrews; 1 in James; and 4 in 2 Peter. It is also used 4× (1 in Acts, 3 in Hebrews) in the associated sense of 'leaders', which might (optimistically!) be taken in the sense of 'those whose construals are authoritative'. Obviously this grammar may be at work without the use of ἡγέομαι itself, as the next examples above indicate.

[45] An X-term which may be something as objectively identifiable as John-the-Baptist, as for instance with Matthew 11:14, 'if you are willing to accept it, he [John] is the Elijah who is to come.'

[46] Moule, *Forgiveness and Reconciliation*, 221–2.

[47] Charles M. Wood, *The Formation of Christian Understanding: Theological Hermeneutics*, Valley Forge, PA: Trinity Press International, [2]1993 (1981), 93.

theological hermeneutic of Francis Watson mentioned above, whose avowed 'intratextual realism' suggests that the key issue is indeed construal, although he terms it 'mediation': 'it is necessary to speak of the text as *mediating* the reality of Jesus rather than as *constructing* it'.[48]

We have isolated, in this section, a certain kind of subject matter which renders the speech act of teaching involved as necessarily a strongly self-involving one. Accounts of a verse such as James 1:2 will typically acknowledge this without pausing to consider the idea of self-involvement to which they appeal, and in one sense all my own account does is demonstrate that what there is to be explained here is an illocutionary act at work. In our final example, we shall attempt to examine a topic where the type of illocution is not predetermined by the subject matter at hand.

§3.3 *Teaching as a multi-dimensional speech act: the kingdom of God in the speech acts of Jesus*

It is not my intention here, even if it were possible, to provide a full study of the much discussed topic of the kingdom of God; and neither am I particularly concerned to trace the various strands of scholarship on the subject.[49] My aim is rather to clarify the kinds of distinction which can usefully be drawn by approaching a topic such as the kingdom of God by way of looking at the speech act of teaching[50] with which it is typically introduced into public discourse. Unlike the two examples considered above, I judge that the illocution involved varies across a range of strong and weak speech acts when teaching about the kingdom of God is in view. As a result the institutional reality of the kingdom of God is constituted differently for different purposes: it is an interpersonal reality neither reducible to nor separable from the self-involvement of those who receive the teaching of Jesus on this topic.

---

[48] Watson, *Text, Church and World*, 225.

[49] For overall background and orientation I have drawn upon Perrin, *Kingdom of God in the Teaching of Jesus*; idem, *Jesus and the Language of the Kingdom: Symbol and Metaphor in New Testament Interpretation*, Philadelphia: Fortress Press, 1976 (a very different work from his 1963 study); G. R. Beasley-Murray, *Jesus and the Kingdom of God*, Grand Rapids: Eerdmans, 1986; Chilton (ed.), *Kingdom of God in the Teaching of Jesus* ; and idem, 'Kingdom of God in Recent Discussion'.

[50] Or preaching. See n. 41 above.

Speech act theory has not been generally considered in connection with this kind of question. For my discussion of the kingdom of God I shall be drawing to some extent on the various exegetical studies of Bruce Chilton, and therefore it is perhaps appropriate to preface this section with a brief discussion of Chilton's own brisk reference to speech act theory and its applicability to kingdom language which, despite its brevity, is still more than most exegetes have attempted.[51]

Chilton develops a theory of 'performance' for understanding Jesus' teaching, by which he 'refers both to the activity which results in the telling of a parable, and to the activity which may attend the hearing of a parable'. The kingdom is performed, parabolically, in both word and deed.[52] Analysing 'Jesus' construal of the kingdom', Chilton warns that the notion of performance should not be taken existentially, and in a lengthy footnote he tries to show that his notion of performance is simply a way of speaking, and not one which 'determines or describes what is true'.[53] In so doing he suggests that Searle and to some measure Austin support the view that 'nothing is performed by speech except a manipulation of language', and he cites Anthony Thiselton in support of an existential grounding for 'performative utterance'.[54] I suggest, however, that he has joined here precisely what Thiselton, in this reference, was trying to rend asunder: the 'language event' approach of Fuchs and Ebeling, and the Austin-Searle stress on states of affairs underwriting speech acts.[55] In conclusion, Chilton writes that

> The philosophy of language can, and has, contributed to . . . the literary study of the New Testament. But linguistic philosophy has not produced a sufficiently coherent account of how words convey meaning to enable us to employ it directly as a description of how the preaching of the kingdom functions.[56]

With our view of 'performative' suitably disentangled from existentialist concerns, I propose to attempt to utilise speech

---

[51] The reference occurs in Bruce Chilton and J. I. H. McDonald, *Jesus and the Ethics of the Kingdom* (Biblical Foundations in Theology), London: SPCK, 1987. The relevant sections are written by Chilton (see xi).

[52] Chilton and McDonald, *Jesus and the Ethics of the Kingdom*, 16, 31.

[53] Chilton and McDonald, *Jesus and the Ethics of the Kingdom*, 110, cf. 131-2, n. 2. All subsequent quotations in this paragraph are from this footnote.

[54] Thiselton, *Two Horizons*, 336-7.

[55] See also Thiselton, *Two Horizons*, 354-5.

[56] Chilton and McDonald, *Jesus and the Ethics of the Kingdom*, 132, n. 2.

act theory for precisely this function (although with regard to *teaching*) in what follows.

It is all too easy for an analysis of synoptic 'kingdom' language not even to get off the ground. The interested interpreter is waylaid immediately by questions of the appropriate translation of ἡ βασιλεία τοῦ θεοῦ, and the apparently self-sustaining momentum of the debate about when the kingdom was expected to come, with its well-known positions of realised eschatology (C. H. Dodd),[57] consistent/futurist eschatology with its imminent but mistaken expectation (Albert Schweitzer),[58] and all in-augurated stations in between.[59] Fortunately it seems that many writers today are willing to allow that such a focus risks missing the more fundamental question of the nature of ἡ βασιλεία τοῦ θεοῦ in the first place, which must be assumed in some sense for the temporal debate even to get under way.[60] Four brief observations will have to suffice here.

First, one clearly needs a refined use of language to address the question of what sort of *thing* the kingdom of God is. It is not, to use the language of Arbib and Hesse, a spatio-temporal reality. Thus, to ask 'Is it real?' forces us to draw on the con-ceptuality of institutional reality, in its speech act sense. The alternative, to suggest that it is not a 'thing' at all, is perhaps more common in the literature, and need not pose any problems in itself, but I suggest that it does not solve the problems of how to discuss the kingdom as something experienced within spatio-temporal reality. Kingdom language operates at the Kantian divide between experience and transcendence, not least because 'the conviction that God is transcendent, beyond the terms of reference of what people see and imagine, is basic within the biblical tradition'.[61]

---

[57] C. H. Dodd, *The Parables of the Kingdom*, London: Nisbet, 1935.

[58] Albert Schweitzer, *The Quest of the Historical Jesus: A Critical Study of Its Progress from Reimarus to Wrede*, London: A&C Black, 1954 (1906); cf. also Johannes Weiss, *Jesus' Proclamation of the Kingdom of God*, London: SCM Press, 1971 (1892).

[59] E.g. G. E. Ladd, *The Presence of the Future: The Eschatology of Biblical Realism*, Grand Rapids: Eerdmans, 1974; and W. G. Kümmel, *Promise and Fulfilment: The Eschatological Message of Jesus* (SBT 1/23), London: SCM Press, ³1957. All the positions of these last three notes are reviewed in Wendell Willis (ed.), *The Kingdom of God in 20th-Century Interpretation*, Peabody, MA: Hendrickson, 1987.

[60] A significant move in this direction is Perrin, *Jesus and the Language of the Kingdom*; see especially 197–9.

[61] Bruce Chilton, *Pure Kingdom: Jesus' Vision of God* (Studying the Historical Jesus), London: SPCK, and Grand Rapids: Eerdmans, 1996, 23.

Secondly, the translation of ἡ βασιλεία τοῦ θεοῦ may of course be partly a function of context in any particular case, but, as is widely noted, its standard translation as 'kingdom of God' certainly risks putting the emphasis in the wrong place by focusing on the rule rather than the one doing the ruling. Various recent suggestions try and redress the balance: God's imperial rule, the 'coming of God' and the saving sovereignty, divine government, even 'The revolution is here!'.[62] Perhaps the most significant proposal is that of Bruce Chilton, who draws on first-century targumic literature (particularly the Isaiah targums) in an effort to find linguistic evidence from a similar time to the Gospels, and demonstrates that 'the kingdom of God' appears as almost a circumlocution for God himself acting in power. Hence the title of his published thesis *God in Strength* or, as his summary article of the same time puts it, 'regnum dei deus est' (the reign of God is God (himself)).[63] Chilton's work has met with criticism, for instance concerning the precise applicability of his suggested linguistic evidence,[64] but certainly his proposal appears to be the obvious way of making sense of at least some of the kingdom parables, such as the parable of the wedding banquet (Matt. 22:1–14) where the kingdom 'may be compared to the king' (NRSV) whose actions are described in the parable. In any case, whether or not one accepts the details of his position, Chilton's case is the starkest of reminders that ἡ βασιλεία τοῦ θεοῦ is about the spatio-temporal world being God's theatre where his glory is staged.

Such a perspective also seems, thirdly, to bypass the debates about realised or imminent eschatology, since God's activity amongst human beings is not, on this account, something which begins at a definite time either in the first century or at the end

---

[62] Offered respectively by Robert W. Funk, Roy W. Hoover et al., *The Five Gospels: The Search for the Authentic Words of Jesus*, New York: Macmillan, 1993; Beasley-Murray, *Jesus and the Kingdom of God*, *passim* and cf. 339; R. T. France, *Divine Government: God's Kingship in the Gospel of Mark*, London: SPCK, 1990, 13; David Wenham, *The Parables of Jesus*, London: Hodder & Stoughton, 1989, 20–5.

[63] Bruce Chilton, *God in Strength: Jesus' Announcement of the Kingdom* (SNTU 1), Freistadt: Plöchl, 1979, reprinted in the Biblical Seminar Series, Sheffield: JSOT Press, 1987, especially 277–98; idem, 'Regnum Dei Deus Est', *SJT* 31 (1978), 261–70.

[64] E.g. the caveats of John P. Meier, *A Marginal Jew: Rethinking the Historical Jesus*, vol. 2, *Mentor, Message and Miracles*, New York: Doubleday, 1994, 264, 287 n. 113. Meier is also concerned about Chilton's non-apocalyptic claims for kingdom language.

of the *eschaton*. The declaration of the kingdom, whether as ἤγγικεν or as ἔφθασεν, is fundamentally about a new orientation rather than a new epoch, on which more in a moment.

And fourthly, the recognition that ἡ βασιλεία τοῦ θεοῦ is God at work in power, perceived upon the earth, explains its multi-dimensional nature in the sense described by Chilton in his study of the background to the term in the language of kingship in the Psalms.[65] Chilton identifies a fivefold polarity in this background:

1. temporal/ultimate (the eschatological dimension, cf. Psalms 44, 47, 96, 98)

2. dynamic/immanent (the dimension of transcendence, cf. Psalms 22, 93, 145)

3. righteous/perfected (the dimension of judgment, cf. Psalms 10, 97, 103)

4. clean/holy (the dimension of purity, cf. Psalms 5, 24, 149)

5. local, in Zion and in heaven/omnipresent (the dimension of radiation, cf. Psalms 29, 47, 48, 114, 145)[66]

The kingdom operates along these various spectra, and it follows that on different occasions or in different situations the language of the kingdom will operate in different ways. In relation to our own concern with the nature of institutional facts which help to construct models of the transcendent, we shall be considering in particular the second of these five dimensions below.[67]

Valid as such an approach undoubtedly is, however, it seems preferable to articulate it in terms of the multi-valency of speech act illocutions which characterise the kingdom,[68] rather than saying that the *concept* of 'kingdom' itself is flexibly adapted to its different uses, which is the well-known position adopted by Norman Perrin in his last work on the parables. Perrin, drawing particularly on the work of Philip Wheelwright (as well as Paul

[65] Chilton, *Pure Kingdom*, 23–44; cf. 146–63.

[66] As summarised in Chilton, 'Kingdom of God in Recent Discussion', 273–4.

[67] Cf. Chilton, *Pure Kingdom*, 66–73.

[68] For this point in relation to parables generally, see T. Aurelio, *Disclosures in den Gleichnisse Jesu: Eine Anwendung der Disclosure-Theorie von I. T. Ramsey, der modernen Metaphorik und der Sprechakte auf die Gleichnisse Jesu* (Regensburger Studien zur Theologie 8), Frankfurt am Main: Lang, 1977.

Ricoeur) suggests a contrast between a 'steno-symbol', which has a fixed reference, and a 'tensive' symbol. A tensive symbol has 'a set of meanings that can neither be exhausted nor adequately expressed by any one referent', or, put more simply, its reference varies according to context.[69] However, Dale Allison correctly points out that Perrin's two types of symbol are made to be artificially mutually exclusive, and that the thesis that Jesus' use of kingdom language operates tensively in contrast to standard Jewish steno-uses is sustained only by limiting the accepted dominical sayings to those which do in fact work most flexibly.[70] It is perhaps fairest to see Perrin's proposal as a step on the way towards a projected hermeneutic of the New Testament which he did not live long enough to see through, a hermeneutic which would have attempted to take seriously the multiple appropriation of a text traditionally exegeted in univocal fashion.[71] Certainly, as it stands, his proposal has generally met with a negative response from critics.[72] I shall suggest that we need neither a theory of 'tensive language' nor of multi-referentiality to account for the ways in which kingdom language is used in the Gospels.

Construing the kingdom

The foregoing remarks are plainly inadequate for addressing all the various interpretive issues raised by this topic, but they are sufficient for the specific task in hand, which is the exploration of 'kingdom' language as it is introduced in the speech act of teaching, with its apparatus of construal. What we require, therefore, are examples of biblical language where construal will be an interesting category, and, as mentioned above, this

[69] Perrin, *Jesus and the Language of the Kingdom*, 29–32, here 30; cf. Philip Wheelwright, *Metaphor and Reality*, Bloomington, IN: Indiana University Press, 1962; Ricoeur, *Symbolism of Evil.*

[70] Dale C. Allison Jr, *The End of the Ages Has Come: An Early Interpretation of the Passion and Resurrection of Jesus* (SNTW), Edinburgh: T&T Clark, 1987 (1985), 107–12.

[71] *Jesus and the Language of the Kingdom* was published in the year of Perrin's death, 1976. His 'pilgrimage' towards this more hermeneutical work is the subject of Calvin R. Mercer, *Norman Perrin's Interpretation of the New Testament: From 'Exegetical Method' to 'Hermeneutical Process'* (StABH 2), Macon, GA: Mercer University Press, 1986.

[72] E.g. Chrys C. Caragounis, 'Kingdom of God/Kingdom of Heaven', *DJG*, 417–30, who wastes no time describing Perrin's view as self-contradictory and plainly inapplicable to the Gospel texts (422)!

seems prima facie most likely in those sayings where the transcendence of the kingdom is, to some extent at least, at issue.

Chilton's discussion of the 'transcendent co-ordinate' of the kingdom focuses on the following Lucan verses: 11:20 and 13:20–21 (with parallels) and 17:21.[73] Indeed, concerns about the presence of the kingdom in Jesus' ministry often start with an examination of his saying that 'if it is by the Spirit//finger of God that I cast out demons, then the kingdom of God has come to you' (Matt. 12:28//Luke 11.20). Here the act of exorcism indicates that the kingdom has come (ἔφθασεν). However, wary lest this line of inquiry should lead us straight into the quagmire of debate about temporal issues in relation to the kingdom, I choose to focus instead on Luke 17:21, a verse unique to Luke and one which, though often assimilated to the temporal debate, is I suggest best viewed as an entrée to the issue of self-involvement in kingdom language.

The Pharisees question Jesus about when the kingdom will come, and he replies,

Οὐκ ἔρχεται ἡ βασιλεία τοῦ θεοῦ μετὰ παρατηρήσεως, οὐδὲ ἐροῦσιν, Ἰδοὺ ὧδε ἤ, Ἐκεῖ, ἰδοὺ γὰρ ἡ βασιλεία τοῦ θεοῦ ἐντὸς ὑμῶν ἐςτιν (Luke 17:20b–21)

This much debated verse clearly presupposes some form of 'present' kingdom, but it is cryptic, hidden in some way.[74] The major interpretive debate concerns ἐντὸς ὑμῶν,[75] and the three main options are clearly set out by Beasley-Murray in his study of this verse under the heading 'the incalculable kingdom'.[76] The translation 'within you' is 'the common interpretation of the church', a view which has overwhelming linguistic support, but which poses for Beasley-Murray the insuperable problem that such an immanent conception of the kingdom cannot be allowed in Jesus' teaching: 'No interpretation of a saying of Jesus

---

[73] Chilton, *Pure Kingdom*, 66–73.

[74] So Wright, *Jesus and the Victory of God*, 469.

[75] μετὰ παρατηρήσεως also attracts its fair share of attention: most straightforwardly it is 'with observation'; cf. 'so that it's approach can be observed', BAGD, 622.

[76] Beasley-Murray, *Jesus and the Kingdom of God*, 97–103. He draws on the major study of B. Noack, *Das Gottesreich bei Lukas: Eine Studie zu Luk. 17.20–24* (Symbolae Biblicae Uppsalienses 10), Lund: Gleerup, 1948, who demonstrates that all the major options pre-date modern biblical criticism.

on the kingdom of God can be right that diminishes its strictly eschatological content.'[77] The standard alternative, to render it 'among you' on the grounds that this fits better theologically, he shows to be untenable, since this reduces the verse to arguing the platitude that 'when the kingdom comes it will be among you' (unless one introduces some such notion as its *sudden* future appearance, but this is clearly not at issue in Jesus' words).[78]

The untenability of this alternative leaves Chrys Caragounis arguing that 'within you' must be the right translation. Not only does this fit the available evidence concerning ἐντὸς, but also it takes into account parallels in the *Gospel of Thomas* (to which we must return below), the consistent Lukan usage of ἐν μέσῳ ὑμῶν to indicate 'among', and the parallel point of Luke 17:20, where the kingdom is said not to be coming with 'signs that can be observed', leading Caragounis to conclude that

> 'Within you,' therefore, seems to be Luke's way of expressing the inward nature and dynamic of the kingdom of God, rather than refer to any actual presence in or among the Pharisees.[79]

Caragounis thus also wishes to defend the view that the kingdom is never already present in the synoptics, but finds an alternative way to Beasley-Murray to uphold this view. In fact, Beasley-Murray finds a third line of interpretation, traced back to Cyril of Alexandria and revived by various modern scholars as strands of linguistic evidence have been unearthed, which leads him to favour some such translation as 'within your grasp' or 'it lies in your power to receive it'.[80] Linguistically possible, and consonant with the overall thrust of Jesus' teaching, this view addresses neither the *when* nor the *where* of the kingdom, but rather focuses on the ensuing implication that Jesus' hearers must avail themselves of the opportunity to enter which is thus presented.[81]

---

[77] Beasley-Murray, *Jesus and the Kingdom of God*, 101.

[78] Would that exegesis were this simple . . . For a recent commentator who finds that this 'somewhat vulnerable' view 'does best justice to the content of v. 21' see John Nolland, *Luke 9:21–18:34* (WBC 35B), Waco: Word, 1993, 853–4.

[79] Caragounis, 'Kingdom of God', 423–4.

[80] Beasley-Murray, *Jesus and the Kingdom of God*, 102–3.

[81] Beasley-Murray, *Jesus and the Kingdom of God*, 103, citing R. Otto, *The Kingdom of God and the Son of Man* (trans. F. V. Filson and B. L. Woolf), London: Lutterworth, 1938 (1934), 136. Significant defences of the 'within your grasp' view have included C. H. Roberts, 'The Kingdom of Heaven (Lk. xvii.21)', *HTR* 41 (1948), 1–8; and A. Rüstow, '*Entos hymon estin*: Zur Deutung von Lukas 17.20–21', *ZNW* 51 (1960), 197–224.

While these various interpretations all seem to be making good points, it is notable that there is no clear correlation between exegetical position and views on the presence or otherwise of the kingdom.[82] Rather it is theological agendas, either explicit or implicit, which drive the discussion. My concern is to ask what contribution may be made by enquiring after the nature of the illocution performed by Jesus in this verse.

The key contribution of a speech act approach, I suggest, is that it enables us to focus on Jesus' own concern with construal on the part of those who grasp the kingdom, without prejudging the question of how far this correlates with any interpersonal or objective criteria for saying that the kingdom is present. At stake in Luke 17:21 is a strongly self-involving declaration: the kingdom cannot be observed objectively; it does not come with outward signs. What is needed is eyes to see, or in other words, *the ability to construe* the perceived phenomena in such a way that God's activity is understood through them. If one can perform such a construal, then the grammar of the illocution involved indicates that the kingdom of God is present, since the institutional state of affairs which 'the kingdom of God' refers to is created by the successful performance of the illocution.

This is the by-now familiar logical grammar which accompanies strong self-involvement. However, what I believe makes this case particularly of interest is that the institutional state of affairs constituted by the illocutionary act, and labelled as 'the kingdom of God', is constituted in different ways by different speech acts,[83] with the unifying feature that all these constructions relate in some way to the activity of God as perceived within the spatio-temporal realm.[84] Jesus performs a strongly self-involving declarative speech act and the direction of fit is world-to-word: the kingdom is right here if you have but

---

[82] Note, for example, Wright, *Jesus and the Victory of God*, 469, who follows Beasley-Murray in translation, but who *does* see the kingdom as present in Jesus' ministry, *contra* Beasley-Murray. We should note, for completeness, that Chilton favours 'in your midst' for ἐντὸς ὑμῶν (Chilton, *Pure Kingdom*, 73), but his discussion is brief.

[83] In Chilton's terms: 'One advantage of seeing the distinct coordinates of the kingdom in Jesus' theology is that we can easily explain why in one aspect (eschatology) the kingdom is near, while in another aspect (transcendence) the kingdom has arrived.' Chilton, *Pure Kingdom*, 68.

[84] I am following Arbib and Hesse here in using construction non-reductively for God-related language located in but pointing beyond the spatio-temporal realm; cf. Arbib and Hesse, *Construction of Reality, passim*; and my discussion in ch. 4 above.

eyes to see it. However, elsewhere his illocutions work with word-to-world direction of fit: the kingdom of heaven is like a merchant in search of fine pearls (Matt. 13:45) where the issue at hand is one's attitude to everything else in comparison with one's estimation of the value of God's personal involvement in one's world. In our terms, this is not a strongly self-involving speech act. Clearly it concerns itself with the topic of one's attitude, but rather as an 'external' feature to be considered whatever one's attitude is, not as a grammatical feature of that attitude itself. In such a case, the illocution is a weak one, and the kingdom is being discussed in terms directly relatable to brute facts. It may be that they are potential and not actual brute facts (there need be no merchant or pearl; and neither need specific 'acts of God' be in view), but the point is that the teaching act concerned is primarily descriptive-assertive, and only declarative in a weak sense.

When Jesus teaches about the kingdom of God, therefore, and especially in relation to its transcendence, he performs declarative and strongly self-involving speech acts which focus on the ability of the hearer to construe God's activity. He also performs assertive and weakly self-involving speech acts which discuss one's stance toward brute facts as characteristic of the kingdom. Across the spectrum of strength of such speech acts, inward transformation is thus inextricably linked with external states of affairs. In the kingdom of God, one might say, there are not only new eyes to see with but also new things to see with them.

The constructed kingdom

N. T. Wright is wise to caution against trying to comprehend the kingdom by starting from isolated verses and their possible linguistic ranges; indeed Luke 17:21 is a particular instance he uses to make this point since he notes that in a sense the translation is underdetermined by linguistic evidence. He argues that instead we need a broader view which does justice to the Gospels as a whole and into which difficult verses can then be fitted in whatever manner seems most plausible.[85] This would follow also from my own observation above that one's view of

---

[85] Wright, *Jesus and the Victory of God*, 225, n. 100.

ἐντὸς ὑμῶν does not apparently correlate with a particular view of the 'presence of the kingdom' or otherwise.

In the light of this, I should say that I am not trying to develop a view of the kingdom based on this one verse, or on the possible translations of ἤγγικεν in Mark 1:15. Rather I am pursuing a four-step argument. First, I am assuming that the kingdom of God is an institutional reality constructed by the performance of illocutionary acts within a particular context, which in this case must be something like the community of those whose discourse is informed by the biblical text. Secondly, the speech act of teaching introduces this institutional reality under a variety of types of illocution. Here is where I suggest the variable element of kingdom language is most profitably located. It follows, thirdly, that as such illocutions vary over the assertive-declarative range, so language about the 'kingdom of God' is to be understood as on the one hand weakly self-involving, addressing itself to states of affairs which hold independently of one's own perspective (thus objective; or better, 'inter-personal'), and on the other hand as strongly self-involving, and dependent upon one's construal for its existence. Finally, we come to a verse such as Luke 17:21, and find that it is describing the activity of construal, and thus we can understand it in speech act terms without having to prejudge in this case what sort of imminence or presence the kingdom may have in other respects.[86]

Wright himself, without using the language of speech act theory, focuses on the way in which Jesus in his teaching *redefines* the kingdom, which is certainly an illocutionary act.[87] A new construal is placed on familiar events; new institutional facts are created out of the redefinition. However, it is important to balance this emphasis with the observation that not all such teaching is strongly self-involving. We can detect a spectrum of different strength illocutions which present the kingdom in the teaching of Jesus as both self-involving and yet also anchored in the world of extra-linguistic fact.

---

[86] This conclusion is compatible with that of Chilton, *Pure Kingdom*, 68, as quoted above, although clearly it rests on a different conceptual model.

[87] Wright, *Jesus and the Victory of God*, 226–42 and throughout; e.g. 'Jesus spent his whole ministry *redefining* what the kingdom meant' (471) or 'he was retelling this familiar story [of the kingdom] in such a way as to subvert and redirect its normal plot' (199).

We may, for instance, return to a verse such as the afore-mentioned Luke 11:20, and note that it combines both fact and stance: Jesus performs exorcism, although even this fact must be considered an institutional fact since it relies on contested practices of naming the demonic and characterising it, and where this is done among his hearers then the kingdom has come (illocution) even if it is not recognised (perlocution). In contrast to Luke 17:21, there is a specific fact around which the focus on stance is organised, but the emphasis still falls on one's willingness or ability to make the requisite construal.[88] Luke 13:20–21 (// Matt. 13:33; *Gos. Thom.* 96), the saying about a woman who takes yeast or leaven and mixes it into the dough, also focuses on ways in which the transcendence of the kingdom may be construed: 'the kingdom is hidden in gestures as common as the woman's',[89] and since no specific evidence such as an exorcism is noted the accent falls again on the stance rather than any fact.

Moving more widely than the particular verses introduced by Chilton under the rubric of 'transcendence', we find again the spectrum of strengths of illocution characterising the kingdom logia. In Jesus' response to those from John asking whether he was the one to come or not, the emphasis is on the fact rather than the stance (although stance remains implicit): 'Go and tell John what you have seen and heard: the blind receive their sight, the lame walk, the lepers are cleansed . . . And blessed is anyone who takes no offence at me' (Luke 7:22–23). In contrast, stance is preeminent, although irreducibly related to assumed states of affairs, in a parable such as Matthew 25:14–30, the parable of the talents.

In sum, different teaching speech acts highlight different combinations of stance and states of affairs. Speech act theory

---

[88] Chilton speaks here of an 'implicit christology' which requires a certain construal to be grasped; *Pure Kingdom*, 68. Although writing about Luke 17:21, Norman Perrin's comments on that verse seem better suited to the verse here discussed: 'One could have photographed an exorcism . . . but the kingly activity of God would not be manifest on the photograph . . . To experience the kingly activity of God one must have *faith*, i.e. one must interpret the event aright and commit oneself without reservation to the God revealed in the event *properly interpreted.*' Perrin, *Kingdom of God in the Teaching of Jesus*, 187. These comments, from his earlier, more exegetical and less self-consciously hermeneutical work on the parables, draw out both the issue of stance and the institutional nature of a fact such as 'exorcism'.

[89] Chilton, *Pure Kingdom*, 71.

facilitates a discussion of the constructed nature of the kingdom of God without reducing the kingdom to stance alone. Finally, it accounts for the variable emphases of kingdom language by way of the inherent flexibility of illocutionary acts, rather than by postulating some ad hoc view of tensive language or multiple referentiality.

Implications: authority and secrecy in the public domain

There are two or three interesting issues which arise from the speech act considerations developed thus far, and which are worth developing briefly. I consider in particular the issues of authority and of Gnostic interpretation, both germane to any interpretation of the verses we have discussed.

First, this approach highlights the role of the speaker as an authoritative voice in the community or context in which the illocutionary construal takes place. The question of the authority to perform speech acts is a multifaceted one which we have considered from various angles throughout this study. Here it must suffice merely to draw attention to its part in the argument: the very fact that Jesus' teaching is preserved as part of the Gospels, to whatever extent historically speaking, provides at least one context in which his words are counted as decisive in the construction of 'kingdom reality'. On a speech act account, teaching authority is the authorisation to construct, with a construal which has a modelling or normative role in some community, but, most significantly, which is predicated on illocutions which address stance towards brute facts and which are therefore open to review and evaluation by other members of the community. In other words, it is the illocutionary link between states of affairs and stance which anchors the authority in a world which extends beyond community-relativity and which does not leave it at the subjective mercy of such perlocutionary effects as powerful, forceful or rhetorically sophisticated speech.

We have suggested in §3.2 above that construal, or reconstrual, lies near the heart of the grammar of Christian belief. Such construals establish certain institutional frameworks which depend both on foundational brute fact and on continued interpersonal accreditation for their ongoing existence.[90] Certain

---

[90] Expressed this way, the account of Searle, *Construction of Social Reality*, clearly offers something of a speech act rendering of Peter Berger's 'plausibility structures'; cf. Berger, *Social Reality of Religion*, 38–60.

types of speech act, in drawing their currency precisely from such frameworks, may thus only take place within them. Authoritative pronouncements are one such type of speech act: inseparable from but not reducible to community accreditation. It is in this carefully constructed sense that it seems appropriate to say that Jesus speaks with authority, and thus that his teaching illocutions are felicitous.[91]

Secondly, although it would take us too far afield, it seems to me that this is also a fruitful direction in which to address the prominent and vexed question of the relationship between the Jesus of the text and the Jesus of history. This is not entirely Martin Kähler's Christ of faith against the Jesus of history: if anything it is a more subtle version of it, memorably contrasted by some recent Catholic writers as the real Jesus as against the historical (i.e. historically-critically constructed) Jesus.[92] Sympathetic to such an approach as I am, it does seem to suppose that a constructed reality must necessarily be entirely separated from brute fact, which as we have seen is not the case.[93]

A final observation concerning this way of addressing the language of Jesus' teaching in the Gospels is that it provides a framework within which construal is given an appropriate but not an exclusive place as a key to understanding the kingdom of God. This is particularly relevant by way of contrast to the widespread tendency to trace certain synoptic sayings back to parallels in the *Gospel of Thomas*, thereby raising the question as to whether my own approach in this chapter might lend support to a kind of proto-Gnostic view of Jesus as a teacher of inner transformation.[94]

[91] Relatively few accounts of speech act theory take up the authority question. For an argument that Jesus' teaching authority is drawn from the non-linguistic backing of states of affairs, see Thiselton, 'Christology in Luke'. He also provides some helpful reflections on the illocutionary as against perlocutionary nature of authority in 'Authority and Hermeneutics'.

[92] Thus John P. Meier, *A Marginal Jew: Rethinking the Historical Jesus*, vol. 1, *The Roots of the Problem and the Person*, New York: Doubleday, 1991, 196–201; Luke Timothy Johnson, *The Real Jesus: The Misguided Quest for the Historical Jesus and the Truth of the Traditional Gospels*, San Francisco: HarperSanFrancisco, 1996, especially 133–66.

[93] An indication of how an account of Jesus might be developed from the text in terms of construal is given by Robert Morgan, 'The Hermeneutical Significance of Four Gospels', *Int* 33 (1979), 376–88.

[94] In particular one notes the parallels between Luke 17:21 and *Gos. Thom.* 3 (and 113, 51, and P. Oxy 654:9–16), cf. Richard Valantasis, *The Gospel of Thomas* (New Testament Readings), London and New York: Routledge, 1997, for discussion

However, it would be a mistake to suppose that Gnostic sympathies are a corollary of a speech act view. There is no denying the substantive similarities in content between Luke 17:21 and *Gos. Thom.* 3, but I contend that the simplest explanation for this is the correct one, that Thomas does not, by and large, maintain an independent tradition going back to the historical Jesus, but represents a development of the canonical Gospel tradition.[95] The key question, therefore, is what Thomas does with this perspective. Even a cursory acquaintance with the kind of sayings predominant in Thomas bears out Valantasis's description of Thomas's theology: 'a performative theology whose mode of discourse and whose method of theology revolves about effecting a change in thought and understanding in the readers and hearers (both ancient and modern)'. The 'central performance' is encapsulated in *Gospel of Thomas* 1: 'Whoever discovers the interpretation of these sayings will not taste death.'[96] The general subject matter concerns itself with the issues of construal which we have considered. As is well known, the sayings of Thomas appear with almost no narrative context, and rarely do they address themselves to historical events and facts. When they do it is generally to urge that this is the wrong way to look.[97] It thus seems fair to conclude that brute fact has largely dropped out of the picture here, and the thrust of the gospel is the attempt to turn construal into an end in itself rather than a mediation between the construer and what is construed.

There thus seems no reason to suppose that the significant overlap between the institutional nature of facts created by illocutions in the canonical Gospels and those in the *Gospel of Thomas* should lead us to reduce the one to the other. In the canonical kingdom logia the illocutions vary across the whole

---

of the relevant texts (33–4; 58–9; 129–30; 193–4). A recent review of relevant issues, from a somewhat 'pro-Thomas' perspective, is G. J. Riley, 'The *Gospel of Thomas* in Recent Scholarship', *CR:BS* 2 (1994), 227–52.

[95] Space precludes discussion of this most central and contested issue in *Gos. Thom.* studies. See Christopher Tuckett, 'Thomas and the Synoptics', *NovT* 30 (1988), 132–57.

[96] Valantasis, *Gospel of Thomas*, 7, 10. Valantasis's reading of Thomas is concerned to explicate the text in its own right rather than use it in constant comparison with the canonical Gospels, and he even eschews the label 'Gnostic' in order to avoid importing what he sees as inappropriate resonances into his investigation (24–7).

[97] Note, almost at random, *Gos. Thom.* 51–3.

spectrum of assertive-declarative speech acts. In Thomas the illocution is almost uniformly strongly declarative. My defence of the important role of construal in teaching about the kingdom does not, therefore, imply anything like a Gnostic approach to the subject. While performative language draws its currency from events in the public domain, the language of inner transformation as an end in itself withdraws from precisely this arena.

§4 Conclusions

This chapter has broadened the investigation of speech acts in the New Testament beyond that of previous chapters by focusing attention on a more general speech act than confessing or forgiving: that of teaching. I have argued that the speech act of teaching, because it is so wide ranging and flexible, offers insights into the speech act dynamics of biblical language in general, particularly in the way in which it highlights the creation of institutional facts in the process of teaching. After developing speech act categories for teaching from a comparison of discussions in the philosophy of education and in studies of teaching in the time of Jesus, I have suggested that a spectrum ranging from assertive to declarative speech acts can be discerned in New Testament teaching, and in particular in the teaching of Jesus.

I have discussed cases at either end of this spectrum: teaching as the assertion of facts, which was found to be always bound up with other performative dynamics, and teaching as the illocutionary creation of states of affairs in strong declarations. This latter type of speech act focuses attention on the important issue of construal in the logic of Christian belief, but does so as part of a balanced account of one aspect only of a hermeneutic of self-involvement.

Finally, I have considered the case of Jesus' teaching about the kingdom of God, which ranges over strong and weak construal by way of the full range of strengths of illocution. This part of the study is envisaged as a contribution towards elucidating the kinds of role played by institutional facts in reading the New Testament. Related issues of the authority of the speaker (to create institutional facts by the accredited performance of the speech act of teaching) and the similarities between strong construal and Gnostic emphases on inner transformation have been addressed briefly in order to show how this account may or may not be developed in other directions.

As suggested at the beginning of the chapter, the fact that teaching is such a different kind of speech act from forgiving has meant that it has raised a different set of issues in developing a hermeneutic of self-involvement compared to our earlier investigations. It is thus hoped that the more specific studies of chapters 6 and 7 have been rounded out in certain ways toward a more comprehensive articulation of some of the possible roles of speech act theory in New Testament interpretation.

Conclusion

9

Some Hermeneutical Implications

If it is true that speech act theory has, as Anthony Thiselton suggests, suffered undeserved neglect in the disciplines of biblical studies and systematic theology,[1] then this study has sought to redress the balance by proposing some ways in which the subject offers hermeneutical resources for the various interpretive tasks of biblical and theological studies. With respect to discussions of religious language and its varying functions, David Hilborn notes that speech act studies have been few and far between, and that the theory 'has been appropriated only sporadically by those working on such discourse, and even then, there has been very little dialogue between those concerned'.[2] In the biblical field, even when speech act theory would appear to be a ready resource, it remains largely untapped.[3]

In terms of theological inquiry, it must be noted that as long ago as 1932 Karl Barth was writing of 'The Speech of God as the Act of God'.[4] Barth's concerns of course were not those of speech

[1] Thiselton, 'Speech-Act Theory and the Claim That God Speaks', 97.

[2] David Hilborn, 'From Performativity to Pedagogy: Jean Ladrière and the Pragmatics of Reformed Worship Discourse', in Stanley E. Porter (ed.), *The Nature of Religious Language: A Colloquium* (Roehampton Institute London Papers 1), Sheffield: Sheffield Academic Press, 1996, 170–200, here 173.

[3] E.g.: William Baker's discussion of speech-ethics in the epistle of James surveys aspects of personal speech in a variety of inter-personal (including divine) contexts, and includes an analysis of the role of truthfulness in speech-ethics, but contains only one indifferent reference to the work of J. L Austin; William R. Baker, *Personal Speech-Ethics in the Epistle of James* (WUNT 2/68), Tübingen: J. C. B. Mohr, 1995, 42, n. 68.

[4] Karl Barth, *Church Dogmatics*, vol. 1, *The Doctrine of the Word of God*, Part 1 (trans. G. W. Bromiley), Edinburgh: T&T Clark, 1975 (1932), 143–62.

act theory, but it is perhaps fair to say that Wolterstorff's treatment of 'divine discourse' with the aid of the categories of speech acts represents a long overdue attempt to explore the dynamics of such a central theological topic from a speech-act perspective.[5]

It seems, then, that theologians and biblical critics have not always known what to make of speech act theory. Appeals to it reflect more or less directly the limited extent to which it is understood on its own terms. If Austin's particular emphasis on convention-governed performatives such as 'I name this ship' is taken as the essence of speech act theory, then theologians are content to leave it to its obvious relevance to liturgical considerations, where it has indeed proved fruitful.[6] Similarly, if it is thought that Austin essentially proposes a 'performative use of language' to set alongside more familiar language-related concerns, then 'performative utterances' are duly noted, but the purpose of such an exercise is not always clear.[7]

In contrast I have proposed that a thorough understanding of speech act theory invites us to take seriously a hermeneutical category of *self-involvement*. As a result, one does not 'apply' speech act theory to biblical texts, and neither does one restrict its scope to certain prominently Austinian types of conventional utterance. Since the work of Donald Evans, self-involvement has not been a widely utilised category. Reader-orientated hermeneutical models have given a certain pre-eminence to the role of the reader's self in contributing to ways of understanding meaning and texts, but often appear to have struggled to articulate criteria for interpretive controls. Other theological traditions have welcomed the idea of the constructed self, or the self who

---

[5] Wolterstorff, *Divine Discourse*, especially 63–74; cf. Vanhoozer, 'God's Mighty Speech-Acts', especially 172.

[6] E.g. Jean Ladrière, 'The Performativity of Liturgical Language', *Concilium*, vol. 2 no. 9 (1973), 50–62; David Crystal, 'Liturgical Language in a Sociolinguistic Perspective', in David Jasper and R. C. D. Jasper (eds), *Language and the Worship of the Church*, London: Macmillan, 1990, 120–46; Geoffrey Wainwright, 'The Language of Worship', in Cheslyn Jones, Geoffrey Wainwright, Edward Yarnold SJ and Paul Bradshaw (eds), *The Study of Liturgy*, London: SPCK, and New York: Oxford University Press, ²1992 (1978), 519–28; and Hilborn, 'From Performativity to Pedagogy'.

[7] See, for example, Stephen Breck Reid, 'Psalm 50: Prophetic Speech and God's Performative Utterances', in Stephen Breck Reid (ed.), *Prophets and Paradigms: Essays in Honor of Gene M. Tucker* (JSOTS 229), Sheffield: Sheffield Academic Press, 1996, 217–30.

is constituted by or in the reading process.[8] I have suggested that a hermeneutic of self-involvement incorporates many of the most helpful insights of such approaches while still navigating between complete independence from the text and complete constitution by it.[9]

The development of such a hermeneutic relies, as I have attempted to show, on the more nuanced and cautious claims of a full understanding of the various categories of speech act theory. In so far as such a philosophy of language does justice to the workings of language, then one may be justified in offering a hermeneutic of self-involvement as something of an advance on other models which have sought, rightly, to move away from the notion of an objectively independent text which stands outside the hermeneutical process. It remains the case, however, that in seeking to articulate precisely the extent to which speech act theory *does* succeed in this way, I have been drawn to a variety of proposals which refine the scope of its primary relevance to certain 'strong' categories: strong illocutions, strong construal, and finally strong self-involvement.

Such a hermeneutic also sheds new light on familiar and currently prominent questions concerned with realism and non-realism.[10] As ever, such an easy polarisation fails to do justice to the complexities of the world in which we live, with all its irreducibly social and interpersonal constituents. In this study I have attempted to demonstrate that the concepts of brute and institutional fact, and their speech act construction mechanisms, are subtle enough to offer appropriately refined formulations concerning what is and is not real, and thus also what is and is not true.

Speech act theory itself is evidently not a theological enterprise, but many significant theological categories are carried by, or in Recanati's terms 'staged' by, speech acts.[11] Confession,

[8] See ch. 5 above.

[9] A rare theological use of the category of 'self-involvement' is George Hunsinger, 'Truth as Self-Involving: Barth and Lindbeck on the Cognitive and Performative Aspects of Truth in Theological Discourse', *JAAR* 61 (1993), 41–56. Despite the title, however, this article makes only minimal and perhaps unduly vague use of the category of 'performative'.

[10] See the recent collection of diverse viewpoints represented in Colin Crowder (ed.), *God and Reality: Essays on Christian Non-Realism*, London: Mowbray, 1997, especially the cautious defence of realism therein by Fergus Kerr, 'What's Wrong with Realism Anyway?', 128–43.

[11] Recanati, *Meaning and Force*, 258–66.

forgiveness and teaching are just three particular examples of (speech) acts which occupy prominent places in Christian traditions. My studies of these speech acts have highlighted the interdisciplinary nature of asking questions about these kinds of phenomena. Speech act theory has proved helpful in demarcating criteria for construing divine activity, for example, where forgiveness relates such activity to interpersonal construals. Again one must stress that such a hermeneutic of self-involvement is precisely fitted only to certain kinds of cases, but, in such cases, I suggest that it represents a model well suited to highlighting theological concerns in biblical interpretation. In so far as the conclusions of chapters 6, 7 and 8 support such a claim, then this kind of 'theological interpretation of scripture' may be offered as a contrasting alternative to other current endeavours with similar concerns.[12]

Finally, I propose that this study should issue in a call for the necessary role of a theology of the imagination in the activity of biblical interpretation. This I see as a direct corollary of the argument that the world envisaged, created and sustained by self-involving biblical texts, and thus accessed in particular via a hermeneutic of self-involvement, is in fact the world in which we live, construed theologically. However, to dwell in such a world is not to sever one's links with physical or social reality, but rather it is to be drawn in by self-involvement to a world whose grammar is that of the theology of the imagination. In chapter 4 I have mentioned various studies which provide useful points of contact with a speech act approach.[13] In the hermeneutics of Paul Ricoeur, and in the biblical work of those such as Walter Brueggemann who follow him, we find further congruences.[14] Nevertheless, while I remain heavily indebted to their ways of articulating the issues, I propose that once again a

---

[12] See the survey of Stephen E. Fowl, 'Introduction', in Fowl (ed.), *Theological Interpretation of Scripture*, xii–xxx. Of course, I do not suggest that a speech act approach could ever represent *the* theological interpretation of Scripture.

[13] In addition one should now note Garrett Green, *Theology, Hermeneutics and Imagination: The Crisis of Interpretation at the End of Modernity*, Cambridge: Cambridge University Press, 2000.

[14] See especially the essays collected in Ricoeur, *Figuring the Sacred*. Brueggemann's actual uses of such an approach (e.g. the essays collected in Brueggemann, *Interpretation and Obedience*) offer more support for my thesis than do his rarer attempts to explore the workings of it as a hermeneutic (Brueggemann, *Texts under Negotiation*).

hermeneutic of self involvement offers resources for appropriating the best of such approaches while offering a more helpful way of anchoring imaginative construals in the interpersonal objectivity of social reality. In the spirit of Fergus Kerr's work on Wittgenstein, this may best be seen as a desire to continue the exploration of 'biblical interpretation after Wittgenstein'.[15]

This study was originally conceived as a relatively straight-forward argument: appropriate the development of speech act theory in biblical interpretation and then apply it to some suitable New Testament text, discovering in the process various hitherto unsuspected interpretive nuggets. Instead I have found myself forced to reconsider just what it is that the development of speech act theory amounts to, and in what ways it could prove relevant to the task of interpreting texts.

In part 1 of this study I therefore attempted to guide the discussion toward certain key issues which needed to be in place for the biblical explorations of part 2. I have proposed that 'speech act criticism' cannot be the way forward, and that the refined criteria of strong and weak illocutions, and strong and weak construals, lead us instead to an eclectic engagement with the biblical text. In the process, the possibility of a radically subject-orientated approach to speech acts presented itself: the reduction of interpretation to the construal of the text by the subject, or, as I have termed it, the 'neopragmatist' challenge. My preferred response was to explore the notion of construal from a speech act perspective. The validity or otherwise of neopragmatist forms of textual non-realism is not perhaps an issue which one needs to settle before appealing to speech act theory in biblical interpretation, but one's view of it certainly affects the point of any such appeal.

In part 2 I went on to make the anticipated turn towards the biblical text, beginning by exploring the 'logic of self-

---

[15] Kerr, *Theology after Wittgenstein*. A recent and illuminating proposal which brings together such an 'after Wittgenstein' approach with the work of writers like Garrett Green mentioned above, alongside a concern to move beyond a simple polarisation between realism and non-realism, is Sue Patterson, *Realist Christian Theology in a Postmodern Age* (Cambridge Studies in Christian Doctrine), Cambridge: Cambridge University Press, 1999. She focuses more on the connections between imagination and the 'language-ridden' nature of the world rather than exploring construction per se (see especially 73–93).

involvement' of Donald Evans. In many ways I regard this study as something of a vindication of Evans's approach, an approach largely overlooked in the intervening years for the various reasons which I have discussed. With a careful reading of Evans in hand, I have gone on to studies of confession, forgiveness and teaching as examples of strong (or at least potentially strong) speech acts. I have not sought to *explain* these practices, but rather to elucidate them and lay bare their various speech act mechanisms. Again, non-realism in varying degrees lies either side of this path, and I have attempted to clarify the ways in which I dine at its (socially constructed) table with rather a long spoon.

If there is any merit in the resultant hermeneutic of self-involvement, then I would judge that all manner of acts represented in and effected by the New Testament text need to be addressed from this speech act perspective. Such a perspective may enable us to articulate how it is that the New Testament text, as a vehicle for divine discourse, remains effective among us, for as long as we have eyes and ears, and the wit and the wisdom, so to construe it.

Bibliography

A second date in brackets indicates the date of the first edition of the book or the original appearance of the article.

Abrahams, Israel, *Studies in Pharisaism and the Gospels*, Cambridge: Cambridge University Press, 1924.

Adam, A. K. M., 'The Sign of Jonah: A Fish-Eye View', *Semeia* 51 (1990), 177–91.

——, *Making Sense of New Testament Theology: 'Modern' Problems and Prospects* (StABH 11), Macon, GA: Mercer University Press, 1995.

Allison Jr, Dale C., *The End of the Ages Has Come: An Early Interpretation of the Passion and Resurrection of Jesus* (SNTW), Edinburgh: T&T Clark, 1987 (1985).

Alston, William P., *Philosophy of Language*, Englewood Cliffs, NJ: Prentice-Hall, 1964.

Amador, J. D. H., 'Where Could Rhetorical Criticism (Still) Take Us?', *CR:BS* 7 (1999), 195–222.

Anderson, Perry, 'Components of the National Culture', *NLR* 50 (July–August 1968), 3–57.

Anscombe, G. E. M., *Intentions*, Oxford: Blackwell, 1957.

——, 'On Brute Facts', *Analysis* 18 (1958), 69–72.

Apel, Karl-Otto, *Understanding and Explanation: A Transcendental-Pragmatic Perspective*, Cambridge, MA, and London: MIT Press, 1984 (1979).

Apel, Karl-Otto, 'Is Intentionality More Basic than Linguistic Meaning?', in Lepore and Van Gulick (eds), *John Searle and His Critics*, 31–55.

Arbib, Michael A. and Mary B. Hesse, *The Construction of Reality*, Cambridge: Cambridge University Press, 1986.

Ashmore, Malcolm, *The Reflexive Thesis: Wrighting Sociology of Scientific Knowledge*, Chicago: University of Chicago Press, 1989.

Aurelio, T., *Disclosures in den Gleichnisse Jesu: Eine Anwendung der Disclosure-Theorie von I. T. Ramsey, der modernen Metaphorik und der Sprechakte auf die Gleichnisse Jesu* (Regensburger Studien zur Theologie 8), Frankfurt am Main: Lang, 1977.

Austin, J. L., *Sense and Sensibilia*, Oxford: Oxford University Press, 1962.

———, 'Performative-Constative', in Charles E. Caton (ed.), *Philosophy and Ordinary Language*, Urbana: University of Illinois Press, 1963, 22–33, with discussion 33–54; reprinted in Searle (ed.), *Philosophy of Language*, 13–22.

———, *How to Do Things with Words*, edited by J. O. Urmson and Marina Sbisa, Oxford: Oxford University Press, ^{2}1975 (1962).

———, *Philosophical Papers*, edited by J. O. Urmson and G. J. Warnock, Oxford: Oxford University Press, ^{3}1979 (1961).

Avramides, Anita, *Meaning and Mind: An Examination of a Gricean Account of Language*, Cambridge, MA, and London: MIT Press, 1989.

Bach, K. and R. M. Harnish, *Linguistic Communication and Speech Acts*, Cambridge, MA: MIT Press, 1979.

Baker, G. P. and P. M. S. Hacker, *Wittgenstein: Understanding and Meaning, Volume 1 of an Analytical Commentary on the Philosophical Investigations*, Oxford: Blackwell, 1980.

———, *Language, Sense and Nonsense: A Critical Investigation into Modern Theories of Language*, Oxford: Blackwell, 1984.

———, *Scepticism, Rules and Language*, Oxford: Blackwell, 1984.

Baker, Jonathan, *How Forgiveness Works* (Grove Spirituality Series 53), Nottingham: Grove Books, 1995.

Baker, William R., *Personal Speech-Ethics in the Epistle of James* (WUNT 2/68), Tübingen: J. C. B. Mohr, 1995.

Barr, James, *The Semantics of Biblical Language*, Oxford: Oxford University Press, 1961.

Barrett, C. K., *A Commentary on the First Epistle to the Corinthians* (BNTC), London: A&C Black, ²1971 (1968).

Barth, Karl, *Church Dogmatics*, vol. 1, *The Doctrine of the Word of God*, Part 1 (trans. G. W. Bromiley), Edinburgh: T&T Clark, 1975 (1932).

Barth, Markus, *Ephesians 1–3* (AB 34), New York: Doubleday, 1974.

Bartholomew, C. G., 'Three Horizons: Hermeneutics from the Other End – an Evaluation of Anthony Thiselton's Hermeneutic Proposals', *EJTh* 5 (1996), 121–35.

Bassler, Jouette M., '1 Cor 12:3 – Curse and Confession in Context', *JBL* 101 (1982), 415–18.

Bauckham, Richard (ed.), *The Gospels for All Christians: Rethinking the Gospel Audiences*, Edinburgh: T&T Clark, 1998.

Bearn, Gordon C. F., 'Derrida Dry: Iterating Iterability Analytically', *Diacritics* 25.3 (1995), 3–25.

Beasley-Murray, G. R., *Jesus and the Kingdom of God*, Grand Rapids: Eerdmans, 1986.

Beasley-Murray, Paul, 'Romans 1:3f: An Early Confession of Faith in the Lordship of Jesus', *TynB* 31 (1980), 147–54.

Beker, J. C., 'Contingency and Coherence in the Letters of Paul', *USQR* 33 (1978), 141–50.

——, *Paul the Apostle: The Triumph of God in Life and Thought*, Philadelphia: Fortress Press, 1980.

Benn, Piers, 'Forgiveness and Loyalty', *Philosophy* 71 (1996), 369–83.

Berger, Peter, *The Social Reality of Religion*, London: Penguin, 1973 (= *The Sacred Canopy*, New York: Doubleday, 1967).

——, *The Heretical Imperative: Contemporary Possibilities of Religious Affirmation*, London: Collins, 1980.

——, *A Rumor of Angels: Modern Society and the Rediscovery of the Supernatural*, New York: Doubleday, expanded edition, 1990 (1969).

Berger, Peter L. and Thomas Luckmann, *The Social Construction of Reality: A Treatise in the Sociology of Knowledge*, London: Penguin, 1967.

Berlin, Isaiah et al., *Essays on J. L. Austin*, Oxford: Clarendon Press, 1973.

Bernstein, Richard J., *Beyond Objectivism and Relativism: Science, Hermeneutics, and Praxis*, Philadelphia: University of Pennsylvania Press, 1983.

Betz, Hans Dieter, *Galatians: A Commentary on Paul's Letter to the Churches in Galatia* (Hermeneia), Philadelphia: Fortress Press, 1979.

Bird, Graham H., 'Austin's Theory of Illocutionary Force', in Peter A. French, Theodore E. Uehling Jr and Howard K. Wettstein (eds), *Midwest Studies in Philosophy VI*, Minneapolis: University of Minnesota Press, 1981, 345–69.

——, 'Relevance Theory and Speech Acts', in Tsohatzidis (ed.), *Foundations of Speech Act Theory*, 292–311.

Black, Max, 'Austin on Performatives', *Philosophy* 38 (1963), 217–26, reprinted in Fann (ed.), *Symposium on J. L. Austin*, 401–11.

Bogen, James, 'An Unfavourable Review of *Language, Sense and Nonsense*', *Inquiry* 28 (1985), 467–82.

Booth, Wayne C., *The Rhetoric of Fiction*, London: Penguin Books, ²1983 (1961).

Bosk, Charles L., *Forgive and Remember: Managing Medical Failure*, Chicago: University of Chicago Press, 1979.

Braithwaite, Richard B., *An Empiricist's View of the Nature of Religious Belief*, Cambridge: Cambridge University Press, 1955.

Briggs, Richard S., 'The Uses of Speech Act Theory in Biblical Interpretation', *CR:BS* 9 (2001).

Brint, Michael and William Weaver (eds), *Pragmatism in Law & Society*, Boulder, CO, and Oxford: Westview Press, 1991.

Brooke, A. E., *The Johannine Epistles* (ICC), Edinburgh: T&T Clark, 1912.

Brown, Colin, 'The Hermeneutics of Confession and Accusation', *CTJ* 30 (1995), 460–71.

——, 'Ernst Lohmeyer's *Kyrios Jesus*', in Martin and Dodd (eds), *Where Christology Began*, 6–42.

Brown SS, Raymond E., *The Epistles of John* (AB 30), London: Geoffrey Chapman, 1982.

Brown, Raymond E., Karl P. Donfried and John Reumann (eds), *Peter in the New Testament*, Minneapolis: Augsburg, 1973.

Brown Jr, Robert L. and Martin Steinmann Jr, 'Native Readers of Fiction: A Speech-Act and Genre-Rule Approach to Defining Literature', in Paul Hernadi (ed.), *What Is Literature?*, Bloomington: Indiana University Press, 1978, 141–60.

Brueggemann, Walter, 'Imagination as a Mode of Fidelity', in James T. Butler, Edgar W. Conrad and Ben C. Ollenburger (eds), *Understanding the Word: Essays in Honor of Bernhard W. Anderson* (JSOTS 37), Sheffield: JSOT Press, 1985, 13–36.

——, 'The Third World of Evangelical Imagination', *HBTh* 8 (1986), 61–84; reprinted in Brueggemann, *Interpretation and Obedience*, 9–27.

——, *Israel's Praise: Doxology against Idolatry and Ideology*, Philadelphia: Fortress Press, 1988.

——, *Interpretation and Obedience: From Faithful Reading to Faithful Living*, Minneapolis: Fortress Press, 1991.

——, *Texts under Negotiation. The Bible and Postmodern Imagination*, Minneapolis: Fortress Press, 1993.

——, *Theology of the Old Testament: Testimony, Dispute, Advocacy*, Minneapolis: Fortress Press, 1997.

Brümmer, Vincent, *Theology & Philosophical Inquiry: An Introduction*, Philadelphia: Westminster Press, 1982.

——, *What Are We Doing When We Pray? A Philosophical Inquiry*, London: SCM Press, 1984.

Bryant, David, *Faith and the Play of Imagination: On the Role of Imagination in Religion* (StABH 5), Macon, GA: Mercer University Press, 1989.

Bultmann, Rudolf, *Theology of the New Testament*, vol. 1, London: SCM Press, 1965 (1952).

——, *The Johannine Epistles* (Hermeneia), Philadelphia: Fortress Press, 1973 (1967).

Burgess, Joseph A., *A History of the Exegesis of Matthew 16:17–19 from 1781 to 1965*, Ann Arbor: Edwards Brothers, 1976.

Buss, Martin J., 'Potential and Actual Interactions between Speech Act Theory and Biblical Studies', in White (ed.), *Speech Act Theory and Biblical Criticism* (= *Semeia* 41), 125–34.

Butler, Joseph, *The Works of Joseph Butler, in two volumes. Vol II: Sermons, etc* (ed. W. E. Gladstone), Oxford: Clarendon Press, 1896.

Cadbury, Henry J., 'The Meaning of John 20:23, Matthew 16:19 and Matthew 18:18', *JBL* 58 (1939), 251–4.

Caird, G. B., *The Language and Imagery of the Bible*, London: Duckworth, 1980.

——, *New Testament Theology* (ed. L. D. Hurst), Oxford: Clarendon Press, 1994.

Campbell, J. Gordon, 'Are All Speech-Acts Self-Involving?', *RelStud* 8 (1972), 161–4.

Caragounis, Chrys C., 'Kingdom of God/Kingdom of Heaven', *DJG*, 417–30.

Cavell, Stanley, *A Pitch of Philosophy: Autobiographical Exercises*, Cambridge, MA: Harvard University Press, 1994.

——, *Philosophical Passages: Wittgenstein, Emerson, Austin, Derrida*, Cambridge, MA, and Oxford: Blackwell, 1995.

Charlesworth, James H., 'Forgiveness (Early Judaism)', *ABD*, II:833–5.

Chilton, Bruce D., 'Regnum Dei Deus Est', *SJT* 31 (1978), 261–70.

——, *God in Strength: Jesus' Announcement of the Kingdom* (SNTU 1) Freistadt: Plöchl, 1979, reprinted in the Biblical Seminar Series, Sheffield: JSOT Press, 1987.

——, 'Jesus and the Repentance of E. P. Sanders', *TynB* 39 (1988), 1–18.

——, 'The Kingdom of God in Recent Discussion', in Bruce Chilton and Craig A. Evans (eds), *Studying the Historical Jesus: Evaluations of the Current State of Research* (New Testament Tools and Studies XIX), Leiden: E. J. Brill, 1994, 255–80.

——, *Pure Kingdom: Jesus' Vision of God* (Studying the Historical Jesus), London: SPCK, and Grand Rapids: Eerdmans, 1996.

Chilton, Bruce (ed.), *The Kingdom of God in the Teaching of Jesus* (Issues in Religion and Theology 5), London: SPCK, 1984.

Chilton, Bruce and J. I. H. McDonald, *Jesus and the Ethics of the Kingdom* (Biblical Foundations in Theology), London: SPCK, 1987.

Chomsky, N., *Syntactic Structures*, The Hague: Mouton, 1957.

Clarke, Paul Barry and Andrew Linzey (eds), *Dictionary of Ethics, Theology and Society*, London and New York: Routledge, 1996.

Coady, C. A. J., *Testimony: A Philosophical Study*, Oxford: Clarendon Press, 1992.

Cohen, L. Jonathan, 'Do Illocutionary Forces Exist?', *PhQ* 14 (1964), 118–37, reprinted in Fann (ed.), *Symposium on J. L. Austin*, 420–44.

——, 'Speech Acts', in Thomas A. Sebeok (ed.), *Current Trends in Linguistics*, vol. 12. *Linguistics and Adjacent Arts and Sciences*, The Hague: Mouton, 1974, 173–208.

Cohen, Ted, 'Illocutions and Perlocutions', *Foundations of Language* 9 (1973), 492–503.

Collin, Finn, *Social Reality* (The Problems of Philosophy), London and New York: Routledge, 1997.

Collini, Stefan, 'Introduction: Interpretation Terminable and Interminable', in Eco, *Interpretation and Overinterpretation*, 1–21.

Conzelmann, Hans, *1 Corinthians* (Hermeneia), Philadelphia: Fortress Press, 1975 (1969).

Corrington, Robert S., *The Community of Interpreters: On the Hermeneutics of Nature and the Bible in the American Philosophical Tradition* (StABH 3), Macon, GA: Mercer University Press, ²1995 (1987).

Cover, Robin C., 'Sin, Sinners (OT)', in *ABD*, VI:31–40.

Cranfield, C. E. B., 'Divine and Human Action: The Biblical Concept of Worship', *Int* 12 (1958), 387–98.

Croft, William, 'Speech Act Classification, Language Typology and Cognition', in Tsohatzidis (ed.), *Foundations of Speech Act Theory*, 460–77.

Crowder, Colin (ed.), *God and Reality: Essays on Christian Non-Realism*, London: Mowbray, 1997.

Crystal, David, 'Liturgical Language in a Sociolinguistic Perspective', in David Jasper and R. C. D. Jasper (eds), *Language and the Worship of the Church*, London: Macmillan, 1990, 120–46.

Culler, Jonathan, *Structuralist Poetics: Structuralism, Linguistics and the Study of Literature*, Ithaca: Cornell University Press, 1975.

Culler, Jonathan, *On Deconstruction: Theory and Criticism after Structuralism*, London: Routledge & Kegan Paul, 1983.

Cullman, Oscar, *The Earliest Christian Confessions*, London: Lutterworth Press, 1949 (1943).

Culpepper, R. Alan, *Anatomy of the Fourth Gospel: A Study in Literary Design*, Philadelphia: Fortress Press, 1983.

Cunningham, Valentine, *In the Reading Gaol: Postmodernity, Texts, and History*, Oxford: Blackwell, 1994.

Danker, F. W., *Creeds in the Bible*, St. Louis, MO: Concordia Publishing House, 1966.

Dascal, Marcelo, 'Speech Act Theory and Gricean Pragmatics: Some Differences of Detail That Make a Difference', in Tsohatzidis (ed.), *Foundations of Speech Act Theory*, 323–34.

Davidson, Donald, 'A Nice Derangement of Epitaphs', in Ernest Lepore (ed.), *Truth and Interpretation: Perspectives on the Philosophy of Donald Davidson*, Oxford: Blackwell, 1986, 433–46.

Davies, W. D. and Dale C. Allison Jr, *A Critical and Exegetical Commentary on the Gospel according to Saint Matthew* (ICC), 3 vols, Edinburgh: T&T Clark, 1988, 1991, 1997.

Davis, Steven, 'Perlocution' in Searle, Kiefer and Bierwisch (eds), *Speech-Act Theory and Pragmatics*, 37–55.

Day, Peggy L., *An Adversary in Heaven: Satan in the Hebrew Bible* (HSM 43), Atlanta: Scholars Press, 1988.

Dennett, Daniel C., *The Intentional Stance*, Cambridge, MA, and London: MIT Press, 1987.

Derrett, J. D. M., 'Binding and Loosing', *JBL* 102 (1983), 112–17.

Derrida, Jacques, *Marges de la philosophie*, Paris: Les Editions de Minuit, 1972.

——, *Of Grammatology* (trans. Gayatri C. Spivak), Baltimore: Johns Hopkins University Press, 1975.

——, 'Signature Event Context', *Glyph* 1 (1977), 172–97.

——, 'Limited Inc abc', *Glyph* 2 (1977), 162–254.

——, *Limited Inc* (ed. Gerald Graff), Evanston, IL: Northwestern University Press, 1988.

DiGiovanna, Joseph J., *Linguistic Phenomenology: Philosophical Method in J. L. Austin* (American University Studies, Series V, Philosophy, vol. 63), New York: Peter Lang, 1989.

Dilman, Ilham, *Mind, Brain and Behaviour: Discussions of B. F. Skinner and J. R. Searle*, London: Routledge, 1988.

Dodd, C. H., *The Parables of the Kingdom*, London: Nisbet, 1935.

——, *The Apostolic Preaching and Its Developments*, London: Hodder & Stoughton, 1936.

——, 'The Kingdom of God Has Come', *ExpT* 48 (1936–7), 138–42.

Downing, F. Gerald, *Christ and the Cynics: Jesus and Other Radical Preachers in First-Century Tradition*, Sheffield: Sheffield Academic Press, 1988.

——, *Cynics and Christian Origins*, Edinburgh: T&T Clark, 1992.

Du Plessis, J. G., 'Speech Act Theory and New Testament Interpretation with Special Reference to G. N. Leech's Pragmatic Principles', in P. J. Hartin and J. H. Petzer (eds), *Text and Interpretation: New Approaches in the Criticism of the New Testament*, Leiden: E. J. Brill, 1991, 129–42.

Dunn, James D. G., 'Jesus – Flesh and Spirit: An Exposition of Romans 1:3–4', *JTS* 24 (1973), 40–68.

Eaton, Marcia, 'Speech Acts: A Bibliography', *Centrum* 2 (1974), 57–72.

Eco, Umberto, *Interpretation and Overinterpretation* (ed. Stefan Collini), Cambridge: Cambridge University Press, 1992.

Edwards, Derek, Malcolm Ashmore and Jonathan Potter, 'Death and Furniture: The Rhetoric, Politics and Theology of Bottom Line Arguments against Relativism', *HHS* 8.2 (1995), 25–49.

Eriksson, Anders, *Traditions as Rhetorical Proof: Pauline Argumentation in 1 Corinthians* (Coniectanea Biblica NT 29), Stockholm: Almqvist & Wiksell, 1998.

Evans, C. A. and B. D. Chilton (eds), *Authenticating the Words of Jesus* (New Testament Tools and Studies 28/1), Leiden: E. J. Brill, 1999.

——, *Authenticating the Activities of Jesus* (New Testament Tools and Studies 28/2), Leiden: E. J. Brill, 1999.

Evans, Christopher F., *Saint Luke*, London: SCM Press, 1990.

Evans, Donald D., *The Logic of Self-Involvement: A Philosophical Study of Everyday Language with Special Reference to the Christian Use of Language about God as Creator*, London: SCM Press, 1963.

Evans, Donald D., *Communist Faith and Christian Faith*, London: SCM Press, 1965.

——, 'Religious Language and Divine Transcendence', unpublished lectures, University of Chicago, 1967.

——, 'Differences between Scientific and Religious Assertions', in Ian G. Barbour (ed.), *Science and Religion: New Perspectives on the Dialogue*, London: SCM Press, 1968, 101–33.

——, 'Barth on Talk about God', *Canadian Journal of Theology* 16 (1970), 175–92.

——, 'Reply to J. Gordon Campbell', *RelStud* 9 (1973), 469–72.

——, *Struggle and Fulfillment: The Inner Dynamics of Religion and Morality*, Cleveland: Collins, 1979 (UK 1980).

——, *Faith, Authenticity and Morality*, Edinburgh: The Handsel Press, 1980.

——, 'Academic Scepticism, Spiritual Reality and Transfiguration', in L. D. Hurst and N. T. Wright (eds), *The Glory of Christ in the New Testament: Studies in Christology in Memory of George Bradford Caird*, Oxford: Clarendon Press, 1987, 175–86.

——, *Spirituality and Human Nature* (Suny Series in Religious Studies), Albany: SUNY Press, 1993.

Evans, Gillian R., *Problems of Authority in the Reformation Debates*, Cambridge: Cambridge University Press, 1992.

Fann, K. T. (ed.), *Symposium on J. L. Austin*, London: Routledge & Kegan Paul, 1969.

Fee, Gordon D., *The First Epistle to the Corinthians* (NICNT), Grand Rapids: Eerdmans, 1987.

Felman, Shoshana, *The Literary Speech Act: Don Juan with J. L. Austin, or Seduction in Two Languages*, Ithaca, NY: Cornell University Press, 1983.

Fish, Stanley, 'How to Do Things with Austin and Searle: Speech-Act Theory and Literary Criticism', *MLN* 91 (1976), 983–1025, reprinted in Fish, *Is There a Text in This Class?*, 197–245.

——, 'Interpreting the *Variorum*', *Critical Inquiry* 2 (1976), 465–85, reprinted in Fish, *Is There a Text in This Class?*, 147–73.

Fish, Stanley, 'Normal Circumstances, Literal Language, Direct Speech Acts, the Ordinary, the Everyday, the Obvious, What Goes without Saying, and Other Special Cases', *Critical Inquiry* 4 (1978), 625–44, reprinted in Fish, *Is There a Text in This Class?*, 268–92.

——, *Is There a Text in This Class? The Authority of Interpretive Communities*, Cambridge, MA: Harvard University Press, 1980.

——, 'With the Compliments of the Author: Reflections on Austin and Derrida', *Critical Inquiry* 8 (1982), 693–721, reprinted in Fish, *Doing What Comes Naturally*, 37–67.

——, 'Anti-Foundationalism, Theory Hope, and the Teaching of Composition' (1987), reprinted in Fish, *Doing What Comes Naturally*, 342–55.

——, *Doing What Comes Naturally: Change, Rhetoric and the Practice of Theory in Literary and Legal Studies*, Oxford: Clarendon Press, 1989.

——, 'Almost Pragmatism: The Jurisprudence of Richard Posner, Richard Rorty and Ronald Dworkin', in Brint and Weaver (eds), *Pragmatism in Law & Society*, 47–81, reprinted in Fish, *There's No Such Thing as Free Speech and It's a Good Thing Too*, 200–30.

——, *There's No Such Thing as Free Speech and It's a Good Thing Too*, New York and Oxford: Oxford University Press, 1994.

Fitzgibbons, Richard P., 'The Cognitive and Emotive Uses of Forgiveness in the Treatment of Anger', *Psychotherapy* 23 (1986), 629–33.

Fitzmyer SJ, Joseph A., 'The Semitic Background of the New Testament *Kyrios*-Title', in Joseph A. Fitzmyer SJ, *A Wandering Aramean: Collected Aramaic Essays* (SBLMS 25), Missoula, MT: Scholars Press, 1979, 115–42.

——, *Romans* (AB 33), London: Chapman, 1993.

Florian, Casiano and Christian Duquoc (eds), *Forgiveness* (*Concilium* 184), Edinburgh: T&T Clark, 1986.

Follesdal, Dagfinn, 'Analytic Philosophy: What Is It and Why Should One Engage In It?', in Hans-Johann Glock (ed.), *The Rise of Analytic Philosophy*, Oxford: Blackwell, 1997, 1–16.

Forguson, L. W., 'In Pursuit of Performatives', *Philosophy* 41 (1966), 341–47, reprinted in Fann (ed.), *Symposium on J. L. Austin*, 412–19.

Forguson, L. W., 'Locutionary and Illocutionary Acts', in Berlin et al., *Essays on J. L. Austin*, 160–85.

Fowl, Stephen E., 'The Ethics of Interpretation; or, What's Left Over after the Elimination of Meaning?', in David J. A. Clines, Stephen E. Fowl and Stanley E. Porter (eds), *The Bible in Three Dimensions: Essays in Celebration of the Fortieth Anniversary of the Department of Biblical Studies, University of Sheffield* (JSOTS 87), Sheffield: JSOT Press, 1990, 379–98.

——, *The Story of Christ in the Ethics of Paul: An Analysis of the Function of the Hymnic Material in the Pauline Corpus* (JSNTS 36), Sheffield: JSOT Press, 1990.

——, 'Introduction', in Fowl (ed.), *The Theological Interpretation of Scripture*, xii–xxx.

——, *Engaging Scripture: A Model for Theological Interpretation*, Oxford: Blackwell, 1998.

——, Review of Francis Watson, *Text and Truth: Redefining Biblical Theology*, Edinburgh: T&T Clark, 1997, in *MTh* 15 (1999), 94–6.

Fowl, Stephen E. (ed.), *The Theological Interpretation of Scripture: Classic and Contemporary Readings* (Blackwell Readings in Modern Theology), Oxford: Blackwell, 1997.

France, R. T., *Divine Government: God's Kingship in the Gospel of Mark*, London: SPCK, 1990.

Frei, Hans W., *The Identity of Jesus Christ: The Hermeneutical Bases of Dogmatic Theology*, Philadelphia: Fortress Press, 1975.

Fuller, R. H., *The Christology of the New Testament*, London: Collins, 1965.

Funk, Robert W., Roy W. Hoover et al., *The Five Gospels: The Search for the Authentic Words of Jesus*, New York: Macmillan, 1993.

Furberg, Mats, 'Meaning and Illocutionary Force', in Fann (ed.), *Symposium on J. L. Austin*, 445–68.

Gadamer, Hans-Georg, *Truth and Method*, London: Sheed & Ward, ²1989 (German original 1960).

Geertz, Clifford, *The Interpretation of Cultures: Selected Essays*, New York: Basic Books, 1973.

Gellner, Ernest, *Words and Things: A Critical Account of Linguistic Philosophy and a Study in Ideology* (with an introduction by Bertrand Russell), London: Gollancz, 1959.

Gestrich, Christof, *The Return of Splendor in the World: The Christian Doctrine of Sin and Forgiveness* (trans. Daniel W. Bloesch), Grand Rapids: Eerdmans, 1997 (1989).

Glock, Hans-Johann, *A Wittgenstein Dictionary*, Oxford: Blackwell, 1996.

Gloer, W. Hullitt, 'Homologies and Hymns in the New Testament: Form, Content and Criteria for Identification', *PRS* 11 (1984), 115–32.

Green, Garrett, *Imagining God: Theology and the Religious Imagination*, San Francisco: Harper & Row, 1989.

——, *Theology, Hermeneutics and Imagination: The Crisis of Interpretation at the End of Modernity*, Cambridge: Cambridge University Press, 2000.

Green, Thomas F., *The Activities of Teaching*, New York: McGraw-Hill, 1971.

Grice, H. P., 'Utterer's Meaning, Sentence Meaning and Word Meaning', *Foundations of Language* 4 (1968), 225–42, reprinted in Searle (ed.), *Philosophy of Language*, 54–70, and in Grice, *Studies in the Way of Words*, 117–37.

——, 'Logic and Conversation', in P. Cole and J. L. Morgan (eds), *Syntax and Semantics*, vol. 3, *Speech Acts*, New York: Academic Press, 1975, 41–58, reprinted in Grice, *Studies in the Way of Words*, 22–40.

——, *Studies in the Way of Words*, Cambridge, MA: Harvard University Press, 1989.

Grondin, Jean, *Introduction to Philosophical Hermeneutics* (trans. Joel Weinsheimer), New Haven and London: Yale University Press, 1994 (1991).

Grudem, Wayne, 'Scripture's Self-Attestation and the Problem of Formulating a Doctrine of Scripture', in D. A. Carson and John D. Woodbridge (eds), *Scripture and Truth*, Leicester: IVP, 1983, 19–59 and 359–68.

Gu, Yueguo, 'The Impasse of Perlocution', *JPrag* 20 (1993), 405–32.

Guelich, R. A., *Mark 1:8:26* (WBC 34a), Waco: Word, 1989.

Gundry, Robert H., *Matthew: A Commentary on His Handbook for a Mixed Church under Persecution*, Grand Rapids: Eerdmans, [2]1994 (1982).

Guthrie, Donald, *New Testament Introduction*, Downers Grove, IL: IVP, [3]1970.

Haber, Joram Graf, *Forgiveness*, Savage, MD: Rowman & Littlefield, 1991.

Hacker, P. M. S., *Wittgenstein's Place in Twentieth-Century Analytic Thought*, Oxford: Blackwell, 1996.

Hale, Bob and Crispin Wright (eds), *A Companion to the Philosophy of Language* (Blackwell Companions to Philosophy), Oxford: Blackwell, 1997.

Hancher, Michael, 'Beyond a Speech Act Theory of Literary Discourse', *MLN* 92 (1977), 1081–98.

Hansen, Steven E., 'Forgiving and Retaining Sin: A Study of the Text and Context of John 20:23', *HBTh* 19 (1997), 24–32.

Hauerwas, Stanley, *Unleashing the Scripture: Freeing the Bible from Captivity to America*, Nashville: Abingdon Press, 1993.

Hauerwas, Stanley and Richard Bondi, 'Language, Experience and the Life Well Lived: A Review of the Work of Donald Evans', *RelSRev* 9.1 (1983), 33–7.

Haugeland, John, 'The Intentionality All-Stars', in James E. Tomberlin (ed.), *Philosophical Perspectives 4: Action Theory and Philosophy of Mind*, Atascadero, CA: Ridgeview Publishing Company, 1990, 383–427.

Hays, Richard B., *The Moral Vision of the New Testament: A Contemporary Introduction to New Testament Ethics*, Edinburgh: T&T Clark, 1996.

Henderson, Ian H., *Jesus, Rhetoric and Law* (Bib Int Ser 20), Leiden: E. J. Brill, 1996.

High, Dallas M., *Language, Persons, and Belief: Studies in Wittgenstein's Philosophical Investigations and Religious Uses of Language*, New York: Oxford University Press, 1967.

Hilborn, David, 'From Performativity to Pedagogy: Jean Ladrière and the Pragmatics of Reformed Worship Discourse', in Stanley E. Porter (ed.), *The Nature of Religious Language: A Colloquium* (Roehampton Institute London Papers 1), Sheffield: Sheffield Academic Press, 1996, 170–200.

Hirsch Jr, E. D., *Validity in Interpretation*, New Haven and London: Yale University Press, 1967.

Hirsch Jr, E. D., 'Reading, Writing, and Cultural Literacy', in Winifred Bryan Horner (ed.), *Composition and Literature: Bridging the Gap*, Chicago and London: University of Chicago Press, 1983, 141–7.

——, 'Meaning and Significance Reinterpreted', *Critical Inquiry* 11 (1984), 202–25.

Holdcroft, David, 'Doubts about the Locutionary/Illocutionary Distinction', *International Studies in Philosophy* (1974), 3–16.

Holmer, Paul, 'Wittgenstein and the Self', in Richard H. Bell and Ronald E. Hustwit, *Essays on Kierkegaard & Wittgenstein: On Understanding the Self*, Wooster, OH: College of Wooster, 1978, 10–31.

Holtz, T., 'Das Kennzeichen des Geistes (1 Kor. xii. 1–3)', *NTS* 18 (1971/2), 365–76.

Hooker, M. D., 'On Using the Wrong Tool', *Theology* 75 (1972), 570–81.

Hornsby, Jennifer, 'Things Done with Words', in Jonathan Dancy, J. M. E. Moravcsik and C. C. W. Taylor (eds), *Human Agency: Language, Duty and Value. Philosophical Essays in Honor of J. O. Urmson*, Stanford, CA: Stanford University Press, 1988, 27–46 and 283–8.

——, 'Illocution and Its Significance', in Tsohatzidis (ed.), *Foundations of Speech Act Theory*, 187–207.

Hunsinger, George, 'Truth as Self-Involving: Barth and Lindbeck on the Cognitive and Performative Aspects of Truth in Theological Discourse', *JAAR* 61 (1993), 41–56.

Incandela, Joseph M., 'The Appropriation of Wittgenstein's Work by Philosophers of Religion: Towards a Re-evaluation and an End', *RelStud* 21 (1985), 457–74.

Iser, Wolfgang, 'The Reality of Fiction', *NLH* 7 (1975), 7–38.

——, *The Act of Reading: A Theory of Aesthetic Response*, Baltimore and London: Johns Hopkins University Press, 1978.

Jacobs, Alan, 'A Tale of Two Stanleys', *First Things* 44 (1994), 18–21.

Jeanrond, Werner G., *Text and Interpretation as Categories of Theological Thinking*, Dublin: Gill & Macmillan, 1988 (1986).

Jewett, R., 'The Redaction and Use of an Early Christian Confession in Romans 1:3–4', in D. E. Groh and R. Jewett (eds), *The Living Text: Essays in Honor of Ernest W. Saunders*, Lanham, MD: University Press of America, 1985, 99–122.

Johnson, Luke Timothy, *The Letter of James* (AB 37A), Doubleday: Anchor, 1995.

——, *The Real Jesus: The Misguided Quest for the Historical Jesus and the Truth of the Traditional Gospels*, San Francisco: HarperSanFrancisco, 1996.

Jones, Ivor Harold, *The Matthean Parables: A Literary & Historical Commentary* (NovTSup LXXX), Leiden: E. J. Brill, 1995.

Jones, L. Gregory, *Embodying Forgiveness: A Theological Analysis*, Grand Rapids: Eerdmans, 1995.

Jones, O. R., *The Concept of Holiness*, London: Allen & Unwin, 1961.

Käsemann, E., 'A Critical Analysis of Philippians 2:5–11', *JTC* 5 (1968), 45–88.

——, *Commentary on Romans*, Grand Rapids: Eerdmans, 1980.

Katz, Jerrold J., *Propositional Structure and Illocutionary Force: A Study of the Contribution of Sentence Meaning to Speech Acts*, New York: Crowell, and Sussex: Harvester Press, 1977.

Kaufmann, Gordon, *The Theological Imagination*, Philadelphia: Westminster Press, 1981.

Kelly, J. N. D., *Early Christian Creeds*, London: Longmans, [3]1972 (1950).

——, *The Pastoral Epistles* (BNTC), London: A&C Black, 1963.

Kelsey, David H., *The Uses of Scripture in Recent Theology*, Philadelphia: Fortress Press, 1975.

——, 'The Bible and Christian Theology', *JAAR* 48 (1980), 385–402.

Kennedy, G. A., *New Testament Interpretation through Rhetorical Criticism*, Chapel Hill: University of North Carolina, 1984.

Kerner, G. C., 'A Wittgensteinian Critique of Some Recent Developments in the Theory of Speech Acts', in Rudolf Haller and Wolfgang Grassl (eds), *Language, Logic and Philosophy: Proceedings of the Fourth International Wittgenstein Symposium*

28 Aug–2 Sep 1979, Kirchberg am Wechsel, Austria, Dordrecht: D. Reidel Publishing Company, and Vienna: Hölder-Pichler-Tempsky, 1980, 423–5.

Kerr, Fergus, 'Language as Hermeneutic in the Later Wittgenstein', *Tijdschrift voor Filosofie* 27 (1965), 491–520.

——, *Theology after Wittgenstein*, London: SPCK, [2]1997 (1986).

—— 'What's Wrong with Realism Anyway?', in Crowder (ed.), *God and Reality*, 128–43.

Knierim, R., *Die Hauptbegriffe für Sünde im alten Testament*, Gütersloh, 1965.

Knight III, George W., *The Pastoral Epistles* (NIGTC), Grand Rapids: Eerdmans, 1992.

Korting, G., 'Binden oder lösen: Zu Verstockungs- und Befreiungstheologie in Mt 16,19; 18,18.21–35 und Joh 15,1–17; 20, 23', *SNTU* 14 (1989), 39–91.

Kramer, Werner, *Christ, Lord, Son of God* (SBT 50), London: SCM Press, 1966.

Kripke, Saul, *Wittgenstein on Rules and Private Language*, Oxford: Blackwell, 1982.

Kselman, John S., James H. Charlesworth and Gary S. Shogren, 'Forgiveness', in *ABD*, II:831–8.

Kugel, James L., 'On Hidden Hatred and Open Reproach: Early Exegesis of Leviticus 19:17', *HTR* 80 (1987), 43–61.

Kuklick, Bruce, 'Seven Thinkers and How They Grew: Descartes, Spinoza, Leibniz, Locke, Berkeley, Hume and Kant', in Richard Rorty, J. B. Schneewind and Quentin Skinner (eds), *Philosophy in History: Essays on the Historiography of Philosophy*, Cambridge: Cambridge University Press, 1984, 125–39.

Kümmel, W. G., *Promise and Fulfilment: The Eschatological Message of Jesus* (SBT 1/23), London: SCM Press, [3]1957.

Kurzon, Dennis, *It Is Hereby Performed . . . Explorations in Legal Speech Acts* (Pragmatics & Beyond VII:6), Amsterdam and Philadelphia: John Benjamins Publishing Company, 1986.

Kurzynski, M. J., 'The Virtue of Forgiveness as a Human Resource Management Strategy', *Journal of Business Ethics* 17.1 (1998), 77–85.

Ladd, G. E., *The Presence of the Future: The Eschatology of Biblical Realism*, Grand Rapids: Eerdmans, 1974.

Ladrière, Jean, 'The Performativity of Liturgical Language', *Concilium*, vol. 2 no. 9 (1973), 50–62.

Lamarque, Peter and Stein Haugom Olsen, *Truth, Fiction, and Literature: A Philosophical Perspective*, Oxford: Clarendon Press, 1994.

Lanser, Susan S., *The Narrative Act: Point of View in Prose Fiction*, Princeton: Princeton University Press, 1981.

——, '(Feminist) Criticism in the Garden: Inferring Genesis 2–3', in White, (ed.), *Speech Act Theory and Biblical Criticism* (= *Semeia* 41), 67–84.

Lash, Nicholas, *Theology on the Way to Emmaus*, London: SCM Press, 1986.

Latour, Bruno and Steve Woolgar, *Laboratory Life: The Social Construction of Scientific Facts*, Beverly Hills: Sage Publications, 1979.

Lauritzen, Paul, 'Forgiveness: Moral Prerogative or Religious Duty?', *JRE* 15 (1987), 141–54.

Leith, John H., 'Creeds, Early Christian', in *ABD*, I:1203–6.

Lentricchia, Frank, *After the New Criticism*, Chicago: University of Chicago Press, 1980.

Lepore, Ernest and Robert Van Gulick (eds), *John Searle and His Critics*, Cambridge, MA, and Oxford: Blackwell, 1991.

Levenson, Jon D., *Creation and the Persistence of Evil: The Jewish Drama of Divine Omnipotence*, San Francisco: Harper & Row, 1988.

Lin, Hong-Hsin, 'The Relevance of Hermeneutical Theory in Heidegger, Gadamer, Wittgenstein and Ricoeur for the Concept of Self in Adult Education', unpublished Ph.D. thesis, University of Nottingham, 1998.

Lindbeck, George A., *The Nature of Doctrine: Religion and Theology in a Postliberal Age*, London: SPCK, 1984.

Litfin, Duane, *St. Paul's Theology of Proclamation: 1 Corinthians 1–4 and Greco-Roman Rhetoric* (SNTSMS 79), Cambridge: Cambridge University Press, 1994.

Lundin, Roger, 'Reading America', unpublished paper at the Crossing the Boundaries conference, Gloucester, MA, 1998.

Lundin, Roger, Anthony C. Thiselton and Clarence Walhout, *The Responsibility of Hermeneutics,* Grand Rapids: Eerdmans, and Exeter: Paternoster Press, 1985.

Lündstrom, Gösta, *The Kingdom of God in the Teaching of Jesus,* Edinburgh: Oliver & Boyd, 1963.

Luz, Ulrich, *Matthew in History: Interpretation, Influence, and Effects,* Minneapolis: Fortress Press, 1994.

Lyons, William, *Emotions,* Cambridge: Cambridge University Press, 1980.

——, *Approaches to Intentionality,* Oxford: Clarendon Press, 1995.

McClendon Jr, James Wm, and James M. Smith, 'Religious Language after J. L. Austin', *RelStud* 8 (1972), 55–63.

——, *Understanding Religious Convictions,* Notre Dame, IN: University of Notre Dame Press, 1975; revised as (1994) below.

——, *Convictions: Defusing Religious Relativism,* Valley Forge, PA: Trinity Press International, 1994.

McDonald, James I. H., *Kerygma and Didache: The Articulation and Structure of the Earliest Christian Message* (SNTSMS 37), Cambridge: Cambridge University Press, 1980.

McFadyen, Alistair I., 'Original Sin in Modern Theology', paper presented to the Nottingham Theological Society, Nottingham, 30 June 1998.

——, *Bound to Sin: Abuse, Holocaust and the Christian Doctrine of Sin* (Cambridge Studies in Christian Doctrine), Cambridge: Cambridge University Press, 2000.

McGinn, Colin, *Wittgenstein on Meaning: An Interpretation and Evaluation,* Oxford: Blackwell, 1984.

McGinn, Marie, *Routledge Philosophy Guidebook to Wittgenstein and the Philosophical Investigations,* London: Routledge, 1997.

McIntyre, John, *The Shape of Soteriology: Studies in the Doctrine of the Death of Christ,* Edinburgh: T&T Clark, 1992.

McKnight, Scot, 'The Hermeneutics of Confessing Jesus as Lord', *Ex Auditu* 14 (1998), 1–17.

McNulty, T. Michael, 'Pauline Preaching: A Speech-Act Analysis', *Worship* 53 (1979), 207–14.

Mackintosh, H. R., *The Christian Experience of Forgiveness*, London: Nisbet & Co., 1927.

Magee, S. J. B., *Philosophical Analysis in Education*, New York: Harper & Row, 1971.

Mananzan OSB, Sr Mary-John, *The 'Language Game' of Confessing One's Belief: A Wittgensteinian-Austinian Approach to the Linguistic Analysis of Creedal Statements* (Linguistische Arbeiten 16), Tübingen: Max Niemeyer Verlag, 1974.

Mantey, J. R., 'The Mistranslation of the Perfect Tense in John 20:23, Mt. 16:19, and Mt. 18:18', *JBL* 58 (1939), 243–9.

——, 'Evidence That the Perfect Tense in John 20:23 and Matthew 16:19 Is Mistranslated', *JETS* 16 (1973), 129–38.

Marcuse, Herbert, *One Dimensional Man: Studies in the Ideology of Advanced Industrial Society*, London: Routledge & Kegan Paul, 1964.

Marrou, H. I., *A History of Education in Antiquity*, New York: New American Library, 1964.

Marshall, I. Howard, ' "To Find Out What God Is Saying": Reflections on the Authorizing of Scripture', in Roger Lundin (ed.), *Disciplining Hermeneutics: Interpretation in Christian Perspective*, Grand Rapids: Eerdmans, and Leicester: Apollos, 1997, 49–55.

Martin, Ralph P., *Worship in the Early Church*, Grand Rapids: Eerdmans, 1974 (1964).

——, *New Testament Foundations. Volume 2*, Grand Rapids: Eerdmans, and Carlisle: Paternoster, revised edition, 1986 (1978).

——, 'Patterns of Worship in New Testament Churches', *JSNT* 37 (1989), 59–85.

——, *A Hymn of Christ: Philippians 2:5–11 in Recent Interpretation and in the Setting of Early Christian Worship*, Downers Grove, IL: IVP, 1997 (= revised edition of *idem, Carmen Christi: Philippians ii.5–11 in* . . . , Grand Rapids: Eerdmans, 1983 (1967)).

Martin, Ralph P. and Brian J. Dodd (eds), *Where Christology Began: Essays on Philippians 2*, Louisville, KY: Westminster John Knox Press, 1998.

Martinich, A. P., 'Sacraments and Speech Acts', *Heythrop Journal* 16 (1975), 289–303, 405–17.

Masterson, P., 'Self-Involvement and the Affirmation of God', in J. Walgrave, A. Vergote and B. Willaert (eds), *Miscellanea Albert Dondeyne: Godsdienstfilosofie; Philosophie de la Religion*, Gembloux: Leuven University Press, 1974, 263–77.

Meeks, Wayne A., 'The Man from Heaven in Johannine Sectarianism', *JBL* 91 (1972), 44–72.

Mehta, Ved, *Fly and the Fly-bottle: Encounters with British Intellectuals*, Harmondsworth: Penguin Books, 1965.

Meier, John P., *A Marginal Jew: Rethinking the Historical Jesus*, vol. 1, *The Roots of the Problem and the Person*, New York: Doubleday, 1991.

——, *A Marginal Jew: Rethinking the Historical Jesus*, vol. 2, *Mentor, Message and Miracles*, New York: Doubleday, 1994.

Mercer, Calvin R., *Norman Perrin's Interpretation of the New Testament: From 'Exegetical Method' to 'Hermeneutical Process'* (StABH 2), Macon, GA: Mercer University Press, 1986.

Meyer, Ben F., *Reality and Illusion in New Testament Scholarship: A Primer in Critical Realist Hermeneutics*, Collegeville, MN: Michael Glazier, Liturgical Press, 1994.

Meyers, Robert B. and Karen Hopkins, 'A Speech-Act Theory Bibliography', *Centrum* 5 (1977), 73–108.

Michel, Otto, 'ὁμολογέω κτλ', in *TDNT* V, 199–220.

Milbank, John, *Theology and Social Theory: Beyond Secular Reason*, Oxford: Blackwell, 1990.

Miller, Arthur, *The Crucible: A Play in Four Acts*, Harmondsworth: Penguin, 1968 (1953).

Minear, P. S., 'Promise', *IDB* 3:893–6.

Mitchell, W. J. T. (ed.), *Against Theory: Literary Studies and the New Pragmatism*, Chicago and London: University of Chicago Press, 1985.

Mohrlang, Roger, *Matthew and Paul: A Comparison of Ethical Perspectives* (SNTSMS 48), Cambridge: Cambridge University Press, 1984.

Moo, Douglas, *The Epistle to the Romans* (NICNT), Grand Rapids: Eerdmans, 1996.

Moore, Stephen D., *Literary Criticism and the Gospels: The Theoretical Challenge*, New Haven and London: Yale University Press, 1989.

Moran, Gabriel, *Showing How: The Act of Teaching*, Valley Forge, PA: Trinity Press International, 1997.

Morgan, Robert, 'The Hermeneutical Significance of Four Gospels', *Int* 33 (1979), 376–88.

Moule, C. F. D., 'Further Reflexions on Philippians 2:5–11', in W. W. Gasque and R. P. Martin (eds), *Apostolic History and the Gospel: Biblical and Historical Essays Presented to F. F. Bruce*, Exeter: Paternoster, 1970, 264–76.

——, *The Birth of the New Testament* (BNTC), London: A&C Black, ³1981 (1962).

——, 'The Theology of Forgiveness', *Essays in New Testament Interpretation*, Cambridge: Cambridge University Press, 1982 (1971), 250–60.

——, '". . . As we forgive . . .": A Note on the Distinction between Deserts and Capacity in the Understanding of Forgiveness', *Essays in New Testament Interpretation*, Cambridge: Cambridge University Press, 1982 (1978), 278–86.

——, *Worship in the New Testament* (Grove Liturgical Study 12/13), Bramcote: Grove Books, 1983 (1961).

——, *Forgiveness and Reconciliation*, London: SPCK, 1998.

Muddiman, John, 'Form Criticism', in *DBI*, 240–3.

Mulhall, Stephen, *On Being in the World: Wittgenstein and Heidegger on Seeing Aspects*, London: Routledge, 1990.

Müller-Fahrenholz, Geiko, *The Art of Forgiveness: Theological Reflections on Healing and Reconciliation*, Geneva: WCC Publications, 1996.

Murphy, Jeffrie G., 'Forgiveness and Resentment', in Murphy and Hampton, *Forgiveness and Mercy*, 14–34.

——, 'Introduction. I. The Retributive Emotions', in Murphy and Hampton, *Forgiveness and Mercy*, 1–10.

——, 'Forgiveness and Mercy', *REP*, 3:697–701.

Murphy, Jeffrie G. and Jean Hampton, *Forgiveness and Mercy* (Cambridge Studies in Philosophy and Law), Cambridge: Cambridge University Press, 1988.

Murphy, Nancey, 'Textual Relativism, Philosophy of Language, and the Baptist Vision', in Stanley Hauerwas, Nancey Murphy and Mark Nation (eds), *Theology without Foundations: Religious Practice & the Future of Theological Truth*, Nashville: Abingdon Press, 1994, 245–70.

——, *Anglo-American Postmodernity: Philosophical Perspectives on Science, Religion, and Ethics*, Colorado: Westview Press, 1997.

Murphy, Nancey and James Wm McClendon Jr, 'Distinguishing Modern and Postmodern Theologies', *MTh* 5 (1989), 191–214.

Nagel, Thomas, *The View from Nowhere*, New York: Oxford University Press, 1986.

Narveson, Jan, 'The Agreement to Keep Our Agreements', *Philosophical Papers* 23 (1994), 75–87.

Nerlich, Brigitte and David D. Clarke, 'Language, Action and Context: Linguistic Pragmatics in Europe and America (1800–1950)', *JPrag* 22 (1994), 439–63.

Neufeld, Dietmar, *Reconceiving Texts as Speech Acts: An Analysis of 1 John* (Bib Int Ser 7), Leiden: E. J. Brill, 1994.

Neufeld, Vernon H., *The Earliest Christian Confessions* (New Testament Tools and Studies V), Leiden: E. J. Brill, 1963.

Newman, Louis E., 'The Quality of Mercy: On the Duty to Forgive in the Judaic Tradition', *JRE* 15 (1987), 155–72.

Nida, Eugene et al., *Style and Discourse*, New York: United Bible Societies, 1983.

Noack, B., *Das Gottesreich bei Lukas: Eine Studie zu Luk. 17.20–24* (Symbolae Biblicae Uppsalienses 10), Lund: Gleerup, 1948.

Noble, Paul R., 'Hermeneutics and Post-Modernism: Can We Have a Radical Reader-Response Theory?', *RelStud* 30 (1994), 419–36, and 31 (1995), 1–22.

Nolland, John, *Luke 9:21–18:34* (WBC 35B), Waco: Word, 1993.

Norris, Christopher, *What's Wrong with Postmodernism: Critical Theory and the Ends of Philosophy*, New York and London: Harvester Wheatsheaf, 1990.

——, *Deconstruction: Theory and Practice*, London: Routledge & Kegan Paul, [2]1991 (1982).

Norris, Christopher, *Reclaiming Truth: Contributions to a Critique of Cultural Relativism*, Durham: Duke University Press, 1996.

Nuyts, Jan and Jef Verschueren, *A Comprehensive Bibliography of Pragmatics*, 4 vols, Amsterdam and Philadelphia: John Benjamins Publishing Company, 1987.

O'Neill, J. C., 'The Unforgiveable Sin', *JSNT* 19 (1983), 37–42.

Ohmann, Richard, 'Speech Acts and the Definition of Literature', *Philosophy and Rhetoric* 4 (1971), 1–19.

—— 'Speech, Literature, and the Space between', *NLH* 4 (1972), 47–63.

—— 'Literature as Act', in Seymour Chatman (ed.), *Approaches to Poetics*, New York: Columbia University Press, 1973, 81–108.

Otto, R., *The Kingdom of God and the Son of Man* (trans F. V. Filson and B. L. Woolf), London: Lutterworth, 1938 (1934).

Pagels, Elaine, *The Origin of Satan*, London: Allen Lane, 1995.

Pannenberg, Wolfhart, *Systematic Theology*, 3 vols, Edinburgh: T&T Clark, 1991–8 (1988–93).

Passmore, John, *A Hundred Years of Philosophy*, Harmondsworth: Penguin, ²1966 (1957).

Patterson, Sue, *Realist Christian Theology in a Postmodern Age* (Cambridge Studies in Christian Doctrine), Cambridge: Cambridge University Press, 1999.

Pears, David, 'Wittgenstein and Austin', in Bernard Williams and Alan Montefiore (eds), *British Analytical Philosophy*, London: Routledge & Kegan Paul, 1966, 17–39.

Pearson, B. A., 'Did the Gnostic Curse Jesus?', *JBL* 86 (1967), 301–5.

——, *The Pneumatikos-Psychikos Terminology in 1 Corinthians: A Study in the Theology of the Corinthian Opponents of Paul and Its Relation to Gnosticism* (SBLDS 12), Missoula, MT: Scholars Press, 1973.

Penelhum, Terence, *Butler*, London, Boston and Henley: Routledge & Kegan Paul, 1985.

Perkins, Pheme, *Jesus as Teacher* (Understanding Jesus Today), Cambridge: Cambridge University Press, 1990.

Perrin, Norman, *The Kingdom of God in the Teaching of Jesus*, London: SCM Press, 1963.

——, *Jesus and the Language of the Kingdom: Symbol and Metaphor in New Testament Interpretation*, Philadelphia: Fortress Press, 1976.

Peterson, David, *Engaging with God: A Biblical Theology of Worship*, Leicester: Apollos, 1992.

Petrey, Sandy, *Speech Acts and Literary Theory*, New York and London: Routledge, 1990.

Phillips, D. Z., *The Concept of Prayer*, London: Routledge & Kegan Paul, 1965.

Pingleton, Jared P., 'Why We Don't Forgive: A Biblical and Object Relations Theoretical Model for Understanding Failures in the Forgiving Process', *Journal of Psychology and Theology* 25 (1997), 403–13.

Placher, William C., *Unapologetic Theology: A Christian Voice in a Pluralistic Conversation*, Louisville, KY: Westminster/John Knox Press, 1989.

Plantinga, Alvin, 'Reason and Belief in God', in Plantinga and Wolterstorff (eds), *Faith and Rationality*, 16–93.

Plantinga, Alvin and Nicholas Wolterstorff (eds), *Faith and Rationality: Reason and Religious Belief in God*, Notre Dame: University of Notre Dame Press, 1983.

Polk, Timothy, *The Prophetic Persona: Jeremiah and the Language of the Self* (JSOTS 32), Sheffield: JSOT Press, 1984.

——, *The Biblical Kierkegaard: Reading by the Rule of Faith*, Macon, GA: Mercer University Press, 1997.

Porter, S. E., 'Vague Verbs, Periphrastics, and Matt 16:19', *FNT* 1 (1988), 155–73.

——, 'Why Hasn't Reader-Response Criticism Caught on in New Testament Studies?', *LT* 4 (1990), 278–92.

Potter, Jonathan, *Representing Reality: Discourse, Rhetoric and Social Construction*, London: Sage Publications, 1996.

Poulain, Jacques, 'Pragmatique de la Communication et Dynamique de la Verité: La fidélité théorique de D. Evans à la révélation chrétienne', *RSR* 69 (1981), 545–72.

Poythress, Vern S., 'Is Romans 1³⁻⁴ a *Pauline* Confession after All?', *ExpT* 87 (1976), 180–3.

Pratt, Mary Louise, *Toward a Speech Act Theory of Literary Discourse*, Bloomington: Indiana University Press, 1977.

——, 'The Ideology of Speech-Act Theory', *Centrum* NS 1.1 (1981), 5–18.

——, 'Interpretive Strategies/Strategic Interpretations: On Anglo-American Reader Response Criticism', *Boundary* 2.11 (1982), 201–31.

Pratt, Mary Louise and Elizabeth Closs Traugott, *Linguistics for Students of Literature*, New York: Harcourt Brace Jovanovich, 1980, 226–71.

Prichard, H. A., 'The Obligation to Keep a Promise', *Moral Obligation: Essays and Lectures*, Oxford: Clarendon Press, 1949, 169–79.

Pyper, H. S., Review of Kevin J. Vanhoozer, *Is There a Meaning in This Text? The Bible, the Reader, and the Morality of Literary Knowledge*, Grand Rapids: Zondervan, 1998, in Lester L. Grabbe (ed.), *Society for Old Testament Study Book List 1999*, Sheffield: Sheffield Academic Press, 1999, 119–20.

Quine, W. V. O., 'Mr Strawson on Logical Theory', *Mind* 62, 248 (1953), 433–51, reprinted in W. V. O. Quine, *The Ways of Paradox*, New York: Random House, 1966, 135–55.

——, *Word and Object*, Cambridge, MA: Harvard University Press, 1960.

——, 'On What There Is', in W. V. O. Quine, *From a Logical Point of View*, Cambridge, MA: Harvard University Press, ²1961 (1953), 1–19.

Quinn, Philip L., 'Sin', in *REP*, 8:791–6.

Ramge, Hans, 'Language Acquisition as the Acquisition of Speech Act Competence', *JPrag* 1 (1977), 155–64.

Recanati, François, 'Some Remarks on Explicit Performatives, Indirect Speech Acts, Locutionary Meaning and Truth-Value', in Searle, Kiefer and Bierwisch (eds), *Speech-Act Theory and Pragmatics*, 205–20.

——, *Meaning and Force: The Pragmatics of Performative Utterances*, Cambridge: Cambridge University Press, 1987.

Recanati, François, 'Contextualism and Anti-Contextualism in the Philosophy of Language', in Tsohatzidis (ed.), *Foundations of Speech Act Theory*, 156–66.

Rée, Jonathan, 'English Philosophy in the Fifties', *Radical Philosophy* 65 (1993), 3–21.

Reeder Jr, John P., 'Forgiveness: Tradition and Appropriation', *JRE* 15 (1987), 136–40.

Reid, Stephen Breck, 'Psalm 50: Prophetic Speech and God's Performative Utterances', in Stephen Breck Reid (ed.), *Prophets and Paradigms: Essays in Honor of Gene M. Tucker* (JSOTS 229), Sheffield: Sheffield Academic Press, 1996, 217–30.

Rendall, Steven, 'Fish vs. Fish', *Diacritics* 12.4 (1982), 49–57.

Richardson, Alan, *Creeds in the Making: A Short Introduction to the History of Christian Doctrine*, London: SCM Press, 1935.

Ricoeur, Paul, *The Symbolism of Evil*, New York: Harper & Row, 1967.

——, *Interpretation Theory: Discourse and the Surplus of Meaning*, Fort Worth: Texas Christian University Press, 1976.

——, 'Evil: A Challenge to Philosophy and Theology', *JAAR* 53 (1985), 635–48, now reprinted in Ricoeur, *Figuring the Sacred*, 249–61.

——, 'Evil', in Mircea Eliade (ed.), *The Encyclopedia of Religion*, 16 vols, New York: Macmillan, 1987, 5:199–208.

——, *Figuring the Sacred: Religion, Narrative, and Imagination* (ed. Mark I. Wallace), Minneapolis: Fortress Press, 1995.

Riesner, Rainer, *Jesus als Lehrer: Eine Untersuchung zum Ursprung der Evangelien-überlieferung* (WUNT II/7), Tübingen: J. C. B. Mohr (Paul Siebeck), 1981.

——, 'Jesus as Preacher and Teacher', in Henry Wansbrough (ed.), *Jesus and the Oral Gospel Tradition* (JSNTS 64), Sheffield: Sheffield Academic Press, 1991, 185–210.

——, 'Teacher', in *DJG*, 807–11.

Riley, G. J., 'The *Gospel of Thomas* in Recent Scholarship', *CR:BS* 2 (1994), 227–52.

Roberts, C. H., 'The Kingdom of Heaven (Lk. xvii.21)', *HTR* 41 (1948), 1–8.

Roberts, T. A., 'Editor's Introduction', in T. A. Roberts (ed.), *Butler's Fifteen Sermons Preached at the Rolls Chapel and A Dissertation of the Nature of Virtue*, London: SPCK, 1970, ix–xxiv.

Rorty, Richard, *Philosophy and the Mirror of Nature*, Princeton: Princeton University Press, 1979.

——, 'The World Well Lost', *JP* 69 (1972), 649–65, reprinted in Richard Rorty, *Consequences of Pragmatism: Essays, 1972–1980*, Minneapolis: University of Minnesota Press, 1982, 3–18.

——, 'Texts and Lumps', *NLH* 17 (1985), 1–16.

——, *Contingency, Irony, and Solidarity*, Cambridge: Cambridge University Press, 1989.

——, 'Pragmatism, Davidson and Truth', *Objectivity, Relativism and Truth: Philosophical Papers Volume 1*, Cambridge: Cambridge University Press, 1991, 126–50.

——, 'The Pragmatists's Progress', in Eco, *Interpretation and Overinterpretation*, 89–108.

——, *Truth and Progress: Philosophical Papers Volume 3*, Cambridge: Cambridge University Press, 1997.

Rorty, Richard (ed.), *The Linguistic Turn: Recent Essays in Philosophical Method*, Chicago and London: University of Chicago Press, 1967.

Rundle, Bede, *Wittgenstein & Contemporary Philosophy of Language*, Oxford: Blackwell, 1990.

Russell, Jeffrey Burton, *The Devil: Perceptions of Evil from Antiquity to Primitive Christianity*, Ithaca and London: Cornell University Press, 1977.

——, *Satan: The Early Christian Tradition*, Ithaca and London: Cornell University Press, 1981.

——, *Lucifer: The Devil in the Middle Ages*, Ithaca and London: Cornell University Press, 1984.

——, *Mephistopheles: The Devil in the Modern World*, Ithaca and London: Cornell University Press, 1986.

Rüstow, A., '*Entos hymon estin*: Zur Deutung von Lukas 17.20–21', *ZNW* 51 (1960), 197–224.

Ryle, Gilbert, *The Concept of Mind*, London: Hutchinson, 1949.

——, *Collected Papers Vol. 2: Collected Essays 1929–68*, London: Hutchinson & Co., 1971.

Sadock, Jerrold M., 'Toward a Grammatically Realistic Typology of Speech Acts', in Tsohatzidis (ed.), *Foundations of Speech Act Theory*, 393–406.

Sadock, Jerrold M., and Arnold M. Zwicky, 'Speech Act Distinctions in Syntax', in Timothy Shopen (ed.), *Language Typology and Syntactic Description*, vol. 1, *Clause Structure*, Cambridge: Cambridge University Press, 1985, 155–96.

Sanders, E. P., *Paul and Palestinian Judaism: A Comparison of Patterns of Religion*, London: SCM Press, 1977.

——, 'Jesus and the Sinners', *JSNT* 19 (1983), 5–36.

——, *Jesus and Judaism*, London: SCM Press, 1985.

——, 'Sin, Sinners (NT)', in *ABD*, VI:40–7.

Sanders, J. T., *The New Testament Christological Hymns* (SNTSMS 15), Cambridge: Cambridge University Press, 1971.

Satterthwaite, Philip E., and David F. Wright (eds), *A Pathway into the Holy Scripture*, Grand Rapids: Eerdmans, 1994.

Saye, Scott C., 'The Wild and Crooked Tree: Barth, Fish, and Interpretive Communities', *MTh* 12 (1996), 435–58.

Schaff, Philip, *The Creeds of Christendom, with a History and Critical Notes*, vol. 1, *The History of the Creeds*, Grand Rapids: Baker, 1983 (1931).

Schmithals, W., *Gnosticism in Corinth: An Investigation of the Letters to the Corinthians*, Nashville: Abingdon Press, 1971 (1956).

Scholer, D. M., 'Sins Within and Sins Without: An Interpretation of 1 John 5:16–17', in G.F. Hawthorne (ed.), *Current Issues in Biblical and Patristic Interpretation*, Grand Rapids: Eerdmans, 1975, 230–46.

Schweitzer, Albert, *The Quest of the Historical Jesus: A Critical Study of Its Progress from Reimarus to Wrede*, London: A&C Black, 1954 (1906).

Scruton, Roger, *Modern Philosophy: A Survey*, London: Sinclair-Stevenson, 1994.

Searle, John R., 'How to Derive an "Ought" from an "Is"', *Philosophical Review* 73 (1964), 43–58, revised and reprinted in Searle, *Speech Acts*, 175–98.

——, 'What Is a Speech Act?', in Max Black (ed.), *Philosophy in America*, London: Allen & Unwin, 1965, 221–39; reprinted in Searle (ed.), *Philosophy of Language*, 39–53.

Searle, John R., 'Austin on Locutionary and Illocutionary Acts', *Philo-sophical Review* 77 (1968), revised and reprinted in Berlin et al., *Essays on J. L. Austin*, 141–59.

——, *Speech Acts: An Essay in the Philosophy of Language*, Cambridge: Cambridge University Press, 1969.

——, *The Campus War: A Sympathetic Look at the University in Agony*, Harmondsworth: Pelican Books, 1972.

——, 'The Logical Status of Fictional Discourse', *NLH* 6 (1975), 319–32, reprinted in Searle, *Expression and Meaning*, 58–75.

——, 'A Taxonomy of Illocutionary Acts', in Keith Gunderson (ed.), *Language, Mind and Knowledge: Minnesota Studies in the Philosophy of Science*, Minneapolis: University of Minnesota Press, 1975; reprinted in Searle, *Expression and Meaning*, 1–29.

——, 'Reiterating the Differences: A Reply to Derrida', *Glyph* 1 (1977), 198–208.

——, 'Literal Meaning', *Erkenntnis* 13 (1978), reprinted in Searle, *Expression and Meaning*, ch. 5, 117–36.

——, *Expression and Meaning: Studies in the Theory of Speech Acts*, Cambridge: Cambridge University Press, 1979.

——, 'The Background of Meaning', in Searle, Kiefer and Bierwisch (eds), *Speech-Act Theory and Pragmatics*, 221–32.

——, *Intentionality: An Essay in the Philosophy of Mind*, Cambridge: Cambridge University Press, 1983.

——, 'The World Turned Upside Down [A review of Jonathan Culler's *On Deconstruction*]', *New York Review of Books* 30.16 (October 1983), 74–9.

——, 'Indeterminacy, Empiricism, and the First Person', *JP* 84 (1987), 123–46.

——, 'Wittgenstein', in dialogue with Bryan Magee in Bryan Magee, *The Great Philosophers: An Introduction to Western Philosophy*, London: BBC Books, 1987, 320–47.

——, *Minds, Brains and Science: The 1984 Reith Lectures*, London: Penguin, 1991 (1984).

——, 'Response: The Background of Intentionality and Action', in Lepore and Van Gulick (eds), *John Searle and His Critics*, 289–99.

Searle, John R., *The Rediscovery of the Mind*, Cambridge, MA, and London: MIT Press, 1992.

——, 'Literary Theory and Its Discontents', *NLH* 25 (1994), 637–67.

——, *The Construction of Social Reality*, London: Penguin, 1995.

——, *The Mystery of Consciousness*, London: Granta Books, 1997.

——, 'Replies to Critics of *The Construction of Social Reality*', *HHS* 10.4 (1997), 103–10.

——, *Mind, Language and Society: Philosophy in the Real World*, London: Weidenfeld & Nicolson, 1999.

Searle, John R. (ed.), *The Philosophy of Language*, Oxford: Oxford University Press, 1971.

Searle, John R., Ferenc Kiefer and Manfred Bierwisch (eds), *Speech Act Theory and Pragmatics*, Dordrecht, London and Boston: Reidel, 1980.

Searle, John R. and Daniel Vanderveken, *Foundations of Illocutionary Logic*, Cambridge: Cambridge University Press, 1985.

Shepherd, Norman, 'Scripture and Confession', in Skilton (ed.), *Scripture and Confession*, 1–30.

Shogren, Gary S., 'Forgiveness (NT)', in *ABD*, II:835–8.

Skilton, John H. (ed.), *Scripture and Confession: A Book about Confessions Old and New*, Nutley, NJ: Presbyterian and Reformed Publishing Co., 1973.

Smart, Ninian, *The Concept of Worship*, London and Basingstoke: Macmillan, St. Martin's Press, 1972.

Smeyers, P. and J. D. Marshall, *Philosophy and Education: Accepting Wittgenstein's Challenge*, Dordrecht: Kluwer, 1995.

Smith, Nicholas H., *Strong Hermeneutics: Contingency and Moral Identity*, London and New York: Routledge, 1997.

Soskice, Janet Martin, *Metaphor and Religious Language*, Oxford: Clarendon Press, 1985.

Sperber, D. and D. Wilson, *Relevance: Communication and Cognition*, Oxford: Blackwell, 1986.

Spivak, Gayatri Chakravorty, 'Revolutions That as Yet Have No Model: Derrida's *Limited Inc*', *Diacritics* 10.4 (1980), 29–49.

Stagaman, SJ, David, '"God" in Analytic Philosophy', in Sebastian A. Matczak (ed.), *God in Contemporary Thought: A Philosophical Perspective* (Philosophical Questions Series 10), New York: Learned Publications, 1977, 813–49.

Stanton, G. N., 'Form Criticism Revisited', in Morna Hooker and Colin Hickling (eds), *What about the New Testament? Essays in Honour of Christopher Evans*, London: SCM Press, 1975, 13–27.

Staten, Henry, *Wittgenstein and Derrida*, Oxford: Blackwell, 1985.

Stauffer, Ethelbert, *New Testament Theology* (trans. John Marsh), London: SCM Press, 1955 (1941).

Steiner, George, *Real Presences: Is There Anything in What We Say?*, London: Faber & Faber, 1990.

Stendahl, Krister, *Paul among Jews and Gentiles and Other Essays*, Philadelphia: Fortress Press, 1976

——, *Meanings: The Bible as Document and as Guide*, Philadelphia: Fortress Press, 1984.

Stiver, Dan R., 'The Uneasy Alliance between Evangelicalism and Postmodernism: A Reply to Anthony Thiselton', in David S. Dockery (ed.), *The Challenge of Postmodernism: An Evangelical Engagement*, Wheaton: Bridgepoint, 1995, 239–53.

Stout, Jeffrey, *The Flight from Authority: Religion, Morality and the Quest for Autonomy*, Notre Dame, IN: University of Notre Dame Press, 1981.

——, 'What Is the Meaning of a Text?', *NLH* 14 (1982), 1–12.

——, *Ethics after Babel: The Languages of Morals and Their Discontents*, Cambridge: James Clarke & Co., 1988.

Strawson, P. F., 'Freedom and Resentment', in Strawson, *Freedom and Resentment and Other Essays*, 1–25 (1962).

——, 'Intention and Convention in Speech Acts', *Philosophical Review* 73 (1964), 439–60, reprinted in Fann (ed.), *Symposium on J. L. Austin*, 380–400, and in Searle (ed.), *Philosophy of Language*, 23–38.

——, 'Critical Notice of Wittgenstein's *Philosophical Investigations*', in Harold Morick (ed.), *Wittgenstein and the Problem of Other Minds*, New York: McGraw-Hill, 1967, 3–42.

——, 'Imagination and Perception', in Strawson, *Freedom and Resentment and Other Essays*, 45–65 (1970).

Strawson, P. F., *Freedom and Resentment and Other Essays*, London: Methuen, 1974.

——, *Analysis and Metaphysics: An Introduction to Philosophy*, Oxford: Oxford University Press, 1992.

Stroud, Barry, 'The Background of Thought', in Lepore and Van Gulick (eds), *John Searle and His Critics*, 245–58.

Surin, Kenneth, *Theology and the Problem of Evil*, Oxford: Blackwell, 1986.

Swartley, Willard M., *Slavery, Sabbath, War and Women: Case Issues in Biblical Interpretation*, Scottdale: Herald Press, 1983.

Synod of the Dutch Reformed Church in South Africa, *Human Relations and the South African Scene in the Light of Scripture*, Pretoria: Dutch Reformed Church Publishers, 1976.

Tavuchis, Nicholas, *Mea Culpa: A Sociology of Apology and Reconciliation*, Stanford, CA: Stanford University Press, 1991.

Taylor, Vincent, *Forgiveness and Reconciliation: A Study in New Testament Theology*, London: Macmillan, 1946.

Telfer, W., *The Forgiveness of Sins: An Essay in the History of Christian Doctrine and Practice*, London: SCM Press, 1959.

TeSelle, Sallie McFague, *Speaking in Parables: A Study in Metaphor and Theology*, Philadelphia: Fortress Press, 1975.

Thiel, John, *Nonfoundationalism* (Guides to Theological Inquiry), Minneapolis: Augsburg–Fortress, 1994.

Thiselton, Anthony C., 'The Parables as Language-Event: Some Comments on Fuchs's Hermeneutics in the Light of Linguistic Philosophy', *SJT* 23 (1970), 437–68.

——, 'The Use of Philosophical Categories in New Testament Hermeneutics', *Churchman* 87 (1973), 87–100.

——, 'The Supposed Power of Words in the Biblical Writings', *JTS* 25 (1974), 283–99.

——, *The Two Horizons: New Testament Hermeneutics and Philosophical Description*, Grand Rapids, Eerdmans, and Carlisle: Paternoster Press, 1980.

——, 'Reader-Response Hermeneutics, Action Models, and the Parables of Jesus', in Lundin, Thiselton and Walhout, *Responsibility of Hermeneutics*, 79–113.

Thiselton, Anthony C., 'Address and Understanding: Some Goals and Models of Biblical Interpretation as Principles of Vocational Training', *Anvil* 3 (1986), 101–18.

——, *Language, Liturgy and Meaning* (Grove Liturgical Study 2), Bramcote: Grove Books, ²1986 (1975).

——, *New Horizons in Hermeneutics: The Theory and Practice of Transforming Biblical Reading*, London: HarperCollins, 1992.

——, 'Authority and Hermeneutics: Some Proposals for a More Creative Agenda', in Satterthwaite and Wright (eds), *A Pathway into the Holy Scripture*, 107–41.

——, 'Christology in Luke, Speech-Act Theory, and the Problem of Dualism in Christology after Kant', in Joel B. Green and Max Turner (eds), *Jesus of Nazareth: Lord and Christ*, Carlisle: Paternoster Press, and Grand Rapids: Eerdmans, 1994, 453–72.

——, 'The Logical Role of the Liar Paradox in Titus 1:12, 13: A Dissent from the Commentaries in the Light of Philosophical and Logical Analysis', *BibInt* 2 (1994), 207–23.

——, *Interpreting God and the Postmodern Self: On Meaning, Manipulation and Promise*, Edinburgh: T&T Clark, 1995.

——, 'Speech-Act Theory and the Claim That God Speaks: Nicholas Wolterstorff's *Divine Discourse*', *SJT* 50 (1997), 97–110.

——, 'Thirty Years of Hermeneutics: Retrospect and Prospects', in Joze Krasovec (ed.), *Interpretation of the Bible*, Ljubljana: Slovenska akademija znanosti in umetnosti, and Sheffield: Sheffield Academic Press, 1998, 1559–74.

——, 'Communicative Action and Promise in Interdisciplinary, Biblical, and Theological Hermeneutics', in Lundin, Walhout and Thiselton, *Promise of Hermeneutics*, 133–239.

Thompson, William G., *Matthew's Advice to a Divided Community: Mt. 17,22–18,35* (Analecta Biblica 44), Rome: Biblical Institute Press, 1970.

Thomson, Oliver, *A History of Sin*, Edinburgh: Canongate Press, 1993.

Thurén, Lauri, 'On Studying Ethical Argumentation and Persuasion in the New Testament', in Stanley E. Porter and Thomas H. Olbricht (eds), *Rhetoric and the New Testament:*

Essays from the 1992 Heidelberg Conference (JSNTS 90), Sheffield: Sheffield Academic Press, 1993, 464–78.

Thyen, Hartwig, *Studien zur Sündenvergebung im Neuen Testament und seinen alttestamentlichen und jüdischen Voraussetzungen* (FRLANT 96), Göttingen: Vandenhoeck & Ruprecht, 1970.

Tilley, Terrence W., *The Evils of Theodicy*, Washington DC: Georgetown University Press, 1991.

——, ' "Lord, I believe: help my unbelief": Prayer without Belief', *MTh* 7 (1991), 239–47.

Tingley, Edward, 'Types of Hermeneutics', *Southern Journal of Philosophy* 36 (1998), 587–611.

Tompkins, Jane P., 'An Introduction to Reader-Response Criticism', in Jane P. Tompkins (ed.), *Reader-Response Criticism: From Formalism to Post-Structuralism*, Baltimore and London: Johns Hopkins University Press, 1980, ix–xxvi.

Torrance, Alan, 'Forgiveness: The Essential Socio-political Structure of Personal Being', *JTSA* 56 (1986), 47–59.

Tryzna, Thomas, 'The Social Construction of Forgiveness', *CSR* 27 (1997), 226–41.

Tsohatzidis, Savas L., 'The Gap between Speech Acts and Mental States', in Tsohatzidis (ed.), *Foundations of Speech Act Theory*, 220–33.

Tsohatzidis, Savas L. (ed.), *Foundations of Speech Act Theory: Philosophical and Linguistic Perspectives*, London and New York: Routledge, 1994.

Tuckett, Christopher, 'Thomas and the Synoptics', *NovT* 30 (1988), 132–57.

Urmson, J. O., 'Performative Utterances', *Midwest Studies in Philosophy* 2 (1977), 120–7, reprinted in Peter A. French, Theodore E. Uehling Jr and Howard K. Wettstein (eds), *Contemporary Perspectives in the Philosophy of Language*, Minneapolis: University of Minnesota Press, 1979, 260–7.

Vaihinger, Hans, *The Philosophy of 'As If': A System of the Theoretical, Practical, and Religious Fictions of Mankind* (trans. C. K. Ogden), New York: Harcourt, Brace & Co., ²1935; reprint: Boston: Routledge & Kegan Paul, 1965.

Valantasis, Richard, *The Gospel of Thomas* (New Testament Readings), London and New York: Routledge, 1997.

Van Unnik, W. C., 'Jesus: Anathema or Kyrios (1 Cor. 12:3)', in Barnabas Lindars and Stephen Smalley (eds), *Christ and Spirit in the New Testament (FS C. F. D. Moule)*, Cambridge: Cambridge University Press, 1973, 113–26.

Vanderveken, Daniel, 'Illocutionary Logic and Self-Defeating Speech Acts', in Searle, Kiefer and Bierwisch (eds), *Speech Act Theory and Pragmatics*, 247–72.

——, *Meaning and Speech Acts*, vol. 1, *Principles of Language Use*, Cambridge: Cambridge University Press, 1990.

——, *Meaning and Speech Acts*, vol. 2, *Formal Semantics of Success and Satisfaction*, Cambridge: Cambridge University Press, 1991

Vanhoozer, Kevin J., 'The Semantics of Biblical Literature: Truth and Scripture's Diverse Literary Forms', in D. A. Carson and John D. Woodbridge (eds), *Hermeneutics, Authority and Canon*, Leicester: IVP, 1986, 53–104.

——, 'Christ and Concept: Doing Theology and the "Ministry" of Philosophy', in John D. Woodbridge and Thomas Edward McComiskey (eds), *Doing Theology in Today's World: Essays in Honor of Kenneth S. Kantzer*, Grand Rapids: Zondervan, 1991, 99–145.

——, 'The Hermeneutics of I–Witness Testimony: John 21.20–24 and the "Death" of the "Author"', in A. Graeme Auld (ed.), *Understanding Poets and Prophets: Essays in Honour of George Wishart Anderson* (JSOTS 152), Sheffield: Sheffield Academic Press, 1993, 366–87.

——, 'From Canon to Concept: "Same" and "Other" in the Relation between Biblical and Systematic Theology', *SBET* 12 (1994), 96–124.

——, 'God's Mighty Speech-Acts: The Doctrine of Scripture Today', in Satterthwaite and Wright (eds), *A Pathway into the Holy Scripture*, 143–81.

——, *Is There a Meaning in This Text? The Bible, the Reader, and the Morality of Literary Knowledge*, Grand Rapids: Zondervan, 1998.

Voelz, James W., *What Does This Mean? Principles of Biblical Interpretation in the Post-Modern World*, St. Louis, MO: Concordia Publishing House, 1995.

Volf, Miroslav, *Exclusion and Embrace: A Theological Exploration of Identity, Otherness, and Reconciliation*, Nashville: Abingdon Press, 1996.

Vorländer, H., 'Forgiveness', *NIDNTT* 1:699–703.

Wagatsuma, Hiroshi and Arthur Rosett, 'The Implications of Apology: Law and Culture in Japan and the United States', *Law & Society Review* 20 (1986), 461–98.

Wainwright, Geoffrey, *Doxology: The Praise of God in Worship, Doctrine and Life*, London: Epworth Press, 1980.

——, 'The Language of Worship', in Cheslyn Jones, Geoffrey Wainwright, Edward Yarnold SJ and Paul Bradshaw (eds), *The Study of Liturgy*, London: SPCK, and New York: Oxford University Press, ²1992 (1978), 519–28.

Walsh, Brian J., 'Anthony Thiselton's Contribution to Biblical Hermeneutics', *CSR* 14 (1985), 224–35.

Walzer, Michael, *Thick and Thin: Moral Arguments at Home and Abroad*, Notre Dame: University of Notre Dame Press, 1994.

Warnock, G. J., *English Philosophy since 1900*, London: Oxford University Press, ²1969 (1958).

——, 'Some Types of Performative Utterance' in Berlin et al., *Essays on J. L. Austin*, 69–89.

——, *J. L. Austin*, London: Routledge & Kegan Paul, ²1991 (1989).

Warnock, Mary, *Imagination*, Berkeley: University of California Press, 1976.

Watson, Duane F., 'Rhetorical Criticism of Hebrews and the Catholic Epistles since 1978', *CR:BS* 5 (1997), 175–207.

Watson, Francis, *Text, Church and World: Biblical Interpretation in Theological Perspective*, Edinburgh: T&T Clark, 1994.

——, *Text and Truth: Redefining Biblical Theology*, Edinburgh: T&T Clark, 1997.

Weigand, Edda, 'The State of the Art in Speech Act Theory (Review article of Savas L. Tsohatzidis (ed.), *Foundations of Speech Act Theory: Philosophical and Linguistic Perspectives*, London and New York: Routledge, 1994)', *Pragmatics & Cognition* 4 (1996), 367–406.

Weiss, Johannes, *Jesus' Proclamation of the Kingdom of God*, London: SCM Press, 1971 (1892).

——, *Earliest Christianity: A History of the Period A.D. 30–150. Volume II*, New York: Harper & Brothers, 1959 (1937).

Wenham, David, *The Parables of Jesus*, London: Hodder & Stoughton, 1989.

West, Cornel, 'The Limits of Neopragmatism', in Brint and Weaver (eds), *Pragmatism in Law & Society*, 121–6.

Westerholm, S., *Jesus and Scribal Authority* (Coniectanea Biblica NT 10), Lund: C. W. K. Gleerup, 1978.

Wheelwright, Philip, *Metaphor and Reality*, Bloomington, IN: Indiana University Press, 1962.

White, Alan, 'Speech Acts', in Thomas Mautner (ed.), *A Dictionary of Philosophy*, Oxford: Blackwell, 1996, 403–4.

White, Hugh C. (ed.), *Speech Act Theory and Biblical Criticism* (= *Semeia 41*), Decatur, GA: Scholars Press, 1988.

Williams, Bernard, *Problems of the Self: Philosophical Papers 1956–1972*, Cambridge: Cambridge University Press, 1973.

Williamson, Hugh, *Jesus Is Lord: A Personal Rediscovery*, Nottingham: Crossway Books, 1993.

Willis, Wendell (ed.), *The Kingdom of God in 20th-Century Interpretation*, Peabody, MA: Hendrickson, 1987.

Witherington III, Ben, *Jesus the Sage: The Pilgrimage of Wisdom*, Edinburgh: T&T Clark, 1994.

——, *Conflict and Community in Corinth: A Socio-Rhetorical Commentary on 1 and 2 Corinthians*, Carlisle: Paternoster Press, 1995.

——, *Grace in Galatia: A Commentary on St. Paul's Letter to the Galatians*, Edinburgh: T&T Clark, 1998.

Wittgenstein, Ludwig, *Tractatus Logico-Philosophicus* (trans D. F. Pears and B. F. McGuinness), London: Routledge & Kegan Paul, 1961 (1921).

——, *Philosophical Investigations*, Oxford: Blackwell, [3]1967 (1953).

——, *The Blue and Brown Books*, Oxford: Blackwell, [2]1969 (1958).

——, *On Certainty*, Oxford: Blackwell, 1969.

——, *Zettel*, Oxford: Blackwell, [2]1981 (1967).

Wittgenstein, Ludwig, 'Remarks on Frazer's *Golden Bough*', now reprinted in Ludwig Wittgenstein, *Philosophical Occasions 1912–1951* (eds James Klagge and Alfred Nordmann), Indianapolis and Cambridge: Hackett Publishing Company, 1993, 115–55.

Wolterstorff, Nicholas, *Works and Worlds of Art*, Oxford: Clarendon Press, 1980.

——, 'What "Reformed Epistemology" Is Not', *Perspectives* (November 1992), 10–16.

——, *Divine Discourse: Philosophical Reflections on the Claim That God Speaks*, Cambridge: Cambridge University Press, 1995.

Wood, Charles M., *The Formation of Christian Understanding: Theological Hermeneutics*, Valley Forge, PA: Trinity Press International, [2]1993 (1981).

Wright, N. T., *Jesus and the Victory of God*, London: SPCK, 1996.

Wu, J. L. and S. C. Pearson,'Hymns, Songs', in *DLNTD* (1997), 520–7.

Wunderlich, Dieter, 'Methodological Remarks on Speech Act Theory', in Searle, Kiefer and Bierwisch (eds), *Speech Act Theory and Pragmatics*, 291–312.

Yates, Roy, 'Colossians 2,14: Metaphor of Forgiveness', *Biblica* 71 (1990), 248–59.

Yoder, John Howard, *The Royal Priesthood: Essays Ecclesiological and Ecumenical* (ed. Michael G. Cartwright), Grand Rapids: Eerdmans, 1994.

Young, Frances, *The Making of the Creeds*, London: SCM Press, 1991.

Zurdeeg, Willem F., *An Analytical Philosophy of Religion*, Nashville: Abingdon Press, 1958.

Index of Subjects

Reference is to main discussions only.
Items indicated by * are particular kinds of speech act.

Index of Modern Authors

Index of References